Essentials / of **Psychological Assessment** Series

Everything you need to know to administer, score, and interpret the major psychological tests.

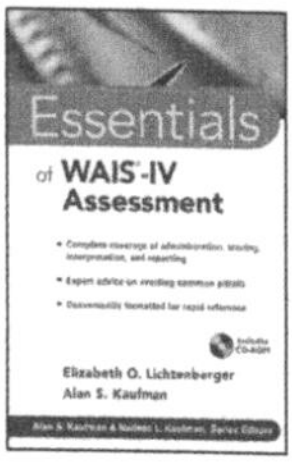

I'd like to order the following *Ess*

- ❑ WAIS®-IV Assessment (w/CD-ROM) / 97...
- ❑ WJ III™ Cognitive Abilities Assessment,
- ❑ Cross-Battery Assessment, Second Ed
- ❑ Nonverbal Assessment / 978-0-471-383
- ❑ PAI® Assessment / 978-0-471-08463-1 •
- ❑ CAS Assessment / 978-0-471-29015-5 • $38.95
- ❑ MMPI®-2 Assessment, Second Edition / 978-0-470-92323-8 • $38.95
- ❑ Myers-Briggs Type Indicator® Assessment, Second Edition / 978-0-470-34390-6 • $38.95
- ❑ Rorschach® Assessment / 978-0-471-33146-9 • $38.95
- ❑ Millon™ Inventories Assessment, Third Edition / 978-0-470-16862-2 • $38.95
- ❑ TAT and Other Storytelling Assessments, Second Edition / 978-0-470-28192-5 • $38.95
- ❑ MMPI-A™ Assessment / 978-0-471-39815-8 • $38.95
- ❑ NEPSY®-II Assessment / 978-0-470-43691-2 • $38.95
- ❑ Neuropsychological Assessment, Second Edition / 978-0-470-43747-6 • $38.95
- ❑ WJ III™ Tests of Achievement Assessment / 978-0-471-33059-2 • $38.95
- ❑ Evidence-Based Academic Interventions / 978-0-470-20632-4 • $38.95
- ❑ WRAML2 and TOMAL-2 Assessment / 978-0-470-17911-6 • $38.95
- ❑ WMS®-IV Assessment / 978-0-470-62196-7 • $38.95
- ❑ Behavioral Assessment / 978-0-471-35367-6 • $38.95
- ❑ Forensic Psychological Assessment, Second Edition / 978-0-470-55168-4 • $38.95
- ❑ Bayley Scales of Infant Development II Assessment / 978-0-471-32651-9 • $38.95
- ❑ Career Interest Assessment / 978-0-471-35365-2 • $38.95
- ❑ WPPSI™-III Assessment / 978-0-471-28895-4 • $38.95
- ❑ 16PF® Assessment / 978-0-471-23424-1 • $38.95
- ❑ Assessment Report Writing / 978-0-471-39487-7 • $38.95
- ❑ Stanford-Binet Intelligence Scales (SB5) Assessment / 978-0-471-22404-4 • $38.95
- ❑ WISC®-IV Assessment, Second Edition (w/CD-ROM) / 978-0-470-18915-3 • $48.95
- ❑ KABC-II Assessment / 978-0-471-66733-9 • $38.95
- ❑ WIAT®-III and KTEA-II Assessment (w/CD-ROM) / 978-0-470-55169-1 • $48.95
- ❑ Processing Assessment / 978-0-471-71925-0 • $38.95
- ❑ School Neuropsychological Assessment / 978-0-471-78372-5 • $38.95
- ❑ Cognitive Assessment with KAIT & Other Kaufman Measures / 978-0-471-38317-8 • $38.95
- ❑ Assessment with Brief Intelligence Tests / 978-0-471-26412-5 • $38.95
- ❑ Creativity Assessment / 978-0-470-13742-0 • $38.95
- ❑ WNV™ Assessment / 978-0-470-28467-4 • $38.95
- ❑ DAS-II® Assessment (w/CD-ROM) / 978-0-470-22520-2 • $48.95
- ❑ Executive Function Assessment (w/CD-ROM) / 978-0-470-42202-1 • $48.95
- ❑ Conners Behavior Assessments™ / 978-0-470-34633-4 • $38.95
- ❑ Temperament Assessment / 978-0-470-44447-4 • $38.95
- ❑ Response to Intervention / 978-0-470-56663-3 • $38.95
- ❑ Specific Learning Disability Identification / 978-0-470-58760-7 • $38.95
- ❑ IDEA for Assessment Professionals (w/CD-ROM) / 978-0-470-87392-2 • $48.95
- ❑ Dyslexia Assessment and Intervention / 978-0-470-92760-1 • $38.95
- ❑ Autism Spectrum Disorders Evaluation and Assessment / 978-0-470-62194-3 • $38.95

Please complete the order form on the back.
To order by phone, call toll free 1-877-762-2974
To order online: www.wiley.com/essentials
To order by mail: refer to order form on next page

Essentials

of **Psychological Assessment** Series

ORDER FORM

Please send this order form with your payment (credit card or check) to:
John Wiley & Sons, Attn: J. Knott, 111 River Street, Hoboken, NJ 07030-5774

QUANTITY	TITLE	ISBN	PRICE
____	_____	_____	____
____	_____	_____	____
____	_____	_____	____
____	_____	_____	____
____	_____	_____	____

Shipping Charges:	Surface	2-Day	1-Day
First item	$5.00	$10.50	$17.50
Each additional item	$3.00	$3.00	$4.00

For orders greater than 15 items,
please contact Customer Care at 1-877-762-2974.

ORDER AMOUNT _____
SHIPPING CHARGES _____
SALES TAX _____
TOTAL ENCLOSED _____

NAME_____

AFFILIATION_____

ADDRESS_____

CITY/STATE/ZIP_____

TELEPHONE_____

EMAIL_____

❑ Please add me to your e-mailing list

PAYMENT METHOD:

❑ Check/Money Order   ❑ Visa   ❑ Mastercard   ❑ AmEx

Card Number _____ Exp. Date _____

Cardholder Name (Please print) _____

Signature _____

*Make checks payable to **John Wiley & Sons**. Credit card orders invalid if not signed.*
All orders subject to credit approval. • Prices subject to change.

To order by phone, call toll free 1-877-762-2974
To order online: www.wiley.com/essentials

Essentials of TAT and Other Storytelling Assessments

Essentials of Psychological Assessment Series
Series Editors, Alan S. Kaufman and Nadeen L. Kaufman

Essentials

of TAT and Other Storytelling Assessments

Second Edition

Hedwig Teglasi

John Wiley & Sons, Inc.

BW

Library of Congress Cataloging-in-Publication Data:

Teglasi, Hedwig.

Essentials of TAT and other storytelling assessments / Hedwig Teglasi. — 2nd ed.

   p. ; cm. — (Essentials of psychological assessment series)

Rev. ed. of: Essentials of TAT and other storytelling techniques assessment / Hedwig Teglasi. c2001.

Includes bibliographical references and index.

ISBN 978-0-470-28192-5 (pbk. : alk. paper)

ISBN 978-0-470-62705-0 (ebk)

ISBN 978-0-470-62717-4 (ebk)

ISBN 978-0-470-62718-2 (ebk)

1. Thematic Apperception Test.   2. Personality assessment of children.   I. Teglasi, Hedwig. Essentials of TAT and other storytelling techniques assessment.   II. Title.

III. Series: Essentials of psychological assessment series.

[DNLM: 1. Thematic Apperception Test. 2. Child. 3. Personality Assessment.

WM 145.5.T3 T261ea 2010]

RC473.T48T44 2010

155.4'182844—dc22

                                                   2009050969

10 9 8 7 6 5 4 3 2

11/18/15

For Saul, Jordan, and Jeremy

Contents

Series Preface

In the *Essentials of Psychological Assessment* series, we have attempted to provide the reader with books that will deliver key practical information in the most efficient and accessible style. The series features instruments in a variety of domains, such as cognition, personality, education, and neuropsychology. For the experienced clinician, books in the series will offer a concise yet thorough way to master utilization of the continuously evolving supply of new and revised instruments, as well as a convenient method for keeping up to date on the tried-and-true measures. The novice will find here a prioritized assembly of all the information and techniques that must be at one's fingertips to begin the complicated process of individual psychological diagnosis.

Wherever feasible, visual shortcuts to highlight key points are utilized alongside systematic, step-by-step guidelines. Chapters are focused and succinct. Topics are targeted for an easy understanding of the essentials of administration, scoring, interpretation, and clinical application. Theory and research are continually woven into the fabric of each book, but always to enhance clinical inference, never to sidetrack or overwhelm. We have long been advocates of "intelligent" testing–the notion that a profile of test scores is meaningless unless it is brought to life by the clinical observations and astute detective work of knowledgeable examiners. Test profiles must be used to make a difference in the child's or adult's life, or why bother to test? We want this series to help our readers become the best intelligent testers they can be.

In *Essentials of TAT and Other Storytelling Assessments, Second Edition,* Dr. Hedwig Teglasi links the projective hypothesis, which is the theoretical foundation of all thematic apperceptive techniques, with current constructs in the study of personality. She also contextualizes the clinical use of storytelling techniques within the study of narrative as the language of experience, reflecting individualistic schemas and social information processing. Emphasizing the Thematic Apperception

Test (TAT), the book also covers the Children's Apperception Test, the Tell-Me-A-Story Test, and the Roberts 2. Specific guidelines, including worksheets and illustrative examples, are provided in each of four areas: Cognitive, emotional, interpersonal, and motivational/self-regulatory processes.

Alan S. Kaufman, PhD, and Nadeen L. Kaufman, EdD, Series Editors
Yale University School of Medicine

Acknowledgments

A story, as the language of experience, may be examined and re-examined, regardless of whether it is told about a picture or recounts a personal memory. The scientific literature across various psychology subfields provides various lenses through which to analyze open-ended narratives, both in terms of content and structure. I continue to be indebted to the scholars whose ideas inform my approach to coding and interpreting stories. This second edition has also benefited from listening to my students who posed insightful questions, thus spurring clarifications. Finally, I am appreciative of the support of my editor at Wiley, Isabel Pratt.

One

Methods for eliciting and interpreting stories told about pictured scenes are known generically as *thematic apperceptive techniques*, traditionally classified as projective instruments but also viewed as performance-based measures of personality. What all projective techniques have in common is that each presents a task that maximizes the imprint of individuality because there is no single correct approach to meeting the performance demands. The broader conceptualization of projective tests as *performance-based measures of personality* recognizes the essential distinction within the field of personality, between measures calling for the individual to navigate a task or to report information sought by a questionnaire or interview (see Meyer & Kurtz, 2006; Teglasi, 1998). Personality performance measures are distinct from the more structured cognitive performance measures. Personality tasks are used to evaluate problem-solving and reasoning under conditions of uncertainty without an obvious correct answer, whereas cognitive tests (intelligence or academic achievement) present clear-cut problems, the answers to which are easily classified as being correct or not. In the absence of a single right or wrong solution, evaluation of the responses to storytelling tasks occurs by qualified professionals in accord with their theoretical framework and training as well as preference for a particular interpretive scheme.

Although subjected to criticism, the set of pictures introduced by Morgan and Murray (1935) as the Thematic Apperception Test (TAT) remains the most popular (Archer, Marnish, Imhof, & Piotrowski, 1991; Watkins, Campbell, & McGregor, 1988; Watkins, Campbell, Nieberding, & Hallmark, 1995). The use of these pictures, however, did not remain wedded to Murray's interpretive system, and a plethora of interpretive approaches was subsequently developed. Additionally, a variety of different picture stimuli and accompanying interpretive procedures were introduced as variations of the TAT.

HISTORY OF THEMATIC APPERCEPTION TECHNIQUES

The introduction of the TAT stimuli (Morgan & Murray, 1935; Murray, 1938, 1943) popularized the idea that telling a story to pictured scenes depicting complex social situations would reveal important aspects of personality. The use of pictures to elicit stories had been reported prior to the introduction of the TAT but only in four obscure studies (cited in Tomkins, 1947).

At the time that the TAT was being developed, the Rorschach technique, emphasizing *perception*, was gaining popularity. For Murray (1938), the TAT offered the advantage of assessing *apperception*. He defined *perception* as recognition of an object based on sensory impression and *apperception* as the addition of meaning to what is perceived. Accordingly, telling stories about pictured scenes was an *apperceptive* task requiring the interpretation of the pictured cues to discern characters' motives, intentions, and expectations. Although Murray introduced a specific, theoretically based system for interpreting the stories told to TAT pictures, the appeal and the flexibility of the storytelling technique led to the introduction of many different sets of picture stimuli and many interpretive approaches for the TAT pictures (see Chapter 8).

Interpretive procedures for the TAT and its derivatives have been designed either for the study of personality (for a summary, see Smith, 1992) or for clinical use (for a summary, see Jenkins, 2008). Personality researchers favored well-defined criteria to assess specific personality constructs (see Smith, 1992), whereas clinicians preferred broader constructs to assess the functioning of the "whole" person. Many insisted that the TAT be interpreted and not scored (see edited volume by Gieser & Stein, 1999). Generally, clinicians preferred to use the technique as a flexible tool for eliciting information that they would then interpret in light of their professional training and expertise. Such an approach is exemplified by Bellak's (1975, 1993) application of psychoanalytic theory to the interpretation of TAT stories. Despite the popularity of the TAT among clinicians, there is no consensus on a particular scoring system and there is no comprehensive set of norms for clinical use. Nevertheless, specific coding procedures have been developed for clinical purposes that are reliably scored and correlate with adjustment (see Jenkins, 2008; McGrew & Teglasi, 1990). Although the psychoanalytic perspective dominated the clinical use of the TAT for over a half-century, other interpretive frameworks were introduced, based primarily in social cognitive theory (Cramer, 1996; Teglasi, 1993, 1998; Westen, Klepser, Ruffins, Silverman, Lifton, & Boekamp, 1991). Rather than undermining its original theoretical foundations, current perspectives expand the basic tenets on which the TAT was grounded.

According to social cognitive theory, real-time information processing is informed by previously organized mental sets or schemas that structure knowledge about the self, others, and the world (Cervone, 2004; Teglasi, 1998). Individuals draw from a storehouse of schemas to interpret current situations, and it is the *interpretation* that drives decisions and actions. What is essential to understand about personality performance measures in clinical use is that they present tasks that are ill-defined as to the desired solution, calling for individuals to impose their mental sets to interpret and respond to ambiguous or novel stimuli.

Subsequent to the formulation of the projective hypothesis (Frank, 1939), the TAT and other measures permitting open-ended responses were designated as projective techniques. A fundamental assumption of all projective methods, including thematic apperceptive techniques, is the "projective hypothesis," which posits that stimuli from the environment are perceived and organized by the individual's specific needs, motives, feelings, perceptual sets, and cognitive structures, and that in large part this process occurs automatically and outside of awareness (Frank, 1948). The pervasive influence of the unconscious on perception, thought, behavior, and motivation is well documented (Bargh & Morsella, 2008; Duckworth, Bargh, Garcia, & Chaiken, 2002). The projective hypothesis bears a striking resemblance to current definitions of the "unconscious" as comprising qualities of the mind that influence conscious thought and behavior through processes that are outside of immediate awareness (James, 1998; Uleman, 2005). Such automatic processes shape responses to projective tests and to similarly unstructured life encounters.

Historically, much of the criticism directed at the TAT was rooted in the incorrect view that the TAT and self-report provide equivalent information. Since self-report methods were viewed as being the more straightforward and less labor intensive way to find out what a person believes (just ask directly), projective tests were challenged to show that they add value beyond self-report. In this context, the low correlations between narrative motive measures and corresponding self-reported traits were misjudged as indicative of lack of validity of one or the other. Trait theorists tended to question the reliability and validity of projective measures (e.g., Lilienfield, Wood, & Garb, 2000), whereas motive theorists took the low correlations to be evidence of the distinctiveness of the constructs assessed with self-report and performance instruments (e.g., Brunstein & Maier, 2005).

Research has established dualities in psychological constructs that inform the use of measurement with self-report and personality performance measures such as the TAT. Explicit versions of constructs are attributed to the self and available to introspection, hence to self-report, whereas implicit versions are not accessible by introspection (see Bornstein, 2002; James, 1998; McClelland, Koestner, & Weinberger, 1989; Westen, 1990, 1991; Winter, John, Stewart, Klohnen, & Duncan, 1998). Changes in the theoretical landscape due to advances in understanding the profound role of the unconscious in human functioning has led to the realization that the human mind is too complex to be characterized by a single assessment method.

DON'T FORGET

Attributes of Projective Techniques (including TAT)

- Stimuli are sufficiently ambiguous to preclude a ready response, thereby requiring individual interpretation.
- There are many "correct" ways to approach the task.
- The response is open-ended and maximizes the imprint of organization.

THEORETICAL FOUNDATIONS

The projective hypothesis and schema theory are similar in their central tenets. Both point to the role of previously organized mental "sets" in the interpretation of current stimuli, and both emphasize the influence of these mental structures as occurring outside of conscious awareness (Fiske, Haslam, & Fiske, 1991; Wyer & Srull, 1994). In essence, schema theory and research may be viewed as elaborating the workings of the projective hypothesis and as supporting performance measures of personality such as the TAT. The story form itself is a schema that captures the organization of prior experience and provides the structure for ordering current experience (Teglasi, 1998). To understand the operation of schemas in guiding responses to personality performance tests, it is necessary to consider basic dualities in psychological constructs and in modes of processing information.

Dualities in Psychological Constructs and Modes of Information Processing

The well-documented distinction between *implicit* and *explicit* versions of psychological constructs appears to correspond to a basic dichotomy between the "experiencing self," driven by emotion that imparts a sense of genuineness, and the "verbally defined self," guided by more dispassionate processing of verbal information (James, 1890). Explicitly attributed constructs express what is important to one's self-definition or identity or what is viewed as socially desirable (being a good student) that may or may not be supported by actual experiences (enjoying the process of learning). In a series of classic articles, McClelland and his colleagues (Koestner & McClelland, 1990; Koestner, Weinberger, & McClelland, 1991; McClelland et al., 1989) argued that implicit achievement motivation (measured with the TAT) and explicit achievement motivation (measured with self-report) develop by different routes and have different patterns of relationships with other variables (see meta-analytic review in Spangler, 1992). Implicit motives are dispositional preferences for particular qualities of affective experiences, grounded in personally significant encounters and spurring spontaneous reactions. In contrast, self-attributed motives are conceptualizations about the self that may be more rooted in logical, cultural, and social bases for a desired self-description than personal inclination. Self-attributed motives forecast responses to situations that provide incentives for expressing socially promoted values or for presenting the self in a particular light but are not necessarily linked to the individual's affective preferences. Implicit motives develop through intrinsic enjoyment generated when doing tasks or experiencing activities or situations and, therefore, predict self-selected, goal-related activities (Biernat, 1989; Koestner, Weinberger, & McClelland, 1991; McClelland et al., 1989). The TAT-assessed implicit motives predicted long-term behavioral trends, whereas questionnaire measures of self-attributed motives predicted short-term choice behaviors. Dual versions of numerous constructs measured with self-report and performance tasks have since been proposed (see Rapid Reference 1.1).

≡ Rapid Reference 1.1

Dual Versions of Constructs: Implicit and Explicit Personality

- **Achievement motivation** (McClelland et al., 1989)
- **Self-esteem** (Bosson, Swann, & Pennebaker, 2000; Spalding & Hardin, 1999)
- **Dependency** (Bornstein, 1998)
- **Anxiety** (Egloff, Wilhelm, Neubauer, Mauss, & Gross, 2002)
- **Attitudes** (Greenwald, Banaji, Rudman, Farnham, Nosek, & Mellott, 2002)
- **Aggression** (Frost, Ko, & James, 2007)

≡ *Rapid Reference 1.2*

....

Dual Process Information Processing Systems (see Evans, 2008)

System One	System Two
Not reflectively conscious	Conscious
Automatic, effortless	Deliberative, effortful
Rapid, intuitive, simultaneous processing	Relatively slow, controlled, analytic processing
High capacity to process a great deal of information	Capacity limited by attention and working memory
Experiential	Rational
Implicit	Explicit

Two distinct ways of knowing and of information processing (see Rapid Reference 1.2) are relevant to implicit and explicit versions of psychological constructs. The essential contrast is between processing that is unconscious (implicit), rapid, automatic, and capable of simultaneously handling a great deal of information and processing that is conscious (explicit), slow, and deliberative (for a review, see Evans, 2008). This dichotomy characterizes information processing that is rational and experiential, and conflict between these modes of thought has been described as a discrepancy between the "heart" and the "head" (see Epstein, 1994; Epstein & Pacini, 1999). The "heart" tends to harbor convictions that do not require new evidence, deriving credibility by virtue of their connection to emotions. The "head" responds to logic and rational ideas that may change more easily with new evidence. Of course, there are points in between the extremes reflecting compromises between the two thought systems.

Individuals bring to any encounter implicit and explicit (self-attributed) motives or convictions as well as automatic and controlled modes of information processing that support both implicit and self-attributed convictions. Although implicit and explicit schemas are salient in different contexts, as noted earlier, they join together in their influences on behavior and adjustment. Under some circumstances, external incentives may override an individual's implicit motives (Rudman, 2004) and conflict between explicit and implicit psychological constructs may lead to various compromises that have implications for well-being. Discrepancy between implicit and self-attributed motives to achieve is associated with decreased subjective well-being and increased symptom formation (Baumann, Kaschel, & Kuhl, 2005).

Discrepancies between implicit and self-attributed inclinations may be resolved differently depending on their social desirability in a culture (achievement or aggression). According to the *channeling hypothesis* (Winter, John, Stewart, Klohnen, & Duncan, 1998), when facing a conflict between their desires to maintain a particular self-image or public reputation and their implicit inclinations, individuals will allow explicit motives to influence the channels for expressing the implicit motives. For instance, a person who does not endorse an aggressive self-image, but implicitly experiences hostile tendencies, would express these tendencies in ways that are indirect (Frost, Ko, & James, 2007). Assessing both versions of psychological constructs enables researchers and practitioners to weigh the relative influence of explicit and implicit versions of the same personality variable as a function of the situational context.

Public and Personal Knowledge Structures

A fuller appreciation of the relationship between schema theory and the projective hypothesis necessitates a distinction between two types of knowledge structures that organize experience. One is independent of the knower, and the other is unique to the knower (Mandler, 1982; Wozniak, 1985). Knowledge that exists independently of the knower is *public*, whereas knowledge that is dependent on the individual's experiences is *personal* (see Fig. 1.1). All schemas, public or personal, are outgrowths of the capacity of human beings to detect, process, and use information about covariations of stimuli and events in their surroundings (such as a change in contingencies), often without deliberate effort or conscious awareness (Dowd & Courchaine, 2002; Lewicki, Czyzewska, & Hill, 1997; Lewicki, Hill, & Czyzewska, 1992). Schemas that capture the regularities of the external world that are amenable to proof by logic, evidence, or social consensus may be called *public*. However, schemas that coordinate perceived regularities in the inner and outer worlds are more aptly characterized as *personal* because they are unique to the individual and subject to confirmation only by like-minded others.

The *public* schemas may be further categorized as *logical* and *social*. Logical schemas such as mathematical formulas or scientific principles describing observed relationships among facts or ideas (such as the formula for calculating the circumference of a circle) develop and change through critical analysis, logical proof, or direct evidence. Social schemas organizing regularities in routine events (how to order a meal in a restaurant, what happens when visiting the dentist), rules or beliefs that are widely held in a culture (raising one's hand in class, tipping the server), or the layout of public spaces (such as an airport) are maintained by consensus, not necessarily logic. Such social schemas provide clear expectations about what will happen and how to behave in commonly occurring situations (Abelson, 1981; Schank & Abelson, 1977).

A twofold classification of *personal schemas* parallels the distinctions between two versions of psychological constructs, *implicit* and *explicit*, described above (also see Payne, Burkley, & Stokes, 2008). *Explicit personal schemas* are models about the self (in relation to others and the world), including motives that a person endorses (self-attributes) on the basis of social values or importance to identity but not necessarily supported by patterns of regularities in actual experience. *Explicit* personal schemas are active in situations that are relatively structured, providing cues or incentives (reminders, supervision) salient for a particular self-image. *Implicit personal schemas* reflect experiential regularities as an ongoing synthesis of bidirectional and reciprocal encounters of individuals with their surroundings (see Teglasi & Epstein, 1998). As individuals notice patterns in the external world such as links between actions and outcomes and regularities in their emotional states in relation to the stream of external events, they form expectations about what actions can or cannot bring about certain effects. Therefore, *implicit personal schemas* include ideas about sources of distress and about one's efficacy to regulate uncomfortable states or to bring about desired outcomes, capturing the reciprocal relations among affect, cognitions, and behavior. Personal schemas, particularly if implicit, change more readily through experiential learning (detecting new regularities, reframing experiences) than through didactic methods (Dowd, 2006).

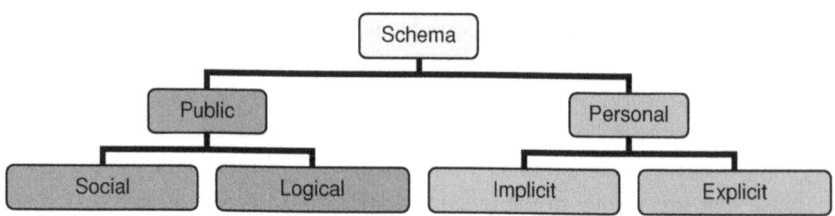

Figure 1.1 Public and Personal Schemas

Each individual develops unique patterns of assumptions about the self, the world, and relationships, arriving at a particular stance toward life through the complex interplay of maturation, temperament, cognitive development, and socialization (Stark, Rouse, & Livingston, 1991). Personal schemas are representations that are idiosyncratic to the knower because their development is influenced by individual differences shaping the transactions with the environment as well as the interpretation of those transactions (see Teglasi, 2006). Individuals' strategies for synthesizing cues provided in the scenes portrayed in TAT pictures and for organizing the response are analogous to the manner in which they apply previously acquired knowledge for adaptive use in novel, stressful, or ambiguous situations. Likewise, schema theory assumes that successful adaptation to unfamiliar situations requires the coordination of what one "perceives" in the present with what one "knows" from previous experience.

The construct of the personal schema brings together models of perception, cognition, memory, affect, action, and feedback, in social and cultural contexts, thereby incorporating the various perspectives for understanding personality. The schema construct also bridges the study of normal personality processes with the study of psychopathology because schema-driven information processing allows previously organized knowledge to influence perception of ongoing experiences in adaptive or maladaptive ways. Knowledge structures that accurately represent reality increase efficiency in identifying perceptions, organizing them into meaningful units, filling in missing information, and devising a strategy for seeking new information as needed. However, maladaptive schemas bias attention and information processing to conform to an initial misconception and resist change despite contradictory evidence (e.g., Beck, 2002; Beck & Clark, 1997; Horowitz, 1991; Riso, du Toit, Stein, & Young, 2007).

Dual theories of information processing account for the development of public and personal knowledge structures and have implications for the use of tools to assess the schemas that represent these two modes of thought.

DON'T FORGET

Projective techniques are concerned primarily with the application of knowledge structures that are unique to the knower to organize responses to ambiguous stimuli.

THE SCHEMA AND THE STORY

The story form and personal schemas are similar in that both are products of prior synthesis of experience and inform subsequent information processing. The story implicitly carries the schemas by which individuals

CAUTION

Personal schemas are resistant to change because the processes that led to their development may still be operating and because schemas tend to organize and modify new experiences to fit the preexisting structures.

order their experiences, structuring the stream of life events as episodes with a beginning, middle, and end (Oatley, 1992). Far more than delineating events that occur at a particular time and place, the story conveys personal meanings by weaving together events, emotions, thoughts, and behaviors in ways that reflect causal, conditional, and temporal understandings (that even preschool children possess; see review, Flavell & Miller, 1998; Fivush & Haden, 1997; Wellman & Gelman, 1998). In essence, the story functions as a tool for thinking (Bruner, 1990; Hermans, 2003), incorporating the narrator's understanding of the mental world, termed "theory of mind," based on the recognition that outward actions are organized by the inner world of thoughts, beliefs, feelings, wishes, and intentions (Fonagy & Target, 2003).

Children's understanding of mental states develops in tandem with their capacity to incorporate psychological causality in recounting autobiographical memories. Narrative accounts of experience reflect understandings of mental states as causally related to behaviors (see review, Reese, 2002). Akin to the schema, theory of mind is not a collection of isolated beliefs but captures the reciprocal relations among mental states, perceptions of environments, decisions, plans, and actions (Wellman, 1990). As do schemas, theory of mind operates outside of consciousness and provides a foundation for processing social information, including classifications and relations among mental elements (thoughts, feelings, intentions) and their connections to external events and actions.

Narrative as Cognition

The contrast between narrative and propositional thought parallels the distinction between public and personal schemas. Propositional thought is public, logical, formal, theoretical, general, and abstract, whereas narrative thought is story-like, concrete, specific, personally convincing, imagistic, interpersonal, and includes characters, settings, intentions, emotions, actions, and outcomes (see Bruner 1986, 1990). Narrative and propositional modes of thought provide distinct ways of ordering experience. Propositional or paradigmatic thought employs operations by which one establishes categorization or conceptualizations (Bruner, 1986; Hermans, Kempen, & Van Loon, 1992; Vitz, 1990) and encompasses logical or scientific universals that transcend personal experience and specific context. Narrative thought also establishes categories, but they are contextualized in relation to specific persons, times, and places and invested with emotion. Logical thought aims to establish truth, whereas the narrative mode convinces by its meaningfulness (Parry & Doan, 1994). (See Rapid Reference 1.3.)

≡ *Rapid Reference 1.3*

Empirical and Conceptual Support for the Assessment of Schemas with Storytelling

1. A growing body of literature urges researchers to focus on stories as the natural mode through which individuals make sense of their experiences (e.g., Bruner, 1990; McAdams, Diamond, de St. Aubin, & Mansfield, 1997). The ability to construct stories with a sensible sequence of events, reasonable causal relationships, and cohesive emotional experiences is an important developmental task of childhood, with implications for mental health (Mancuso & Sarbin, 1998). Storytelling is closely linked to listening and to reading comprehension (Blankman, Teglasi, & Lawser, 2002).

2. The principles that organize experience are evident through various narrative procedures including early memories, autobiographical recollections, and stories told to picture stimuli (Demorest & Alexander, 1992; McAdams, Hoffman, Mansfield, & Day, 1996). Thematic coherence (agency and communion) was evident across narratives written by adults and college students about personally important scenes in their lives and their TAT stories (McAdams, Hoffman, Mansfield, & Day, 1996). Scripts extracted from autobiographical memories and from stories told to TAT cards a month later supported the conclusion that scripted knowledge structures are superimposed on new affective stimuli (Demorest and Alexander, 1992).

3. Socially competent behavior involves complex skills starting with accurate encoding and interpretation of relevant cues from external and internal sources, formulating intentions, maintaining goals, generating appropriate responses, and using strategies to enact and evaluate the chosen response (Dodge & Price, 1994; Elias & Tobias, 1996). Although these components of social problem solving may be conceptually separated, they are linked together in the story form as a framework for thinking about social situations (e.g., Teglasi & Rothman, 2001; Teglasi, Rahill, & Rothman, 2007).

4. Schemas that represent relationships maladaptively are functionally related to psychopathology (e.g., Downey, Lebolt, Rincon, & Freitas, 1998; Oppenheim, Emde, & Warren, 1997). Schematic processing problems that reduce flexibility in processing information promote vicious cycles where ineffective schemas are preserved, thereby maintaining dysfunctional emotions, attitudes, and behaviors (Greenberg, Rice, & Elliott, 1993). Cognitive therapeutic approaches are increasingly grounded in schema theory (e.g., Riso, du Toit et al., 2007).

5. Stories are important structures that organize experiences. Mental and physical benefits derive from expressing feelings associated with adverse events in an organized way, such as telling a story (Hemenover, 2003; Pennebaker, 1997). However, the experience need not be one's own. Writing about someone else's trauma as if it were one's own produced effects that were similar to writing about one's own traumatic experience (Greenberg, Wortman, & Stone, 1996).

The ability to organize experience into narrative form is a central developmental task, related to children's adjustment (Mancuso & Sarbin, 1998). At about 5 years of age, children's narratives move beyond temporal sequences of events to identify the problem or psychological issue in a situation, and by ages 9 to 11, approximate adult levels (Applebee, 1978; Botvin & Sutton-Smith, 1977; Peterson & McCabe, 1983). Children who do not provide cohesive narrative accounts of events or experiences are perceived as less competent academically and socially (Bloome, Katz, & Champion, 2003). Exchanging stories is a fundamental mode by which people share their subjective reality, and telling the right story at the right time in a social conversation has been viewed as a hallmark of social intelligence (Schank, 1990). As the language of experience, it has been argued that virtually all meaningful social knowledge is learned in the form of stories (Schank & Abelson, 1995).

TAT and Autobiographical Narrative

The story is the primary means by which episodes in daily life are represented in memory (Schank, 1990), providing a structure for ordering the sequences of events, situating them in a particular place and point in time, and connecting them to feelings, thoughts, and behaviors. According to script theory, the *scene* or recollection of a specific episode in one's life contains at least one basic affect (e.g., joy, excitement, fear, anger) and one object of that affect (Tomkins, 1987; Carlson, 1981). Scenes become organized into families or groupings, comprising *scripts* that govern the interpretation, creation, and organization of new scenes and recollections of prior scenes. Tomkins' notion of *script* corresponds to the *personal schema*. The ability to recall scenes (episodic memory) and to organize them into scripts (general event memory) serves adaptive functions (see review, Nelson & Fivush, 2004). Giving a coherent account of a specific experience is necessary for communication, whereas the synthesis of events into general narrative structures (scripts or schemas) aids the recall of prior episodes (filling in the gaps) and informs interpretations of subsequent ones.

Recalled episodes are not expected to correspond with what actually happened. Rather, the greatest value in autobiographical studies lies in their illumination of *current* life meanings (Tomkins, 1987). Likewise, experiences described by clients to their therapists do not correspond to historical facts but constitute "story lines" that have been transformed by psychological processes (Schafer, 1992). Similarly, according to the life-story model of adult identity (McAdams, 1985, 1993; McAdams & Pals, 2006), individuals selectively value past experiences that are continuous with the present, thereby lending coherence to their lives. Memories that are relevant for individuals' implicit and explicit goals or motives are more accessible (Woike, Mcleod, & Goggin, 2003). Implicit motives operate in the recall of emotionally charged experiences (Woike, Gershkovich, Piorkowski, & Polo, 1999), whereas explicit motives operate in the recall of experiences and information relevant to maintaining the self-concept (DeSteno & Salovey, 1997; Singer & Salovey, 1993; Woike et al., 2003). The details of stories told to TAT stimuli are not assumed to represent actual experiences. However, like other sources of narrative (the interview, autobiographic stories, specific recollections, diaries), TAT stories are amenable to analysis in terms of the categories and principles that organize experience such as causal understandings, means-ends sets, abstract themes, affective scripts, and complexity in the representation of persons (e.g., Alexander, 1988; Arnold, 1962; Demorest & Alexander, 1992; Leigh, Westen, Barends, Mendel, & Byers, 1992; McAdams, Hoffman, Mansfield, & Day, 1996; Schank, 1990). Early memory narratives of patients at the start of therapy and TAT stories were coded with the *Social Cognition and Object Relations Scale* (SCORS; Westen, 1995) and both predicted the therapeutic alliance, a variable crucial to outcomes (see Pinsker-Aspen, Stein, & Hilsenroth, 2007). Broad motivational themes (agency and communion) coded from TAT stories are congruent with thematic content of diaries of daily memories (Woike & Polo, 2001). Through unconscious processes, individuals apply the categories for thinking about significant others to new encounters (Andersen, Reznik, & Glassman, 2005), and these categories may be gleaned from analysis of stories about early experiences and about TAT cards.

The categories built into schemas depend on individuality in detecting patterns of regularities across experiences. The raw materials for detecting patterns are the observed distinctions. As individuals interact with their social and physical worlds, they construe reality (expectations, causal understandings) by registering patterns in what they notice as relevant in their surroundings. When co-occurring thoughts, emotions, and action tendencies are noticed in a given environmental context, the brain clusters them together (see Mischel & Ayduk, 2004) such that, when one element of the cluster is brought to mind, it activates the others (a visit to one's childhood home calling forth certain feelings and thoughts).

An examination of neural networks involved in autobiographical memory (using event-related functional Magnetic Resonance Imaging) demonstrated that TAT stimuli activated brain areas known to be involved in autobiographical memory retrieval (Schnell, Dietrich, Schnitker, Daumann, & Herpertz, 2007). The TAT cards produced similar activation in those with Borderline Personality Disorder (BPD) and control participants but, unlike the control participants, those with BPD showed hyperactivation of these areas for both the affectively loaded TAT and for neutral stimuli. This finding that those with BPD did not differentiate between emotional and neutral stimuli means that such distinctions are not available in daily life to enrich the implicit process of schema development. What is not noticed, even implicitly, cannot be classified into categories that are built into the schemas.

When the individual is actively contemplating an interpersonal situation or task, such as telling stories about pictorial stimuli, he or she constructs a working model that combines internal and external sources of information (see Rapid Reference 1.4). Stories evoked by pictures permit the evaluation of the categories applied to information processing that contribute to well-being as well as to distress or counterproductive behavior. Structural features of children's TAT stories reveal distortions and deficits in processing information that are associated with emotional disability identified in the school system (Lohr, Teglasi, & French, 2004; McGrew & Teglasi, 1990). Qualities of children's schemas such as their accuracy, organization, and complexity have been related to temperament (Bassan-Diamond, Teglasi, & Schmidt, 1995; Lohr et al., 2004), empathy (Locraft & Teglasi, 1997; Teglasi, Locraft, & Felgenhauer, 2008a), as well as to listening and reading comprehension (Blankman, Teglasi, & Lawser, 2002).

≋ *Rapid Reference 1.4*

The Relationship of TAT Stories to Life Experiences

1. Individuals learn "lessons" from the regularities of day-to-day experiences. When a lesson repeatedly occurs, it may become a type of structure (like grammar) that exists apart from the specific incidents from which the lesson arose (Schank, 1990; Tomkins, 1987). Because abstracted schemas are based on numerous experiences (real or vicarious), they are readily activated (Murray, 1938), particularly in ambiguous situations or by tasks such as the TAT.

2. Individual differences in the synthesis of experiences applied to daily life are paralleled by variations in the construction of TAT stories as (a) piecemeal associations, (b) a direct replay of actual experiences selected from memory, (c) imposition of narrative patterns borrowed from books, other media, or stereotypes, or (d) application of convictions or lessons "abstracted" from experience (Teglasi, 1993) to meet task demands.

3. The inner logic and cohesiveness of the stories together with their content represent how individuals learn from day-to-day experiences and how they apply their knowledge to meet the task demand (e.g., accurately interpreting the stimuli and following instructions).

4. Content that is repeated provides clues about the narrator's concerns or preoccupations (Henry, 1956). However, addressing both the structure and content overcomes the pitfall of attributing too much weight to content (that may be pulled by the stimuli or recent experiences) but not meaningfully incorporated into structures that guide the synthesis of experience (Teglasi, 1998).

Use of the TAT to Measure Narrative Cognition

Once established, personal schemas are vehicles to compare incoming information with existing knowledge. The pre-existing schemas automatically provide the categories and structures for organizing stories told to TAT pictures in line with the instructions and the pictured scenes. Just as one would expect a person to give a coherent account of a prior experience, the stories about TAT pictures are expected to be organized productions rather than fantasies or random associations (Holt, 1961). The narrator's schemas used to interpret the pictured scene and organize ideas when telling TAT stories are applicable to the interpretation of similarly unstructured life situations (Bellak, 1975, 1993). The pictures provide the "givens" to be explained and the instructions call for producing a complete story. The construction of the story entails the superimposition of narrative patterns that apply to the internal representations of prior experience serving as the schemas for ordering the individual's ongoing encounters with the world (see Rapid Reference 1.5). Although permitting a wide range of responses, TAT stimuli are sufficiently structured to detect problems with interpreting the scenes. Overlaps between structural and thematic features of TAT stories with accounts of significant autobiographical episodes are expected because both are constructed according to the principles by which the narrator organizes experiences. However, there is no expectation of resemblance of the surface content of TAT stories to actual happenings.

≡ Rapid Reference 1.5

Social Problem Solving and Standard Questions for Eliciting TAT Stories

What is happening in the picture? Before a concern or problem is resolved, it must first be identified. The individual's storehouse of memories and schemas for understanding social situations is the source for generating ideas about the tensions depicted in the scene and for organizing these ideas. Describing isolated stimulus features does not satisfy the demands of the instructions.

What happened before? The sequence of unfolding events including those prior to the scene depicted reveals the narrator's schemas about social causality (e.g., cause-effect reasoning) and time perspective. The narrator's style of processing social information is seen not only in the interpretation of the immediate circumstances presented in the stimuli but in placing events in a historical context by postulating sequences of events leading up to the scene.

What is the person (or people) thinking and how is that person (or people) feeling? These questions evoke the narrator's understanding of the inner world and capacity to coordinate the inner life and external circumstances of the

(continued)

various characters portrayed in the scene or introduced into the story. Reasoning about intentions, values, and goals is a key component of social information processing. A cohesive story requires the narrator to incorporate each character's thoughts, feelings, or intentions in ways that fit the circumstances, actions, and outcomes.

How does the story end? In a well-constructed story, the details cohere around the ending. Although TAT instructions do not specifically ask for actions or plans to resolve the dilemmas set before the characters, the means to resolving tensions or accomplishing goals are implicit in the storytelling task. The perceived means-ends connections are crucial aspects of schemas and of narratives and are therefore considered the basis for understanding the lesson, moral, or import of the story (Alexander, 1988; Arnold, 1962; Schank, 1990). The narrator's resources for problem solving are indicated not only by the manner in which the characters resolve the dilemmas introduced into the story but also by the manner in which the narrator meets the problem-solving demands of the storytelling task.

Individuals vary in the accuracy, complexity, and organization of autobiographical narratives (see Nelson & Fivush, 2004) as well as of their TAT stories. Some tell stories that reflect coherently organized internal representation of experience presenting a detailed, balanced, and flexible panorama of feelings and intentions promoting an accurate and nuanced map of reality. Others tell stories that reflect an inner world organized according to gross categories or polarized dichotomies that simplify perceptions of the environment. Still others tell stories reflecting piecemeal ideas rather than cohesive patterns of thought. Given that schema development is the product of the individual's synthesis of prior experience, the accuracy and completeness of the schemas may be constrained if information processing is chronically disrupted by problems with the regulation of attention, cognition, or emotion, or by a poor fit between the individual's temperamental tendencies and environmental expectations or by adverse social-environmental conditions. Children with temperamentally high negative emotional reactivity told TAT stories reflecting less complex, more short-term self-regulatory strategies than children with average reactivity (Bassan-Diamond, Teglasi, & Schmidt, 1995; Lohr, Teglasi, & French, 2004).

Schema Activation

Schemas stored in memory are inert until activated. The particular schemas activated are those that have been useful in the past (chronic accessibility) and deemed relevant (by association) to the current context (Anderson, Bothell,

Byrne, Douglass, Lebiere, & Quin, 2004). Once activated, the schemas shape real-time information processing, in part by directing attention, memory, and perception. In some instances, activated schemas promote errors in judgment that are not conducive to adaptive responses. However, executive functions enable the individual to monitor their schemas and, when necessary, to deliberately override one that is activated and substitute alternative schemas (see MacDonald, 2008). Higher order executive functions may be related to the availability of meta-schemas (Singer & Salovey, 1991) that allow the individual to deal constructively with activated schemas. These superordinate schemas are relevant to adjustment and resilience because they influence how individuals reshape their schemas when confronted with daily stress, unforeseen failure, or unexpected upheaval.

Schemas have been viewed as psychological vulnerabilities underlying psychopathology. Dysfunctional schemas are maintained by tendencies to process information in ways that confirm existing schemas, discounting or distorting schema-discrepant information and readily accepting schema-consistent ideas. For instance, the belief that one is generally incompetent may be maintained by tendencies toward harsh self-scrutiny, selective attention to mistakes, discounting successes, or overvaluing mistakes. Cognitive therapy has focused on underlying schemas (see Riso, du Toit et al., 2007) with particular emphasis on overcoming resistance to information that is out of tune with the schema.

Schema Complexity

Cognitive complexity is commonly understood in terms of two components of information processing: *differentiation*, or the ability to perceive and think about multiple dimensions of a phenomenon, and *integration*, or the ability to recognize connections between differentiated dimensions of a phenomenon (e.g., Schroder, Driver, & Streufert, 1967; Suedfeld, Tetlock, & Streufert, 1992). Those with more complex schemas, characterized by more distinctions and more connections among them, may be more prepared to replay negative information constructively by exploring various dimensions rather than ruminating on a single track or making all-or-none judgments. Those with less complex schemas may tend to overestimate the impact of a negative situation because they do not see different aspects of life as separate (see Linville, 1987; Luo, Watkins, & Lam, 2009).

Evidence documenting the link between schema complexity and adjustment has been mixed (Woolfolk, Gara, Allen, & Beaver, 2004), and inconsistencies are due, in part, to how the construct is conceptualized and measured. The schemas may be complex in two distinct ways. In attitude research, the structural complexity of statements may involve *dialectical* complexity, focusing on the tension between two perspectives, or *elaborative* complexity, focusing on the details of a single perspective (Conway et al., 2008).

Schemas that structure autobiographical memory and TAT stories reflect the processes of differentiation and integration (Woike, Lavezzary, & Barsky, 2001). However, similar to statements about attitudes, complexity in narratives may be evaluated in two ways: the distinction and coordination of different *conceptual domains* (the problem, feelings, thoughts, actions or circumstances, and resolutions) or *elaborations* within a single domain (nuances of negative or ambivalent feelings). A story organized around the sense of oneself as an anxious person would be characterized as *elaboratively complex* if it were dominated by ruminative details about the nuances of potential threats or of anxious states, and as *conceptually complex* if it specified the conditions evoking the anxiety and included goals, coping strategies for the anxiety and the problem, and appropriate connections between means and ends.

DON'T FORGET
....

TAT stories may be characterized by two forms of complexity—termed *conceptual complexity*, referring to the number of different domains that are distinguished, and *elaborative* complexity, referring to the number of *details* within domains. The latter involves being caught up in nuances and intricacies of a single psychological construct without considering others. For example, in telling a story, an individual might distinguish and connect nuances of negative emotions but give little consideration to other domains such as coping with those emotions. Likewise, an individual may tell an action-packed TAT story but not consider goals or intentions or other domains of experience.

Schema Development

The emergence of mental models about the world is central to human development, allowing individuals to use what they have learned in the past to inform their encounters in the present. The foundation for schema growth is the organized and systematic processing of information that permits the individual to discern regular patterns and rules inferred through experience. Individuals detect, synthesize, and use covariations in patterns of information in the course of myriad interactions with persons in various contexts (Dowd & Courchaine, 2002; Lewicki, Czyzewska, & Hill, 1997; Lewicki, Hill, & Czyzewska, 1992). Pattern detection is supported by individual differences in systems that regulate basic processes such as attention, emotions, cognition, and behavior that

≣ *Rapid Reference 1.6*

Attention-Deficit/Hyperactivity Disorder (ADHD), characterized by deficits in core cognitive functions such as sustained attention, inhibition, and executive planning, is associated with limitations in appraising others' emotional states (Corbett & Glidden, 2000). Among male adolescents with ADHD, emotion recognition of anger and fear (signals of potential threat) improved after taking medication but remained impaired relative to control participants. Medication may increase readiness to make distinctions, but schema development takes place over time (Williams et al., 2008).

are often studied in the field of temperament or neurosciences (e.g., Posner & Rothbart, 2007). The regulation of attention and emotion is linked to sets of knowledge structures such as emotion understanding that promote children's social competence (see Spinrad et al., 2006; Trentacosta, Izard, Mostow, & Fine, 2006). Selective attention or the ability to be attuned to some things while screening out others keeps an individual from being bombarded with information that is not relevant to current activity and from focusing too narrowly, ignoring important cues. Attentional regulation (sustain, focus, and shift) allows the individual to process the complexities needed to make adequate decisions or perform some tasks (see Rapid Reference 1.6).

Chronic affective states as conceptualized in temperament research are related to schema development. Emotions influence information processing by alerting the individual to emotion-relevant aspects of the environment and guiding the interpretations of those events. Negative emotional reactivity is associated with greater attention to negative events (Derryberry & Reed, 1994) and with perceiving those events as more aversive or stressful (Rothbart & Bates, 2006; Costa, Somerfield, & McCrae, 1996). Self-regulatory schemas measured with TAT stories showed that elementary school children with high negative emotional reactivity were more focused than those with average reactivity on the immediate short-term resolutions to tensions (Bassan-Diamond et al., 1995). Over time, negative emotionality contributes to the development of schemas that confer vulnerability to depression. However, schemas of individuals with chronic and non-chronic forms of depression are distinct (Riso et al., 2003). The schemas associated with chronic depression suggest impaired autonomy (low coping efficacy and view of environment as challenging) and hypervigilance (to one's mistakes or to departure from rigid performance expectations). Such schemas are consistent with the tendency of those with chronic depression to report a general malaise and dissatisfaction with life rather than to present clear-cut problems to be resolved.

≡ Rapid Reference 1.7

Basic self-regulatory processes (of attention, emotion, and behavior) shape schema growth, operating directly, indirectly, bidirectionally, and hierarchically (see Teglasi, 2006): (a) *directly*—by guiding the information that enters awareness to be classified and organized; (b) *bidirectionally*—by influencing exposure to information by selective attention and selective approach or avoidance; (c) *reciprocally*—by the goodness of fit between the person and various environments (resources to meet demands) and by the responses the individual elicits from others (acceptance, support, harshness); and (d) *hierarchically*—by driving the mental representations of experiences as shaped by the foregoing direct, indirect, and bidirectional influences. Once developed, the schemas take their place among the variables that guide person by environment encounters.

Complaints about multiple life areas are difficult to resolve in piecemeal fashion and it is useful to conceptualize the various issues under a common theme of generalized maladaptive schemas (Riso, Maddux, & Turini-Santorelli, 2007).

A history of faulty information processing reinforces incomplete or distorted mental sets and interventions need to address the schemas (gaps or distortions), how they are used (selective processing of information), and the processes by which they developed and continue to be maintained (see Rapid Reference 1.7). Schema-related impediments contributing to maladaptive behaviors include cognitive distortions (e.g., biased interpretation of situations and intentions) and cognitive deficits (e.g., poor problem solving). As noted earlier, situations vary in the demands made for motivation and information processing (including for the regulation of emotion and attention). Therefore, dysfunctional schemas are often situation specific. Individuality and situation-specificity of schemas contribute to the heterogeneity of schematic processing difficulties within disorders such as anxiety and depression (Foa & Kozak, 1991; Greenberg, Elliott, & Foerster, 1991; Safran & Greenberg, 1988) that may be targeted for intervention (Goldfried, Greenberg, & Marmar, 1990; Shirk, 1998; Riso et al., 2007; Shirk & Russell, 1996).

EMPIRICAL FOUNDATIONS OF STORYTELLING TECHNIQUES

The empirical foundation of any instrument depends on its validity or capacity to measure what it purports to assess and to do so reliably. Validity and reliability are not established generically for the storytelling technique but demonstrated separately for each set of pictures, administrative procedure, and interpretive method.

Therefore, evidence supporting or disconfirming a specific approach to narrative assessment is the property of that particular method. Psychometric standards apply with equal rigor to every assessment strategy, whether reliant on questionnaires or performance tasks but, in their application, psychometric principles are tailored to the nature of the technique. Users of open-ended performance tasks depend on the establishment of valid and reliable criteria for coding and interpretation just as users of questionnaire techniques count on previously developed items and scales with demonstrated validity and reliability (see Cramer, 1996; Jenkins, 2008; Teglasi, 1993, 1998).

Construct Validity

Clarity about the construct that a test purports to measure is essential to its proper use. The idea of construct validity rests with the assumption that the phenomenon being measured such as "intelligence" exists in the real world, influencing responses to circumstances regardless of whether or not it is measured. This separation between constructs as real phenomena and measures as attempts to capture those phenomena acknowledges multiple possibilities for assessment of a construct and allows ongoing refinements to be made both to the construct and to its various measures. On the other hand, defining a construct as synonymous with a particular measure (i.e., operational definition) leaves little room for revising the construct. An example of construct refinement, discussed earlier in the chapter, is the formulation of *explicit* and *implicit* versions of psychological phenomena as distinct because of their differential influences on real-life behaviors. This advancement was enabled by the use of diverse measurement approaches for seemingly similar constructs that were eventually found to provide unique information. The notion that performance and self-report instruments are alternative measures of the same construct is no longer theoretically defensible. Likewise, low agreement by different informants on questionnaires raise questions about their equivalence across informants (De Los Reyes & Kazdin, 2005).

For a test to be valid (see Borsboom, Mellenbergh, & Van Heerden, 2004), the construct measured must refer to a "real" phenomenon that causes variation in responses in actual life settings and also causes variation in responses to the test. According to Borsboom and colleagues (2004), "validity" as a concept is distinct from "validation" as the activities to establish validity. A commonly used validation activity, the "multi-trait-multi-method" correlation matrix, has been used to tease apart variance due to methods and constructs (Campbell & Fiske, 1959). Although providing important information, this matrix does not directly address the core issue of validity, the existence of an attribute, and its causal influence on real world and test responses. Evidence bearing on "validity" comes from knowledge of the causal influences exerted by the construct on item responses.

Construct "validation" refers to "an integration of any evidence that bears on the interpretation or meaning of test scores" (Messick, 1989, p. 17), including all forms of reliability and other indicators that a test measures what is intended. The evaluation of validation evidence must be in tune with the theoretical conception of the phenomenon in question. For instance, "intelligence" is real because it influences responses not only to the test items but also in real-life contexts. However, if intelligence tests are limited to highly structured items, then responses are generalizable only to similarly structured real-world contexts. In keeping with the emphasis of Borsboom and colleagues, patterns of convergences or divergences of various measures of aggression (multi-trait-multi-method matrix) would not inform validity without accounting for the influences of various aggression-related phenomena on responses to the various measures. These phenomena may include forms (overt and relational) and functions of aggression (proactive and reactive; see Card & Little, 2006) as well as implicit and explicit versions of the aggression construct (Frost, Ko, & James, 2007). In essence, the validity of constructs is not provided by tables of correlations but by substantive psychological theory.

Ascribing *validity* to the TAT for clinical use starts with the formulation of meaningful psychological constructs that are causally related to responses in the real world and to story construction. The categories for coding stories then must reflect current understandings of the construct. Accordingly, frequency counts of aggressive story content, even if reliable across raters, are of limited value in assessing the construct of aggression (see Teglasi, 1993, 1998) because they fail to take important distinctions into account such as the stimulus pull for aggressive content, intent of aggression, outcomes of aggression, as well as forms and functions of aggression. As explained in subsequent chapters, all content, including aggression, takes on meaning in reference to the eliciting pictured stimulus, evoking circumstances, intentions, and outcomes.

Developing and validating units for interpreting TAT stories also require careful attention to measurement issues such as the possible confounding influence of number of words or story length in some interpretive systems (e.g., Veroff, Atkinson, Feld, & Gurin, 1960). Two proposals to resolve this problem are the use of a correction factor for story length (e.g., Cramer, 1987; Murray, 1943; Winter, 1982) and the use of interpretive units that are not referenced directly to the words in the story but to underlying structures (Teglasi, Locraft, & Felgenhauer, 2008a, b).

Above all else, conceptual clarity should guide the evaluation of the evidence supporting the usefulness of a measure.

Face Validity

The concept of face validity refers to whether the "appearance" of a test is consistent with what it is designed to measure. Because the test taker does not know how the stories are to be interpreted, face validity is a matter of acceptability of the storytelling procedure on its "face." Telling stories about social scenes that depict tension does appear to be a "face valid" measure of social information processing. However, face validity, according to the Standards for Educational and Psychological Testing, is not an acceptable basis for drawing conclusions from a test.

Criterion Validity

Criterion validation of a measure includes activities to establish a correlation, concurrent or predictive, between the instrument and a designated set of criteria. However, since the same constructs are assumed to underlie variation in responses to the measure in question (e.g., TAT) and to criterion variables (real-life responses), it would seem logical that both would be subject to construct validation (Messick, 1989). Accordingly, a given performance measure would be understood in terms of its functional demands, and responses would be expected to generalize to other tasks and life situations only if they make similar functional demands (i.e., measure the same dimension of the construct). This emphasis on construct validity places equal value on prediction and explanation as fundamental to validation efforts. The need to distinguish between prediction and explanation is demonstrated by findings that TAT and self-report measures of achievement motivation both correlate with external criteria, but in different ways (discussed earlier).

Incremental Validity

An instrument has the property of incremental validity if it adds information to other measures in the battery by raising the overall correlation with the criterion (Mischel, 1968). An example of incremental validity is the prediction of grade point average (GPA) or job success from a combination of IQ and TAT scores, noting the contribution that each adds to the other. The more multiply determined and complex a criterion, the more important it is to account for the role of multiple constructs. The limitations of any single construct (and its associated measures) to explain functioning is evident in the frequent use of multiple assessment measures and the notion of "incremental validity," which refers to the capacity of a test to provide unique information to the prediction of a criterion after controlling for contributions of other measures (Mayer, 2003). According to such a practical view of incremental validity, a test would be valued if it accounts for variance in a criterion not obtained by other instruments in a given battery. On the other hand, if incremental validity were rooted in construct validity, value would be placed on the unique contributions of constructs, as variously measured, rather than on single instruments. In other words, the practical question of which tests should be selected would be transformed to the question of which constructs are pertinent to a given phenomenon, what are the unique contributions of each construct to variance in that phenomenon, and what are the best ways to measure each construct? Emphasis on construct validity would allow incremental validity activities to independently consider the adequacy of the constructs and of their measures as both predictor and predicted variables. The overriding question would be about the nature of the constructs that underlie variation in the predictor and the predicted variable.

Content Validity

The content validity of thematic apperception techniques may refer to picture stimuli or to the interpretive units. Regarding picture stimuli, content validity refers to sufficiency of sampling thematic domains (e.g., types of relationships, emotions, or situations), whereas the content validity of the interpretive strategy concerns the adequacy of the coding units applied to narrative content to measure the phenomenon under consideration (e.g., object relations).

Conceptual Validity

Whereas construct validity and incremental validity connect measures and constructs across individuals, "conceptual validity" (from Maloney & Ward, 1976) centers on patterns within single individuals. The formulation of a *case conceptualization* yields hypotheses about how an individual has arrived at a particular stance toward life at a given point in his or her development. Given that similar outcomes may be traced to different causal pathways (equifinality) and different outcomes may be caused by similar factors (multifinality; Cicchetti & Rogosch, 1996), the case conceptualization is not a simple matter. It is not possible to consult a list of specific risk or protective factors in persons or environments to anticipate certain outcomes for all individuals, and similar behaviors in a given setting are explained by different causes. Therefore, a case conceptualization is basically a procedure to fashion a working model of the individual's ongoing interactions with various contexts and the growth of schemas synthesizing those interactions. In so doing, an exclusive focus on documenting behavioral variations across settings (as in functional behavioral analysis) is limited because it does not include procedures to examine causal influences beyond the immediate circumstances (Haynes

& O'Brien, 1990). Likewise, assessments that are narrowed to descriptions of diagnostic symptoms do not consider other characteristics of the individual such as coping resources and do not clarify the mechanisms by which a given disorder (e.g., anxiety) limits functioning.

Conceptual validity of a case formulation is grounded in procedures that yield causal hypotheses for the relevant phenomena by examining information about individuals' current and prior interactions contributing to the presenting concerns. Regardless of the theoretical orientation guiding the professional's views on assessment or intervention, the case conceptualization takes into consideration the heuristic that behavior is a function of the person, environment, and the dynamics between them (Lewin, 1935). Individual functioning in current contexts is informed by what has been learned (schemas) in previous encounters. Due to their impact on how individuals interact in their current contexts, schemas are considered important targets of intervention (e.g., Shirk & Russell, 1996), and both implicit and explicit schemas need to be addressed (Dowd, 2006).

Reliability

The general concept of reliability in psychological assessment refers to the attribute of consistency in measurement.

Rater Reliability

The product of storytelling is an open-ended response that requires interpretive judgment and documentation of the reliability of that judgment. Interrater reliability addresses the question of whether the interpretive procedure applied by different raters to identical responses yields the same result. Interrater reliability for thematic techniques tends to be high when interpretive criteria are clearly designated and interpreters are well trained in the rating procedure (Karon, 1981). Under such conditions, agreement calculated between two (or more) raters or a rater and a set of practice materials scored by an expert often exceeds the .80 to .85 range, which is generally considered adequate (Lundy, 1985). With training and practice, interrater reliability in each of the coding parameters described in this book is .80 or higher (Blankman, Teglasi, & Lawser, 2002; Teglasi, Locraft, & Felgenhauer, 2008a). Clear criteria and adequate training reduce the bias by differential experience of the interpreter and by variation in values or assumptions about what responses reflect (see Jenkins, 2008). Though not generally reported in the literature, in clinical use, it may be important to establish the reliability of a single rater over time.

Decisional Reliability

Another way of evaluating the reliability across raters is to examine the agreement in global judgments or decisions derived from the protocol rather than focusing on specific units. This form of reliability more accurately reflects the clinical use of the TAT, where clinicians apply their knowledge of research and theory to draw conclusions. One problem is that professionals with different theoretical foci tend to emphasize different aspects of the protocol. However, Shneidman (1951) demonstrated that 16 clinicians using their own methods came to similar conclusions. An important influence on reliability of decisions relates to the number of performance samples or cards administered. For a reliable assessment with the TAT, it has been recommended that clinicians obtain at least six stories from each respondent (Lundy, 1985; Smith, 1992).

Test-Retest Reliability

Two important considerations in documenting reliability upon retesting are (a) whether the focus is on similarity of story content or similarity of the clinician's judgment (Karon, 1981), and (b) whether the personality construct under consideration is relatively stable or fluctuating (Cramer, 1996). The reliability of the specific content is less relevant than consistency of the interpretive meaning of the response with the passage of time. Moreover, given that personality may be subject to change, the time interval between testing and retesting is crucial, and the degree of consistency must be viewed in light of data and theory about expected change in the particular unit on which reliability is sought. Structural characteristics of TAT stories tend to remain stable (at least in the short term) as shown by test-retest correlations (Locraft & Teglasi, 1997).

Internal Consistency

Items of a test measuring a particular construct are expected to correlate with each other. The higher the

CAUTION

The terms *objective* and *projective* imply that the former is less subjective. However, as George Kelly (1958) points out, both objective and projective methods have subjective elements, though they occur in different parts of the assessment process: Reliability of items on a rating scale is essentially a matter of consistency in the respondents' interpretation of questions, whereas reliability of inferences based on thematic apperceptive methods rests on a combination of the stimulus, the response, the method of interpretation, and the skill of the interpreter. Meyer and Kurtz (2006) offer editorial guidelines for authors submitting manuscripts to the *Journal of Personality Assessment* to shift away from use of the terms projective and objective.

correlation among the items as indicated by coefficient alpha, the more consistently each item measures the construct under consideration. Split-half reliability (in which scores on one half of the test such as odd and even items are correlated with the other) is another way of estimating the internal consistency. When documenting internal consistency of the TAT, each picture is considered as one item. The number of TAT stories obtained may not be sufficient to establish split-half reliability. A more general problem concerns all approaches to internal consistency in TAT type measures. Given that the pictures are designed to elicit different themes (Morgan & Murray, 1935), it would be inappropriate to rely on story content to establish internal consistency (Lundy, 1985). Indeed, with respect to thematic content, the TAT does not meet the tenets of classical psychometric theory because test-retest reliabilities have been higher than measures of internal consistency (alpha coefficients)—a pattern that is contrary to traditional psychometric assumptions (Lundy, 1985). However, consistency of structural variables, not influenced directly by the picture, is conceptually defensible and seems acceptable (Atkinson, Bongort, & Price, 1977). Internal consistency appears to be high with structural or formal qualities of the story, such as the accuracy of the match between the story and the stimulus or the degree of cohesiveness among story details (Blankman, Teglasi, & Lawser, 2002; Teglasi, Locraft, & Felgenhauer, 2008a).

TEST YOURSELF

1. **The Rorschach is primarily a test of perception, whereas the TAT is a test of apperception.**

   True or False?

2. **Historically, criteria for coding stories have been most clinically useful if**
   (a) they were narrowly specified and psychometrically validated.
   (b) they provided broad interpretive guidelines.
   (c) both "a" and "b."
   (d) neither "a" nor "b."

3. **Schema theory supports the following assumptions that are central to the "projective hypothesis":**
   (a) importance of previously organized "sets" for the interpretation of current experience.
   (b) importance of mental processes that operate outside of awareness.
   (c) both "a" and "b."
   (d) neither "a" nor "b."

(continued)

4. **Knowledge structures or schemas organize information that is**
   (a) independent of the knower and amenable to public verification.
   (b) limited to the knower and not amenable to validation by logical analysis.
   (c) both "a" and "b."
   (d) neither "a" nor "b."

5. **TAT stories may constitute**
   (a) a replay of actual experiences.
   (b) ideas borrowed from the media.
   (c) abstractions synthesized from life experiences.
   (d) all of the above.

6. **Storytelling is useful to assess schemas and social problem-solving strategies in**
   (a) highly familiar scripted situations.
   (b) novel, stressful, complex, or emotionally charged situations.
   (c) both "a" and "b."
   (d) neither "a" nor "b."

7. **Dual theories of information processing contrast**
   (a) the "experiencing" self, influenced by emotion, and the verbally defined self.
   (b) emotion-driven thinking and rational analytic mode of thinking.
   (c) narrative thought and propositional thought.
   (d) all of the above.

8. **Individual differences in emotional, cognitive, and attentional processes influence the development of schemas.**
   True or False?

9. **All reliability and validity evidence may be subsumed under the rubric of construct validation.**
   True or False?

10. **Storytelling and self-report measures may be used interchangeably.**
    True or False?

11. **Documenting the psychometric qualities of the TAT is complicated by**
    (a) the need to establish validity and reliability for each interpretive method.
    (b) the need to demonstrate reliability for each rater.
    (c) both "a" and "b."
    (d) neither "a" nor "b."

Answers: 1. True; 2. b; 3. c; 4. c; 5. d; 6. b; 7. d; 8. True; 9. True; 10. False; 11. c.

Two

ESSENTIALS OF STORYTELLING ADMINISTRATION

Thematic apperceptive techniques have been characterized as performance measures of personality with the pictured stimuli and the instructions constituting standard elements of the storytelling task (Teglasi, 1998). If thematic apperceptive techniques are to reveal competencies, such as sizing up social cues and reasoning about social situations, then the pictured stimuli along with the instructions must impose those demands.

STIMULI

The name Thematic Apperception Test (TAT) refers to the specific stimuli and instructions introduced by Murray (1943). However, the term *thematic apperception* has been used in a generic sense and is not restricted to one set of picture cards (Keiser & Prather, 1990). Subsequent to the introduction of the TAT, various sets of stimuli have been developed to elicit themes according to a given theoretical orientation (Blacky Test, Blum, 1950; Tasks of Emotional Development, Cohen & Weil, 1975) or to sample attitudes in a specific situation (School Apperception Method, Solomon & Starr, 1968; Education Apperception Test, Thompson & Sones, 1973). Pictures were also introduced for use with specific populations such as children (Children's Apperception Test, Bellak & Bellak, 1949; Roberts Apperception Test for Children, McArthur & Roberts, 1982—currently, Roberts 2, Roberts & Gruber, 2005; Children's Apperceptive Storytelling Test, Schneider, 1989); adolescents (Symonds Picture Story Test for Adolescents, Symonds, 1939, 1949; senior adults (Senior Apperception Test, Bellak & Bellak, 1973; Gerontological Apperception Test, Wolk & Wolk, 1971); and specific ethnic groups (Tell-Me-A-Story, Constantino, Malgady, & Rogler, 1988; Thompson, 1949). Sets of stimuli have also been introduced in response to criticisms that the TAT pictures are achromatic, negative in emotional tone, and lacking in racial diversity (e.g., Holmstrom, Silber, & Karp, 1990; McArthur & Roberts, 1982; Schneider, 1989; Thompson & Sones, 1973).

The TAT pictures also have been criticized for featuring people wearing dated clothing and hair styles (Henry, 1956; Murstein, 1968) and for their predominantly negative tone (Ritzler, Sharkey, & Chudy, 1980). Despite these criticisms, the TAT stimuli remain the most popular (see Teglasi, 1998). The introduction of different stimuli because they are colorful or because they are more modern has not led to the abandonment of the original set because the new pictures did not incorporate the strengths of the original TAT stimuli. A better understanding of the stimulus qualities may lead to more effective use of thematic apperceptive techniques (Murstein, 1965; Zubin, Eron, & Schumer, 1965).

Stimuli play an important role in shaping the stories, and the value of the pictures resides in their ability to elicit responses with interpretive meaning for important areas of functioning. However, desired stimulus variables differ according to what is being assessed. To date, the introduction of new stimuli has not brought us closer to a theoretical understanding of the role of various properties of pictured stimuli nor to an agreed-upon scoring system. Broad conclusions about the advantages of various characteristics of stimuli, such as their ambiguity (the number of cues guiding the response and the definitiveness of the cues), cannot be drawn without reference to the scoring system, the nature of the population, or intended use. When studying hostility, researchers have argued that pictures with low relevance for unacceptable behavior measure drive toward its expression, whereas pictures with high relevance measure inhibition or guilt about its expression (Salz & Epstein, 1963). Low ambiguity may be preferable in the assessment of a single motive (Singer, 1981), but higher ambiguity may be advantageous in the relative assessment of two motives (Atkinson, 1992). Richness of personality content varied as a function of three levels of ambiguity (high, medium, low) within the TAT set, with cards of medium ambiguity yielding stories with the most personality information (Kenny & Bijou, 1953). However, studies of ambiguity are inconclusive because investigators compare various degrees of ambiguity that are not standard in regard to an underlying dimension of ambiguity.

Although the development of sets of thematic apperceptive stimuli has focused on their relevance to thematic content (e.g., a particular motive), it is likely that the structural features of stimuli contribute to their usefulness in clarifying psychological functioning apart from their content (Teglasi, 1993, 1998). These structural elements of stimuli include degree of complexity, ambiguity, affective tone, number of distinguishing details, or disparate cues to be reconciled. These aspects of stimuli could be systematically varied, along with important elements of content (e.g., age, gender, racial features, type of interaction), to permit conclusions about the respondent's performance in varying degrees of structure and about the schemas pertaining to specific types of interactions. Sets of stimuli with graded levels of ambiguity permit the evaluation of the response along a continuum of structure.

The TAT set (Morgan & Murray, 1935; Murray, 1938) is comprised of 30 pictures and one blank card. These cards are organized into four parallel sets of 20 pictures tailored to the age and gender of the respondent. Accordingly, the cards are numbered from 1 to 20, with some containing letter suffixes to designate them as suitable for boys (B), girls (G), males over 14 (M), females over 14 (F), or combinations of those groups (MF, BG, BM, GF). Cards that have no letters following their numbers are considered suitable for both genders and for any age, 4 or above (for a review of the history of the images depicted in TAT pictures, see Morgan, 1995).

Characteristics of the Respondent in Relationship to the Stimulus

The assumption that the storytellers become more invested in the task, telling longer and richer stories if they identify with the characters, provided the rationale for designating "male" and "female" TAT cards. Clinicians thought that the respondents' identification would be enhanced if respondents perceived themselves as being similar to the character or characters depicted in the stimulus. However, college students did not identify more with pictured characters of their own gender (Katz, Russ, & Overholser, 1993). The data showed no gender-based differences in story length, amount of fantasy, or nature of the affect. Furthermore, it is not possible to ascertain on the basis of stimulus similarity that the storyteller does or does not identify with the character. For example, regardless of their gender, most children telling stories about Card 2 of the TAT focus on the young woman in the foreground, although there is a male in the background. Thus, the centrality of the figure seems to be the basis for its prominence in the stories. Currently, TAT cards are not administered according to their original designation as appropriate for adult males and females or boys and girls (e.g., B = boy; M = man; G = girl; F = woman). Thus Card 3BM, which is designated as appropriate for a boy or a man, is just as often used for a girl or a woman.

In general, adaptations of stimuli for specialized populations do not elicit richer, more productive stories than do the traditional TAT figures (Bailey & Green, 1977; Weisskopf-Joelson, Zimmerman, & McDaniel, 1970). The Gerontological Apperception Test (GAT) introduced for use with aged patients (Wolk & Wolk, 1971) was based on the assumption that many individuals at an advanced age would find it difficult to identify with the situations and characters depicted in the TAT. The GAT depicted "problems specific to the aged such as loss of sexuality, loss of attractiveness, physical limitations, and family difficulties [that] are not usually elicited" (p. 3). However, a comparison of the GAT with the TAT showed no advantage to the GAT (Fitzgerald, Pasewark, & Fleisher, 1974; Pasewark, Fitzgerald, Dexter, & Cangemi, 1976). Similar reasoning was applied to the development of the Senior Apperception Test (Bellak, 1975), which, likewise, did not fare better than the TAT. The essential issue may not be one of similarity but the capacity of the narrator to grasp the meaning of the experience portrayed.

The original set of TAT cards depicted Caucasian characters, and questions have been raised regarding their applicability to other populations. Bailey and Green (1977) modified Murray's TAT cards to provide a more realistic depiction of characters of African descent than the previous attempt by Thompson (1949), which superimposed dark skin on white features. They compared stories told to the newly developed stimuli, the original TAT cards, and the Thompson modification. Although African American respondents (ages 25 to 45) rated both sets of modified cards as facilitating their production, the response content was not affected. Moreover, there were no differences across the three sets of stimuli on ratings of respondents' ability to relate personal feelings. Indeed, perceived similarity of the narrator and pictured character corresponded more to the affective tone of the relationship depicted in the TAT card than to the content of the themes that are frequently elicited (Alvarado, 1994). The concern regarding the issue of similarity between stimulus figures and storyteller may have more to do with sensitivity to the feelings of the respondent than with the utility of the information derived from the assessment.

As stimuli are shaped to incorporate the diversity of the population, it is important for professionals not to abandon other theoretical and empirical considerations. One example is the introduction of the TEMAS ("themes" in Spanish), an acronym for a projective storytelling technique called Tell—Me—A—Story by Constantino, Malgady, and Rogler (1988). The TEMAS stimuli are not equivalent to the TAT pictures, differing in at least two important respects: structure and the number of characters portrayed. First, the TEMAS stimuli are structured by presenting two sides of a dilemma as alternatives to be reconciled, thereby providing more clues to guide the narrative than the TAT cards. Second, the busier stimuli and greater number of characters in the TEMAS encourage longer stories, particularly if the narrator takes a descriptive approach. Constantino and Malgady (1983) administered two versions of the TEMAS, minority and nonminority, along with the standard TAT pictures to three groups of children: Hispanic, African American, and European American. Minority children told longer stories to both versions of the TEMAS than to the standard TAT cards. However, minority students' story length did not differ across the two versions of the TEMAS, minority and nonminority, suggesting that other aspects of the stimulus besides the social/ethnic features of the characters accounted for the difference. The European-American children showed equal verbal productivity regardless of stimuli. Moreover, African American and European American children demonstrated equal verbal productivity on the TAT. The point here is not to denigrate the TEMAS nor tout the superiority of the TAT but to emphasize the conceptual distinctions and similarities among various methods of assessment rather than to assume them based on superficial resemblance or differences.

Qualities of the Pictured Stimulus

The task of telling a story about a pictured scene implicitly calls for a story that "explains" the stimulus and develops a "context" for the interpretation through an appropriate network of events, thoughts, feelings, intentions, actions, and outcomes. For the assessment of personal schemas, it is most useful to present stimuli depicting scenes that are difficult to explain in terms of the common cultural stereotypes or canned stories. One of the advantages of the TAT set is that the pictures portray situations conveying unfinished business that do not fit the stereotypic mold (Henry, 1956). For instance, Card 4 of the TAT calls for the narrator to reconcile the discrepancy between the close physical proximity of the man and woman portrayed and the contrast between the angry expression on the man's face and the conciliatory expression of the woman. A scene that can be explained easily in terms of schemas representing familiar, scripted knowledge may be handled by imposing a canned story, whereas an unusual or complex scene calls for more flexible use of knowledge structures to explain the scene and comply with instructions.

There are two basic ways to evaluate stimulus pull: (a) types of themes frequently elicited and (b) qualities of the pictured scene (Peterson & Schilling, 1983). Descriptions of typical themes elicited by various TAT cards are available (Bellak, 1975; Bellak & Abrams, 1997; Henry, 1956; Holt, 1978; Murstein, 1968; Stein, 1955). The thematic pull of the cards has been important to clinicians who are interested in exploring an individual's style of response to identified areas of psychological functioning. However, some cards elicit a wider range of themes than others (e.g., Cooper, 1981; Newmark & Flouranzano, 1973). Perhaps such cards are more useful because they provide greater leeway for the respondent to express psychologically meaningful content. Indeed, Haynes and Peltier (1985) found that nine of the cards that were identified by Newmark and Flouranzano as eliciting a wide range of themes were rated by clinicians as most frequently used.

Attitudes revealed in any particular story may be specific to the interaction of the characters portrayed in the picture presented. Relationships among peers, adults, and children, or between males and females, may engender different schemas. Therefore, an adequate sampling of pictures depicting individuals of various ages, genders, and types of interactions is useful. In addition, the structural qualities of the stimulus influence the ease or difficulty in finding an appropriate explanation for the scene. Stimulus details that are not usually mentioned often influence the story implicitly. Flowers or books in Card 5 are not prominently featured, but they may suggest something about the room. Likewise, the jacket and tie worn by the young man in the foreground in Card 8BM is a detail that may provide cues that shape the story (e.g., "on his wedding day"). Other stimulus details are irrelevant (an "eyebrow" in Card 1 or "the man's underwear" in Card 2). The demands of the task vary according to the qualities of the picture stimuli, and clinicians must evaluate performance in the context of these demands (see Rapid Reference 2.1).

≡ *Rapid Reference 2.1*

Four Structural Components of TAT Pictures

1. **Minor or irrelevant details**— Rarely mentioned explicitly and usually having little influence on the narrative (suggests narrow focus on detail characterizing concrete thought; Card 1 "someone has an eyebrow" or card 2 "there are lines in the ground").

2. **Context**— A relatively central object or clothing that usually influences the interpretation of the scene but may or may not be explicitly mentioned (violin in Card 1, books being held by the girl in Card 2). Some objects, such as the gun in Card 3BM, are meaningful but may recede into the background (not noticed or deliberately ignored) or may be identified as something else (such as keys) without misinterpreting the overall gestalt of the picture.

3. **Postures and facial expressions**— Most salient in guiding interpretation of the scenes are the postures and facial expressions that convey characters' emotions and relationships as well as their apparent attitude or activity. For example, in Card 1, a certain mood is suggested by the boy's touching his face as well as by his posture and facial expression. These aspects of the stimulus implicitly guide the narratives but are rarely mentioned explicitly.

4. **Configuration**— A precise interpretation, grounded in the relations among the details, context, postures/facial expressions, captures the psychological issue or subtext of the scene, incorporating the stimulus components without directly (descriptively) focusing on them.

Content and Structure of the Pictured Stimulus

Characteristics of Picture Content

1. *Characteristics of the people.* Central to the narrative is the portrayal of the characters, in terms of age, gender, or general appearance, feelings, and activities. A thematic apperceptive set should sample different types of relationships to elicit a range of schemas from the respondent. The set should also include pictures that vary in the number of persons portrayed.

2. *Characteristics of the background scene or objects.* The type of setting, such as a rural background, or objects, such as a gun, are pertinent to the story content but are not as central as the basic emotions or relationships.

3. *Psychological issue.* The underlying psychological dilemma conveyed by the stimulus configuration (nature of the background, objects, facial expressions, and postures of the characters) constitutes the emotional issue raised or latent meaning of the stimulus (Henry, 1956). For example, Card 1, depicting a boy and a violin, raises the possible conflict between personal inclination and demands of outside agents. Furthermore, perceptions of family relationships may come to the forefront because the violin implies a task that is not required by the educational system but is typically promoted by the family.

4. *Similarity to the respondent.* The match between the age, gender, race, or ethnic background of the respondent and those of characters portrayed in the stimuli has been considered a possible factor influencing the response. Although more research is needed, evidence to date suggests that physical similarities (such as age, gender, race) may not be critical (Murstein, 1963). What may be paramount is how meaningful the psychological issues portrayed are to the respondent.

Characteristics of Picture Structure

1. *Ambiguity.* Murstein (1963, 1965) distinguished between structure and ambiguity of the TAT pictures. Structure is the property of the stimulus (e.g., clarity about who and what is depicted; provision of cues or props), whereas ambiguity is a function of variation in themes elicited by the card (Newmark & Flouranzano, 1973). Pictures of moderate ambiguity permit variability in response but provide anchors to guide the professional's interpretation (Lindzey, 1952; Murstein, 1965). In

contrast, stimuli that present a clear depiction of what might be happening in the picture reduce the variability in responses. For example, one of the cards in the Tasks of Emotional Development (TED) portrays a middle-aged woman pointing to a child's possessions on the floor while the child looks on. This scene constrains the response more than TAT Card 5, which depicts an older woman looking into a room (various objects in the room, such as books or flowers, are present but are not central). The TED stimulus defines the characters and the conflict by pulling for a story about a parent chastising a child about a specific transgression. The Roberts 2, Card 14, is similarly structured to portray parent-child conflict, intending to pull for maternal limit setting. The TAT picture does not preclude this theme but permits the selection of numerous others. A quality of the stimulus related to ambiguity is its stereotypicality, or the extent to which the stimulus configuration portrays commonly recognized social contexts within a culture that are amenable to a conventional or "scripted" explanation. A stimulus may contain many cues constraining the narrative, and these cues may be more or less in line with the cultural stereotypes. Stimuli that are explained easily by a stereotypic story downplay the demand on the narrator to marshal internally organized schemas in favor of social schemas. The Roberts 2 uses stimuli that reflect structured situations that are recognizable real-life events (Roberts & Gruber, 2005). Given that the pictures clearly portray the "meaning" of the situation, the authors removed the term "apperception" from the name of the test, indicating that the Roberts 2 is not a projective technique.

2. *Affective tone.* Theoretically, the general mood of pictures used in thematic apperceptive techniques may be positive, negative, or neutral. The TAT cards have been criticized for their predominantly negative tone (Ritzler, Sharkey, & Chudy, 1980), in part because the pictures are black and white. Given the common association of color with positive feelings, the presence or absence of color is thought to contribute to the emotional tone of the pictured scene. However, systematic evidence is not sufficient to warrant conclusions about the potential influence of color on stories told about otherwise identical scenes. Moreover, the negative tone may be advantageous because it presents unfinished business or a dilemma to be resolved, providing the opportunity to observe how the respondent appraises and deals

with the tensions depicted in the picture. Essentially, the negative scenes make it possible to observe how the narrator moves from the sadness or conflict to an adaptive resolution. The Apperceptive Personality Test (APT) was designed to avoid the negative tone of the TAT stimuli (Holmstrom, Silber, & Karp, 1990). Nevertheless, judges rated outcomes of the TAT stories as more favorable than those of the APT stories (participants did not differ in their ratings of the story outcomes). This finding suggests that whether the story ends happily or unhappily is a function of the narrator rather than the stimulus. In ambiguous situations, the schemas associated with potent emotions may come to the surface. Thus, one of the advantages of presenting stimuli with many possible responses (such as the TAT) is to allow the emergence of the most salient schemas.

3. *Complexity.* Degree of stimulus complexity varies according to the number and type of discrepant elements that need to be synthesized into a cohesive story (e.g., foreground and background, facial expressions and posture). Unusual details (gun in a surgery scene) call for ingenuity to develop a story that is in tune with the stimuli because they cannot be readily explained.

4. *Intensity.* A dramatic portrayal of the conflict or of the emotion as evident in the TAT stimuli is likely to give the impression of unfinished business and, thereby, draw in the respondent (Henry, 1956). Other stimuli that utilize line drawings (Roberts 2) or colorful pictures (TEMAS) fall short of the life-like rendering of the people portrayed in the achromatic TAT set.

5. *Universality.* The generality of the emotions or experiences depicted may overcome the necessity of creating separate sets of stimuli that portray different ages, genders, and racial or ethnic groups. It has been suggested that pictures representing relatively universal social situations that most people encounter are suitable across various age and subcultural groups (Veroff, 1992).

ADMINISTRATION

Any open-ended task is sensitive to cues and instructional sets that may guide the response (Dana, 1982). Therefore, it is necessary to establish standard administrative procedures for structuring the task, for providing encouragement, and for prompting responses. It is also important to represent faithfully the narrator's performance of the task. The sequence of cards in the TAT set has an inherent logic, and, generally, they should be administered in numerical order (Arnold, 1962; Bellak, 1986; Karon, 1981). For instance, the first two cards (1 and 2) are relatively benign, whereas cards 3BM and 4 depict more intense emotions. However, as described in the next section, each card has unique qualities, and the professional may use judgment in determining the sequence.

Instructions

The instructions for the TAT ask respondents to construct a complete story that includes the following components (Murray, 1943): What is happening in the picture? What happened before? How are people (persons) in the picture feeling? What are they thinking? How does everything turn out at the end? These story components are relevant to social cognitive theories, incorporating the various elements of social information processing involved in social problem solving (see Rapid Reference 2.2).

Rapid Reference 2.2

TAT Instructions and Social Problem-Solving Components Embedded in the Schema (Teglasi, 1998)

Problem-Solving Component	Instructions (and information processing)
Identify Problem: The narrator identifies the problem implied in the scene by sizing up the stimulus (context, objects, clothing, people, facial expressions, and postures). The task is to coordinate internal and external sources of tension in the interpretation of the scene.	What is happening in the picture? (encoding and interpreting stimuli to distill the central problem or dilemma from the perspectives of the various characters)
Understanding Causal Sequences: The narrator establishes logical and cohesive sequences of events, connecting causes with effects and ordering stream of events in a realistic timeframe.	What happened before? (placing events in historical context)

Problem-Solving Component	Instructions (and information processing)
Understanding the Inner World: The narrator connects the inner world of characters, their thoughts, feelings and intentions, with their overt actions and with sequences of events.	What are the characters thinking and how are they feeling? (understanding the influences of mental states on responses, establishing goals, or intentions)
Understanding Means-Ends Connections: The narrator proposes appropriate means to resolve the tensions or problems set before the characters in ways that coordinate the above.	How does the story end? (forging causal links among intentions, behaviors, and outcomes, thereby conveying expectations of what responses produce what effects)

Similar instructions apply to other thematic apperception techniques developed after the TAT, including those described in Chapter 8. As long as directions to include specific components of stories are clearly communicated, the exact wording is not crucial. The professional should use language that is appropriate to the narrator's level of understanding.

Instructions for adults are (Murray, 1943, adaptation from pages 5–6):

I am going to show you some pictures, one at a time, and your task will be to make up a story for each card. In your story, be sure to tell what has led up to the event shown in the picture, describe what is happening at the moment, what the characters are feeling and thinking, and then give the outcome. Tell a complete story with a beginning, middle, and end. Do you understand? I will write your stories verbatim as you tell them. Here's the first card. (The examiner hands the picture to the client.)

The following modification of the general instructions for younger children is given by Murray (1943, adaptation from pages 5–6):

I am going to show you some pictures, and I would like you to tell me a story for each one. In your story, please tell: What is happening in the picture? What happened before? What are people thinking and how are they feeling? How does it all turn out in the end? So, I'd like you to tell a whole story with a beginning, middle, and ending. You can make up any story you want about the picture. Do you understand? I'll write down your story. Here's the first card. (The examiner hands the picture to the client.)

Rapid Reference 2.3

TAT Administration Guidelines for Clients with Intellectual Disability (Hurley & Sovner, 1985)

1. The examiner should use concrete vocabulary when giving directions.
2. The examiner may demonstrate by making up a story to a sample card.
3. Beyond prompting as needed for each component of the directions, the examiner may ask clarifying questions as needed without being "suggestive."

If the examiner is also audiotaping, he or she may say: "I will write down your stories as you tell them, but I am also tape-recording them in case I miss some of what you say."

Instructions for telling TAT stories do not provide new information but simply reiterate the elements of the familiar story form. Even young children are aware of the basic story structure (Applebee, 1978) and, at least theoretically, it would be sufficient to ask the respondent to tell a whole story with a beginning, middle, and end. However, giving systematic instructions, as proposed by Murray, is advantageous because they set standards for the narrative product and provide a vehicle for standard queries by the examiner. Prompts, especially with children, are frequently necessary to obtain sufficient material for interpretation. Professionals have proposed departures from the generally accepted procedure to administer the test to clients who have mild or moderate mental disabilities (see Rapid Reference 2.3). Peterson (1990) suggests this variation of the instructions, which gives as few cues as possible: "Tell me a story about what might be happening in this picture" (p. 194). A modification of Murray's instruction, substituting "what is the problem" for "what is happening" in the picture (Ronan, Colavito, & Hammontree, 1993; Ronan, Date, & Weisbrod, 1995), was intended to facilitate scoring according to a problem-solving conceptualization.

Settings and Materials

The testing room should be comfortable and free of distracting sounds and objects (toys, clutter). Some examiners avoid a direct face-to-face position to minimize the possibility of giving inadvertent cues to the client. However, there is no compelling reason to change seating position or other routines established earlier in the administration. The examiner needs the selected picture cards, tools for writing, and tape recorder.

Encouragement

Although the TAT is considered suitable for children as young as age 4, even older children and adults sometimes have difficulty developing a story that includes all of the elements requested in the directions. It is suggested that examiners follow a standard procedure for prompting at all ages. If the individual has difficulty getting started and instructions have been repeated and clarified, the examiner might say something like, "Start by saying what might be happening in the picture." If the respondent starts the story but hesitates, the examiner should nod encouragingly or prompt the storyteller to "go on" in preference to specific questions. Such general prompts are meant to convey the expectation that the storytelling process is not a series of questions and answers (though on some occasions, this is unavoidable). If the narrator seems "stuck" after describing what is happening in the picture, the next prompt might be, "What might have happened before?" Next, the examiner might inquire about how the sequence of events proceeds and if necessary prompt for an ending to the story by asking "How does everything turn out at the end?" If omitted by the narrator, at this point, the examiner should inquire about how the characters are feeling and what they are thinking. The examiner may query as needed to clarify ambiguities such as a vague pronoun reference (e.g., "Who is she?"). To produce a faithful record, the examiner notes all queries as well as the respondent's nonverbal behaviors, remarks, or pauses in storytelling. If the narrator does not respond to encouragement or specific queries, the examiner may suggest coming back to the card later.

DON'T FORGET

- You may repeat the directions if asked or if you feel it is needed.
- Be sure to prompt for story components if not already given by the respondent; each component may be requested only *once per story*. The components are: what is *happening* in the picture, what happened before, what is the character (or characters) *thinking*, how is the character (or characters) *feeling*, and how does it all turn out in the end?
- Make sure the narrator gives an ending to the story.
- Write down *everything* that the narrator says verbatim—whether or not it is part of the story—and *everything* that you say. Also write the narrator's non-verbal responses (pauses in the narration, scowling, big smile, pointing to the lady holding the books, unusual posture, tone of voice, relevant behavior).
- Also, tape record so that you don't miss anything.

(continued)

- Be interested and generally encouraging nonverbally and with statements such as "go on, hmm, then what ..."
- Transcribe the stories as soon as possible after administration (typing during the narration is not conducive to rapport).

DON'T FORGET

Prompts are limited to the four areas of the instructions.

- If the narrator has difficulty getting started, please refrain from a general statement such as, "it is your story, you may tell any story you want." Your encouragement should focus the narrator on the picture by saying, "Tell me a story about this picture." If more is needed, you might say, "Tell me what you think might be happening in the picture." or "You may begin by telling me what might be happening in this picture." If the respondent expresses self-doubt about not telling a good story, don't say "there are no right or wrong or good or bad stories, just make up any story you want." You might say "there are many ways to tell good stories."
- Ask "What happened before?" if the examinee seems stuck after describing the events in the stimulus.
- Ask "What is he/she thinking or how is he/she feeling?" choosing words carefully. For example, don't ask what the person is *thinking about*, as this might prompt a one-word answer (e.g., his mother, the violin).
- ".....and then what happened" or "go on ..." are good general prompts to try to avoid question-answer sets.
- It is important to elicit an ending to the story with queries such as "How does it all turn out? What happens in the end?"
- For any prompt above, if the narrator does not respond, you can repeat the prompt, give an encouraging nod, and say "okay, what else"? However, if the narrator attempts the response, accept whatever is said, without further prompting.
- Wherever possible, use general encouragement in lieu of specific prompts such as nodding, "hmm," or "go on" to avoid a question-answer set.

Recording Responses

A tape recorder may be used to back up the examiner's written notes. There are several advantages to this two-pronged procedure. First, the examiner's handwriting retains the interpersonal component of the interaction, calling on the respondent to pace the story to the requirements of the writer. However, if the respondent speaks too quickly and the examiner cannot keep up, the tape recorder becomes essential. Second, even if the examiner is able to keep up with the respondent's pace, the use of the tape recorder relieves the pressure to write down every utterance because missing words or sentences or parenthetical comments can be filled in later. Third, despite every effort to assure that the tape recorder works properly, the written protocol provides a back up.

DON'T FORGET

When transcribing the stories, common words may be abbreviated, including: Looks like = ll; Long pause = LP; Short pause = SP; What is happening in the picture query = H?; What happened before query = B?; Thinking query = T?; Feeling query = F?; Ending query = TO?.

Selecting Cards

The TAT Manual (Murray, 1943) instructs that 20 cards be administered from the TAT set, which includes 30 pictures and one blank card. Eleven of the cards are designated for all respondents, and nine are selected according to age and gender. It is not required, nor even preferable, that all 20 TAT cards be administered to examinees. A survey of clinicians in juvenile and forensic settings indicated that the mean number of cards used was 10.25 (Haynes & Peltier, 1985). Generally, clinicians administer from 8 to 12 cards. The cards are not selected in accord with their original designations as appropriate for specific ages and gender, but according to clinician's judgment regarding their usefulness to elicit psychologically meaningful material.

Clinicians choose cards based on the "pull" for certain themes or psychological processes under consideration. Peterson and Schilling (1983) offer a theoretical discussion of stimuli. Description of themes most frequently elicited by each TAT card (e.g., Bellak, 1975; Bellak & Abrams, 1997; Henry, 1956; Holt, 1978; Stein, 1955) and a review of perceived usefulness of various cards (Teglasi, 1993) are also available. The first 10 cards of the TAT set depict basic interpersonal relationships that are more likely to elicit emotionally relevant material and are more likely to be used by clinicians than the second set (Cooper, 1981; Ehrenreich, 1990; Worchel, Aaron, & Yates, 1990).

Suggestions for picture selection within the TAT set (Bellak, 1975; Henry, 1956; Teglasi, 1993) indicate that many of the male cards are preferable for both

≡ Rapid Reference 2.4

TAT Card Selection

There is considerable agreement among clinicians regarding preferences for specific TAT cards. Arnold's (1962) preferred cards (1, 2, 3BM, 4, 6BM, 7BM, 8BM, 10, 11, 13MF, 14, 16, and 20) include all but one (12M) of Bellak's (1986) essential and male cards (1, 2, 3BM, 4, 6BM, 7BM, 11, 12M, and 13MF). Preferences indicated by Rabin and Haworth (1960) for children between the ages of 7 and 11 (1, 3BM, 7GF, 8BM, 12M, 13B, 14, and 17BM) and for adolescents (1, 2, 5, 7GF, 12F, 12M, 15, 17BM, and 18GF) include many of the cards favored by Arnold and Bellak. Hartman's (1970) survey of preferred cards with children under the age of 17 in rank order are 1, 3BM, 6BM, 7BM, 13MF, 7GF, 8BM, 4, 10, 12M, 16 (blank), and 18GF. Teglasi (1993) indicated the following cards as most useful for children and adolescents of both genders: 1, 2, 3BM, 4, 5, 6BM, 7GF, and 8BM but also noted that others have been useful depending on age and referral issues (7BM, 10, 12M, 13B, 13MF, 14, and 17BM).

genders because they elicit richer and more complex themes (see Rapid Reference 2.4). In agreement with others, Bellak and Abrams (1997) have proposed a standard set of 8 to 10 cards for use with adults that can be supplemented as needed: 1, 2, 3BM, 4, 6BM, 7GF, 8BM, 9GF, 10, and 13MF. With one exception (13MF), the productive cards seem to work equally well across ages and genders. Cards that do not depict emotions or relationships very clearly or that portray a person immersed in thought with no additional cues (3GF) are not as useful as those that do.

Murray's (1943) description of important stimulus properties and elaboration based on Henry's (1956) review and the author's experience are summarized below for each of the most frequently used TAT cards.

Card 1

Murray's description: "A young boy contemplating a violin which rests on the table in front of him."

Elaboration: 1. Other details are a sheet of music, table, or cloth under the violin. 2. Stimulus demand: Depiction of one character and one major object requires an explanation that accounts for the boy's facial expression in relation to the violin.

Card 2

Murray's description: "Country scene: In the foreground is a young woman with books in her hand; in the background, a man is working in the fields and an older woman is looking on."

Elaboration: 1. Other details include features pertaining to the farm (rocks, buildings, horse) and to the three characters. 2. Stimulus demand: The scene requires integration of the three characters and the background scene as well as the wealth of detail 3. Seldom noted details are: possible pregnancy of the older woman, the furrows in the field, dress of the woman, musculature of the man.

Card 3BM

Murray's description: "On the floor against a couch is the huddled form of a boy with his head bowed on his right arm. Beside him on the floor is a revolver."

Elaboration: 1. The object on the floor beside the huddled figure is most generally seen as a gun or weapon, but people have reported other objects such as keys. Many respondents identify this figure as female. 2. Stimulus demand: The figure and the "gun" are the only forms. Many respondents do not concern themselves with the object, focusing on the posture of the person depicted. Some merely indicate awareness of an object without identifying it.

Card 4

Murray's description: "A woman is clutching the shoulders of a man whose face and body are averted as if he were trying to pull away from her."

Elaboration: 1. On rare occasions, a second woman in the background is reported as a real person, a poster, or picture of a woman. 2. Stimulus demand: An adequate accounting explains the discrepant and dramatic emotions of the man and woman. The two primary characters are in physical proximity (touching) but their emotions are discrepant.

Card 5

Murray's description: "A middle-aged woman is standing on the threshold of a half-opened door, looking into a room."

Elaboration: 1. Other details are objects in the room such as flowers. 2. Stimulus demand: An adequate accounting of this relatively simple scene requires an explanation of why the woman is entering the room. Additional characters may be introduced. Objects in the room may be mentioned, suggesting that attention is diverted by minor detail.

Card 6BM

Murray's description: "A short, elderly woman stands with her back turned to a tall young man. The latter is looking downward with a perplexed expression."

Elaboration: 1. The woman is facing a window, and the man is holding a hat. The hat and window may be mentioned by those who are bolstering their responses by external detail. Otherwise, these remain as implicit cues to the interaction. 2. Stimulus demand: An unusual relationship (e.g., son leaving or imparting bad news) between the man and the woman needs to be explained. The other details are incidental.

Card 7BM

Murray's description: "A gray-haired man is looking at a younger man who is sullenly staring into space."

Elaboration: 1. There are no other details besides the main figures, but facial features may be noted. 2. Stimulus demand: An explanation of the relationship between the two men that accounts for their facial expressions and age differences is needed.

Card 7GF

Murray's description: "An older woman is sitting on the sofa close beside a girl, speaking or reading to her. The girl, who holds a doll in her lap, is looking away."

Elaboration: 1. The girl appears to be disengaged from what the woman is doing. The doll is sometimes perceived as a pet (e.g., "cat"). Details of furniture or clothing are sometimes noted. 2. Stimulus demand: An explanation of the relationship between the two main figures (why the girl is looking away) is needed.

Card 8BM

Murray's description: "An adolescent boy looks straight out of the picture. The barrel of a rifle is visible at one side, and in the background is the dim scene of a surgical operation, like a reverie image."

Elaboration: 1. Often noted details are aspects of the surgical scene, the "knife," the tie and jacket worn by the figure in the foreground. Window or book-case in the upper right is rarely mentioned. 2. Stimulus demand: This is a complex scene demanding an explanation of the relationship between the foreground and the background, which appear to be in different realities. The scene is complicated by the relatively clear depiction of a rifle and various subtle details.

Card 10

Murray's description: "A young woman's head against a man's shoulder."
Elaboration: 1. The gender of the two figures depicted is sufficiently vague to accommodate various interpretations. Thus, the main issue in this card is physical closeness. 2. Stimulus demand: This card has a relative absence of cues to guide interpretation of the relationship.

Card 12M

Murray's description: "A young man is lying on a couch with his eyes closed. Leaning over him is the gaunt form of an elderly man, his hand stretched out above the face of the reclining figure."
Elaboration: 1. Stimulus demand: An explanation of the unusual position of the two figures is needed.

Card 13MF

Murray's description: "A young man is standing with downcast head buried in his arm. Behind him is the figure of a woman lying on the bed."
Elaboration: 1. The woman's nudity is an important detail. 2. Stimulus demand: An explanation of the relationship between the man and the woman is needed.

Card 13B

Murray's description: "A young boy is sitting on the door-step of a log cabin."
Elaboration: 1. Details include aspects of the cabin, the boy's bare feet, a possible object in the boy's hands. 2. Stimulus demand: The stimulus is simple, portraying only one character. As all stimuli with a single figure, this one raises the opportunity for introducing other characters or for explaining what the boy is doing alone. In this way, the card may bring out the sense of relatedness to the larger world. Pictures portraying more than one character compel the respondent to deal with the relationships as depicted.

CAUTION

It is best to administer thematic apperceptive tasks toward the end of a comprehensive battery after rapport has been established because (a) the respondent will feel more comfortable with the examiner as a result of earlier interactions; (b) the respondent's general concerns about the testing can be clarified prior to administering a task that is anxiety provoking for both adults and children due to its ambiguity (Newmark, Hetzel, & Freking, 1974; Newmark, Wheeler, Newmark, & Stabler, 1975); and (c) any resistance or anxiety generated will not interfere with performance of subsequent tasks.

 TEST YOURSELF

1. **Clinicians select TAT stimuli on the basis of**
   (a) their original designation of being appropriate for children or adults and for males or females.
   (b) "pull" for specific thematic content.
   (c) both "a" and "b."
   (d) neither "a" nor "b."

2. **Stimuli play an important role in thematic apperception techniques because**
   (a) they present the emotional, social, and contextual cues to be addressed.
   (b) they vary in the richness and clinical utility of responses they elicit.
   (c) they set the problem-solving demand of the task.
   (d) all of the above.

3. **Individuals tell more clinically useful stories if they are similar in age, gender, or race to the characters depicted.**
   True or False?

4. **When administering the TAT, the standard instructions simply reiterate what one would typically include in a complete story.**
   True or False?

5. **Professionals should provide the narrator with as much encouragement as possible to assure the "best" story possible.**
   True or False?

Answers: 1. d; 2. d; 3. False; 4. True; 5. False

Three

ESSENTIALS OF STORYTELLING INTERPRETATION

The TAT was originally designed for ages 4 and up (Murray, 1938). In her review of studies using the TAT, Cramer (1996) concluded that "the same interpretive perspectives that have been found to be useful in the interpretation of adult TAT stories have been found to be equally informative when used with stories of children" (p. 209). Bellak's interpretive systems for adults (TAT) and for children (CAT) are virtually identical (Bellak & Abrams, 1997). Likewise, procedures to assess schemas provided in this book are applicable to both children and adults as well as to a wide range of picture-story methods, provided they use stimuli that portray tensions to be identified and resolved. The role of schemas in facilitating information processing is detailed in other chapters. The aim of story interpretation is to evaluate the schematic structures and information processing applied to the organization of ill-defined situations. It may be said that schemas enable "intelligent" decisions, particularly in circumstances that require complex judgment. As tools for thinking about experiences, schemas are useful if they are sufficiently accurate and complex to meet the information processing requirements of the situation or task at hand.

Consider the following riddle (source unknown): There was a man one night. He started to run straight forward. Then he turned left. Soon after, he turned left again. Then he started running toward home. When he got home there were two masked men waiting for him. Who were they?

Activation of the baseball schema gives coherence to the facts enabling the solution to the riddle. The man running is a baseball player and the two masked men are the catcher and the umpire. Although individuals vary in the ease with which the baseball schema comes to mind, the schema itself does not change with the individual's experience, hence it is public.

Now consider the following vignette. Alison, an 8-year-old, enthusiastically tells her teacher about her family trip to Disneyland during the preceding long weekend, to which the teacher playfully responds "get out of here." Without hesitation, Alison walked out of the classroom. Despite a well-above-average IQ score, Alison's schemas do not provide a sufficiently nuanced representation of this interaction to allow her to coordinate the emotional cues implicit in the teacher's tone of voice and facial expression with the literal meaning of the words and with the situational context. Whereas the baseball game schema coordinates information about sequences of events in the external world, the schema for grasping this situation requires understanding of mental states.

Alison responded to the teacher's words at face value rather than to the communicative intent. An understanding of mental states, termed "theory of mind" (Premack & Woodruff, 1978), allows a statement such as "get out of here" to be interpreted in light of the entire interaction rather than in isolation. Without a well-developed theory of mind, social perceptions are not contextualized in cognitive frameworks that connect behaviors with intentions, thoughts, or feelings (Malle, 2001), and these limitations are evident in the above vignette and in children with autism (Baron-Cohen, 1995; Frith, 2000; Leslie, 1992).

Both theory of mind and the schema construct assume that mental models are basic tools for social cognition because they organize otherwise disconnected stimuli into units that are easily understood (Baird & Baldwin, 2001; Fiske & Taylor, 1991; Schank & Abelson, 1977). The capacity to infer mental states allows humans (including young children) to make sense of, anticipate, and respond appropriately to others' behaviors. Theory of mind has been formulated by studying instances where it is limited, such as young children and those with autism. Of less concern to schema researchers, but central to theory of mind, is the phenomenon of intentionality or human agency to take action on the basis of mental states (Rapid Reference 3.1).

To understand intentions, it is necessary to distinguish them from desires or wishes (see Malle & Knobe, 2001). Intent is based on the specific beliefs that an individual's action will result in a particular outcome, thereby representing both the intended outcome and paths to taking action, whereas desire is a wish for an outcome but with no commitment to take the initiative. (See Rapid Reference 3.2.)

The major focus of this chapter is on the basics of formulating the underlying import (borrowing the term from Arnold, 1962) or message of TAT stories. The *import* refers to the narrator's schema based on subjective synthesis of experiences rather than to actual life events. The organizational principles imposed on the narrative encapsulated in the import resemble those that structure ongoing experiences. Human memory functions as a filing system for organizing relevant experiences in narrative form (Schank, 1990), including external circumstance, inner tensions or psychological problems, intention, means to pursue them, and outcomes. When certain patterns of relations are repeatedly observed among external events, inner tensions,

≣ *Rapid Reference 3.1*

Intentions, Means, and Ends in Developmental Research

1. The general definition of "theory of mind" is the understanding that behavior is organized by individuals' mental states such as motives, beliefs, or goals (Premack & Woodruff, 1978). In turn, this theory of mind makes it possible to predict others' actions (Astington, 1991; Flavell, 1988) by differentiating between what is objective (outer world of events and actions) and subjective (the inner world of thoughts, beliefs, and intentions). Understanding intentions is supported by a "theory of mind." Longitudinal associations have been found between infant attention to intentional action and theory of mind at age 4, controlling for IQ, verbal competence, and executive functioning (Wellman, Lopez-Duran, LaBounty, & Hamilton, 2008). Moreover, infants selectively attend to and recall features of actions that are relevant to intentions (Wellman & Phillips, 2001). Even though human actions are not broken up in terms of discrete intent-related actions, infants as young as 10 to 11 months are attuned to structure in behavior that corresponds to the initiation and completion of an intention (Baldwin, Baird, Saylor, & Clark, 2001).

2. By age 5, children distinguish between actions that are intentional and those that are not as depicted in stories (Astington & Lee, 1991). Whereas 3- and 4-year-olds had difficulty distinguishing between desires and intentions, by age 5 children were able to do so (Schult, 2002). Understanding false beliefs emerges at age 4 but complex emotions such as surprise and pride are understood later (see reviews, Flavell & Miller, 1998; Wellman, 2002). Problems with the development of a narrative theory of mind (inability to form intentions or generate cohesive ideas) are empirically associated with childhood pathology (Baron-Cohen, 1991, 2000).

3. A child's ability to verbalize an understanding of the connections among intentions, means, and ends lags behind implicit comprehension, just as a 4-year-old's ability to discuss the rules of grammar lags behind the use of language. Despite difficulty verbalizing emotions such as anger or hurt, young children manage to act constructively on their own and others' emotions (Dunn, 1991). Thus, young children differ from adults not in the basic processes of social interaction but in the size of the gap between their implicit and explicit knowledge bases (Premack, 1992). Piaget points to areas such as logico-mathematical thinking as showing the greatest discrepancy between children and adults, whereas those who study the theory of mind point to the ways in which adults think remarkably like their 5-year-old selves (e.g., Gardner, 1991). Children's understanding of intentions is demonstrated implicitly at younger ages through their actions and explicitly at older ages by verbalizing their understanding.

≡ Rapid Reference 3.2

Intention versus Desire

1. Desires are rooted in a culture, embedded in knowledge about ends toward which members of the culture generally strive (Bruner, 1990). Intentions are grounded in the more personal process of forming connections among intentions, actions, and outcomes based on experienced regularities. These intention-action-outcome schemas are more sophisticated than desires because they incorporate means-ends relations and causality.

2. A true intention that is distinct from wish or desire involves an individual who (Knobe, 2003): (a) wants a certain outcome; (b) believes that a given action will lead to that outcome; (c) intends to perform the action; (d) has the capacity to perform that action; and (e) relates the performance of the action to the intention it serves. Most children with autism have difficulty attributing beliefs/ intentions to others but have less difficulty ascribing desires (Baron-Cohen, 1995). Attribution of desires is less sophisticated than ascribing beliefs, emerging earlier developmentally (Wellman & Woolley, 1990).

3. Differences in sophistication in theory of mind are not only seen across age but also across individuals. Although 3-year-old children may make explicit reference to intention, this early view of intentionality is fused with the concept of desire (Baird & Astington, 2005). By age 5, children's conceptions of intention resemble those of adults. Nevertheless, there are older children (and adults) who continue to fuse the idea of desire and goal-directed intention.

intentions, actions, and outcomes, they become a type of structure or schema that exists independently from a particular experience. As noted in Chapter 1, these schemas may become activated as the default in ambiguous situations. Schema activation depends on a base level of chronic accessibility, based on its salience due to its past usefulness and to its relevance, by association, to the current context (Anderson, Bothell, Byrne, Douglass, Lebiere, & Quin, 2004). Although the import that carries the subtext or message of the story is usually derived from the structure of its content, it is also informed by the storytelling process or manner in which the narrative unfolds (see Rapid Reference 3.3).

CAUTION

Although limited development of theory of mind impedes social cognition, a person who has difficulty interpreting mental states may not have similar difficulties with causal reasoning about physical events.

≋ Rapid Reference 3.3

Content and Process in Formulating the Import

Content	Process
External dilemma or circumstance: What is happening, what happened before?	**External dilemma or circumstance:** How is the response related to what is depicted in the stimulus card (reaction, interpretation)? How realistic is the connection between the current circumstance and prior history?
Psychological problem or tension: What is the psychological "issue" or problem? What is the connection between external and internal sources of the problem? What are characters' thoughts, feelings about their circumstances or the problem?	**Psychological problem or tension:** Is the problem or psychological issue (thoughts and feelings) in tune with the stimulus configuration? Are sources of feelings internal or external? How adequately is the problem or tension formulated in reference to what is happening in the scene depicted and to what occurred earlier?
Intentions or goals: What are the characters' intentions or goals vis a vis the problem?	**Intentions or goals:** How well does the narrator understand social causality in setting goals? What are the qualities of the intentions or goals (immediate wish, desire, or well-formulated purpose)?
Plot complications: What, if any, factors complicate the characters' circumstances or view of the dilemma? Are there a series of twists in the events, a string of mishaps or ineffectual actions? Is there something about the history of the problem that complicates matters?	**Storytelling complications:** How does the narrator develop complexity, if at all, in constructing the story (by elaborating on a single idea that does not advance the plot or coordinating multiple ideas)?
Means: What are the means (decisions, plans, actions, coping strategies) taken by characters or helpers to resolve the problems or tensions?	**Means:** Are means realistic and sufficient to accomplish the aims? Are means reactive or proactive?
Outcome: How does everything turn out in the end? Are the problems resolved to everyone's satisfaction? For the short and long terms?	**Outcome:** Does the outcome come about through realistic transitional processes? Is there a coherent framework connecting events, intentions, decisions, actions, and outcomes? Does the ending address the entire problem or only part of the problem?

NARRATIVE FORM, PROCESS, AND CONTENT

Patterns in "how" a narrator tells a story and "what" he or she tells elucidate the narrator's schemas. Form and content in the TAT have been distinguished (Henry, 1956; Holt, 1958; Rappaport, 1947) as products of the storytelling process (Teglasi, 1993). Because formal qualities of the story and the narrative process provide information about the cohesiveness and reality base of the narrator's schemas, they should be evident across cards within a protocol. In contrast, content is expected to vary with specific stimuli that have been designed to elicit particular themes (Morgan & Murray, 1935; Murray, 1938).

Story Form

Given that much of the story content is set by the stimulus, a key to story interpretation is to analyze the structure of the content (McGrew & Teglasi, 1990; Teglasi, 1993) by abstracting a higher-order principle for its organization rather than specific thematic interpretation (Holt, 1958). Three types of formal or structural qualities of stories are distinguished: The first is the *import*, which is a generalized property of content constituting the subtext, underlying message, or "moral" of the story (elaborated later in this chapter); the second is *abstracted content*, or any higher-order designation of content such as time perspective, social appropriateness, or internal or external sources of affect. Abstracted properties of content reflect psychological processes. For example, inappropriate content (regardless of the specifics) is expected to be screened out, and its inclusion suggests impaired functioning. The third type is *structural organization*, in which the organization of the narrator's thought processes and the cohesiveness of his or her schemas are revealed by structural properties such as internal logic, compliance with instructions, or accuracy of stimulus interpretation.

Process of Story Development

The process of constructing and organizing the narrative translates into the story structure. Accordingly, the juxtaposition of ideas as driven by disconnected associations or by a logical synthesis of ideas is evident in the structural organization of the story. The narrative process includes (a) the sequence in which ideas are introduced and elaborated (e.g., reaction to stimulus, examiner's inquiries, previous story elements), (b) apparent plan in developing the story, (c) the monitoring of the unfolding details, and (d) flexibility in responses to examiner queries.

Story Content

Content analysis identifies the specific concerns and themes that are salient for the narrator. For example, a recurring description of characters as "tired" or as feeling burdened may have relevance to the experience of the narrator and should be investigated. However, content interpretation is a complex endeavor. Specific content may not express relatively enduring concerns if they are cued by the picture stimuli or constitute fleeting associations of the storyteller. Therefore, simple frequency counts that isolate content from the pull of the stimulus or other aspects of the story are misleading. Despite similar content, a story that evolves through a patchwork of memories or loosely connected associations reveals different psychological processes than a narrative that is constructed through a creative reorganization of ideas represented in memory and in keeping with the stimulus. Thus, aggressive content that is congruent with the stimulus or serves a constructive purpose has different implications than aggression introduced spontaneously with antisocial or unclear intent. The nature of the individual's experiences and concerns (content) is influenced by how those experiences and concerns are organized (form).

STORY IMPORT

A commonly used interpretive strategy is to recast the details of a TAT story into more abstract themes that constitute its import, or "moral" (e.g., Arnold, 1962; Bellak, 1975; Teglasi, 1993). The professional's formulation of the import aims to clarify the narrator's stance on life by taking into account the content and structure of the story as well the process of narration. In other words, the import encapsulates all of the content and structural details to convey the convictions or principles (or lack thereof) guiding the organization of the story. However, if these narrative elements are disorganized, they do not constitute "convictions" in the usual sense of guiding thoughts, feelings, and actions in a systematic way. Thus, the narrative process and structure are critical in determining the "import" of the story. In condensing TAT stories and life narratives into their "import," the emphasis has been on the connections between means and ends because these links constitute the "lessons" learned from life experiences (Arnold, 1962; Bruhn, 1992; Schank, 1990).

On the basis of daily encounters, individuals discern patterns that connect intentions, plans, actions, and outcomes in particular circumstances to form expectations about how their own or others' actions produce positive emotions, ameliorate tensions, or create meaningful outcomes. These patterns, including complexities such as internal or external barriers that hinder the pursuit or attainment of desired outcomes, are filed in memory and subsequently retrieved as lessons based on the individuals' ideas about how intentions, means, and outcomes "go together" (Schank, 1990). The central role of intentions, means, and ends in extracting the message of the story parallels the importance accorded to these variables in developmental research. Judging from their daily interactions, children implicitly understand social causality and act on these understandings well before they can grapple with these concepts verbally. The story import reveals implicit understandings rather than verbally organized knowledge of inner states or of social causality.

Instructions for TAT stories require the narrator to coordinate the inner world of intentions, thoughts, and feelings with outward actions and sequences of events. Regardless of thematic content, the coordination among intentions, actions, and outcomes constitutes a basic structure for organizing information about self, others, and the world (e.g., Schank, 1990) and, therefore, conveys the moral or import of the story. However, the narrative process must be factored into the import, particularly if story content is disjointed, insubstantial, or based on an inaccurate reading of the stimulus.

The next section describes two types of imports: *content import* (Arnold, 1962), which expresses the subtext of the narrative content, and *process import*, which is based on the narrative process and structural properties of the story (Teglasi, 1993).

Content Import and Process Import

The import distills the story content and storytelling process in relation to the five structural pillars of the narrative: *circumstance, the identified problem, intention, means,* and *outcome.* The initial premises of the story, including the nature of the problem, provide the backdrop for evaluating the appropriateness of the connections of intentions to actions and of means to ends. The range of possible or appropriate actions depends on both the external circumstance and the character's inner world. The import captures the logic of the unfolding events and cohesiveness of inner states with circumstances and actions. If one aspect of experience (such as actions or feelings) is overemphasized relative to others, the import likewise reflects that emphasis. In formulating the *content import,* most weight is given to how the initial premises and subsequent events relate to the outcome. The reason the outcome of the story is pivotal in determining the import is that a satisfactory ending ties up all the loose ends, thereby imparting coherence to the details. Thus, a story about a bank robbery carries a different message according to whether the robber ends up living happily ever after ("crime pays") or winds up in prison ("crime doesn't pay"). Finally, logical inconsistencies as well as gaps in information processing limit the narrator's understanding of social causality and of the connections between means and ends. Therefore, the interpreter considers not only the story details that are included but also what is missing.

The message or import of the story may be general, going beyond the specifics of a given plot, or may be situation-specific, applicable only to the context or circumstances described. A conditional or situation-specific import is worded in an "if ... then" format. Special circumstances in the story or an unusual state of the character (e.g., during war, when drunk or confused) constitute the "if." Additionally, the interpreter should be alert to systematic variations in the imports describing specific relationships (peer, parent, child) or involving different ages or genders. Variation in responses according to structural qualities of the stimulus (complexity, background) or emotional reaction of the narrator (frightened by the scene) may limit generalization. An import may be written in the first, second, or third person. It may be a simple statement or it may express a complex set of premises. Although a content import is generally written from the perspective of the character described in greatest detail (as the following examples show), the basic conviction representing the narrator's schema should be similar regardless of perspective. A story about a bully implies a victim and vice versa, just as a general conviction such as "might makes right" applies to both the strong and the weak. A *process import* captures the principles used by the narrator to organize the response, apart from the content. When the content per se is not substantial enough to abstract a conviction, the import is derived largely from the narrative process. Finally, the storytelling process has a bearing on the meaning of the content, hence the import. For instance, the meaning of the content import changes if the story is based on an inaccurate reading of the picture.

In sum, the import is an abstraction that conveys the subtext of the story from the viewpoint of the narrator rather than from the character's vantage point. This basic unit of inference emphasizes the nature of the outcome in relation to the problem set, the goals, or intentions and the connection between means and ends. Content imports not only capture the structure of the content but also incorporate the narrative process. At times, the import is constructed entirely on the basis of the storytelling process.

For those learning to formulate *imports*, it may be helpful to diagram the structural pillars of the story: *External circumstance* (what is happening in the picture and what happened before); *problem or psychological tensions* (the inner world of thoughts, feelings, tensions, doubts); *intentions, motives, or goals* of the characters to deal with the problem, the psychological dilemma, or tension; *complicating factors*, if any (anticipated or unexpected turn of events, internal or external barriers to goal pursuit, previous failed efforts); *means* such as actions, decisions, or other coping strategies to address tensions or pursue goals; and *outcomes*, or how things turn out at the end with respect to external circumstances and psychological issues. After diagramming a story into its structural underpinnings, the clinician derives the import by abstracting the relationships among the structural elements. In doing so, the focus is on the cohesiveness among the external circumstance (dilemma, situation, demands), the characters' inner worlds (thoughts, feelings, intentions, goals), and the characters' plans or actions in relation to the outcome.

To illustrate the contrast between content imports and process imports, two stories told by Zelda (complete protocol is presented at the end of this chapter) follow.

Card 1. The boy ... is getting ready for a violin lesson but he ... doesn't know what to ... where the bow is. So he doesn't know what to do. And his violin lesson is in 10 minutes. And this is his first lesson, and he doesn't want to miss it. And ... and he had been already looking around the whole house for his ... bow. And now his lesson was only in 5 minutes. Finally he found his bow and went to violin lessons.

> **External circumstance (current and prior events leading up to the dilemma):** Boy getting ready for violin lesson but does not know where bow is and does not know what to do.
>
> **Problem or psychological tensions:** Does not want to miss lesson to begin in 10 minutes.
>
> **Intentions or goals:** Wants to go to the first lesson.
>
> **Complication** (optional): Already searched the whole house.
>
> **Means:** Search again, without new strategy.
>
> **Outcome:** Found bow in the nick of time; went to lesson.

Content Import: If a boy has not planned ahead and doesn't know what to do, last minute actions (repeating an earlier strategy) can work out.

Content emphasizing last minute pressure is consistent with qualities of the storytelling process indicating imprecision and difficulty with anticipating and planning ahead. First, the facial expression of the boy shown in the picture as contemplating a violin is not a precise fit with someone agitated about a misplaced bow. Moreover, the entire story takes place in the span of 10 minutes (no indication of a broader context or goal), suggesting that a focus on the immediate situation may interfere with setting priorities and following through on long-term intentions.

Card 8BM. I can't think of anything. [E: What is happening in the picture?] There is a lady standing up and there is a man. There are two men, and they're trying to do something to another man. [E: What might the people be thinking and feeling?] The man . . . the woman . . . the man that's not doing anything. I think he's feeling good and the other man . . . feeling okay, but the other lady isn't feeling as good either. [E: How does it end?] I can't think of anything for that.

Circumstance: Naming people in isolation; no interpretation of the stimulus configuration.

Problem or tension: Some people are feeling good and others are not; no dilemma is formulated.

Intention: No purposeful intent.

Complication (optional): none.

Means: none.

Outcome: none.

Process Import: If a situation is complicated or uncomfortable, you just don't deal with it, but take note of isolated bits of information, including how people feel in the moment.

Zelda does not deal with the relations among the pictured elements, referring to the people's actions and feelings in isolation, without ties to each other or to a context. Her vague treatment of the stimulus corresponds to her description of characters who formulate only vague intentions, who display feelings that are not tied to meaningful experience, and who do not act in a purposeful manner. Her relatively greater difficulty responding to this card, which is more complex than others, suggests that she may be experiencing more problems processing information that is more complex and ill-defined.

The pull of the stimulus varies not only according to what is portrayed in the scene but also the structure of the stimulus such as its complexity and inclusion of elements that could potentially divert attention. Complex stimuli, such as TAT Card 8, make it possible to note whether the narrator attends to various elements in isolation or unifies the clues in the scene by inferring meaningful relations among them.

The following story told by Mary, a 21-year-old woman with WAIS IQ 81, incarcerated for drug possession and prostitution, illustrates interpretation of a complex stimulus that is not guided by a conceptual process, and meaning is gleaned more from the process by which the narrative unfolds than by its content:

Card 8BM. They cutting the man open. They cutting a man, and they in the hospital, and that's a gun. Ain't that a gun? They cutting a man open, and it looks like they gonna kill him. [E: End?] I don't know. Tragedy. [E: Feeling?] I can't see. I don't know how they feel. He looks like he is a lawyer or something.

Process Import: When faced with a complex (or unfamiliar) stimulus, you attend to isolated bits of information without understanding causes and effects. Rather than imposing an interpretation that explains the discrepant elements, Mary responds directly to parts of the picture. For instance, "cutting the man open" is a literal translation of part of the scene. After noting the presence of the gun, the narrator assumes that the intention is to kill the man. Finally, the figure in the foreground, who looks like a lawyer (he's wearing a tie and jacket), is not clearly related to the rest of the scene.

The following story told by Ken, aged 8 1/2, of average intelligence, and diagnosed with ADHD, is also best understood in terms of the storytelling process rather than its content.

Card 8BM. They're chopping him, Fred, open and the spirit came out. [E: Before?] Don't know. [E: Thinking?] Get the knife off me.

Process import: You react to isolated stimuli that provoke intense feelings without considering all of the cues provided.

The content is an idiosyncratic association to the stimulus. The narrator begins with a violent description that is a literal translation of one part of the scene (the background, "they're chopping him") without considering the prominent figure in the front. Moreover, he does not develop a context (e.g., prior events, intentions) for the situation described. Because of the inaccurate interpretation of the scene and meagerness of the narrative, the content of the story is less useful in formulating the import than the style of the response. The following import captures the narrator's approach to the task: "You are very reactive to initial impressions of the immediate circumstances without considering all of the relevant information." This import can be restated as follows: "When faced with complex or threatening stimuli, the child overreacts on the basis of appearance without carefully processing the information."

When content is limited to what is pulled by the stimulus or represents fleeting associations rather than meaningful synthesis of prior experience, the content is relatively unimportant in understanding the narrator's conviction. In these instances, the story structure or the manner in which the story is developed (or the task is avoided) is the template for the ongoing organization and reorganization of experience, thereby constituting the import based on the process of storytelling.

Different imports of stories with similar content

Two stories told to Card 1 by children of similar age have superficial similarities in content but the subtext or import is clearly distinct. January, age 10, a sixth grader with average IQ, was evaluated due to parents' concerns about their daughter's increasing difficulty completing school work in a timely manner without extensive adult support (also see Chapter 8). Although January is receiving good grades currently, she struggles and expresses growing self-doubt about her ability to do the work demanded and to deal with tests that are important, particularly when they are timed. Benjie, age 9-11, a fifth grader with superior IQ, was a participant in a research study.

January
Card 1. Once upon a time there was a boy who liked, who didn't like to play the violin. But he was obligated to play the violin. When, now he is looking around and thinking if he should play it to get a good grade in school or if he shouldn't cuz he doesn't like to do it. And at the end he says I'd rather not play it because I don't like it. The end. [*Feeling?*] He's feeling like the fact that he is not playing the violin. He feels quite satisfied that he doesn't have to do it because he doesn't really care about it.

> **Circumstance:** Boy is obliged to play the violin to get good grades but he does not want to.
>
> **Problem or tension:** Boy needs to make a decision—whether or not to do what he dislikes because his grades in school depend on it.
>
> **Intention:** Make a decision between obligation and feelings.
>
> **Complication** (optional): none.
>
> **Means:** none.
>
> **Outcome:** Decides not to play (perhaps going along with stimulus, where the boy is not actually playing) but does not deal with potential consequences of getting a bad grade.

Content import: When faced with an obligation that carries significant implications for your future, you are satisfied to decide not to do it because you don't care about it and don't like it.

Benjie
Card 1. The boy has a violin except he can't play it very nicely. So he's kind of upset because he can't figure out how to play it well. (You want to know what I think this thing is? Points to the paper under the violin.) [Up to you] He's thinking whether he should keep trying or quit it because he doesn't know how to play it. (T/0) he gives up because he decides that he'll never be able to do it.

> **Circumstance:** Boy has a violin but can't play it nicely.
>
> **Problem or tension:** Upset because he can't figure out how to play it very well.

Intention: Make a decision about whether he should keep trying or to quit because he doesn't know how to play.

Complication (optional): none.

Means: Deliberate decision and thinking based on his own sense of standards.

Outcome: Gives up the violin based on the expectation that he will never be able to play nicely (but there is no external pressure).

Process import: It is very important to do things well even on a leisure activity, and when you have determined that you will never be able to meet your own standards, you give up the activity.

Although the themes of both stories revolve around making the decision to play or not, the message or import conveyed are distinct. The protagonist of each story makes the decision not to play the violin, but the way in which the problem is defined, the manner in which the decision is made, and consequences of the decision vary. In January's story, the character abandons the obligation to carry on a disliked activity but ignores the consequences of the unmet obligation. In Benjie's story, the child is not pressured by obligation but by his own standards. The character's reluctance to pursue a voluntary activity in which he feels he cannot excel may be a reasonable decision.

Although the story outcome figures prominently in the imports of the stories told by January and Benjie, the outcome is judged in reference to the problem at hand. January's definition of the problem as an obligation to do a disliked task in order to attain good grades is not easily resolved by deciding not to do it. On the other hand, Benjie's view of the problem as a decision to expend effort on an activity that is not obligatory allows for a decision not to pursue it (in the absence of talent to attain one's standards). Benjie's protagonist has deliberated prior to making the decision, whereas January's character simply abandons a disliked task that is necessary to get good grades, ignoring its implications for the future.

Specificity or Generality of the Import

If a story is about a person having to give in to someone more powerful, a general import such as "might makes right" may be formulated. However, whenever possible, the import should include the nature of the dilemma or circumstances. In that way, when all the imports are reviewed, it is possible to ascertain the specific conditions under which this conviction applies (such as between children and authority figures or among peers as well). Initial versions of the imports may be considered as more conditional, but if similar subtext underlies a number of stories depicting different circumstances, analysis of the entire protocol may suggest a more general conviction.

For instance, consider the following story told by Brian, age 15, with superior IQ score.

Card 5. Jake lives with his grandmother. His grandmother is a really strict person who wakes him up at 5 AM every day to do his chores. They don't go to school and they're home-schooled, so they have all of their books hanging up on the wall. Right now his grandmother is coming in and waking them up. Jake has to wash the dishes, clean his clothes, and fold them. The grandmother thinking, "why are they so lazy?" Jake's thinking, "why is she so strict?" And they both feel unhappy that the other is not cooperating. /TO/ In the end, the elder has the power over the child and he has to get up and do his chores.

> **Circumstance:** Grandmother is strict with home-schooled charges, waking them early to do chores.
>
> **Problem or tension:** Grandmother and children feel unhappy, former feeling that the children are uncooperative and lazy and latter feeing grandmother is too strict.
>
> **Intention:** No intention or goal, characters are wondering why...
>
> **Complication** (optional): none.
>
> **Means:** Gets up and does chores as demanded.
>
> **Outcome:** None, the tensions and burdens continue.

Process import: When others more powerful than you make burdensome demands that you don't understand, you have no option but to comply.

The generality or specificity of this import would be determined in the context of the entire protocol.

IMPORT ANALYSIS

Each import is evaluated in the context of the others in a given protocol as illustrated by the stories told by Zelda, age 8-10, WISC IQ 113. Although experienced interpreters need not diagram each story prior to formulating the import, the diagrams are presented below to assist the learner. The stories were obtained in the context of an evaluation prompted by parental concerns about Zelda's poor school performance (grades of C and lower) and teachers' complaints about her slow pace of work and disorganization. Parents indicated concern about her frequent daydreaming but also described her as relaxed, good-natured, and adept interpersonally.

Card 1. The boy... is getting ready for a violin lesson but he... doesn't know what to... where the bow is. So he doesn't know what to do. And his violin lesson is in 10 minutes. And this is his first lesson, and he doesn't want to miss it. And ... and he had been already looking around the whole house for his ... bow. And now his lesson was only in 5 minutes. Finally he found his bow and went to violin lessons.

External circumstance (current and prior events leading up to the dilemma): Boy getting ready for violin lesson, does not know where bow is and does not know what to do.

Problem or psychological tensions: Does not want to miss lesson to begin in 10 minutes.

Intentions or goals: Wanting to go to the first lesson.

Complication (optional): Already searched the whole house.

Means: More searching without new strategy.

Outcome: Found bow in the nick of time, went to lesson.

Process import: If a boy has not planned ahead and doesn't know what to do, last minute actions can work out.

Content emphasizing last minute pressure is consistent with qualities of the storytelling process, indicating imprecision and difficulty with anticipating and planning ahead. First, the facial expression of the boy shown in the picture as contemplating a violin is not a precise fit with someone agitated about a misplaced bow. Moreover, the entire story takes place in the span of 10 minutes (no indication of a broader context or goal), suggesting that a focus on the immediate situation may interfere with setting priorities and following through on long-term intentions.

The next story also shows that Zelda has difficulty acting on her intentions.

Card 2. The lady ... she's walking by a place where there are ... where they are trying to teach horses to do certain things. And she like ... but she doesn't really understand what they're doing. And she has to go somewhere. But she wants to know what the people are doing with the horses. So she decides to ask the man, even though she doesn't want to. And then she decides not to ask the man because she's too shy and she's got to get somewhere. And then she goes.

In diagramming the story, the content that is pulled by the stimulus is not repeated. The import or moral of the story hinges on the connections among the diagrammed elements.

Circumstance: Girl walking by a place on her way somewhere.

Problem or tension: Does not understand what people are doing and she wants to know.

Intention: Decides to ask the man, but does not want to.

Complication (optional): Feels too shy to ask the man so she does not.
Means: Abandons intent to ask and goes along her way.
Oucome: Presumably gets where she is going.

Process import: If a lady is curious about what she sees along the way to somewhere else (vague), she thinks of asking but, finding that difficult, she will forget about it and keep going.

The import suggests an inactive stance toward the process of learning from her environment as an initial intention (to understand) is abandoned. The "lady" has no strategy to find another way to answer her question and loses interest as she shifts her attention to her vague destination ("somewhere"). Generally, intentions are more difficult to sustain when they are vague (wishes) than when they are well-defined and linked to actions. The next story is about a girl who ignores the external world, remaining in her daydreams, but only as long as they are pleasant.

Card 7GF. [E: What is happening in the picture?] There is . . . a mother and a daughter, and the daughter is holding her little sister or brother. Well, her mother is trying to tell her something, but the girl is daydreaming . . . and the girl's not [there] because she's just daydreaming . . . and what the mom wants to tell her is important. And . . . the girl . . . she's dreaming nice thoughts so she doesn't really want to answer her mother. And all of a sudden, the girl . . . she dreamed bad thoughts so she answered her mother finally.

This story is diagrammed twice, once from the perspective of the child and again from the vantage point of the mother. Typically, when a story is examined from the perspectives of different characters, both versions yield a similar import or belief because the interactions are reciprocal (e.g., a story about a child ignoring her mother implies a mother being ignored).

Daughter

Circumstance: Daughter holding little sister or brother and mother has something important to tell her.
Problem or tension: Daughter is having a nice daydream and does not want to answer.
Intention: None in reference to the concern.
Complication (optional): none.
Means: When her daydream turned bad she answered her mother.
Outcome: She did what her mother wanted; tension resolved.

Mother

Circumstance: Mother wants to tell something important to the daughter who is holding little sister or brother.

Problem or tension: Daughter is lost in her thoughts; unresponsive.
Intention: Not clear; she seems to just wait.
Complication (optional): none.
Means: No action taken by mother; daughter eventually comes around.
Outcome: She gets an answer.

Process import from the child's perspective: If a child is engrossed in happy daydreams, she tunes out her parent (mother), even when the parent is saying something important, paying attention only when she feels like doing so (because the daydream turns bad).

Import from the mother's perspective: If a mother disturbs her daughter's daydreams, even if important, the mother tolerates being ignored until the daydream passes.

What is common to both perspectives is the tenuous connection between intentions, actions, and outcomes. The daughter does not respond to her mother until her daydream turns bad, and the mother seemingly waits. No purpose-driven action is taken. Imports formulated so far (last minute effort pays off; if something is hard, do not do it; do not leave a pleasant activity to respond to mother) are consistent with the presenting concerns of Zelda's parents and teacher. Similar to others, this story has a vague quality by not specifying what the mother is trying to say (other than its being important) or what might be required of the daughter (an "answer"). This general vagueness suggests that Zelda does not actively process the details of her surroundings.

The next story is based on a complex stimulus to which Zelda responds with vague and avoidant content.

Card 8BM. I can't think of anything. [E: What is happening in the picture?] There is a lady standing up and there is a man. There are two men, and they're trying to do something to another man. [E: What might the people be thinking and feeling?] The man . . . the woman . . . the man that's not doing anything. I think he's feeling good and the other man . . . feeling ok, but the other lady isn't feeling as good either. [E: How does it end?] I can't think of anything for that.

Circumstance: Naming people in isolation; no interpretation.
Problem or tension: Some people are feeling good and others are not.
Intention: No purposeful intent.
Complication (optional): none.
Means: none.
Outcome: none.

Process import: If a situation is uncomfortable, you just don't deal with it, but you notice how people feel in the moment.

The content per se is not substantial enough to abstract a conviction. Therefore, the above import is derived largely from the narrative process (explained earlier in this chapter). However, as is often the case, the story line and the storytelling process are parallel. Zelda does not deal with the details of the scene but refers to the people apart from the context portrayed in the picture. Her vague treatment of the stimulus corresponds to her description of characters who formulate only vague intentions, who display feelings that are not tied to meaningful experience, and who do not act in a purposeful manner. Her relatively greater difficulty responding to this card (more complex than others) suggests that she may be experiencing more problems with complex and less defined situations.

Card 13B. There's a boy, and he's thinking about what he's going to do during the day 'cause he's bored. He doesn't know what to do. Finally he . . . decides to . . . play with some of his friends but that wouldn't take the whole day because one of his friends is going out before the day is over. So he's trying to think of something to do at the afternoon and then he remembers that not one of his friends are going out in the afternoon. He decides to play with a different friend in the morning and a different friend in the afternoon.

Circumstance: Boy thinking about what he might do.
Problem or tension: He's bored and does not know what to do.
Intention: Decides to play with friends.
Complication (optional): Plan only works for the morning, not the whole day.
Means: He remembers something that helps plan for the whole day.
Outcome: Decides to play with different friends in the morning and afternoon.

Process import: If a boy is bored and wants to play all day, he can decide to play with different friends when they are available.

In this story, Zelda uses problem-solving strategies: The character sets a goal (play with friends to counteract boredom) and makes an appropriate decision. However, her vague style is evident as neither the activity nor the specific friend is pertinent.

Card 4. [E: What is happening in the picture?] A man . . . he's trying to look at something else, while the woman is trying to look at the man. And the man is feeling that he doesn't love the woman but the woman is feeling that he does . . . that she does love him and he loves her. And then she's got a feeling that he doesn't love her that much because he won't stay with her. But the man had done so much for her and been a nice friend so she didn't think that he didn't like her. And she was troubled. So finally she decides that the man likes her but that he also likes some other people too. And she decides that he can go and be with his other friends and it's okay. She can't make him think differently. This story typically would be diagrammed from the woman's perspective because her viewpoint is emphasized. However, the import applies to both characters.

Circumstance: A man and woman feel differently about each other.

Problem or tension: Woman realizes man does not love her because he won't stay with her but she thinks he likes her and is a friend.

Intention: To allow the man to see other friends because she can't make him think differently.

Complication (optional): none.

Means: Making a decision that allows the relationship to continue in a different way.

Outcome: Tension is resolved.

Process import: Relationships remain intact if people don't make excessive demands and keep expectations within boundaries that respect their own feelings, and those of others.

The woman reflects on the entire relationship and accepts the man's right to his feelings. Despite a "vague" quality to the narrative, the reasoning about relationships is sophisticated.

Card 6BM. A lady has a visitor, and the visitor knows the lady's a maid, but he doesn't remember his name . . . her name, and he's troubled . . . because he knows that the maid's someone important that he knows, and the maid feels the same way about the man. And . . . the man wants to say hello to the maid, and the maid wants to say hello to the man but neither of them can remember each other's name and who each other are and how they know each other. So they just keep on thinking until finally the man remembers but the maid doesn't. So the man says hello to the maid and then the man remembers . . . and then the maid remembers the man by his voice and how he looks and they both start talking to each other.

Circumstance: A lady has a visitor.

Problem or tension: Neither can recall the other's name but both want to say hello.

Intention: Both keep on thinking, wanting to recall the name.

Complication (optional): none.

Means: Man remembers and says hello and the sound of his voice makes her remember.

Outcome: Both start talking to each other.

Process import: It's hard to remember people's names, but if a man and woman think hard, one can suddenly remember and then they can talk to each other.

There is a clear desire by the characters to be respectful to each other, but difficulties such as recalling each other's names (or in Card 7GF, problems disconnecting from a pleasant daydream) complicate their carrying out the intended social behaviors. The explanation for the scene does not fit precisely with the stimulus, and difficulty attuning responses to the nuances of the situation may hinder the pursuit of social goals. Also, the logic of the story is strained in that it is not likely for a man to visit a woman whose name he cannot recall.

Analysis of Imports

As stated earlier, the import of each story is formulated as a general or situation-specific "moral." Subsequently, the examination of the entire set of imports permits further refinement in the distinction between conclusions that are general or specific. The repetition of similar patterns across cards suggests a characteristic style of responding in less structured circumstances or tasks (Henry, 1956), whereas systematic variation suggests situation-specific responses. For instance, negative expectations may apply only in specific instances (such as when a single character is portrayed) or there may be a general pessimism. Interpersonal relationships may vary according to characters' ages, genders, or roles suggesting similar patterns with peers, parents, or authorities. Variations in narrative process and structural aspects of stories also may be noted across picture stimuli that differ in complexity or present potentially distracting cues such as books, flowers, or a gun. Certain patterns may be observed in abstracted characteristics in the content of stories across cards. Thus, characters' goals may be considered in terms of what is emphasized, such as getting the task done, meeting social expectations, or satisfying an immediate need. Likewise, characteristics of actions, such as being reactive or proactive, may be noted. The sequence of imports may also be analyzed (Arnold, 1962).

This set of stories told by Zelda captures her difficulty planning ahead and her tendency to avoid frustrating activities. Awkward circumstances arise because of forgetfulness or lack of planning. Goal-directed activities are limited in that the desired goal, such as the resumption of the moment-by-moment give and take of social interaction (answering mother or remembering a name to say hello), is often very immediate. Moreover, positive outcomes are often anticipated in the absence of sufficient effort, planning, or strategic action (e.g., finding the bow at the last second). Together, these patterns suggest that the connections between means and ends are not sufficiently well-developed to motivate self-directed effort toward long-term goals. Problems with attention, organization, planning, and attuning responses to subtle cues in the surroundings may interfere with sustaining independent effort on academic tasks. Zelda experiences more difficulty when faced with complex and undefined situations than when expectations are clear. She displays interpersonal strengths, including adaptive problem-solving strategies in peer situations (between two adults and among children) and willingness to compromise. In close relationships, Zelda considers the needs and perspectives of others and takes a long-term view rather than overreacting to isolated encounters.

Explanatory Hypotheses for Imports

The import of each story is eventually understood in light of other stories and other sources of information. However, initially the interpreter seeks possible explanations for the import by carefully examining the clues within the story itself. As described earlier, sometimes the content of a story is too confusing or limited to permit the examiner to discover the narrator's conviction. In such instances, the import is formulated on the basis of the narrative structure and storytelling process. These types of imports, described earlier as process imports, reveal the storyteller's style of approaching the task (interpreting the stimulus and developing the story) rather than the conviction typically derived from the content imports. However, all stories, including those with adequate content, are amenable to analysis in terms of the storytelling process and structural organization of the narrative. Indeed, as shown earlier, formal and stylistic aspects of the story tend to parallel the content and suggest possible explanations for the conviction expressed. For instance, in Zelda's stories, the failure of characters to plan ahead and to pursue durable goals is consistent with her preoccupation with relatively immediate concerns. Stylistic factors, such as Zelda's imprecision in accounting for the stimulus configurations and vague processing of information, may play a role in her difficulty with setting and pursuing long-term goals. The aims of the interpreter are to discover the guiding rules (scripts or schemas) for organizing life experiences encapsulated by the "import" as well as to identify the relevant psychological processes and specific concerns of the narrator that may explain the import and are relevant to the purpose of the assessment. Thus, the interpreter may explore several possible explanations for the narrator's schema as captured by the import. First, as already noted, the interpreter examines each import in relation to the narrative process and story structure. Second, the interpreter reviews the other stories in the protocol for corroborating information. Finally, at a later stage, the interpreter examines other pertinent information, such as other tests, behavioral observations, school or job performance, social-emotional history, and life circumstances of the narrator. Thus, Zelda's distractibility and inattention reported by her parents and teachers are consistent with the content imports and with narrative process and structure. In following this interpretive procedure, initial emphasis on the individual's style of processing information is subsequently integrated with the social context to answer the referral questions.

Regardless of the story content, the stylistic and organizational features remain relatively constant within a protocol, with some variation attributable to the nature of the stimulus or to individualistic reactions to specific scenes. Such stylistic features focus on patterns of information processing that unify many different domains of functioning, link performance of the storytelling task with other measures in an assessment battery, and explain variation in adjustment across different life situations. Subsequent chapters of the current volume provide guidelines for coding specific cognitive, attentional, and emotional processes that are useful on their own but also contribute to understanding the story imports. Corroboration for conclusions is found in consistency of content, structure, and narrative process across several stories in the protocol as well as in the patterns of responses to other measures in the assessment battery. The combination of performance data elucidates situation- and task-related variability in functioning that corresponds to adjustment in various life domains. Throughout the evaluation, the interpreter takes a scientific hypothesis-testing stance, systematically relating patterns in the data (within and across measures) to relevant psychological constructs.

CAUTION

In the interpretation of thematic content, the examiner should consider:

1. The relationship of content to the stimulus configuration.
2. The formal characteristics of the narrative (logic, coherence) and process of story construction.
3. The import or message expressed by the story as a whole.

DON'T FORGET

The convictions and organizing principles captured by the imports generally operate outside of the narrator's awareness.

CAUTION

When interpreting imports, keep in mind that:

1. Negative content may be activated by the picture and may not correspond to the narrator's characteristic affect (e.g., anxiety, depression).

2. The details of the narrative may correspond more to stereotypes or well-known scripts (e.g., story, movie) evoked by the scene portrayed in the picture than to lived experience.

3. The story may detail a specific experience or fleeting association rather than actual convictions.

DON'T FORGET

It is important to distinguish between wishes and intentions. What one desires is based on content of outcomes (wanting good grades, an education), but what one intends is based on content of actions—or means to attain the desired outcomes. Intentions are predicated on what is believed to be possible, whereas desires may not be linked to actual expectations that it would happen (Malle & Knobe, 2001). It is not possible to "intend" what one cannot control (the weather, the actions of others).

 **TEST YOURSELF**

1. **Which statement concerning the story import is false?**
   (a) It is formulated by the interpreter.
   (b) It captures the main concerns of the central character.
   (c) It encapsulates the convictions of the narrator.
   (d) It delineates the principles that organize the narrative.

2. **Briefly define the narrative form, process, and content.**

3. **How does the interpreter distinguish between a general and situation-specific import?**

4. **The story structure and narrative process are relevant if**
   (a) content is not amenable to interpretation.
   (b) content is amenable to interpretation.
   (c) both "a" and "b."
   (d) neither "a" nor "b."

5. **Explanatory hypotheses for imports are found in all but**

    (a) story details, structure, and narrative process.

    (b) examinee's explanation.

    (c) performance on other tests.

    (d) background information and current circumstances.

6. **Young children's TAT stories reveal their tacit understanding of social causality**

    (a) better than they can verbalize this knowledge.

    (b) as well as they can verbalize this knowledge.

    (c) worse than they can verbalize this knowledge.

    (d) understanding varies from child to child.

Answers: 1. b; 2. Form: generalized property of content based on its organizational or structural characteristics. Form includes (a) the import, (b) any abstracted quality of content (e.g., higher-order designation such as time perspective), and (c) structural organization (e.g., logic or consistency with the stimulus). Process: manner of sequencing, planning, and monitoring the flow of ideas. Content: specific themes or concerns; 3. The examiner seeks consistency and variation in the narrator's expression of how key elements of the import "go together." These elements include dilemma or circumstance (the problem), intention (inner world of thoughts, feelings, motives, goals), complications, means (actions or decisions), and outcomes; 4. c; 5. b; 6. a.

Four

ESSENTIALS OF TAT ASSESSMENT OF COGNITION

Storytelling tasks such as the TAT that present standard instructions and moderately ambiguous scenes are personality performance measures that reveal aspects of thinking and problem solving in similarly unstructured social situations. Therefore, their use in the assessment of cognitive processes is not meant to replace or validate the more structured tests of cognitive ability or achievement. Problems in reasoning evident in narratives, though related to adjustment, are not necessarily corroborated by Full Scale IQ scores or various subscores. Standard IQ tests were intended to assess the *ability* to solve well-defined (academic) problems but not the capacity to solve ill-defined problems (Pretz, Naples, & Sternberg, 2003). Reasoning under ill-defined conditions involves *dispositions* such as *sensitivity* to recognize the moments that call for reasoning and the *inclination* to invest the necessary energy (Perkins & Ritchhart, 2004). Individuals may be more or less inclined to scrutinize the available cues, to seek new information, and to think about or act on the information that is available. A dispositional view of thinking focuses on *how* the person typically reasons in real-life conditions and *when* the person reasons, not on whether the person is *able* to reason under maximal performance conditions such as when provided with a clear problem or prompted to respond (Ritchhart, 2002). Rapid Reference 4.1 contrasts maximal and typical performance conditions.

The constructs measured with storytelling are not meant to confirm but to supplement information provided by more structured tasks. To generalize a construct from a measure to real-life functioning, it is necessary to consider the performance conditions of both. For instance, two forms of sustained attention (see Barkley, 1997), *contingency-shaped attention* and *goal-directed persistence,* apply respectively to maximal and typical circumstances.

This chapter describes procedures for evaluating schema-guided qualities of thinking and information processing with picture-elicited storytelling tasks. Schemas guide the narrative process including the interpretation of the pictured

≡ Rapid Reference 4.1

Maximal and Typical Conditions of Performance (see Cronbach, 1970; Sackett, Zedeck, & Fogli, 1988)

Maximal Conditions:

- Perceived importance of the task promotes heightened level of effort and attention;
- Clear expectations and performance standards guide responses; and
- Observations are restricted to short time span, allowing for an uncharacteristic spurt of effort that cannot be sustained.

Typical Conditions:

- Lack of awareness of being observed or evaluated reduces likelihood of individuals' exerting their best effort;
- Responses are monitored over a long period of time;
- Responses require competencies learned over time through concerted effort, enabling performance of complex tasks that reflect a history of more typical exertions; and
- Evaluation criteria and performance guidelines are not specified, leaving individuals to impose characteristic ways of responding.

scene, the weaving together of sequences of events with thoughts, intentions, and emotions, and arrival at a reasonable resolution for the problem set before the characters. Styles of information processing are evident in how narrators interpret the stimuli to formulate the central problem or tension, plan and monitor the logic and coherence of the unfolding story, connect ends with the means to accomplish them, incorporate cause-effect understandings and time perspective, and relate the inner (thoughts, feelings, intentions, goals) and outer circumstances (actions, events, stimuli) within and across story characters.

PERCEPTUAL AND CONCEPTUAL MEANING OF THE STIMULI

A basic function of the schema is to impose meaning on what is perceived in the TAT pictures. Hence, an essential question pertains to how the narrator formulates the central dilemma conveyed by the scene: Does the narrator draw meaningful, abstract conceptualizations from perceptual inputs or remain focused on those inputs? Object permanence and the various conservations are common examples of conceptual structures that coordinate multiple aspects of what is perceived (Flavell, 1963; Piaget, 1954). Piaget reasons that *centration*, a focus on a narrow aspect of an object in perceptual processes, leads the perceiver to distort the object by formulating partial impressions, apart from the context. Centration is not a purely developmental phenomenon because it can occur at any age due to cognitive or attentional limitations as well as emotional duress. A smoothly operating conceptual framework applied to the TAT task would guide attention to the most relevant stimulus elements and enable the narrator to grasp the "gist" of the stimulus configuration.

ABSRACT AND CONCRETE THINKING

Concrete thinking is constrained by the immediate context or specific personal experiences, whereas abstract thinking involves relative freedom from the immediate context in favor of abstracted "lessons" derived from experiences (Geary, 2005; Johnston & Holzman, 1979). Behaviorally, abstractness is manifested by using an inner framework to initiate and sustain independent action rather than being compelled by the situation.

Being tied to the immediate circumstance, concrete thinking does not integrate the present perspective with past experience and future considerations. If a behavior has relevance only for the present, there is little incentive to tolerate frustration, and external sources of motivation are needed. Moreover, when experience has little to do with what preceded it and with what is expected to follow, the individual is unprepared to apply lessons from the past to the present and to the anticipated future. Without an abstract inner framework to interpret situations and guide behaviors, the individual is likely to engage in trial-and-error problem solving rather than use cause-effect analysis to plan actions or anticipate outcomes or reactions of others. Furthermore, the individual is unlikely to look inward to reflect on intentions, goals, motives, or actions.

CAUTION

An individual who tends to be anxious or is threatened momentarily by the stimulus or the task or who is perhaps averse to risk may be reluctant to depart from the concrete cues in the TAT picture despite being able to do so in less ambiguous or emotionally charged situations. Thus, emotions generated by the task may restrict flexibility and promote concrete strategies for responding.

CAUTION

Concrete thinking (bound by the stimulus, instructions, or specific personal experience) is common to individuals with very low IQ scores but occurs independently of IQ scores at higher levels.

CAUTION

Phrases that suggest insight (e.g., "will work harder" or "talk about the problem") may reflect "words" that the narrator has heard or read but has not integrated in ways that are useful. Examiners should note the fit between specific content and overall framework of the story (coherence, logic, appropriate linkages among intentions or wishes, actions, and outcomes).

Manifestations of abstract-concrete cognitions in TAT stories are evident in how the narrator interprets the pictured stimuli, as well as in the content and structure of the story. Concrete thinking includes interpretations that are not detached from the specific cues shown in the cards (e.g., "there is a gun so he must have killed someone") and story characters whose thoughts, feelings, and actions are provoked by immediate events or wishes without accompanying psychological processes. Abstract cognitions afford flexibility, enabling the narrator to construct stories that transcend the perceptual features of the stimulus and, hence, to coordinate the progression of external events not only with characters' overt actions but also with their psychological processes (including thoughts, feelings, and intentions). The greater the flexibility in thinking, the more freedom to draw from experiences by combining constituent parts of different "stories" housed in memory. Such flexibility reduces reliance on the superimposition of an intact story based on a single episode or one that is borrowed (stereotypes, scripts, movie plot) in favor of active construction of stories that provide a nuanced interpretation of the pictured scene.

Difficulty with abstracting and symbolizing affective experiences does not necessarily suggest a similar problem in the impersonal domain. Children with autism exhibit a deficiency in understanding the social world even when their comprehension of the physical world remains intact (Baron-Cohen, Leslie, & Frith, 1986). To study young children's understanding of causal relations, Baron-Cohen and her colleagues used a previously developed picture-sequencing task followed by a request to narrate a story. They presented three types of story sequences: (a) mechanical, depicting physical-causal relations; (b) behavioral, depicting sequences of overt behavior without requiring reference to mental states; and (c) intentional, requiring an intuitive and immediate understanding of a mental state (false belief) to explain the sequence of behaviors. The first two types of sequences were relatively well understood by children with autism and high ability levels, but the intentional stories were poorly understood relative to the comparison groups. Compared to children without cognitive impairments and children with Down's Syndrome, those with autism rarely used mental state expressions (e.g., desire, knowledge, emotion, or action implying an inner state). Given the pattern of findings, the authors concluded that the problem was not the inability of the children with autism to make an inference about "behind the scenes" causes but a specific deficit in conceiving of mental states.

DON'T FORGET

The coherence of the narrative is a reflection of the organization of the schemas guiding their construction. Breakdowns can occur at the following junctures:

- Attention: The narrator may find it difficult to focus attention due to problems engaging or sustaining attention, shifting flexibly, or disengaging.
- Conceptualization: The narrator may experience difficulty with making inferences to "explain" the central conflict or dilemma implicit in the pictured scene, as well as with generating a plan for constructing the story.
- Strategic application of knowledge: If the narrator has learned rote response patterns (i.e., without discerning general principles, patterns, rules, or implications), he or she may be unable to generalize the knowledge to a new situation.

Abstraction-Concreteness in Stimulus Interpretation

The most abstract explanation assigns meaning to the "gestalt," accounting for, but transcending the particular details of the stimulus. The most concrete responses focus on the minor or irrelevant details or show reasoning directly from isolated features of the stimulus. Concrete appraisals of the stimulus suggest that the narrator's ideas are heavily reliant on the immediate cues from the environment or details of a given experience rather than on symbolic representations of lessons consolidated from multiple prior experiences. For example, describing the boy in Card 13B as "he has no shoes," "he's poor," or "he's an orphan" entails increasing distance from the perceptual features of the stimulus and reliance on increasingly abstract schemas. Likewise, feelings of characters may be described as emanating directly from the stimulus (e.g., "he looks unhappy"), external events (e.g., "the string broke"), or psychological processes (e.g., "he's upset because he can't play the violin nicely"). When responses are closely bound to the stimulus or instructions of the storytelling task, the narrator is looking to explicit clues from the environment for structure and may perform better in a rehearsed or routine situation and well-learned task. With respect to interpretation of the stimulus, concrete and abstract thinking concerns the relative focus on the perceptual cues versus the overall meaning of the scene.

Abstraction-Concreteness in Narrative Structure

Abstract thinking is evident in the organization of the story content. Certain structural dimensions of the narrative reflect thinking beyond the here-and-now, including: (a) *transitional events*—reasonable causes to explain a change in feeling or realistic sequences of events in relation to outcomes (versus magical or arbitrary turnabout); (b) *context for events*—reasonable history to explain tensions pictured in the stimulus; and (c) *coordination of inner life with external circumstances*—linking external events with characters' ideas or feelings (e.g., weaving together actions, intentions, thoughts, feelings, and outcomes).

Coding Level of Abstraction-Concreteness in Narrative Content

A narrative indicates concrete thinking if the characters' concerns center on the here-and-now (daily routines), content borrows heavily from fictional plots or stereotypes in an attempt to match a "ready-made" template to the current task, or ideas are limited to associations to the stimulus features without a coherent theme. Abstraction in TAT stories is classified below into four levels, starting with the most concrete: Piecemeal description of the stimulus; Literal description of the stimulus; Stimulus bound interpretation; Abstract interpretation.

Descriptive responses (levels one and two) adhere closely to the stimulus, whereas interpretive responses (levels three and four) provide explanations beyond the features of the pictured scene (Byrd & Witherspoon, 1954). Expectations about degree of abstraction in children vary from a predominance of interpretive ("apperceptive") responses by kindergarten (Lehman, 1959) or by age 7 (Schwartz & Eagle, 1986) or 8 (Byrd & Witherspoon, 1954). Others report that descriptive stories are common in third grade (Gardner & Holmes, 1990).

LEVEL OF ABSTRACTION

Level One: Piecemeal description of the stimulus. Content is limited to enumerating isolated or irrelevant details or elements of the picture without relating various components to each other or to a common theme. Feelings are tied literally to the stimulus.

- Naming or describing parts of the pictures, rather than interpretation (holding head and therefore sad; a boy looking at a violin; a woman opening the door).
- Instructions are taken literally (each component of the directions is addressed rather than telling a story, with or without prompting).
- Storytelling concept is not understood (story is to be made up by the narrator rather than inherent in the picture).   *(continued)*

- Story is restricted to statements about what the characters are doing, going to do, or wanting to do and these are the same as what is happening in the picture (hence no interpretation).
- No content beyond what is pictured in the scene (boy is looking at the violin).

Level Two: Literal description of the stimulus. Although the narrator uses the stimulus more holistically than above, the narrative is closely bound to the stimulus or to a literal reading of the scene.

- Interpretations on the scene that remain close to the stimulus and immediate time frame ("this is a woman opening the door to see what is inside"— nothing is anticipated).
- No transitional events for change in circumstance (no prior context and no explanation of change from current circumstance or feeling).
- Concerns are extremely trivial, restricted to daily routines typically taken for granted.
- Feelings emanate literally from properties of the picture, not from interpretation of the picture ("that's a gun so he must have killed someone"; "they are cutting him"—rather than performing surgery or other interpretive explanation).

Level Three: Stimulus bound interpretation. Various parts of the pictured scene are coordinated in the interpretations, but the focus is on the short term such as desires and wishes rather than well-conceived intentions.

- Unfolding story is overly justified by the stimulus properties.
- Inner states stem from events that remain closely tied to the picture.
- Inner states are vague or highly stereotypic.
- Limited insight or sense of a bigger picture influencing thought.
- Limited transitional events or limited understanding of causality for altered feelings or circumstances.
- Desires or wants are salient (being rich, famous, wanting a toy) without realistic means to attain them.
- Sequences of events do not depart meaningfully from the short term or from what is depicted in the picture.

Level Four: Abstract Interpretation. An "explanation" of the scene is provided in terms of inner attributes and outward appearance of characters (e.g., a boy is sad because he can't play the violin nicely—implying a standard—versus he tried to play but couldn't, so he got really sad), where psychological processes are understood as distinct from external events (e.g. intent of actions versus outcomes or impact of actions). Long-term durable commitments make it possible to transcend the tensions depicted in the scenes. The narrator may not have the resources to imagine taking constructive proactive steps to resolve tensions (hence does not imbue characters with these strengths) but is able to interpret the scene in ways that make this possible.

Illustration of Levels of Abstraction-Concreteness in Thinking

Level One: Piecemeal Description
Content is limited to the naming of isolated or irrelevant details of the picture without a framework to connect various components to a meaningful interpretive unit (e.g., "boy has an eyebrow"). Content may be tied directly to various parts of the picture in succession without capturing the gestalt of a single character (e.g., "the girl is carrying books, the lady is leaning against the tree, and the man is working with the horse"). Feelings are tied to the stimulus rather than to story events. This level, suggestive of deficits in abstract thinking, often characterizes those with intellectual disability.

Tonya, age 16-5, Stanford-Binet IQ score of 42.
Card 1. I can't tell if he's asleep or looking down. What is this? . . . [E: Whatever you see.] He's sitting at the table sleeping with his elbows on the table . . . This is hard . . . Can't tell . . . It's the only thing I can think of in this picture. [E: Before?] I don't know. [E: Turns out?] That's hard. [E: Thinking?] Another hard one. [E: Feeling?] He's sad. [E: Why?] I don't know, I can't tell.

Anna, age 7-3; Wechsler Intelligence Scale for Children, Full Scale IQ score of 86 (VIQ = 91; PIQ = 82).
Card 1. I think this boy is fixing something. And, um, he has his hands up into his ears. And, um, he has kind of blondish hair, a white table, and the back is black paper. [E: What is he thinking and feeling?] He's thinking that his thing will work and he's feeling his head.

Both narrators focus on irrelevant, concrete details without providing a meaningful depiction of a single character.

Level Two: Literal Description
Emphasis remains on the perceptual features of the picture, but the narrator connects emotions to single external events linked closely to the stimulus. Attributing an emotion to a single event without a cohesive tie to the inner world or to a broader set of circumstances is not sufficient to demonstrate an understanding of intentions or the role of emotions in experience.

Jim, age 16, Wechsler Full Scale IQ score of 96, diagnosed with Conduct Disorder, being treated in a residential setting.
Card 1. He's looking at a violin. Probably bored—doesn't want to do. Somebody put it in front of him. Feeling angry and mad 'cause somebody asking him to do it. So he doesn't do it.

The interpretation of the stimulus is more closely tied to the perceptual features of the stimulus than to inner psychological processes. The boy "is looking," "probably bored," and "somebody put it in front of him." The absence of context (preceding event, purpose) for interpreting the pictured scene creates the impression of an individual who is reactive to his angry feelings and is bereft of inner resources to represent experience beyond the moment. Likewise, there is no consideration of the intention or identity of the person who put the violin "in front of him."

Amy, age 14-10, Wechsler Intelligence Scale for Children, Full Scale IQ score of 70, provisionally diagnosed with Asperger's Syndrome.
Card 1. He looks kinda, um, looks kinda down because it looks like his guitar broke. He looks depressed. [E: Before?] I think he was probably happy. [E: Ending?] I think he, um, just accidentally broke his guitar.

This story favors a perceptual rather than a conceptual emphasis. The "boy" looks down because it "looks like his guitar broke." Such a one-to-one connection between a feeling and relatively minor event does not adequately explain the emotion. If the "guitar" had broken moments before an important solo performance, the implicit meaning of the situation in terms of its emotional impact would have been sufficiently explained.

Aspects of this story point to problems with abstraction, with cause-effect reasoning, and with understanding intentions. For instance, when asked what happened before, Amy was unable to provide a context, simply stating that the boy was "probably happy." Her response to the question, "what happened at the end?" suggests that she may not fully understand the concept of an "ending" to the story.

Level Three: Stimulus Bound Interpretation
The interpretation is tied to the stimulus in that the events corresponding to the depicted scene have limited links to internal psychological processes and long-term considerations, suggesting that the narrator's ideas are stuck in the scene. As shown in the story below, told by Brian, a 14-year-old ninth grader, this mode of thinking may characterize individuals despite high IQ test scores (Wechsler Intelligence Scale for Children, 135). Brian was referred for academic difficulties and defiant, angry, hostile behaviors at home and in school. At the time of the referral Brian was failing classes, not completing homework, and frequently arriving late to classes.
Card 1. Earlier, Billy's mom decided to tell Billy to go practice his violin. But when Billy got to his violin, one of the strings was missing. He didn't know what to do and he didn't have any money to buy a string so he sat there and practiced the songs in his head. /T/ He's thinking about the songs and practicing them in

his head. /F/ He feels upset that he can't play the violin. /TO/ After, the next day, his mom drove him up to the music store and they bought a whole new set of strings.

Brian provides a complete sequence of events, explaining what is happening as well as what preceded and followed. However, the entire story takes place within a 2-day timeframe and the impetus for action is entirely external, with a remarkable absence of intentions, goals, or initiative. The mother prompts Billy to practice and drives him to the music store to replace the broken string, with no investment on the part of her son.

Level Four: Abstract Interpretation

An abstract interpretation of the scene "explains" the underlying meaning of the stimulus configuration weaving together external events and psychological processes. The story below was told by Gayle, a 15-year old tenth grader, who obtained a Wechsler Full Scale IQ score in the high average range (118) and was referred for anxiety about school, lack of confidence, and difficulty sustaining focus at school and at home. Although frequent illnesses had led to many school absences, at the time of the evaluation Gayle was doing well academically (earning mostly B's), expressing anxiety about math and strengths in the humanities. In the context of a warm and loving relationship with her family, her parents describe Gayle as being sweet, generous, and well-liked by teachers and peers and also as being introspective and internalizing negative feelings such as anger or disappointment rather than expressing them.

Card 1. Well, there's a little boy named Henry and he has gotten a package in the mail from his grandfather. He took it open, put it on the table, and inside the package was a violin. Um, he sat looking at it for a long time because it was his grandfather's violin. He was kinda sad because his grandfather did not have it anymore, but he was happy because his grandfather decided to give it to him and he wants to learn how to play. So after he sits down thinking for a little while he goes off to learn how to play the violin.

The tension depicted is explained and resolved in terms of the external event and psychological process, without specific reference to the pictured details.

PERCEPTUAL INTEGRATION

The concept of *perceptual integration* overlaps with the levels of abstract-concrete thinking described above in that both focus on how the narrator coordinates the *perceptual* (details of the scene) and *conceptual* (meaning of the scene) processes. The construct of perceptual integration combines three considerations: *accuracy* of the story in accounting for the nuances of the stimulus; narrator's understanding of *social causality*; and narrator's *psychological mindedness* in coordinating the inner and outer world. To determine *accuracy*, defined as the fit between the story premise and the stimulus configuration, the examiner refers to the stimuli presented (described in Chapter 2).

To accomplish the storytelling task, the narrator determines how the various perceptual features "go together" to identify the central dilemma or theme of the story, thereby imposing a conceptual framework on what is perceived. A conceptual process applied to the interpretation of perceived information dictates that specific stimuli derive meaning from the relationship among the various perceptual elements (a knife in the kitchen is a tool, but in the classroom it is a weapon). An accurate and integrated accounting of the stimulus would include a conceptual relationship among the perceptual elements of the stimulus rather than focusing on each in isolation. Thus, a high level of perceptual integration requires organization of the emotional and interpersonal cues (facial expression, posture) and the features of the stimulus that set the context (objects, background, or clothing). Conceptual structures (mental sets, expectations, or schemas) organize perceptual inputs into meaningful information.

Professionals have described the social scenes depicted in the TAT set of stimuli as ambiguous because they are amenable to diverse interpretations. Yet the identity of the characters and the nature of their feelings are clearly discernible on many of the cards (Murstein, 1965). Therefore, clinicians may evaluate how the narrator interprets the stimulus apart from the quality of the story. The posture and facial expression suggest some conflict or negative feeling to be identified more specifically by the narrator. Distortion of basic emotions of TAT stimuli must be examined closely (Rappaport, Gill, & Schafer, 1975; Teglasi, 1993; Tomkins, 1947) because they reflect problems with calibrating responses to situations due either to intense preoccupation or faulty information processing. Omitting or misidentifying minor stimulus features (e.g., gun in Card 3BM) or even major features (e.g., violin in Card 1) is less problematic than misperceiving characters' emotions or relationships to one another (McGrew & Teglasi, 1990) as conveyed through their posture or facial expression (e.g., people hugging in Card 4).

The five levels of perceptual integration described next overlap with the concrete-abstract dimensions of thought, but three additional considerations are emphasized: (a) accuracy in the interpretation of the pictured cues; (b) understanding of social causality evident from the sequence of events and action-outcome links; and (c) psychological mindedness in coordinating between the inner and outer worlds of the characters.

LEVELS OF PERCEPTUAL INTEGRATION

One: Discrepant. The premise of the story is not appropriate to the overall picture, due to any of the following: exclusion of a major character, disregard or misperception of characters' ages or roles, focus on irrelevant details, or significant misrepresentation of emotions or relationships.

Any of the following:

- Disregard or misperception of basic emotions or relationships portrayed in the scene (e.g., misreading facial expression or posture or ages of the people).
- Poor fit with the stimulus configuration (e.g., problem identified is unrelated or poorly related to the stimulus, such as when characters with clearly different postures or facial expressions are identified as feeling the same way).
- A major character is omitted from the story.
- Emphasis is on minor, irrelevant details (eyebrow) without perceiving the gestalt.

Two: Literal. At this level, the primary misperception is in the *inferential* or *implicit* meaning of the stimulus. The story details are not "wrong," but the interpretation of the scene is closely bound to the background or contextual elements or may be based almost entirely on what appears in the stimulus, giving the story a descriptive flavor. Emotions are identified but without understanding psychological processes (simplistic associations to the scene or an external event). Wishes and desires spark immediate reactions with no durable intentions. The narrator's favoring perceptual cues over conceptual processes is evident in difficulty grasping the psychological implications of the pictured scene.

Any of the following:

- Emotions and tensions of each character may be identified as portrayed in the scene, but without coordination of the various cues about emotions and relationships into a cohesive interpretation of the stimulus configuration.
- Descriptive use of the stimulus, without meaningful links among various elements of the scene, and without sufficient connection of the external cues with psychological (inner) processes such as intentions, purposes, or long-term plans.
- Emotions are evoked simplistically by external sources without being anchored in ideas that are beyond the moment pictured in the scene or immediate event.
- Sequence of events does not transcend the "moment" captured in the stimulus or simplistic connection between emotions or tensions and story events.
- The intensity of the emotions portrayed is not adequately captured (though not incorrect).

(continued)

- Narrator's difficulty coordinating perceptual with conceptual processes leads to unresolved vacillation or indecision about how to interpret the stimulus (not wondering what an object is).
- Reliance on the perceptual features of the stimulus in lieu of conceptual interpretations results in absence of (or vague) causal inferences or causality is at odds with social reality.
- Reliance on intact scripts (stories, movies, stereotypes) in ways that don't accord with social causality.

Three: Superficial. Characters' basic emotions and relationships are recognized but the interpretation of the scene is hampered by superficially understood psychological processes (e.g., emotions or relationships are elaborated by associations to the scene that may be vague, scripted, or stereotypic).

Any of the following:

- The narrative structure is characterized by simple logical patterns guided by stereotyped social schemas that reflect simplistic regularities of experience (may be borrowed from the media, fairy tale, routines, social scripts, or familiar series of events).
- Perceptual elements of the scene are given undue emphasis with limited interpretation of the psychological process.
- Different characters' emotions are recognized and linked appropriately to external events, but the connections to psychological processes are superficial.
- The view of emotion is constrained within the context of the pictured scene, with little consideration of prior history of the current dilemma or of the role of intentions, goals, or plans.
- Match between the picture and the unfolding story may be imprecise as the narrator may not grasp relevant contextual cues, subtleties of facial expressions, or implications of background scene or clothing.
- Pictured elements are adequately related, but the fit between the stimulus and unfolding story details conveys a simplistic, superficial, or stereotyped grasp (by the narrator) of psychological process or of social causality.

Four: Accurate. More complex reasoning systems are applied to the interpretation of the stimuli where the narrative indicates understanding of the role of the individual's emotions or intentions as well as social norms in reference to external events. The story generally captures the implications of the picture, but a central object or some contextual cues may be ignored or misread. Most importantly, the interpretation of feelings and relationships provides an accurate "reading" of the stimulus configuration. Characters are described as facing external demands or challenges as well as having durable intentions (in contrast to short-term reactions) that could potentially guide responses (even if constructive actions are not taken).

This level is coded if:

The narrative is in accord with the stimulus configuration and integrates inner and outer sources of tension in ways that suggest awareness of psychological processes and solid grasp of social causality. However, the fit between the stimulus configuration and the story falls short of being nuanced due to either of the following:

- Emotions and relationships do not fully capture *subtle* contextual cues in the stimulus or a *major stimulus element* (but not the central tension) is ignored or misperceived.

- Social causality is generally understood but depiction of psychological processes or sequences of events is not fully precise.

Five: Nuanced. The interpretation of feelings and relationships captures the nuances of the pictured cues. Story details are precise, specific, and realistic, despite possible omissions or misidentification of minor stimulus elements. The entire narrative is cohesive in coordinating the nuances of the picture with the unfolding story in ways that capture the psychological issue (or subtext) and convey understanding of social causality. The subtext of the stimulus is accurately understood and causal relations among story details are precise and nuanced.

Reasoning is flexible, involving synthesis of experience to fashion a story that incorporates a nuanced interpretation of the scene and conveys a precise and realistic understanding of social causality and of psychological processes. In other words, the narrator is adept at constructing new schemas to size up and adapt to ambiguous situations.

All of the following:

- Story is consistent with all cues and subtleties of the stimulus configuration (despite possible omission of a minor stimulus element).

- Narrative conveys a clear and realistic understanding of causes and their effects and complexities of psychological process (balancing the details with the "big picture").

- Precise, meaningful, and realistic coordination of the features of the scene (particularly characters' emotions and relationships) with the unfolding story in tune with social causality and psychological process.

Illustrations of Levels of Perceptual Integration

In assigning the levels, the interpreter should give most weight to how well the story explains "what is happening in the picture" as conveyed by the emotions and relationships. The interpreter should accord less weight to omission, overinclusion, or misperception of other less central stimulus features. Each of the five levels is illustrated with examples of stories told to TAT Cards 4 and 8BM (see Chapter 2 for description of cards).

1. *Discrepant*

Two stories told by Aaron, age 8-3, illustrate this level. Aaron has a WISC, Full Scale IQ score of 119 (discrepancy between Verbal = 102 and Nonverbal = 133 reasoning) and is receiving special educational services in a self-contained classroom as treatment for an emotional disability. He also receives services for speech and language as well as specific learning disability.

Card 4. The man with the big frowny face. There was a man who had a, who always wore a frowny face and he was wearing it for years and years. He done it in his bed, he done it all night, he did it all day, I don't know why he does that frowny face but he does it anyway. And he blinks one second before and he doesn't have any money. He likes being kissed in the big, big, neck and he likes, always gets a sloppy kiss and he always likes frowning all the time. One day he smiled and they lived happily ever after. The end. [E: Tell me what he was thinking.] He was thinking he'd get a big sad face on his face and he wondered if he will just blink minute after minute. Then he will be a regular guy.

The title Aaron gave the story and the narrative in general centers on one of the persons portrayed—the man with the "frowny face." The woman is vaguely acknowledged in the phrase "they lived happily ever after." Neither the emotion described nor the relationship between the two people portrayed is an appropriate match with the stimulus configuration.

Card 8BM. The man who always had to go to the doctors. And has to look at his mom there. There was a little kid who always hears his mom get little cuts on her. And she wanted to do something else and he was, is doing, not doing nothing, but watching his mother. Then he was trying to get out but he couldn't. One day he ran away, far away. And he had, and then he forgot all about his mother. And then he wandered back home and he was thinking about doing something else but this boring thing and he lived happily ever after. The end. [E: Feeling?] He was feeling a little bored.

Aaron identified the picture as a scene having something to do with a man who "always had to go to the doctors." Presumably while at the doctor's office, the child "hears his Mom get little cuts on her," an unusual way to describe the "surgery" depicted in the scene. The narrator does not accurately identify the components of the scene (e.g., person being cut appears to be a man), nor does he meaningfully relate the clues to each other (e.g., does not make an appropriate inference unifying the scene).

2. *Literal*

The primary misperception is in the failure to grasp the implicit meaning of the stimulus. The narrator identifies emotions and ages of characters but does not grasp the psychological processes that connect events, feelings, intentions, and actions. The narrative may be grounded in the "moment" that describes the scene without implied causal connections among past, present, or future events. The narrator may tell separate vignettes to various elements of the stimulus without incorporating them into a common context (e.g., the narrator may acknowledge foreground and background but not relate them meaningfully). Relationships or emotions are not grossly incompatible with the stimulus nor are prominent characters omitted. Generally, the narrator emphasizes the "perceptual" rather than the "conceptual." Often there is a superficial, concrete, descriptive use of the stimulus and difficulty cohesively relating the major elements. Alternatively, the narrator may superimpose events borrowed from scripts (stories, movies, stereotypes) in ways that do not accord with social causality or features of the stimulus.

Kip, age 9, WISC Full Scale IQ score of 98.
Card 4. He looks like he's mad, like she did something to him, and she's trying to apologize for what she's done and he's not going to forgive her. [E: Feeling?] Sad, like he's going to cry. [E: Ending?] He ain't going to forgive her and they are going to separate.

The narrator accurately labels feelings, but the story does not convey the psychological processes behind the feelings or actions, nor does it provide sufficient context to explain the feelings and relationships portrayed.

Card 8. The little boy is [laughs] confused. Looks like he doesn't care, his dad is lying on the table, getting operated on. The doctor is scared for the guy's life and looks like the little boy couldn't care less and he's walking out. [E: Ending?] The father is going to live.

Again, the narrator identifies the elements of the picture, but he attributes feelings to what characters look like or seem to be doing in the picture (walking out) rather than inferring about their psychological world, interpersonal relationship, or sequence of events. In these two stories, the narrator is "stuck" by the characters' portrayal in the scene; the literal interpretation seems to mirror a serious inflexibility in functioning.

3. Superficial

Although the interpretation is in accord with the pictured scene, the story does not fully capture the emotions and relationships as depicted or conveys a simplistic understanding of social causality, means-ends connections, and psychological processes.

Brian, age 14, Wechsler IQ score, 135.
Card 4. Alf's wife had an affair with him last night and he's really upset. He's a forgiving person so he won't hit her, but he can't stay with her anymore so he's

leaving. His wife is trying to hold him back, but she can't because he has already made up his mind. Later on, the guy, the husband thinks about it and he gets really upset. And he finds the person she had an affair with and beat him up. /T/ She's thinking "what did I do?" and he's thinking, "why did she do that?"

Both spouses remain baffled by the actions of the other as the narrative conveys limited understanding of intentions behind actions. The wife is physically trying to hold him back (as pictured), providing no explanation, and the angry husband has made up his mind to leave (as pictured).

Card 8. Hank was a soldier in the WWII, and right now he's thinking about the times when he was in the war, when he was on the field and he got shot in the arm. They had to dig into him and take out the bullet. When he's thinking about it, he remembers that he wasn't under anesthesia and that it hurt so bad. He's feeling upset that they didn't put him under anesthesia, but he's also glad that they did what they could, because he would have lost his arm if not. /TO/ Turns out he gets the medal of honor for saving those two men from an ambush. The two men got purple hearts for saving him.

The narrator appropriately separates the foreground from the background, composing a story about a soldier thinking about the details of his wartime surgery, dwelling on the pain but appreciating the successful outcome. When asked how the story turns out, the narrator focuses on the stereotypical outcome of receiving a medal without clarifying the current meaning of the recollection.

4. *Accurate*

The narrator recognizes the tension state and the story generally captures the implications of the stimulus vis-à-vis emotions and relationships. However, the narrative does not provide a precise fit with contextual cues or does not convey reasoning about causality or psychological process that is sufficiently complex to code at level 5.

This level is illustrated by the story to card 7GF and 8BM told by Gayle (high average IQ, see details above). The story Gayle told to card 4 is coded at level 3 because it underplays the intensity of the feelings depicted in the scene.

Card 4. Um, there is a man in the picture who has just come home after a long time away. He comes back to his wife and he has changed a little bit, and she doesn't know how or why, but they don't seem to get along anymore. They are not fighting but they don't really talk anymore. [LP] Do I need more?

Although the narrator identifies tensions between the man and the woman, the story does not account for the facial expressions and postures of the characters.

Card 7GF. Um, this woman is supposed to be teaching the little girl French. But the girl doesn't want to learn to speak French; she wants to go play outside. So she is always distracted and whenever the teacher asks her questions she never knows the answer, which means she has to spend more time learning French and has less time to play outside. And, uh, she never really learns and keeps on not paying attention and never learns how to speak French and they eventually give up.

The story captures the emotions and attitudes of the characters and the relations between them. There seems to be an ongoing tension that is never directly confronted but eventually resolves. Although the sequence of events is in accord with social causality, characters do not use active reasoning to cope with the dilemma (similar to Card 4).

Card 8. Um, the boy in the picture had, um, accidentally ran into the, um, man getting surgery with his car. It was an accident, it wasn't either of their faults, but he feels really guilty and obligated to stay in the hospital while the man gets surgery. And the man is okay; he survives. [Thinking?] He is thinking that he doesn't really want to be there but he feels obligated to.

The story fits the scene, providing the relevant background and relating the scene to the character in the foreground. However, reasoning about causality is a bit strained. There is no mention of other family members of the accident victim and no sense of what the presence of the "boy" accomplishes in carrying out an obligation.

5. *Nuanced*
The narrator accounts for all cues and subtleties in the interpretation of feelings and relationships (despite possible omissions or misidentification of minor details). There is a meaningful interpretation of the stimulus configuration that accurately and specifically captures the "gist" of the pictured scene.

Benjie, age 9-11, WISC Full Scale IQ score of 139.
Card 4. Well, there's a man that looks very mad at someone who annoyed or offended him, and his wife is trying to stop him from doing anything he'll regret such as attacking the person who was offending him. At the end, she'll restrain him and he'll stop and get over his anger.

Here, the narrator precisely articulates the nature of the relationship between the man and woman as well as the nature of the conflict between them. The psychological world is well understood with the woman restraining her husband not because of her own agenda but because the man would regret an impulsive action. In turn, the husband is not only influenced by his wife to stop but also takes responsibility for getting over his anger.

Card 8BM. A boy, yeah a boy, more like an adolescent has to have surgery and he's dreaming about how it's going to be and he's a little scared so he's thinking how it's going to be. So he sees what's going to happen to him, and it makes him even more scared. I don't know why there's something that looks like a rifle there. [E: End?] He goes through it, and he realizes he was worried about nothing because he didn't even feel it.

The narrator clearly relates foreground and background ("dreaming"), and the story is congruent with the emotions portrayed and the major contextual cues. The narrator notices the rifle but does not work it into the story. Given that the story described a "dream," this omission is not significant. The ending of the story relates the dream to the real-life circumstance of the boy.

High levels of Perceptual Integration suggest that flexible and sophisticated conceptual schemas promote the imposition of a meaningful interpretation to identify the central dilemma, based on accurate perceptions. Stereotypic schemas are templates for organizing perceptions of stimuli according to features most salient in the culture. Concrete, rudimentary, or disorganized schemas foster responses that are immediate, unmodulated, and not mediated by a conceptual process.

PLANNING AND MONITORING RESPONSES

The narrator's resources for planning and monitoring responses are conveyed in several ways: modulation of behavior during testing, organization of the story, and planfulness of the story characters. The storytelling task involves on-the-spot decisions to formulate a dilemma that fits the stimulus configuration and a resolution that addresses the central tensions. The narrator improvises the general storyline according to the nuances of the stimulus, weighing alternative details, or modifying the initial approach based on insight or examiner's queries. The narrator's schemas guide the juxtaposition of ideas just as the rules of grammar lend structure to sentences and paragraphs. The schema-guided progression of ideas typically occurs outside of awareness, but the narrator may exert strategic effort to monitor the inclusion and exclusion of detail for cohesiveness and logic while complying with the instructions. As discussed in the earlier section, mental models that enable the individual to impose abstract conceptions on perceptual details of TAT stimuli also enable real-life coordination between immediate presses and longer term considerations. This capacity to see a given event in light of the "bigger picture" of future possibilities supports the formulation of plans and enables the individual to set goals, perhaps to juggle and prioritize multiple goals. Without well-organized schemas to guide the development of the story, the narrator may react to the stimulus, get lost in the detail or in personal thoughts, and manifest difficulty balancing possibility (wishes) with probability (realistic intentions).

Planning is supported by self-regulatory resources to shift from one mindset to another as needed, to focus on what is most relevant, and to regulate attentional and emotional processes. Difficulty maintaining attentional focus interferes with planning and monitoring the progression of the story, as well as the activation of organized schemas (due to disruptions in prior learning) to guide story construction. When asked to retell a complex and unfamiliar story, the narratives of boys diagnosed with ADHD were more poorly organized, less cohesive, and contained more inaccuracies than those of the control group boys (Tannock, Purvis, & Schachar, 1993). Differences in narrative production were explained as a function of difficulties with organization and monitoring of information relating to problems with executive control. Story content, in terms of how well characters plan their actions, often mirrors the story structure. Narrators who take an unplanned trial-and-error approach to the storytelling task also describe characters without goals or plans. Instead, characters react to unexpected events that should have been anticipated or to immediate provocation. Thus, planning and monitoring on the part of the narrator is reflected in the construction of the story as well as in the actions or reactions of the story characters.

The narrator's understanding of cause-effect connections is indicated by the sequence of events (e.g., probable versus highly unlikely set of circumstances) and by the tie between characters' efforts and outcomes. Individuals plan and monitor their actions in accord with their understanding of social causality. If representations of the world (schemas) lack appropriate cause-effect connections to anticipate future events and likely consequences of action or inaction, the individual will need external structures (e.g., clear and reasonable expectations along with consequences) and cues to guide behavior. In structurally coherent stories, characters typically act on intentions or goals to address the central problem through means that are sufficient for the anticipated ends. Characters may keep in mind a number of considerations that apply in a given circumstance (long- and short-term implications of an action) for various parties. The next section describes story characteristics that indicate problems with planning and monitoring.

DON'T FORGET

The task and the environment in which assessment observations take place must be functionally similar to the contexts to which they can be generalized (Messick, 1983). The TAT measures planning and monitoring in less structured settings and applies only to relatively ill-defined situations or tasks.

DON'T FORGET

Stories told in the course of TAT administration are not planned in advance in the sense that written stories may be thought about and edited. Rather, narrators' planning and monitoring resources are implicit in three sources of information:

1. Narrator's behavior during test administration—Generally, behavior that is out of tune with social expectations or resistant to the task foreshadows difficulty planning and monitoring responses in ill-defined contexts.
2. Narrator's plan for telling the story—Clues about the narrator's resources for planning and monitoring are seen in the coherence of the story progression and absence of contradictions and inconsistencies.
3. Characters' feelings, thoughts, intentions, and behaviors—Depiction of characters conveys patterns pertinent to the narrator's planning and monitoring behaviors. Difficulty planning is indicated when characters do not anticipate but are taken off guard by events that would normally be averted (hence would not pose a challenge), when characters are without investment (bored), are not goal directed, or react to provocation or to previous events without regard to broader issues, without being able to change course, or without visioning strategies to get beyond the here and now.

The checklist on the next page details impediments to narrator's planning and monitoring that apply to ill-defined contexts.

TIME PERSPECTIVE

Time perspective has been defined as "the manner in which individuals and cultures partition the flow of human experience into the distinct temporal categories of past, present, and future" (Zimbardo, Keough, & Boyd, 1997, p. 1008). An individual's framework for time is an outgrowth of preferred modes of information processing that become solidified into a functional cognitive style, though it may vary according to the situation. Those who are grounded in the present base decisions on the most salient aspects of the immediate stimulus or setting and are more likely to engage in a broad spectrum of risky behaviors (see More & Gullone, 1996; Zaleski, 1994; Zimbardo & Boyd, 2008). A teenager who is more concerned about parental punishment than about the long-term consequences of actions such as

1. Narrator behavior

(Check as many as apply for each story)

Cards →	1	2											
Resists task by making silly or irrelevant responses while narrating the story, such as making fun of or blaming the cards.													
Negative reaction to the stimuli—where the narrator is uncomfortable looking at the cards or is frightened or has an extreme emotional reaction to the scene.													
Significant discomfort, boredom, or frustration with the task (wants to stop, keeps asking how many more).													
Off task by chatting in a friendly manner while receiving instructions or narrating the story.													
Unusual behaviors such as throwing the cards or making noises.													

2. Narrator's plan for telling the story

(Check as many as apply for each story)

Cards →	1	2											
Associative or reactive generation of ideas (each idea relates to a previous one but do not connect to an overall theme).													
Personal reactions (he's looking at me, this is scary) or first person stories suggesting difficulty distancing self from objective demands of the task.													
Narrator loses the set for telling the story (drawn away from initial focus by Examiner's inquiry or personal associations; switches sets from initial premises without transition; arbitrary shifts in perspective; abrupt changes from third to first person).													
Inconsistencies or contradictory details in the story.													
Narrative implies poor understanding of social causality (motives, intentions, means–ends connections).													

Figure 4.1 Checklist: Impediments to Planning and Monitoring

95

2. Narrator's plan for telling the story

(Check as many as apply for each story)

	Cards →	1	2							
No tension and/or no outcome. (If checked, ignore the two items below.)										
Outcome or change occurs without adequate transition.										
Outcome does not adequately address the central conflict, tension, or dilemma as posed by the narrator.										

3. Characters' feelings, thoughts, intentions, and behaviors

(Check as many as apply for each story)*

	Cards →	1	2							
Characters don't care, are unable to overcome boredom, are bored, or engage in wishful thinking or short-term solutions.										
Characters are preoccupied with immediate gratification or material gain without sufficient effort to attain it.										
Characters act or react without clearly defining the problem or goal. Actions occur in response to a previous event or previous action without planning or anticipation.										
Characters take actions that are haphazard, unplanned, or without having anticipated outcome (consequences of their actions or inactions).										
Characters face challenges or situations that are ordinarily anticipated.										
Characters jump to inappropriate or premature conclusions; can't figure things out; fail to consider reasonable alternatives; or overreact.										
Characters desire to avoid/escape legitimate, age-appropriate restrictions/responsibilities considered unfair or incomprehensible.										
Characters continue to behave in ways that contradict how they think they "should" act.										

**Content may be too limited for any to apply.*

Figure 4.1 (Continued)

skipping classes is stuck in an immediate timeframe. An individual's concept of time is integral to understanding cause-effect connections, antecedents of current circumstances, or vision of the future. A realistic time perspective permits individuals to anticipate, plan ahead, and subordinate immediate concerns to long-term considerations. A realistic time perspective is supported by abstract thought defined earlier as transcending the pulls of the immediate context.

Faulty integration of time perspective occurs in three basic ways. The first is the restriction of the timeframes to the immediate, the second is an unrealistic timeframe, and the third is a vague sense of time. Intermediate and appropriate timeframes reflect higher levels of conceptualizing the time dimension. Coding timeframe is pegged to the narrator's conceptualization of time, as inferred from the events in the story.

(Check as many as apply for each story) **Cards →**	1	2								
Immediate timeframe that does not transcend the stimulus cues or short-term emphasis on the "here-and-now."										
Unrealistic or vague timeframe.										
Appropriate timeframe for the problem set in the story.										

Figure 4.2 Checklist for time perspective

PROCESS OF REASONING/COHERENCE OF STORY STRUCTURE

Difficulties in the process of reasoning, mirrored in the narrative progression and resultant story structure, occur along a broad continuum. For instance, difficulty with planning and monitoring (noted earlier) that impedes purposeful and sustained effort, though problematic, is not as dysfunctional as a thought disorder that leaves the person with diminished inner resources to make sense of many ordinary life situations. In principle, any verbal sample can be examined for the presence of thought disorder, and the thought disorder index (TDI) has been systematically applied to the Rorschach responses. Indicators of thought disorder on the Rorschach are uncorrelated with IQ (Johnston & Holzman, 1979), whereas TDI based on the WAIS are modestly and negatively correlated with IQ (Gold & Hurt, 1990; Johnston & Holzman, 1979). Research on thought disorder has led to the identification of deficits and distortions in thinking (see Rapid Reference 4.2).

≡ *Rapid Reference 4.2*

Deficits and Distortions in Thinking (Kendall, 1993)

Cognitive distortions refer to biased, dysfunctional, or disorganized processing of information, such as when thought process is dominated by personalized and tangential associations. Cognitive deficits refer to information processing that is incomplete or limited, resulting in failure to consider intentions or alternative explanations and in simplified understanding of experiences. Stories told to picture stimuli provide an opportunity to characterize both deficits and distortion in cognition by noting both what is incorporated and what is missing. Problems with narrative thought among children classified with emotional disability were evident in stories with content involving significant misperceptions of stimuli or logical flaws, such as sequences of ideas that are contradictory, highly improbable, socially inappropriate, or unrelated to previous ideas (e.g., McGrew & Teglasi, 1990). On the TAT, the capacity to judge reality apart from one's own preoccupations (reality testing) is poor when: stimulus is inaccurately sized up; responses are not socially acceptable; or stories include illogical, incompatible details or highly implausible sequences of events.

Indicators of thought disorder in stories include poor logic; loose associations; distorted grammar; incoherent, incomplete, or fragmented ideas; and descriptions of aspects of the card that are not in the picture (Fish & Ritvo, 1979; Rund, 1986; Shapiro & Huebner, 1976).

A related concept, Communication Deviance (CD), also informs the assessment of reasoning with TAT stories. The term CD was introduced based on the observation that, when telling stories, certain individuals fail to establish or maintain a shared focus of attention with the listener and manifest problems with the organization and logic of the ideas (Singer & Wynne, 1966; Wynne, Singer, & Toohey, 1976). The CD construct has been measured in a variety of ways including short speech samples (Kymalainen, Weisman, Rosales, & Armesto, 2006) and with the TAT (see Chapman, 2008). CD appears not to be a culture-bound phenomenon but is relevant across cultures (Doane, Miklowitz, Oranchak, & Flores de Apodaca, 1989).

Three categories for classifying structural elements of TAT stories as characterizing CD are described below:

1. *Closure problems*—failing to develop a complete story with a beginning, middle, and end; inclusion of passages with incomplete thoughts, unintelligible sequences, and inconsistent or contradictory details; omission or confusion about central aspects of the picture.

2. *Disruptive behavior*—interrupting the examiner while receiving instructions, abandoning the storyline to express a tangential thought, or losing the storytelling set (misconstruing the task, thoughts wander away).

3. *Peculiar logic and misperceptions*—or significantly misperceiving the pictured cues, assigning idiosyncratic meaning to details in the picture, peculiar reasoning, and repeating words, phrases, or ideas unnecessarily.

Based on the foregoing, the following characteristics of TAT stories indicate problems with reasoning that disrupt the organizational structure of the stories and impair functioning (also see McGrew & Teglasi, 1990).

1. *Disorganized narrative process or a story discrepant from the stimulus (see Perceptual Integration)*. The story may be unrelated to the picture or may center on a wide range of irrelevant stimuli without attending to the most important cues. The narrative may be dominated by meaningless detail or disrupted by the intrusion of personal thoughts, perseverations, or inconsistencies. The narrator may be unable to maintain personal distance from the stimulus, may be overly reactive or frightened by the picture, or may be unable to inhibit associations (e.g., nonsense rhyming, repetition of phrases, introduction of examiner into the story, peculiar or incoherent ideas). The story is made up piecemeal without an organizing schema to focus the progression of ideas (e.g., earlier premises are contradicted by subsequent ideas).

2. *Socially unacceptable* response. The story content deviates from the socially accepted norm or behavior is inappropriate. The story portrays a gruesome, hostile, sadistic, or highly unrealistic or unusual sequence of events, leaving a character in an extremely helpless state, or the examinee's behavior during testing is unacceptable or highly unusual (e.g., "If the card falls forward, I'll tell the story. If it falls backwards, I can't"). Story content is a product of cognitive processes brought to bear on the interpretation of experience. Extremely hostile or bizarre content suggests difficulty presenting the self in a socially appropriate manner that may stem from maladaptive thought processes.

3. *Incompatible levels of conceptualization*. The clinician should note problems with orderly matching of schemas to the situation at hand, such as when the story contains ideas that are conceptually incompatible, when relatively concrete and abstract concerns are seemingly interchangeable (e.g., needing drawing materials and thinking that everyone will laugh at the picture), or when abstract problems have concrete solutions (e.g., a candy bar takes care of homelessness or nightmares).

4. *Faulty logic, major contradiction, magical thinking, confusion, or fragments of ideas left incomplete.* Impaired reasoning is suggested by problems adhering to conceptual boundaries in thinking and serious misunderstanding of social causality. Thus, idiosyncratic reasoning or highly unrealistic cause-effect relationships may be evident in story content, story structure, or narrative process. For example, the outcome is jarringly out of line with actions, thoughts, or feelings of characters; a character is left, baffled or immobilized, to wallow helplessly in dire circumstances; the situation deteriorates, and the character is devoid of coping mechanisms to understand or react; or the narrative task is misunderstood (e.g., "can't tell stories because cards are black and white and not colored"). Sequences of events are not only unlikely (improbable) but virtually impossible (implausible). Thus, story content has significant gaps in logic and may include major contradiction in the storyline (versus contradictory detail due to lack of precision in monitoring the narrative progression). Stories may include overspecific, overgeneralized, or personalized statements or lack transitions. The content may appear confused, contradictory, or illogical (incompatible details, unrealistic ideas, or fragments of thoughts that remain incomplete).

CAUTION

To prevent over- or underidentification of thought disorder in children with immature conversational skills, professionals must rely on their own sense of norms of children's speech to differentiate between disorganized thought from imprecision in the expression of ideas or from normal speech in young children. Among normally developing children, the frequency of illogical thinking and loose associations decreases sharply after about the ages of 6 to 7 (Caplan, 1994).

DON'T FORGET

Difficulties in reasoning are viewed along a continuum from being relatively mild (immediate timeframe, poor planning, minor lapses in monitoring the story progression for consistency) to serious disruptions in logical thought (loose associations, incoherent, incomplete, or fragmented ideas, including descriptions of aspects of cards that are not in the picture). Reasoning difficulties fall into two categories. Distortions: biased, dysfunctional, or disorganized processing of information such that it is dominated by idiosyncratic, tangential associations. Deficits: information processing limited by schemas that are incomplete or simplified (failure to consider intentions, alternative explanations, long-term implications). To note deficits, it is necessary to consider not only what is present but also what is absent in the narrative.

(Check as many as apply for each story)	Cards →	1	2									
Disorganized narration, including level one PI, unfocused progression of ideas (personalized thoughts, perseveration, or emotional reactivity to the picture).												
Socially unacceptable content or conviction (e.g., bizarre; extreme helplessness, hostility, or violence).												
Incompatible levels of conceptualization (ideas don't "go together," seem bizarre).												
Faulty logic; major contradictions; magical thinking; confusion; fragments of ideas left incomplete; implausible sequences of events.												

Figure 4.3 Checklist for process of reasoning/coherence of story structure

PRODUCTION OF IDEAS

The sequence of ideas in the evolving story is generated through a combination of two types of thought processes: associative and rule-based. *Associative* thoughts are characterized as automatic, and *rule-based* thoughts are characterized as deliberate (Sloman, 1996). The two systems of thought serve complementary functions. The associative system draws on the probabilistic structure of information, whereas the rule-based system specializes in analysis or abstraction and guides the focus of thinking to relevant features that can be logically examined. However, the complexities of the thought process are not adequately captured by dichotomizing rule-based versus associative thinking. Indeed, automatic thoughts are often rule-based for two reasons. First, the recurring patterns of experience have an inherent structure (e.g., the laws of nature) and, provided that they are coherently represented in memory, associative thought is logical and internally consistent. Second, rational inferences about the stream of experiences become automatic over time (Smolensky, 1988). Thus, rather than being devoid of logic, associative thoughts are typically sensitive to hierarchical and causal relations because they are based on representations of recurring events and experiences that are orderly or bound by cause-effect relations (Sloman, 1996). Accordingly, the associative thinking applied to the storytelling task is expected to be rule-based and logical. However, the logic and causal relations implicit in the sequence, content, and organization of associative ideas (automatic) may not be explicitly understood by the narrator (not subjected to rational analysis).

Associative paths may stimulate creativity, whereas logical analysis can direct thoughts toward goals. The combination of creativity and rigorous rule application is needed in all disciplines. Logical reflection on an inner world of richly elaborated and nuanced association is a source of "intuitive" wisdom. In daily life, individuals reconcile associations and rule-governed thought (Sloman, 1994) by establishing local (or explanatory) coherence or general (or conceptual) coherence. Local coherence applies rules and explanations to the temporary contents of working memory where individuals are more influenced by what they "see" than by what they "know." Conceptual coherence or framing current information in light of long-term knowledge is usually established selectively as deemed relevant. Thus, most individuals tend to explain their feelings or behaviors according to the peculiarities of the current predicament without reflecting on the possibility that their reaction is typical for them in a certain class of situations. Conceptual coherence may result if a disappointment spurred the individual to seek explanations that involve reflection on patterns of thoughts, feelings, and actions across time and settings.

To meet the storytelling task demand, there must be some coordination between being "reminded" (by the pictured cues) through an associative process and ordering the ideas to construct a logical story that explains the stimulus and satisfies the instructions. Such channeling of associations may not necessarily be deliberate and effortful. The flow of ideas may be automatically organized by its being mapped onto activated schemas such that the associations themselves follow schematic patterns. The five levels of associative thinking described below focus on how successive thoughts are generated, with the assumption that the sequences of ideas are grounded in the underlying schemas that organize their automatic associations. Ideas may be triggered by a previous thought, the stimulus, feeling, specific experience or stereotype, or well-organized personal schemas that lend coherence to the unfolding story. Story construction not only calls for an organized set of associations but also for inhibiting associations that are not relevant to the task (being reminded of something personal) or that are not in tune with the task demand (discrepant from the picture or out of tune with social causality). Problems may occur with organization of associations or with inhibiting associations (and these may be linked to self-regulatory limitations of attention, emotion, and behavior).

Levels of Associative Thought

1. *Tangential Association*
The narrator makes up the story as one idea triggers another without apparent causal linkages and without anchorage to a central concept. Loose or tangential associations suggest difficulty focusing on relevant stimuli, a problem with flexibly

changing mental sets, or a difficulty inhibiting strong associations not pertinent to the current task (Weiner, 1966). Poor control over the attentional and cognitive process interferes with strategic and organized integration of ideas. Therefore, content of stories may be highly idiosyncratic (out of tune with expected regularities in experience), irrelevant, personalized, overly specific, or unrelated to the picture. Responses may initially match the stimulus but subsequently veer away. The narrative creates the impression that thoughts are fluid as the storyteller moves from topic to topic without transition, seemingly carried away in the stream of thoughts or details. In the extreme, the narrator appears to slip into an inner world or lose the focus of the task. The narrative may be characterized by difficulty attending selectively to appropriate stimuli as the narrator may be vague or imprecise in gearing the story to the pictorial cues or may focus on irrelevant detail.

Adam, age 9-8, with high average IQ, referred to clarify the source of his resistance to going to school.

Card 5. Okay, there's this plant. It's really weird. It's real small except whoever comes in the room they disappear. People started to go into the room and they disappear. Finally, this lady peeked in and saw plant eating people. Then she screamed and the plant ran around and ate her. Finally, it ate everyone in the house. Then it went to next house and next house and ate everyone. Then started having babies. They all spread out and ate everyone in the neighborhood. Then went to other states and countries. Soon there were no more people in world. The one plant this only plant started to take over world and now they did. So that's the end of the world.

Although this sequence may have been borrowed from a fictional plot, it meets the criteria for tangential association. The stimulus showing a woman looking into a room serves as a point of departure for a series of associations to a minor detail (plant). The ideas generated have no apparent causal connections to each other or to a unifying concept.

Similarly, the following story, comprised of a series of personal associations evoked by the woman in the picture, does not satisfy the task demand.

Stephanie, age 7-8, Stanford Binet IQ score of 113.

Card 5. Ooo, I got one. Once my grandmother and grandfather went to New Jersey to see my aunt, and then my aunt went to New York to see my other one, and then my aunt went to see my uncle in Annapolis, and then my uncle went to see my great-grandmother in New York, and then my great-grandfather went to see me and my mom and my mom and my dad and nobody, and then we went to see you. The end. But that's really not a true story. [E: Feeling?] Oh yeah. The grandmother feels okay even though she just had a cold and my grandfather has a pain in his leg so he doesn't feel so well, and he's going to the hospital . . . in 1997.

After considerable associative verbiage, the narrator realizes she didn't tell a "true story." This realization may be an important starting point for helping her develop strategies to organize ideas. However, in response to questions about feelings, she refers to physical discomfort, pointing to problems understanding the inner world and providing a clue about the nature of her difficulty with this task.

2. Linear Association

Associations may be described as linear when each idea is triggered by the preceding ones rather than being woven around an implicit organizing framework or plan for accomplishing the task. Linear association reflects difficulty shifting from one dimension of experience to another. Thus, the ideas introduced have some causal link to the preceding and subsequent ideas but are not geared to support a larger pattern. Difficulty with shifting from one aspect of experience to another is evident when the narrator overelaborates one component as thoughts, feelings, or action without a cohesive balance among them or when the storyteller associates ideas to the stimulus, previous story event, or emotion rather than deliberately balancing various dimensions of the task demand. The story progression does not grossly violate logical expectations, but causal connections between proximal story details do not bring conceptual coherence to the narrative as a whole. The narrator may associate different possible explanations for what the picture might be (e.g., giving two or more possible scenarios), and various alternatives may remain undeveloped. Ideas may be introduced as piecemeal responses to the directions, thereby showing some attempt to deal with the task (albeit in an associative fashion).

Johnny, age 9-2, WISC IQ score of 114.
Card 5. Once there was a woman who went in the bathroom to take a shower. She thought she heard a noise. The noise sounded like footsteps coming up the stairs. She got her bathrobe and went out of the shower to see what it was. And she said, "Anybody there?" But no one answered. Then she got back into the bath. Then she heard some more noise thought coming upstairs. Then the woman came back out of the shower and said, "I mean it, is anybody there?" Still she heard no answer. She got back into the shower, and she heard more creaking noises like it was coming up the stairs. And she, then she yelled, "I mean it, get out of here or I'll call the police." Then there was no answer again. She got back into the shower, then she heard the noise coming to tops of steps, then she came out of shower the last time and it was just her dog Fido. The end.

The first response by the woman hearing footsteps while taking a shower is to put on her robe and check it out. Finding nothing, she returns to her bath (previously she was showering so a minor inconsistency) only to hear the noise again, check again and again until finally discovering that it was only the dog. This sequence of ideas comprises repeating the same action without introducing other dimensions of experience such as thoughts (about possible sources of the noise) or feelings (perhaps being afraid) or a strategy (other than returning to the shower). Logically, the sounds made by Fido should have been familiar to the woman. So the premise of the entire sequence of events is a bit "off." Having landed on a theme, the narrator repeated the ideas with only slight variation. Thus, the causal connections among the ideas are vague. Moreover, the stimulus is not a good match to the story. The narrator follows a linear track until he lands on a seemingly satisfactory end.

The narrative need not be long or rambling to be linearly associative, as the following story told by Jeremy (age 12, with low average WISC IQ score) shows.

Card 5. She's going through the door; she finds the light on, okay, she cuts the light off.

This story is an example of linear association reflecting minimal efforts of the narrator, who provides simple associations to the stimulus that are sequentially organized but do not shift from one dimension of experience to another (thoughts, feelings, actions, outcomes). The woman "going through the door" does not think about why the light is on. She simply turns it off. The story is devoid of intentions or causal connections that would provide an organizational framework for the story. Proximal details such as finding the light on and turning it off have an associative connection. One thought simply leads to the next without an interconnected network of ideas.

3. *Patterned Association*

The narrator introduces ideas according to patterns of regularities in experience or prefabricated storylines. Thus, a ready-made schema (scripted or experienced) is reproduced without carefully calibrating the response to the task demand (instructions, nuances of the stimulus, active planning). Borrowing a sequence of ideas from a familiar source such as a story, movie, television show, or a literal replay of what is recalled from a previous experience is a strategy to deal with the task without having to generate an original story. Individuals who rely on such strategies tend to encode the regularities in the stream of events without actively organizing information. Thus, in responding to the TAT task, the individual searches his or her memory to find a "canned" narrative that marginally fits the stimulus and complies with the storytelling instructions. Often this formulaic approach leads to the production of a "stereotypic" story with the feel of a bad movie that is lacking in depth and missing a sense of genuineness of the characters. The narrator may include unnecessary details or, conversely, the story may be sparse with few or vague details. The reasons for characters' actions and reactions and causes for events are at least superficially incorporated but may not be precisely understood. In effect, the patterns of events that easily come to mind (familiarity, salience) are related without actively monitoring the progression of the story and with limited understanding of social causality. In an attempt to reconcile the story with the stimulus, the logic may be mildly strained or the match with the picture may seem like a "stretch."

Micah, age 14, with a WISC Full Scale score of 105, was evaluated due to concerns about rages that he had been experiencing since the age of 2. His parents wanted to understand what Micah needs to keep his anger from escalating.

Card 5. A man and a woman's son didn't come home one night, and they got really worried. So that night the sheriff came and started talking to the husband, and the woman kept on trying to come in and see what the heck was going on, but the sheriff kept telling her to get out, and the husband did too. And it turned out that the kid was kidnapped by some guy. And . . . I don't know . . . the son had been caught stealing something from the store, and the sheriff picked him up and brought him into jail, and so the lad . . . the husband and the wife went to go bail their kid out of jail, but they didn't have enough money, so the kid had to stay in jail for a couple of days. And the wife and the father were worried and upset that their son had done it, and mad at the son. [E: Ending?] Their son finally got out of jail and got grounded for a long time. [E: What are the parents thinking/feeling?] They were thinking that they were going to kill him or something . . . not literally kill him. Get him in a lot of trouble, but when they got to their son, they were just worried about him, wondering if he was okay. [E: What is the son thinking/feeling?] He was mad that he got caught, and he was sorry for what he did. He realized that it wasn't worth it. He was scared that his parents were going to get at him.

This story of parents concerned about their child's being arrested reflects Micah's recurring conflict with authorities. Micah's understanding of this conflict situation emphasizes immediate consequences (concerns about being caught and punished by his parents) instead of possible long-term impact of his arrest or the wrongness of his actions (except that it wasn't worth it given the consequences of getting caught). Micah acknowledged parental viewpoint by association rather than reflective understanding. Parents worry and bail out their son, but their good intentions are not meaningfully incorporated into the son's conclusions (emotional and cognitive) about the situation.

4. Synthesized Association
The narrator introduces ideas in ways that convey understanding of connections between causes and effects and between means and ends. The succession of

ideas suggests anticipation, planning, and response monitoring and the narrative includes details and transitions that tie various dimensions of experience as well as the stimulus cues into a common context. The focus of the narrative is evident—events, thoughts, feelings, actions, and outcomes are compatible with a central theme despite some possible tangents or overelaborations. Causal reasoning governing associations is realistic though story premises may be a bit naive or idealized.

Mathew, age 11-8, WISC IQ score of 126 (Verbal reasoning = 137;
Nonverbal reasoning = 110).

Card 5. A boy promised his mother that he would clean up his room, which he hadn't done for quite a very long time. So, his mother felt very relieved that he comes to clean it up. But when she came to check, the room was even dirtier than before, and she feels very angry at him. She feels she's going to punish him, um, and her son had ran away for a little bit and when he came back she made him clean up not only his room but also several other rooms in the house because he had been bad.

The premise is that the child disappoints his mother by not keeping his promise. Expecting to be punished, the son runs away but "only for a little bit." This indication that the son's disappearance would be brief signals some planning of the story's progression as the narrator anticipates a reconciliation. Upon his return, the son realizes that he will have to pay the consequences for being "bad." This set of associations is logical but falls short of the highest level because the reason the son abandons his intentions to clean up his room ("dirtier than before") remains unclear.

5. *Integrative Association*

Story elements are cohesive and tightly organized around a central theme. Ideas shift conceptually in accord with well-integrated, complex, internalized representations that connect intentions, actions, and outcomes within and across characters. Given that the storytelling process and structure of narratives are related, this level presumes a well-organized narrative (that corresponds to a high level of cognitive-experiential integration described in a later section of this chapter). Although the level of associative thinking generally corresponds to the level of cognitive-experiential integration, the two coding rubrics have distinct foci. Associative thinking focuses on the sequence of ideas in the developing story, whereas cognitive-experiential integration emphasizes the coordination of various dimensions of experience into a cohesive narrative structure.

At age 9, Benjie's story to Card 5, shown on the next page is not particularly dramatic or complex but evolves from establishing a purpose (looking for someone) to taking appropriate action (searching) with the expectation of a reasonable outcome (of finding the person because of the implicit premise that the person is at home). Despite the simplicity of the story, the schema is well developed in terms of the intention-action-outcome set and serves as an implicit organizational structure that guides the introduction of ideas.

Card 5. A lady comes home or rather she comes into a room and she's looking for someone so she searches the house and that's it. [E: Who?] Maybe someone else who lives in the house and maybe she wants something of that person. [E: Happens?] She keeps searching 'till she finds him.

The following story told by a student in kindergarten also develops through a set of integrative associations.

Subject 203 (#90).
Card 5. The mother comes looking for her little boy. And he wasn't there. He might of runned away because his mother told him she was going to spank him. His mother was sad when he ran away. He feels sad, too. She thinks something bad might have happened to him. He might of got lost. He finds a friend and his friend helps him and his mother. His mother gives him a spanking for running away. Then he doesn't do it anymore.

Despite the unsophisticated style of telling the story (e.g., age-appropriate language, sentence structure), the conceptualization of the details in relation to an underlying theme is quite mature. The ideas are logically linked and cohere into an organized schematic structure. In contrast to the story told by Mathew, this one provides a long-term resolution as the boy learns not to run away in the future. Both mother and son take responsibility for their own feelings and actions and appreciate the feelings of the other. Each feels sad about the situation and seems aware of these emotions in the other. This balance of viewpoints is the backdrop for seeking a third party to facilitate the reconciliation. Subsequently, the child accepts punishment for an impulsive action and learns a lesson. In contrast to the story told by Mathew, this one incorporates external provocation, inner states, actions, and resolutions.

LEVELS OF ASSOCIATIVE THINKING

Level One: Tangential Association. Story rambles and is made up as one idea triggers another without apparent causal linkages to each other or to a central concept. Responses may initially match the stimulus but subsequently veer away. The content may be tangential to the stimulus and/or personalized.

Level Two: Linear Association. Ideas are introduced linearly in association to the stimulus, previous story event (e.g., repetitive elaborations on one idea such as a series of actions), or emotion. Responses may center on addressing the specific components of the directions rather than the production of a "story." Narrator may try to connect proximal ideas but overall causal connections among the story details are nonexistent, vague, or implausible.

Level Three: Patterned Association. Ideas are introduced according to scripted regularities in experiences or cultural stereotypes. The sequence of ideas is formulaic and may be borrowed (from a story, movie, or television show) or may be a literal replay of familiar, scripted experiences. The story progression is somewhat like a bad movie lacking in depth or a sense of genuineness of the characters. Details that might be expected to be implicitly understood may be explicitly stated; details may not "add up" or few or vague details may be given. The superimposition of scripted patterns may involve some subtle distortion of the nuances of the stimulus or imprecise logic.

Level Four: Synthesized Association. Ideas are introduced in ways that tie various dimensions of experience into a common context, leading to the production of a coherent narrative that conveys understanding of social causality. The story premises and supporting detail are clearly related and realistic though they may be a bit naive. Relations are congruent among events, thoughts, feelings, actions, and outcomes.

Level Five: Integrative Association. Story elements are cohesive and tightly organized around a central theme with clearly prosocial and realistic convictions guiding the story progression. Ideas shift conceptually in accord with well-integrated, complex internalized representations. Well-developed schemas are implicit in the subtext of the story, which concludes without significant "loose ends."

Coding for associative thinking emphasizes how one thinks and not what one thinks about. Each TAT story is examined in terms of the underlying organizational structure governing the introduction of ideas. Associations are governed by some principles. The five levels convey increasing coherence among the ideas that come to mind in reference to the storytelling task demand.

COORDINATION OF INNER AND OUTER ELEMENTS OF EXPERIENCE

Much of psychopathology may be understood in terms of the failure of cognitive controls to integrate information between the inner and outer environments (Santostefano, 1991). The process of distinguishing between stimuli originating in the outer versus the inner world permits the individual to judge the realities of the environment apart from personal preoccupations. Thus, reality testing requires the individual to coordinate information that is internally represented (i.e., schemas) with external cues. The narrator demonstrates poor reality testing when he or she does not inhibit responses that are socially unacceptable or at odds with the picture presented (both in the Rorschach and the TAT) as well as when stories include logically incompatible details or implausible sequences of events (see previous section on process of reasoning).

Stories that progress through a series of external events or actions with no link to inner states suggest that the narrator is not coordinating the inner and outer dimensions of experience. Similarly, highly trivial or stereotyped (scripted) content suggests that the narrator is not looking beneath the surface. Describing a character as someone who is bored but practices the violin for hours would suggest a disconnection between feelings and actions. The narrator demonstrates coordination of inner and outer perspectives when the characters acknowledge internal and external sources of tension (e.g., remorse or guilt as well as external punishment following hurtful action) and when characters' outward actions are guided by durable intentions (motives, goals, principles) rather than external provocations or immediate desires. Inner representations such as strivings, goals, or a sense of conviction or commitment give meaning and coherence to external reality, allowing individuals to reflect on past experiences, to deliberate before acting, and, ultimately, to act purposefully.

DON'T FORGET

Inner representations such as strivings or goals, conviction, or commitment are resources that:
- give coherence and meaning to external events and to one's own actions
- allow for reflection on past experience
- allow for deliberation before taking action
- ultimately allow for purposeful action

Coordination of perspectives across individuals allows:
- resolutions of the "problem" to address the views and needs of all concerned
- persons to retain their individuality in a cooperative relationship with appropriate boundaries, allowing independent aims

Balanced coordination of inner and outer worlds permits realistic, deliberate problem solving, where emotions are embedded in a rich cognitive context that provides perspective. Problems with coordinating the inner and outer elements of experience are reflected in difficulties making connections among circumstances, intentions, means, and outcomes (see Fig. 4.4).

(Check as many as apply for each story) Cards →	1	2									
Exclusive external impetus— characters' concerns and actions respond to demand, greed, wishes, rebellion, or to previous story event rather than being prompted by inner purpose or realistic attempt at problem resolution.											
Exclusive internal impetus— characters' concerns and actions are ruminative associations or reactions that are not coherently connected with circumstances in the external world; emotions drive story events with little regard to the circumstances or to solving the problem at hand.											
Absence of moral dimension of experience—characters or narrator lack concern for consequences of acts, do not take responsibility for their actions, or disregard the welfare of others; irresponsible acts do not have appropriate consequences											
Socially inappropriate behavior— narrator behavior strains acceptable bounds in relating to the examiner or characters' actions are out of tune with social conventions (antisocial, morbidly helpless).											

Figure 4.4 Checklist: Limitations in coordinating inner and outer experiences

COORDINATION OF PERSPECTIVES OF DIFFERENT INDIVIDUALS

Intrapersonal or self-schemas are structures that connect various components of the inner and outer worlds of one individual, whereas interpersonal schemas coordinate the inner and outer worlds of different individuals. Both intra- and interpersonal schemas are products of cognitive-emotional processes of a given individual. Therefore, individuals who reason simplistically about their own feelings or motives in various situations apply similar reasoning to understand others (unless in the grip of intense emotions). Interpersonal schemas organize perspectives of different individuals by coordinating their inner and outer experiences (intrapersonal schemas). What dominates the organization of intrapersonal schemas (such as standards or principles of fair play versus compliance with social obligations or "duty") will also organize interpersonal encounters. Full coordination of others' intrapersonal schemas would require an implicit understanding that each person brings to the current situation a unique history of experiences and perspectives. TAT cards portraying only one character (1, 3BM) have the potential to reveal coordination of perspectives because intrapersonal schemas include expectations of support or hindrance from others, as well as abstract values or standards (e.g., empathy, courage, commitment) that govern interpersonal relatedness. The following checklist in Figure 4.5 includes characteristics of TAT stories indicating that the narrator meaningfully coordinates perspectives of different individuals:

(Check as many as apply for each story) Cards →	1	2								
Wishes and fantasies are distinct from realistic appraisal (external demands, rules).										
Intent of an action is distinct from its impact.										
Actions and outcomes are clearly and specifically linked with motives and intentions, in line with realistic social causality.										
Characters are meaningfully and reciprocally related to one another (not entrenched in separate concerns or insights that are not relevant or not communicated).										
Resolutions of the "problem" coordinate views and needs of all characters.										
Characters retain their individuality (intentions, goals) while interacting cooperatively.										

Figure 4.5 Checklist: Assets in coordinating inner and outer experiences within and across individuals

COGNITIVE-EXPERIENTIAL INTEGRATION

Stories about pictures permit assessment of the complexity of the cognitive-experiential schemas by revealing the extent and clarity of differentiation of dimensions of experience (e.g., in circumstances, thoughts, feelings, actions, intentions, relationships) and the cohesiveness of the integration of the differentiated elements (e.g., causes-effects, means-ends, feelings-thoughts, intentions-actions). What is differentiated is a function of what is salient for the individual, whereas the integration of what is differentiated demonstrates the principles that bring coherence to the narrator's experiences, both moment to moment and in the long term (see Chapter 1 for detailed discussion). Briefly, cognitive complexity is a product of differentiation and integration applied to information processing (e.g., Streufert & Nogami, 1989). *Differentiation* is the process of distinguishing different dimensions within a domain or taking different perspectives. This process of differentiation may be qualified according to the clarity or vagueness of the distinctions. *Integration* is the process of relating conceptually the dimensions that are distinguished. Thus, long- and short-term views may be reconciled, and intentions and impact of actions may be clearly differentiated yet coordinated.

In determining the level of cognitive-experiential integration, the specific details of the story are considered in relation to each other, to the overall themes, and to the pictured stimulus (e.g., feelings and intentions tied to each other, action, and events versus just describing feelings portrayed in the picture). Realistic appraisal of circumstances suffers when the narrator fails to differentiate and coordinate various elements of experience such as the intent and impact of actions or possibility and probability.

DON'T FORGET

A narrator's difficulties with flexibly applying schemas to accomplish the storytelling task signal that he or she may have problems dealing with situations making similar demands.

Well-developed schemas enhance adjustment because they permit the individual to engage in complex information processing by promoting awareness of intricacies and ambiguities. Individuals who maintain more complex distinctions among various aspects of themselves (self-schema) are better able to cope with stressors (Linville, 1985, 1987; also see discussion in Chapter 1), presumably because their well-differentiated mental sets enable them to organize external threats and inner states and marshall resources to deal with them. Less complex schemas would foster more extreme appraisals of events as all good or all bad (see Rapid Reference 4.3).

≡ *Rapid Reference 4.3*

Schema Complexity and Adjustment

Complexity of the cognitive-experiential schemas is based on:

- clarity of *differentiations* among dimensions of experience (circumstances, thoughts, feelings, intentions, motives or goals, decisions, plans, actions, and outcomes)
- cohesiveness of the *coordination* among them (causes-effects; means-ends; feelings-thoughts; intentions-actions)

Well-developed schemas enhance adjustment because they:

- permit individuals to engage in complex information processing by promoting awareness of different domains of experience
- permit individuals to size up ambiguities according to more complex "rules" about how ideas "go together"

Those with more complex self-schemas cope better with stress. Complicated, ambiguous, or stressful situations require the individual to draw on various schemas resourcefully. Structured, routine, or familiar situations (or tasks) may be managed by scripted schemas (ready-made, well-rehearsed).

Coming to grips with complicated, ambiguous, or stressful situations (or tasks) requires the individual to draw systematically from schemas, whereas the individual may manage familiar or routine events (or tasks) by applying ready-made or well-learned schemas (e.g., Derry, 1996; Hammer, 1996). It should be noted that the complexity of the thought process may be disrupted during stressful episodes where the individual may function below characteristic levels. Stressful events may activate schemas that amplify the feeling of threat and evoke a sense of the self as vulnerable and unable to cope with the distressing emotion or situation (Shirk, Boergers, Eason, & Van Horn, 1998; see Rapid Reference 4.4).

≡ *Rapid Reference 4.4*

Stress and Thought Processes

Certain dimensions of thinking are vulnerable to change during stressful episodes (Pennebaker, 1990):

- Breadth of perspective—The focus of attention and thought is narrowed to immediate concerns.

- Self-reflection—Individuals are less likely to reflect on the causes and effects of their actions, thoughts, and feelings.
- Awareness of emotion—Individuals are less aware of fluctuations in their mood states.

The levels of thought assessed with thematic apperceptive narratives reflect previously organized schemas that are indicative of the individual's characteristic ways of functioning under the relatively unstructured conditions presented by the task. Stress or other unusual circumstances may restrict the thought process.

DON'T FORGET

The same behavior in a given situation may grow out of schemas that differ in their complexity. For example, some individuals may refrain from expressing anger because they anticipate a negative reaction, whereas others may refrain from venting because they understand its emotional impact on others.

Five Levels of Cognitive-Experiential Integration (choose the level that fits best)

1. *Disorganized*

The narrator's schemas for understanding experiences are impaired (distorted or simplified) due to limitations in deciphering social cues, grasping implications of situations, or distinguishing causes and effects as indicated by any of the following: (a) discrepant level of perceptual integration; (b) problems with reasoning and conceptualization such that ideas that "don't go together" are combined; (c) highly idiosyncratic or illogical assumptions about the self or the world, such as highly implausible or unrealistic events and incompatible or contradictory ideas in the story; (d) inability of the narrator to monitor the flow of ideas (perseveration such as repeated phrases, uncorrected fragments or incomplete ideas, incompatible story components such as jarring contradictions among feelings, thoughts, intentions, or actions); (e) gross departure of content from social expectation (extreme helplessness of any character; bizarre, gruesome, or socially unacceptable story content; or inappropriate behavior during test administration); (f) the narrator's inability to understand the task as opposed to finding it difficult; and (g) the narrator's inability to maintain distance from the stimulus by being overly reactive to or frightened by the picture.

Lapses in logical thinking, including marked distortion in understanding of cause-effect relationships or difficulty separating fantasy from reality, may be evident even when content per se is not inappropriate. The stories illustrating this level were told to TAT Card 1 by children who were diagnosed with emotional disorders and were being served in a special education program.

Roger, age 9-8, WISC IQ score of 66.
Card 1. Are there any colored pictures? [E: No, they're just black and white.] He's like painting. [E: He's painting?] He's thinking of something. I don't know what that is because it's not in color. He's thinking. [E: What's happening?] Nothing. This is a violin. He's thinking about playing the violin. [E: Turns out?] Then he plays the violin. [E: Feeling?] That he want to play the violin.

The narrator's comments about not knowing what something is because of the color suggest faulty understanding of the task and difficulty explaining the scene presented. Although initially baffled, he goes on to tell a simplistic story (boy wants to play the violin, then plays) with the help of prompts. The degree of concreteness coupled with the request for the more familiar colored pictures suggests impaired functioning.

Elizabeth, age 10-9, WISC IQ score of 100.
Card 1. [Yells] I don't know! Ung . . . [E: Is this pretty tough?] Um-huh. [E: Well, why don't you start by telling me what is happening in the picture?] The . . . person is thinking. [E: What was happening before?] I don't know . . . Maybe he's having trouble. [E: Turns out?] I don't know . . . [E: Well, the story is not in the picture, so it's up to you to make guesses.] No! I don't want to make guesses! [E: There are many ways to give right answers.] Uck . . . ckk . . . ckkk . . . ck . . . [E: What are some things he might be thinking?] I don't know! Feels very, very sad. [burps] [E: Turns out?] He's happy againnnnnnnnnahhhh!

The child's behavior during testing and style of not telling the story are important considerations. Elizabeth's expression of difficulty with the task by yelling and making random noises is not socially acceptable.

Johnny, age 9-2, WISC IQ score of 114.
Card 1. A kid was making a violin [child dropped card] [E: That's okay.] and he was bored. He didn't know what to do with it. He didn't, he didn't know what to do with it. He was getting tired. It was almost his bedtime, and he wanted to know what to do with it but he didn't know what to do with it. He kept thinking of what to do. He didn't think of anything; he just sat there and thought of what to do. He didn't know what to do with the violin. He didn't know very much about music. It was getting dark, and he didn't know what to do so he just sat there and was thinking thinking. It was almost midnight. And he fell asleep before he could think of anything.

The sophistication required for "making a violin" is incongruous with being bored and with not knowing what to do with it. The character's having no idea of what to do with the violin that he made and his helpless (perseverative) immobility is paralleled by the narrator's inability to generate constructive coping responses to the task.

2. *Rudimentary*

Serious limitations in integrative reasoning are due to a highly simplified process of reasoning (deficit) indicated by any of the following: (a) Feelings or other inner states are not explained beyond simple connection to the stimulus or isolated event; (b) Causal inferences are minimal, extremely basic, or vague (e.g., "something bad happened"); (c) Characters are distinguished by the way they look in the picture ("descriptive") or by outward actions without grasping differences in their intentions, feelings, history, or circumstances. Characters may focus on immediate or self-centered concerns and respond to situational provocation or vague emotions rather than being guided by deliberate intention or anticipation of realistic consequences; (d) Outcomes are vague, insufficiently related to a transitional process (means to ends), or fail to resolve the problem beyond the moment. Solutions to problems may be characterized by wishful (improbable but not impossible) or mildly unrealistic (naive) strategies or avoidance of conflict; (e) The narrator ignores important perceptual cues or leaves feelings or transitions unexplained with "gaps" in communication or understanding.

Consider again Jim's response to Card 1:

Jim, age 16, WAIS IQ score of 96, diagnosed with Conduct Disorder.
Card 1. He's looking at a violin. Probably bored, doesn't want to do. Somebody put it in front of him. Feeling angry and mad 'cause somebody asking him to do it. So he doesn't do it.

Jim's story illustrates two integration problems at this level: (a) He is "stuck" in the needs of one character's reaction to immediate circumstance or provocation without considering intentions or other contextual factors. Intentions are not attributed to the person looking at the violin or to the one who "put it [the violin] in front of him." Indeed, the identity of this person and the nature of the relationship between the person and the boy remain unknown; and (b) he fails to generate or follow through on strategies to meet demands, resolve problems, or anticipate negative consequences. The protagonist does not plan and, likewise, the story progresses in piecemeal fashion without an overall plan on the part of the narrator. Lack of conceptual clarity is reflected in vagueness or fuzziness of story details and in the imbalance among feelings, actions, and thoughts. The boy's reaction ("doesn't do it") is prompted by boredom and anger without considering longer-term strategies such as finding an alternative activity or compromise. These limitations in cognitive integration have hampered Jim's judgment and led to inappropriate behavior.

3. Superficial

The content of the stories is socially appropriate, but the narrative lacks "depth" and specificity. Reasoning coheres around relatively short-term purposes or external demand, often in keeping with the cultural stereotypes or specific experiences of the narrator. The framework for understanding experience is dominated by naive, stereotyped, or wishful thinking and a superficial view of events or relationships. Characters are tuned in to external incentives or consequences with little satisfaction from intrinsic sources or from commitment to standards. Thus, instrumental actions are extrinsically driven rather than motivated by interest, curiosity, or enjoyment of the activity. Characters' actions are responsive to their needs and wants or to external pressure rather than directed by principle or long-term goals. Characters may want to alleviate their immediate distress or to obtain the usual things associated with the "good life" such as happiness, money, education, success, friends, or family. At the same time, characters may look for an "easy" course of action or avoid age-appropriate responsibilities perceived as demanding. Therefore, actions and resolutions of tensions fail to balance long- and short-term perspectives, such as a stereotypic view of people and events or limited coordination of viewpoints of different characters. There may be a sense that the story is "borrowed" or "canned." The narrative may be based on a movie, a book, or a replay of actual experience without the flexibility to draw from various schemas to fashion an original narrative that fits the stimulus precisely.

Joe, age 10-3, above average IQ, diagnosed with Attention-Deficit/Hyperactivity Disorder (ADHD).

Card 1. Well, a kid joins violin, the strings, because he thought it would be easy and fun. But it wasn't because he had to make up all the homework he didn't do when he was in strings and the other kids were in class. When he found out they were having a concert, he hadn't practiced, so he tried to get out of it, but his parents wouldn't give him a note. They thought he should give it his best effort. Just before the concert, he broke the violin. He told his parents it broke accidentally, but they found out because he told his friends and their parents found out and told his parents. So they made him buy a new one. For the next 2 years he had to play violin, and he was bad at it, and he got really bad grades.

The kid who joined the band thinking that playing the violin would be easy and fun doesn't anticipate the frustrations, and when his parents refuse to let him out of his commitment, he breaks the violin. In covering up this action (tells parents it was an accident), the character is short-sighted, again failing to anticipate the consequences, and suffers the price. The parents' intentions are given lip service (want son to give it his best effort), but parent-child perspectives are not coordinated (son deceives parents, gets punished, and gets bad grades). The narrator does connect actions with their consequences but views the negative outcomes as the culmination of a vicious cycle between the child and authority figures. This sequence of actions and reactions does not seem guided by underlying principles such as intrinsic values or realistic problem solving.

4. Realistic

The framework for understanding experience is organized around realistic and practical considerations, with narrative construction guided by coherent principles rather than progressing by a series of actions and reactions (showing poor planning) or by borrowed details (stereotype, movie, book, or personal recollection). The story is conceptually clear and specific; the sequence of events reconciles inner states, actions, and outcomes and coordinates the individuality of different characters. Characters act deliberately toward a clear purpose, although intrinsic sources of motivation or satisfaction (e.g., enjoying the task), the balance between long- and short-term perspectives, and the coordination of viewpoints across different characters are not as prominent or nuanced as at the highest level.

Ian, age 8-11, above average IQ, nonreferred and well adjusted.
Card 1. That's a violin? All right. Well, he came back from school and he didn't want to play the violin because he doesn't like it. Later, he'll probably play it because he wants to watch TV and do his homework and play.

The narrator's schemas include the setting of priorities and tolerance for unpleasant activities to meet responsibilities or goals. However, the storyteller doesn't reconcile the ultimate purpose or value of playing the violin in light of the boy's negative feelings about it.

5. Complex and Responsible

Multiple considerations are clearly differentiated and cohesively reconciled so that events are placed in a context that integrates various dimensions of the inner and outer worlds. Thus, feelings, thoughts, actions, and outcomes are well-coordinated within and across characters. Actions and concerns reflect long-range interests, are precisely in accord with the stimulus, incorporate a well-conceptualized timeframe, and show consideration for others. The narrative conveys an understanding of the complexities of the psychological world, including the intricacies needed to balance long- and short-term needs, aspirations, intentions, actions, and outcomes of various characters. Resolutions are mindful of the dignity of all parties and suggest flexible problem solving. Goals are more abstract than at the realistic level and may involve objectives such as self-development, consideration of others' feelings, or realistic desire to contribute to improving social conditions.

Benjie, age 9-11, nonreferred, well adjusted, very superior IQ (other stories are discussed in Chapter 3, and the entire protocol is presented later in this chapter).

Card 1. The boy has a violin except he can't play it very nicely. So he's kind of upset because he can't figure out how to play it well. You want to know what I think this thing is? [Points to the paper under the violin] [E: Up to you.] He's thinking whether he should keep trying or quit it because he doesn't know how to play it. [E: Turns out?] He gives up because he decides that he'll never be able to do it.

The boy's dilemma involves a decision about continued commitment to an activity that he cannot master according to his own standards. Unlike Ian's story, the meaningfulness of the activity is central to the decision. It is important to note that learning to play the violin is optional and, unlike other skills such as reading, is generally not considered essential for success. Therefore, it is socially acceptable for the child to a make a decision, and this process of decision making is important for assigning the level of cognitive-experiential integration. The boy's decision is not based on momentary frustration with the task but on the conviction that he will never play the instrument up to his standards.

LEVELS OF COGNITIVE-EXPERIENTIAL INTEGRATION

Level One: Disorganized. Characteristics of this level pertain to the narrator's behaviors and to the unfolding narrative. The narrator's behavior grossly departs from social expectation and the narrative progression signals disorganized thought processes. Schemas for understanding experiences are impaired (distorted or simplified), as evidenced by limitations in deciphering social cues, grasping implications, or understanding social causality. Any of the following:

- discrepant level of Perceptual Integration
- highly idiosyncratic or illogical assumptions about the world shown by bizarre, gruesome, socially inappropriate content or distorted understanding of cause-effect relationships
- problems with reasoning and conceptualizations—incompatible ideas, implausible (not merely improbable) or grossly illogical events major contradictions in story content
- gross departure of behavior from social expectations such as throwing test materials
- gross departure of story content from social expectations such as leaving a character in an *extreme* state of helplessness or deprivation

- narrator not able to grasp the task (versus finding it difficult)
- narrator cannot maintain distance from stimulus, overly reactive or frightened by the picture

Level Two: Rudimentary. Rather than idiosyncratic distortion, there is a markedly simplified process of reasoning incorporating minimal causal connections. Accordingly, feelings or inner states are not explained beyond simple reactions and causal inferences are nonexistent, extremely rudimentary, or vague. Characters are distinguished by the way they look in the picture (important perceptual cues may be ignored) or by outward actions with minimal differentiation in their intentions, feelings, history, or circumstances. Characters respond to the situational provocations rather than act with deliberate intention or anticipation of realistic consequences. Outcomes are vague, insufficiently explained, or fail to resolve the problem beyond the moment. Solutions to problems or conflicts are characterized by wishful (improbable but not impossible) or unrealistic strategies or avoidance of conflict.

Feelings and inner states are simplistically understood—simple labels such as happy, sad, and angry are associated to the stimulus or to isolated events.

- Minimal causal inferences, extremely basic or vague (something bad happened).
- Characters are distinguished by how they look in the picture or by outward actions without grasping differences in intentions, feelings, history, or circumstances.
- Outcomes are vague, insufficiently related to a transitional process (means to ends), or fail to resolve the problem beyond the moment. Wishful thinking may prevail (improbable but not impossible as in the previous level) or mildly unrealistic (naïve) strategies or avoidance of conflict.
- Gaps in communication or understanding; omitting transitional events.

Level Three: Superficial. Narratives portray more complex coordination of ideas than above. However, lack of specificity (vagueness) and conformity with cultural "scripts" convey a stereotyped view of events or relationships. Relatively greater emphasis on external incentives or consequences than on inner life and lack of commitment to standards promote actions that are geared to needs and wants. Characters may want to alleviate their immediate distress or to obtain the usual things associated with the "good life" (feeling good, money, education, success, relationships). The narrative lacks "depth" and specificity, suggesting a stereotypical or superficial view with possible "gaps" in understanding seen in the story progression or in sizing up the stimulus.

This level is characterized by socially appropriate content that lacks depth or specificity where purposes are short term, actions are evoked by immediate external demand, and ideas are stereotypic, naïve, or wishful, portraying a superficial view of events and relationships:

- Characters are tuned to external incentives or consequences—little or no intrinsic satisfaction or commitment to standards.

(continued)

- Instrumental actions are extrinsically driven without genuine interest, curiosity, enjoyment of the activity, or commitment to standards.
- Characters' actions are responsive to their needs and wants or to external pressure rather than by principle or long-term goals.
- Actions and resolutions do not balance short- and long-term perspectives.
- Narrative may be borrowed or canned.

Level Four: Realistic. Events are realistically depicted and the story conveys coherence between inner states and external circumstances, within a character and across different characters. Characters' durable intentions guide appropriate actions directed toward clear purposes or problem-resolution. However, the emphasis is more on realistic and practical considerations than ideals, standards, principles, and/or intrinsic sources of satisfaction, which characterize the highest level. Contextual cues may be ignored, but emotions and relationships are accurately interpreted. The framework for understanding experience is organized around realistic and practical considerations with narrative construction guided by coherent principles rather than proceeding by a series of actions and reactions (poor planning) or borrowed details (stereotypes, movie, book, or replay of a single experience).

- Story is conceptually clear and specific.
- Sequences of events reconcile inner states, actions, and outcomes and coordinate the individuality of different characters.
- Characters act with intent and deliberateness to accomplish their intentions.
- Characters balance intrinsic sources of motivation or satisfaction with long- and short-term considerations and interests of all characters.

Level Five: Complex and Responsible. The narrative conveys an understanding of the complexities of the psychological world and resources for flexible problem solving that balances long and short terms, needs and aspirations of various characters, as well as feelings, thoughts, intentions, actions, and outcomes within and across characters. Resolutions are mindful of the needs and rights of all parties; goals are more abstract than above and may involve objectives such as self-development or realistic desire to contribute to improving social conditions. The story flows smoothly, depicts events in a conceptually clear and specific manner, and places events in a context that integrates multiple dimensions and perspectives.

The inner and outer worlds are well-differentiated and well-coordinated. Actions and concerns reflect long-range interests, are in accord with subtleties of the stimulus, and incorporate a well-conceptualized timeframe and consideration among individuals. Multiple dimensions of experience are clearly differentiated and external events are cohesively coordinated with understanding of the intricacies of the psychological world.

- Narrative balances long- and short-term needs, feelings, intentions, aspirations, thoughts, actions, and outcomes of various characters in relation to one another, the context, or problem set by the stimulus and to social causality.

- Actions and concerns reflect long-range interests, are precisely in accord with the stimulus, incorporate a well-conceptualized timeframe, and show a nuanced consideration of others (well-differentiated inner life and external circumstance).
- Resolutions are respectful of all parties, suggest realistic and flexible problem solving, and incorporate multiple viewpoints.
- Goals are more abstract, balanced, or complex than the above level and spur appropriate actions and outcomes. The goals may involve self-development, concerns about others' feelings, or realistic desire to improve social conditions.

CASE ILLUSTRATION

To provide opportunities to contrast two protocols on the variables elaborated in this chapter, Appendix 4.1 presents the coding of stories told by Oscar (O), referred with attentional concerns whose protocol is discussed at length, and stories told by Benjie (B), a focused and attentive participant in a research study similar in age to Oscar.

CAUTION

Analysis of stories does not aim to make or confirm a diagnosis but to clarify the personal schemas relevant to the individual's functioning and to the presenting concerns. For example, problems with the regulation of attention or of emotion are associated with various diagnoses. In the context of a comprehensive assessment, TAT stories clarify how these self-regulatory difficulties are manifested in the schemas that act as templates for reasoning about day-to-day experiences.

Oscar

Oscar was referred for evaluation by his parents at the age of 9 because of increasing concerns about behaviors suggestive of attentional problems first noted when he was 7. Parents reported behaviors such as forgetting to do homework unless reminded and neglecting to turn in the work even if completed. His current and previous year's teachers also reported problems with completion of class-work and homework. Despite Oscar's distractibility when doing school-related tasks, he has done well academically, having earned mostly A's with constant parental supervision and home-school collaboration.

During the testing sessions, Oscar was generally responsive and eager to complete tasks despite some difficulty maintaining his attention. When distracted (by a variety of stimuli), his attention was easily directed back to the task by a verbal prompt. He seemed more engaged and less distractible when performing the unstructured tasks such as drawing and storytelling than the structured academic tasks. However, his actual performance was more organized with greater structure. His Full Scale WISC IQ score was in the high average range (114; 82nd percentile), with little discrepancy among the Index scores. Performance on the Woodcock-Johnson Achievement Test ranged from average in broad written language to very superior in broad reading and broad math. Oscar completed the visual form of the Test of Variables of Attention–Revised (TOVA-R) as a continuous performance test measuring sustained attention. The TOVA is a computerized test presenting a series of stimuli in quick succession and requiring a response only to target stimuli. Although his performance was within the normal range, the rate of commission errors (incorrectly responding to the nontarget stimulus) increased significantly as the test session progressed. Elevated rates of commission errors suggest difficulty inhibiting responses to comply with the task demand. It should be noted that the TOVA was not designed to be used as the sole diagnostic criterion in determining the presence of Attention Deficit Hyperactivity Disorder.

Oscar's TAT protocol is examined in terms of the variables introduced in this chapter to address the referral issues. His stories, imports, and explanatory hypotheses are followed by a narrative summary.

Card 1. Um. Once upon a time, a boy was looking at his violin thinking that he would never be able to play it. Then his father came in and brought in a private music teacher to so she could teach him how to play his violin and . . . she said, "well, young man I see that you want to play the violin." And the boy said, "yes, I guess so," and the lady said, "well, I am your private music teacher, you can call me Ms. Bosh." And she gave him something to play and taught him the notes and then she asked him to play it. The song was "Twinkle, Twinkle, Little Star." And then she said, "that's the first basic violin music. Now, can you please play that?" And the boy played and made several mistakes and she said . . . made him practice until he got it perfect. He played over and over and over and over. And then he had to play so long that he went into overtime and the lady had to get paid extra. And so there was a recital coming up and the lady had told him . . . and Ms. Bosh had told him and then he . . . the boy started to practice very hard and then one day no, and then one week. One week, he was playing very well and then he was able to go on to another song. And she said, "you are doing very well for a beginner, how would you like to be the star of the beginning class." And he said, "would I ever!"

And then she taught him even more music so he would know what to play for the upcoming program and then she also told him that it was a Christmas program. And he said, "Okay." And then he had to practice Christmas songs, like "Jingle Bells" and all those other songs. And then he had to be in . . . he had to be Joseph in a play and, no, he had to be baby Jesus and his parents were Mary and Joseph and after the play he had to play songs with the beginners. And then after the class . . . then after the recital . . . after the Christmas program, she made him advanced and after a while he became the top student in his advanced class. [E: Before?] Um, he was playing around and then his father came in, playing around with his toys, and his boats in the pond in his backyard . . . his pool in his backyard . . . playing with his toys . . . he was playing jump off the ship. [E: Feeling?] In the first part of the story, he was feeling depressed. Then, in the center, he started feeling better and then, at the end, he felt very good and proud of himself.

Content import: If discouraged and lacking interest, a boy can become the best if he receives private help and works hard.

Process import: When telling a story about a picture, you rely on specific details from experience rather than on lessons or abstractions derived from them (this applies to all subsequent stories).

Explanatory hypotheses: After defining the tension in the scene, Oscar loses the focus of the task, replaying concrete details from memory as a script without giving them priority and without a plan for constructing the story. When redirected by the examiner ("what happened before?"), Oscar switched to a different train of thought without connection to the previous sequence of events (describing how the boy was playing around in the backyard). This pattern of stringing together the concrete details of his experiences through an associative process without organizing them conceptually to meet the requirements of the task suggests problems with deliberate organization of behavior in open-ended tasks or situations with few inherent guidelines. This narrative process is consistent with the content that the boy thinks he will never learn the violin but succeeds when he receives help from a private teacher. (It is interesting to note that Oscar receives weekly violin lessons and is making good progress according to his parents.)

Motivational and emotional issues are not covered in this chapter, but this story (and others in the protocol) gives no indication of intrinsic enjoyment of the task as the character seems motivated by recognition for doing well (becoming the star of the class). Possibly, praise and encouragement are effective extrinsic incentives in combination with guidance and structure to maintain attentional focus.

Card 2. This story is about a family trying to survive in the wild. Once upon a time, there was a man, a mother, and a daughter. They lived on a farm out in the mountains. The man was the farmer and he had to plant all the food and take care of the animals. The mother was the helper for the father and the daughter went to school and also helped her father. One day, on the daughter's way to school, she got lost and then she met a boy in the wild and he helped her out because he had lived in the wild for almost all of his life. And then he told her his story and he said that he used to live like her. Then on his way to school he got lost too and he ended up a green man. Green Man. And then he helped her back out of the wild and showed her the way from there to her school. And she got to school and then all day she was thinking about the boy and then all the time that she went back she was still thinking about him. Then she went out into the wild to visit him. And then when she got back home her father and mother were very angry. They said, "Rose," that was her name, "Rose, what were you doing out there so long?" And she said, "nothing, really" and then her father could tell that she was lying because her face always gets really red and she always has water dripping down when she's nervous and she's lying, and her father said, "Rose I can tell that you are lying. Now, tell me what, what happened out there." And she said, "Um . . . well, I was out in the wild . . ." And her father and mother cut her off right there and they said it at once, "What were you doing out in the wild?" And she said, "I gotta go inside and do my homework." And then they, her parents wouldn't let her inside and when they finally found out the truth they grounded her and "No more going to the wild. You can only go to school. We are going to be there every day for a month. And we are going to be there with you when you go to school too so we can make sure that you don't play in school, that you don't go to the wild, that you have no fun for a month." And she said, "That's not fair," and he said, and they said, "Rose, it doesn't matter if it's fair or not, we are trying to protect you." And she said, "That's so unfair" [unclear] and they said, "Rose, just go to your room." And she went to her room and laid down and started doing her homework and cried. Then later on after the month was done their parents felt very sad for what they did . . . they were ashamed of themselves and let her go out into the wild whenever she wanted to but they made one deal that they would have to supervise her. And she said, "Okay." And they lived happily ever after and they got to meet the boy and later on they got married [sings "Wedding March"] and that's the end. [In this story Oscar used different voices for the characters. The voice for the girl was high pitched and was difficult to understand on the tape in certain spots.]

Content import: If a girl violates parental rules, she temporarily accepts her parents' restrictions and supervision but assumes that they ultimately will let her do what she wants.

Explanatory hypotheses: The process of narrating the story is similar to that of Card 1, proceeding from statements about the stimulus to a story that develops through concrete details including verbatim exchanges between characters.

Oscar's problems with monitoring and directing his own ideas and behaviors are evident in the story content and structure as well as narrative process. Just as the main character "got lost" on the way to school, Oscar seems lost in the details of his fantasy and dialogue. Parental supervision in the story likely compensates for the character's (and narrator's) difficulty with self-regulation but may not always be welcome (the character is happy when parents back away from their restrictions). Again, there is no indication of the girl's engagement in schoolwork or devotion to a goal other than to live "happily ever after" with parents regretting their actions rather than the child being concerned about meeting expectations.

Card 3. Once upon a time, there was a little girl. Her name was Miss Latitia. And the people called her Miss Latonya because her full name was Latitia Latonya. And then after a while she had to go down the road to pick up some food and everyone kept saying, "Hello, Miss Latonya." And then she said, "Hello." And she had to pick up all of her groceries and she came back to her house and went outside. [E: Tell me what's happening in the picture.] Well, it looks like she's crying. [E: Are you telling me about the picture? Let's start over and tell me a story about what's in the picture.] Once upon a time, there was a lady named Miss Latitia and she was outside talking to her neighbors and then someone came up and started and said that the landlord came up and told her that she had a few days to pay the rent or else she would have to leave her house. And then she went back to her bedroom and started crying and she said, "What am I going to do? I don't have money. I don't have enough money." And then she started to look around in the city for a job. Then she found one. When she came back home she sat down on her bed and she sat down on the floor by her bed and said, "Oh, I have to start work tomorrow morning." And then, after a while, she thought, "I guess it is worth it because I do have to pay the landlord's rent and I think I would rather live in my home instead of living on the street." And so she went downstairs . . . she went down to the bank and begged the bank people for a few dollars. And they gave her twenty . . . a twenty-dollar bill out of their money, everyone each, and they had four . . . there was ten people there which means she got . . . a lot of money. And then the landlord asked for one thousand dollars and now she only had to pay eight hundred. And then the landlord said, "Do you have the rest of the money," and she said, "No, but I'm going to . . . but, I got a job so I could pay for it." And he said, "All right." And then he left and she said, "Whew." And the landlord said . . . then when the landlord was walking away he said, "That woman . . . she thinks it's no fun to work." And then she said, "Oh, am I ever going to think it's fun to work?" And then she sat down by the side of her bed and started crying again. Then, after a few minutes, she got up and started lying down. And then she asked, she asked herself, "What have I gotten myself into? I could have gotten a job earlier and paid the landlord the money he wanted. But, now I have to pay him eight hundred dollars." And every year, the landlord would come around and demand four hundred dollars. No wait. All right, the landlord wanted one thousand two hundred and then she only had to pay one thousand and the landlord needed one thousand dollars more. And every year the landlord would come around and demand . . . , and the landlord would demand four hundred dollars. And she never paid and she kept saying, "I'll do it next year." And then after three of four years, she had to pay all the money and she said, "Oh, I was so careless, I could have paid so long ago." And then after a while, she ended . . . after three years, no, after five weeks, no, after eleven months, she was able to pay the landlord back. And she did. And she didn't realize that she paid the landlord more than enough. She had paid him five thousand dollars. The landlord gave her back her change and she said, "Thank you." Not knowing that it was her money still. And then . . . [E: If you feel like you are done just let me know.] Okay.

Content import: Without a plan for meeting life's burdensome obligations (keeping a job to pay the rent), a person relies on others not only for help in a crisis but for relief from ongoing responsibilities.

Explanatory hypotheses: Oscar had to be directed to gear his story to what is happening in the picture just as the main character had to be reminded to pay the rent. The story is a repetitious series of associations with details not providing a conceptual shift. Being carried away by the details and having no strategy for ending the story, Oscar abandoned the narrative as soon as the examiner hinted that he might wind it up. Again, the need for external direction to organize ideas and behaviors is evident. Difficulty planning ahead is suggested by the manner of constructing the story and by the failure of the woman to anticipate the need for paying rent until she was in jeopardy of being thrown out of her residence. The complicating factors are the characters' use of ineffective (reactive) strategies to deal with the situation (e.g., paying the wrong amount) and the view that work is "no fun."

Card 4. Once upon a time, there was a man named Rocky and his wife was called Lily. Then, after a few days, Rocky had to go to work and he said, "Gotta go Lily." And she said, "Okay. Have a good time dear." And he said, "Okay." And then after a while, Rocky got called to um, across the world and she said, "Rocky, when will you come back?" And he said "I don't know, maybe in a few months." And she said, "Oh, okay, have a good time dear." And he said, "Bye." And then he got called . . . after that he got called to China and he had to call his wife and said, and he said, "Honey, I'm gonna have to be here a little bit longer." And she said, "For how long?" And he said, "About a year." And she fainted and then she got off the phone and she said, "Bye, honey" and fainted. And then he fainted.

And then after a few minutes, they both got back up and Rocky had to help some Chinese kids because they were being attacked by some gangsters. And he saved their lives and ended up in the hospital. Then after a while, he called his wife and said, "Honey, I think . . . the doctor said that I shouldn't go anywhere now for a while, so I may be coming back home earlier than I expected." And she said, "That's great." And then she started planning a big surprise party for him. She invited everyone in her neighborhood. [Examiner prompts] I don't know how to describe this. [E: Feeling?] She was . . . in the beginning, she was feeling a little bit happy. And then, in the middle, she started to feel a little bit more sad. In the sort of end, she was feeling very sad. Then in the very end, she was feeling very happy. That's all I can think of.

Content import: One way for a husband to get out of his business responsibilities and return to his wife (and a surprise party) is to get hurt while doing something heroic.

Explanatory hypotheses: This meandering story is significantly out of tune with the stimulus (husband and wife amicably saying goodbye is not consistent with the pictured scene). Shifting external circumstances control the relationship between the husband and wife. Accordingly, a fortuitous opportunity to perform a heroic deed enables the characters to do what they want. On a more general level, the import of this story is that ordinary people have little free choice, but heroes do as they please. The happy ending (surprise party) seems a bit unrealistic considering that the husband is coming home because "the doctor said I shouldn't go anywhere for a while." Similar to previous stories, feelings are not interwoven with circumstances but added later in response to inquiry.

Card 5. Once upon a time, there was an old lady called Agatha. Agatha lived alone. She tried to keep her home as neat as possible. But, whenever . . . whenever someone in her apartment came over they always messed up her place because everyone besides her was sort of drunk. And Agatha said, "You people must stop drinking," and they said, "You know, we shouldn't, it's not like it's affecting us." And she said, "Yes, it is, see, you used to be nice and so did you." And then there was this man that was always mean to everyone. And she said, "Well, it's not affecting you, you were always mean." And then she said . . . after him she said, "You were nice too. Everyone except for him was nice. You guys have changed a lot ever since you started drinking. You guys must stop." And then they tried to stop, but it wouldn't work. And then one of them started smoking. And then Agatha took . . . started making a . . . started making a vote for and it went worldwide for everyone that sells guns and everything like that and alcohol and stuff like that to shut their stores down, every store. As long as the alcohol doesn't . . . as long as the alcohol doesn't help people then they couldn't sell it anymore and it helped.

People stopped selling guns and alcohol. And started selling good things like protein, juice, and calcium, and sodas and they were no longer selling guns. Instead of guns they were selling water guns. And then amazingly the rates of every store that stopped selling those things went up very high. Their rates went up quadrupled and then everyone wanted to thank her so they let her own their businesses. And then she was still old but she was, she was favored by everyone around the world. [E: Feeling?] In the beginning, she was feeling sad for the people. In the middle, she feeling a little bit angry and in the end, she was feeling very happy. [E: Before?] She, when she first moved in, she used to have it quiet and then after a week it started.

Content import: If one is concerned about a specific problem, one may go on a general crusade to tackle all the bad things in the world and become (unrealistically) a world-class hero.

Explanatory hypotheses: Rather than resolving the character's initial concern about keeping her apartment neat, the story proceeds as a flight of fancy where the character becomes a heroine. By now, the associative pattern of narrative development is familiar; the story progresses through a series of unlikely events with details that are poorly monitored. The details are incorporated as they come to mind rather than through the use of a more active process of selecting and subordinating the details in the interest of constructing a cohesive story to meet the task demand. Thus, ideas are associatively connected but not conceptually organized.

Card 6. Once upon a time, there was a man named George. He was a very tidy and clean man and he had . . . he . . . he was also rich but still kind. And then he had hired a maid and her name was Miss Phillips. And Miss Phillips was about I think . . . she was about fifty-six years old . . . now that's ancient. And she had said, "You are a very clean man Mr . . . Mr. George. Are you ever going to get a bigger house because you . . . you know that you have a wife and several children. Why you have more children than the Brady Bunch themselves." He said, "I know, I am not sure if I want to get a bigger house. I mean, all our memories are in this house. I'm thinking about it." And then she said, "You have to get a bigger house." He said, "I know but I am not sure if I want to leave this house." And after the next day, she said, "I have an idea, why don't you just take all of your valuables and take them and . . . take them with you . . . every single thing?" And he said, "But, but what about my memories?" And she said, "Your memories will live on with you; they won't be left in here, they will be with you." And he said, "Well, that's a good point." And then he said, "Okay, we'll start moving tomorrow." And she said, and then she said, "But how can you move that fast?" And he said, "Well, we'll get the fastest people in the universe to move us. And then on Earth . . . on the face of the planet to move us." And then, they did. They were moved in less than one day. They had moved to a big mansion. Bigger than this whole school complex. And after a while everyone said . . . after a while the kids finally found their parents and said, "Daddy, I, where's our bedrooms?" and they had been living there for three years. And he said, "I don't know, we'll have to get a . . . we'll have to put a map somewhere in here." And they said, "Yeah." And then after while, they had to post maps almost everywhere. And they did. The end. [E: Feeling?] In the beginning, the father was feeling a little bit sad and happy. And in the middle, the father was feeling okay, pretty good. And in the end, the father was feeling very happy, at the very end.

Content import: If a person is rich, he or she can make a fanciful decision such as moving his or her family to a mansion, but unexpected complications arise that are unrealistically resolved.

Explanatory hypotheses: Again, this is a far-fetched story beginning with a character's concern about neatness and ending with a family moving to a mansion and being so lost that it is necessary to post maps (external structure). As with previous stories, in the absence of planning or anticipation, events unfold through successive reactions to earlier events.

Card 8. Once upon a time, there was a young man and his father. The young man's father was very ill and they had to cut him open to see what was wrong with him. And they said, "Well, young man I don't think we should have cut your father open. The thing is he has an ulcer and also he had the flu, amnesia, and what's it called . . . cancer." And then he said, "What cancer, the flu, amnesia, and all those other things!" And then he said, "I'm afraid so." And then his father was just lying there. And then he said, "Dad, Dad, hello Dad." And then his Dad woke up and said, "Ah, what's the problem?" He said, "Dad you have several problems." And then he wouldn't tell him any more. Then, his father said, "Is he mad at me?" And then they said, "No sir, it's just a problem that we can't help." And he said, "What is the problem. Is it . . . is it something I got in trouble with?" And they said, "No, it's much worse than that, you may . . . you have the chance of dying." And he was like, "WHAT?" And then they were still cutting him open. I mean closing him. And then the guy was had a knife in his hand and accidentally ripped off all his stitches and he was like, "AHH!" And then they had to start all over with the stitching. And so, after a while his son had grown up and then his father died of natural . . . natural reasons. And also because that's the reason . . . and also because of the flu, cancer, and other things. And so he wished and wished and wished and wished that his father would come back. And then after a while they . . . during his father's burial the doctors ran up to the boy and said, "Hey kid, we had made a mistake, your father is not dead." And he said, "What?" And then he . . . and then they said, "He's just sleeping." And then he was like, "Then how come when he was awake he didn't he didn't realize that?" And they said, "Well, I don't know." And then he said, "Yes, my father's alive." And then when his father woke up and got out he said, then the boy said, "Hi dad, you're alive, you have no problems." And he was like, "Phew!" The end. [E: Feeling?] In the beginning, the boy was feeling sad. In the middle, the boy was feeling still sad. And in the end, the boy was feeling real happy.

Content import: When it is difficult to accept what seems inevitable, a boy gets his wish and finds out that there was a big mistake and everything is fine, after all.

Explanatory hypotheses: This story progresses like a bad movie with one-dimensional characters and unlikely sequences of events, including a magical ending. Not having planned ahead, Oscar comes to a point where he is not satisfied with the remaining possibilities for a logical ending to the story. So, he grants his character's wish by bringing his father back from the dead. As with previous stories, people do not face the consequences of their actions, and things turn out fine despite serious mistakes.

Narrative Summary

In constructing the TAT stories, Oscar enjoyed expressing his ideas as they entered his awareness without a plan for strategically subordinating the unfolding details to accomplish the task at hand. Sometimes, when the stimuli were particularly complex, the story content was not a good fit with the pictured scene, indicating that, without clear guidelines, Oscar has difficulty gearing his responses to the cues in the surroundings. Oscar's difficulties monitoring the progression of the stories parallel the description of characters as requiring external supervision and guidance or as encountering problems meeting obligations or resolving their dilemmas due to lack of planning or anticipation. His heroic characters are exempt from life's humdrum requirements. These patterns are in line with Oscar's reported distractibility, inattention, and problems with organization. Oscar's tendency to get carried away with associated details (a style often characterizing individuals with attentional deficits) suggests significant distractibility. In contrast to Oscar's performance on more structured tasks where he was easily redirected, the examiner's prompts usually did not help him to improve the story. Oscar's above average performance on the structured tasks contrasted with his relatively less organized performance on tasks such as the TAT that permitted him to set his own standards and goals for the product. Ironically, he enjoyed the less structured measures and experienced some boredom and frustration with the more structured academic tests.

Although Oscar's stories demonstrate some difficulty monitoring thought process and resisting the pull of less relevant ideas, content was generally socially appropriate. Moreover, Oscar's motivation to please others and to be recognized as successful was evident despite minimal indication of intrinsic investment in goal-directed activities. This motivational pattern, coupled with better performance on tasks with inherent structure and clearly designated response standards, suggests that Oscar will benefit from guidance (at school and at home) to complete assignments that involve planning and self-monitoring. Although at times Oscar perceives external limits as intrusive, he does respond to encouragement, praise, and recognition. Should recommendations discussed with the family and teachers prove insufficient, a trial of medication may be considered.

Benjie

The contrast between stories told by Benjie and Oscar are evident in the coding shown in Appendix 4.1.

Card 1. The boy has a violin except he can't play it very nicely. So he's kind of upset because he can't figure out how to play it well. You want to know what I think this thing is? [Points to the paper under the violin] [E: Up to you] He's thinking whether he should keep trying or quit it because he doesn't know how to play it. [E: Turns out?] He gives up because he decides that he'll never be able to do it.

Card 2. It looks like a family in the mid to late 1800s, and there's the mother who looks like she's taking a rest and there's either one of the sons or the father who's taking the horse and one of the girls looks like she has just read a book and she's coming back to the house with the book she read. I'm not sure they let girls go to school at that time. Otherwise, I would have said she's coming home from school. [E: Anything going on in the family?] Just looks like they're trying to get the day's work done so they can make a living.

Card 3BM. There's a person, and she looks very tired or sad. I have to decide . . . sad, very sad. Someone close to her probably had something bad happen, and she's trying to get over it. Is that a gun? [E: Does it look like a gun to you?] No, a vague object, could be a gun. I don't know if she was depressed and shot herself but it looks like a vague object. That's why I asked because it could be a possibility. [E: What happened?] Maybe one of her family members died. [E: Ending?] She ends up getting over it. Lets out her grief and goes on with life.

Card 4. Well, there's a man that looks very mad at someone who annoyed or offended him, and his wife is trying to stop him from doing anything he'll regret such as attacking the person who was offending him. At the end, she'll restrain him and he'll stop and get over his anger.

Card 5. A lady comes home or rather she comes into a room and she's looking for someone so she searches the house and that's it. [E: Who?] Maybe someone else who lives in the house and maybe she wants something of that person. [E: What happens?] She keeps searching 'till she finds him.

Card 6BM. Have to think. [short pause] A grandmother's son just came home and told her some bad news that he was very sad about and she was both surprised and sad hearing this. That's it. [E: If making up story, what would be the news?] Well maybe . . . I don't really know, just something she's surprised and sad to hear. [E: Ending] She heard the bad news, and they're both a little sad and life goes on. I sound like a tv show.

Card 7GF. Okay. On the story before, I think they did let girls go to school . . . in a one-room schoolhouse. In this picture, the teacher is trying to teach the girl her lessons, but the girl doesn't seem very interested and the girl doesn't learn her lesson and whoever is teaching her gets mad for not paying attention to the lessons. [E: Happens eventually?] The teacher gets mad at her like I said. [E: Future?] Well, after she was scolded, she paid attention more to her lessons.

Card 7BM. A boy comes home with his report card and his father isn't very happy and he punishes him and the boy is very sad because of the punishment. [E: Then what happens?] Then he serves his punishment, and he's not very happy doing it but has to live with it.

Card 8BM. A boy, yeah a boy, more like an adolescent has to have surgery and he's dreaming about how it's going to be and he's a little scared so he's thinking how it's going to be. So he sees what's going to happen to him, and it makes him even more scared. I don't know why there's something that looks like a rifle there. [E: Ending?] He goes through it, and he realizes he was worried about nothing because he didn't even feel it.

Card 12M. A person is sick, and his grandfather comes to see him and his presence there helps the boy get better. [E: Grandfather think?] He's sad that the boy is sick and hopes that he can help in any way. Actually rather, his grandfather being there doesn't cure his illness but it makes him feel better that a person's there by his side.

Card 12BG. Looks like a field with trees and grass and lots of vegetation, river or stream winding through it and an old boat used once in a while if ever and looks like a peaceful place where a person would want to come when they're feeling depressed or stressed or when they just want peace and quiet. It's different from all the rest because there are no people.

Card 13B. There's a boy sitting outside of his log cabin and he looks bored and he's trying to figure out what to do and he's a little sad because he doesn't have anything to do and he can't find anything to do. [E: Ending?] He just doesn't get to do anything because he can't think of anything.

 **TESTYOURSELF**

1. **Which statement is not true of perceptual integration?**
   (a) It is unrelated to cognitive-experiential integration.
   (b) It refers to the accuracy and precision in explaining the scenes in the pictures.
   (c) A high level requires positing conceptual relationships among the perceptual elements.
   (d) All of these are true.

2. **Which statement does not characterize concrete thinking?**
   (a) It is tied to immediate situational cues.
   (b) It is closely linked to specific personal experiences.
   (c) It fosters trial-and-error problem solving.
   (d) All of these statements are true.

3. **Which statement does not belong with cognitive-experiential integration?**
   (a) Integration of past, present, and future time perspectives.
   (b) Organization of ideas according to causes and effects and other logical frameworks.
   (c) Coordination of stimuli from the inner and outer worlds.
   (d) All of these statements apply.

4. **Why is time perspective important in TAT stories?**

5. **What are the essential differences between associative and rule-based thinking?**

6. **How do deficits and distortions in thinking manifest in TAT stories?**

7. **Disrupted schema development (due to attentional or other processing difficulties) is evident in TAT stories.**
   True or False?

Answers: 1. a; 2. d; 3. d; 4. Instructions specifically cue time sequences, which are essential to the story structure. Moreover, timeframe organizes thought; 5. Associative thinking refers to a stream of ideas that is not deliberately organized (automatic) but reflects the inherent regularities of experience, whereas rule-based thinking refers to deliberate analytical or logical thought process geared to a purpose; 6. Deficits are evident in what is left out or remains vague, whereas distortions manifest in content that is contradictory, illogical, or socially inappropriate; 7. True.

APPENDIX 4.1 CODING OF PROTOCOLS OF BENJIE AND OSCAR

Level of Abstraction

Card	1	2	3BM	4	5	6BM	7GF	8	13
Benjie	4	4	4	4	4	4	4	4	4
Oscar	3	3	3	3	3	3		2	

Level of Perceptual Integration

Card	1	2	3BM	4	5	6BM	7GF	8	13
Benjie	5	5	5	5	5	5	5	5	5
Oscar	2	2	2	1	2	1		2	

Level of Associative Thinking

Card	1	2	3BM	4	5	6BM	7GF	8	13
Benjie	5	5	5	5	4	5	4	5	5
Oscar	2	2	2	2	2	2		2	

Level of Cognitive-Experiential Integration

Card	1	2	3BM	4	5	6BM	7GF	8	13
Benjie	5	5	5	5	4	5	4	5	5
Oscar	3	3	2	1	2	1		2	

Five

ESSENTIALS OF TAT ASSESSMENT OF EMOTION

Picture stimuli, such as those in the TAT set that display dysphoric affect, require the respondent to demonstrate capacity to experience, modulate, express, and resolve negative emotion. Difficulty symbolizing and representing affect results in stories that minimize, overplay, or distort the affect-laden aspects of the pictured stimuli. Such difficulties are evident when narrators overreact to, misperceive, or ignore the emotional cues rather than situating feelings in the context of events, intentions, and behaviors in line with the pictured stimuli and social causality. The focus of this chapter is on the principles by which individuals conceptualize and regulate negative emotions.

EMOTION AS STORY

Emotions are complex narrative structures that give shape to bodily (e.g., muscle tension) and affective (e.g., sadness) experiences by connecting the feelings to eliciting conditions and action plans. The "core" of an emotion is an affective state that is positive or negative that has become transformed into an emotion through repeated conceptual acts (for a review, see Barrett, Mesquita, Ochsner, & Gross, 2007; Lazarus, 1991a). A "feeling" becomes an "emotion" when it is embedded in a network of justifying experiences that translates a physiological event into a "story." As Shweder (1994) explains, "The 'emotion' is the whole story, the whole package deal—a kind of somatic event (fatigue, chest pain, goose flesh) and/or affective event (panic, emptiness) experienced as a kind of perception (of loss, gain, threat, possibility) and linked to a kind of plan (attack, withdraw, confess, hide, explore)" (p. 38). A "story" is created when feelings, perceptions, and conceptions converge, revealing the role of emotion as an organizer of an otherwise undifferentiated pleasant or unpleasant feeling state. The story structure connects causes and effects (what causes the emotion) and means with ends (how best to deal with the emotion and with its elicitors to reduce tension and attain one's aims). As a result of becoming associated with cognitions, the affective or somatic reaction develops into an emotion.

Day to day, as individuals encounter changing circumstances along with the ebb and flow of core affects, the transformation of these affective states into emotions becomes automated through the development of the emotion story. Although multiple routes contribute to their development, once consolidated, the emotion stories take on a life of their own. What is automatically experienced as an emotion is a state of mind in which affect (pleasant or unpleasant mood state) and cognition (conceptions about causes and potential actions) are woven together (Barrett et al., 2007). A situation that provokes a feeling activates both the emotion and its related cognitions so that repeated experiences with specific affects, their associated situations, and actions become routinized into automatic cognitive patterns or schemas (e.g., Beck, 1976). These schemas link together the affective and cognitive aspects of mental representations with physiological reactions, as well as with expressive and instrumental behaviors (Lazarus, 1991a; Schwartz & Shaver, 1987). Any one of the elements in the network triggers the other elements to which it is associatively connected (Berkowitz, 1990). For example, dysphoric affect tends to evoke physiological reactions, ideas, memories, and expressive motor reactions associated with that state as well as to prompt other negative feelings.

Individuals differ in the extent to which they characterize their inner states as broad affective experiences ("low granularity") or as well-differentiated, discrete emotions ("high granularity"), but these differences are not fully explained by verbal intelligence or understanding the meaning of words (Barrett 1998, 2004). Often (but not always), particular emotions are tied to specific appraisals according to an "if-then" formula whereby an individual perceiving a demeaning action will feel angry, and a person facing uncertainty or existential threat will feel anxious. However, if "anger" is a response to being demeaned, then the individual, in a given cultural milieu, must recognize and impute meaning to the demeaning signals (Lazarus, 1994). The emotion "story" is governed by culturally bound rules (Lazarus, 1991c; Lutz & White, 1986; Scherer, 1992; Smith & Scott, 1997). Nevertheless, individualistic processes linking affect states with cognition preclude one-to-one correspondence between a specific situation and emotion (Nezlek, Vansteelandt, Van Mechelen, & Kuppens, 2008; Kuppens, Van Mechelen, Smits, De Boeck, & Ceulemans, 2007; Parkinson, 1999).

APPRAISAL AND EMOTION

As noted above, affective states are transformed into emotions as they become embedded in a network of cognitions. Appraisal theorists focus on emotions that arise as individuals automatically size up the implications of affectively charged situations for relevance to their well-being (see Lazarus, 1991a). Although these judgments occur in real time as individuals encounter situations, they are influenced by the schemas (see Cervone, 2004), or the "story" in which the affect is situated. In other words, schemas are the distal elicitors of emotions, and appraisals are the proximal elicitors (Lazarus, 1991a). The emotion is a mental representation, story, or schema that connects an otherwise undifferentiated pleasant or unpleasant affective state with information in the current situation that sets its psychological meaning for the individual. Cognition and affect structure each other reciprocally, both contributing to the regulation of emotion (see Rapid Reference 5.1).

≡ *Rapid Reference 5.1*

Schemas and Emotion Regulation

1. *Complexity and organization of schemas.* Two related sources of difficulty with self-regulation of emotion (including problems with recognition, interpretation, and expression) are insufficient organization and complexity of the schemas (deficits) and dysfunctional organization (distortion). Deficits involve problems of regulation due to underdevelopment of control structures, whereas distortion involves problems of dysregulation due to maladaptive control structures that direct emotions toward inappropriate goals (Cicchetti, Ackerman, & Izard, 1995; Rubin, Coplan, Fox, & Calkins, 1995).

2. *Retrieval of schemas from memory.* Access to prior experience from memory depends on the schemas that are activated. The diathesis-stress model of depression posits that negative life events are more likely to activate dysfunctional schemas but only in the presence of negative affect (Miranda, Gross, Persons, & Hahn, 1998). Depressed mood activates maladaptive schemas (Higgins, King, & Mavin, 1982). More research is needed to address mood-dependent schema retrieval to understand the influence of schemas on psychopathology. Cognition and affect structure each other reciprocally, neither causing the other. Depressive schemas are one component of a complex system involving reciprocal relations among affect, cognition, and behavior (Swallow, 2000). Although there is no agreed-upon view of the schema and its operations, it is increasingly recognized as playing a key role in positive adaptation and in the development and maintenance of psychopathology.

3. *Coordination of activated schemas with on-line information processing.* The individual's "on-line" problem-solving resources (e.g., attention, working memory) influence how schemas are confirmed or reshaped in light of the cues in the current situation. For example, individuals who ruminate on negative

(continued)

emotions rather than focusing on regulatory strategies are at greater risk for serious bouts with depression through the three following mechanisms (see Nolen-Hoeksema, 1999). First, ruminations encourage the dominance of awareness by negative thoughts that exacerbate the negative affect, which, in turn, increases access to depressive thoughts and memories (schema activation). Second, the ruminative process drains energy and impairs concentration, thereby impeding more constructive thinking and problem solving (further disrupting "on-line" processing). Third, unsolved problems and failure to meet current expectations (due to problems with "on-line" processing) feed the vicious negative cycles.

Appraisals that generate emotions and associated responses are constrained by the schemas that are activated. Automatic appraisals are adaptive to the extent that they are informed by adaptive schemas. Seemingly effortless, intuitive appraisals may be based on rich and nuanced considerations, informed by well-developed schemas (e.g., Lazarus, 1995; Reisenzein, 2001; Scherer, 2001; Smith & Kirby, 2001a,b). On the other hand, maladaptive schemas that underlie distorted and dysfunctional appraisals engender emotional experiences and action plans that fuel vicious cycles of distress or conflict. Emotion-focused therapeutic interventions often target the processes transforming core affects into emotions (Greenberg, 1993; Moses & Barlow, 2006).

Consider Kyle, a 17-year-old high school junior whose schemas frame parental restrictions as indicative of their disrespect and distrust. This schema would not directly cause Kyle to become angry. Rather, anger is caused indirectly by the application of this schema to the appraisal of a particular limit (e.g., curfew) as demeaning. A more nuanced set of schemas about parental limits would confer flexibility to appraise some instances as reflecting reasonable parental care, unwarranted worry (or distrust), legitimate differences in perspectives, or misunderstandings. A storehouse of conditional schemas to guide automatic appraisals provides individuals with a panorama of categories with various implications for generating emotional and behavioral responses.

The development of Kyle's schemas may be understood in reference to the dual-process models of appraisal that distinguish between automatic, associative appraisals and conscious, deliberate reasoning (see Smith & Kirby, 2001a, b; Smith & Neumann, 2005). After having repeatedly appraised parental limit setting as insulting, this appraisal is built into Kyle's schemas along with other information, and as soon as he associates an incident with this schema, the appraisal and the emotion immediately follow (see Reisenzein, 2001). At the time of his evaluation,

Kyle automatically experienced anger when faced with or even anticipating parental limits. It seemed to him that the situation directly triggered the anger, as Kyle was not aware of having made an appraisal.

The vicious cycles contributing to the development of these appraisal patterns for Kyle included attentional difficulties manifested in early academic struggles spurring parental vigilance and involvement (choosing the best schools, providing tutors, encouraging homework completion). During the evaluation, Kyle acknowledged his appreciation and continued desire for his parents' support but his ongoing experiences of frustration with academics and feelings of being burdened escalated over the years, resulting in increasingly extreme appraisals and almost constant anger, which he suppresses in an effort to present an easy-going façade. Kyle openly shared his experiences with the examiner, expressing dissatisfaction with his "constant" anger but also explaining these emotions as justified resentment toward the pointless achievement orientation that he perceived as driving his family and society in general.

Even as Kyle was deliberately trying to make sense of his situation, formulating explanations, the regularities of his day-to-day encounters reinforced his automatic schemas. His dichotomous thinking in general contributed to his appraisal of parental limits in "either-or" fashion (they let me or they don't), and his tendency to assume that parental limits were synonymous with being disrespected generated anger and conflict. At the same time, Kyle struggled with daily frustration, difficulty concentrating, and a growing sense of meaninglessness of his classes and academic tasks. Given that the implicit schemas guiding Kyle's ongoing appraisals are reinforced on a daily basis, cognitive interventions encouraging conscious reappraisal would not suffice, without also addressing the implicit processes maintaining the schemas (e.g., Campos, Frankel, & Camras, 2004; Linehan et al., 2002). Changing what Kyle verbalizes will not alter the realities of his experiences or his automatically activated schemas. Prior to the evaluation, Kyle's focus was on trying to get by in high school with minimal effort so he can escape to college. His parents opened a discussion about easing his transition to college by planning proactively to choose the right school and investigating the supports he would need to succeed. Kyle was in accord with the idea and was eager to participate in the evaluation (see Chapter 10).

A premise of appraisal theory is that individuals evaluate affectively charged situations in terms of their relevance for well-being and that the categories for making these judgments are housed in the schemas. Although cultural and linguistic contexts influence the categories used to classify incoming information (e.g., Mesquita, 2001a,b; Mesquita & Ellsworth, 2001), there is convergence across different appraisal models (see Ellsworth & Scherer, 2003) about

≡ Rapid Reference 5.2

Abstract Dimensions of Situations that Guide Appraisal (Frijda, 2006)

Novelty and changes (from expectancy)
Intrinsic pleasantness/unpleasantness
Obstacles or facilitators to one's goals
Predictability
Agency (responsible agent)
Controllability
Compatibility with societal norms or personal values, including evaluative standards

some abstract categories that establish the relevance of a situation for the self (see Rapid Reference 5.2; Frijda, 2006). For example, emotions generated by the appraisal of a stressful situation are moderated by the implicit sense that one has the resources to cope effectively (see Lazarus, 1999; Scherer, Schorr, & Johnstone, 2001).

EMOTION REGULATION

Personal schemas that integrate information from the internal environment with cues from the external environment function as the individual's tools for cognitive control over emotions (Santostefano, 1991). Consider two children in the same family who responded differently to a canceled family outing. Josh, the 10-year-old, was angry about missing the trip and did not stop pouting until he was given a date when the trip would be rescheduled. His 8-year-old brother Joe was more concerned about the "baby" sister's sudden fever and did not express any disappointment about the trip. His "appraisal" of the situation allowed Joe to accept departures from expectations more easily than did Josh. Without such flexibility, Josh regarded this planned trip as akin to a "contract" that was broken, hence engendering anger and disappointment. Likewise, expected behaviors (associated with anniversaries, birthdays, holidays) may have the demanding flavor of a "contract" that must be fulfilled with little regard to the circumstances.

≡ Rapid Reference 5.3

Increasing Structure of Information Processing Applied to Appraisal of Ongoing Encounters (adapted from Frijda, 1986)

- Register or encode isolated information—pain, heat, threat, startle without explanation or association beyond reflex (e.g., "*I am hot, I am afraid*").
- Learned stimulus response patterns—associated stimulus response patterns are fragmented from the larger context. These include simple contingencies such as punishment or situation-specific, nongeneralized associations (e.g., "*If I hit my brother, my mom will be angry*"; "*I will be hurt when I touch the stove*").
- Simple structural patterns such as stereotypes—social schemas that reflect frequent regularities of experience (such as information borrowed from the media or simple right-wrong associations) or are referenced to simple logical patterns (fairy tale, stereotyped story, series of events in a routine situation; e.g., "*Something happens, I do something, all is well*").
- Interpretive structure. Similar to above but includes more complex reasoning systems such as norms, long-term vision, and more elaborate role of emotion or intention in actions or decisions. Individuality is recognized in history, feelings, and values.
- Synthesized structure. Involves drawing resourcefully from life experiences to fashion new schemas and drawing from multiple experiences to size up ambiguous situations.

The accuracy, complexity, and organization of the schemas are critical in the appraisal of emotionally significant events and in generating coping and other self-regulatory responses. At a relatively simplistic level, events are judged by their immediate emotional impact on the perceiver without understanding causes (internal or external), intentions, or perceptions of relevance to goals (immediate or long-term). Such simplified appraisals spawn similarly simplified coping responses (e.g., exploding; fight/flight reactions elicited by fear). Complex appraisals enable the individual to use broader schemas including motivational structures and long-term principles to marshal strategies for handling the situation or managing the emotions (see Rapid Reference 5.3; Frijda, 1986, 2006).

Clinical cognitive theorists view biases, including simplifications or distortions in processing of emotional information, as playing a central role in the onset and maintenance of psychological disorders (Beck, 2005; Williams, Watts, MacLeod, & Mathews, 1997). Problems with emotion regulation are at the core of child psychopathology (e.g., Cole, Michel, & Teti, 1994), involved in both internalizing and externalizing disorders (Achenbach & Edelbrock, 1983), and the majority of disorders experienced by adults have their origins in childhood (Kessler, Berglund, Demler, Jin, & Walters, 2005). Regulation of emotion is necessary for the individual to monitor, evaluate, and modify emotional reactions over time to accomplish goals and maintain relationships. Challenges to and resources for emotion regulation reside in temperament (see Rapid Reference 5.4) and in the schema-guided appraisals. These two sources of regulation or dysregulation are woven together in the course of development. As reviewed in Chapter 1, individual differences in temperamental reactivity and self-regulation are associated with variations in schema qualities that support emotional self-regulation (Bassan-Diamond, Teglasi, & Schmidt, 1995; Lohr, Teglasi, & French, 2004; Teglasi, 2006).

 *Rapid Reference 5.4*

Temperamentally Rooted Effortful and Reactive Control of Emotion

Two aspects of temperament are reactivity (low threshold for arousal of physiological, affective, or behavioral systems) and regulation (automatic and effortful processes that moderate reactive tendencies, including attentional control and approach or avoidance of stimuli-evoking reactivity). Emotion regulation in children has been studied in relation to effortful and reactive control components of temperament. *Effortful* control is deliberate whereas *reactive control* is less voluntary (Derryberry & Rothbart, 1997; Eisenberg & Morris, 2002; Eisenberg, Smith, Sadovsky, & Spinrad, 2004; Spinrad et al., 2006).

By definition, *effortful control*, a function of the executive attentional system, is used by the individual to plan responses, to detect errors, and to inhibit a dominant response or activate a subdominant response (such as emotional expression as needed, even when contrary to preferences; Rothbart & Bates, 2006; Posner & Rothbart, 2007). These effortful functions are supported by the individual's capacity to focus and shift attention flexibly.

Reactive regulatory processes include *overcontrol* (behavioral inhibition, such as being timid, constrained, lacking flexibility) and *undercontrol* (such as impulsive approach behaviors, without anticipation or planning). Whereas effortful control tends to promote positive functioning and development, at the extremes of both types of reactive control processes impede healthy development (Eisenberg & Morris, 2002).

Temperament influences the growth of schemas that regulate emotion and attention (see Teglasi & Epstein, 1998; Teglasi, 2006). The schemas provide the categories used to evaluate emotional experiences (see Barrett, 2006), influencing regulation by guiding ongoing appraisal processes, including the coordination of affective, cognitive, behavioral, and physiological systems (Mauss, Levenson, McCarter, Wilhelm, & Gross, 2005).

Problems with emotion regulation arise in multiple ways with concomitant implications for interventions that may be aimed at: (a) implicit processes that generate the emotions in the first place or (b) deliberate, explicit regulation processes to cope with the emotions themselves (Campos, Frankel, & Camras, 2004; Fosha, 2000; Hunt, 1998; Linehan, 1993; Schore, 2003).

As reviewed above, emotions begin with a particular appraisal of an affect state, becoming embedded in cognitive networks that incorporate response tendencies. Two categories of emotion regulation exert their influences at different points of the unfolding emotional response. *Antecedent-focused* regulation occurs prior to activation of emotional experience and associated response tendencies, whereas *response-focused* regulation takes place after the emotion is experienced and the response tendencies are generated (Gross, 1998, 2001). According to this conceptualization, emotion regulation involves appraisal processes that take place before and after the emotion is experienced (see Rapid Reference 5.5).

≡ *Rapid Reference 5.5*

Antecedent-Focused and Response-Focused Regulation

1. *Antecedent-focused regulation*—Ongoing automatic appraisals that moderate emotions preempt the need for subsequent regulation. For instance, appraisal of a parental limit as legitimate forestalls anger. Even more complex preemption reduces the need for external regulation such as when the youngster, having internalized the limit, regulates his own behavior in line with accepted boundaries. Laboratory procedures have been developed to alter appraisals without explicitly disputing the original appraisal tendencies. Compared to control participants, those engaged in computer-assisted practice with appraisal instructions that promote awareness of the bigger picture (*cognitive bias modification*, CBM) subsequently experienced less distress to negative films and upsetting autobiographical memories (Schartau, Dalgleish, & Dunn, 2009; Wilson, MacLeod, Mathews, & Rutherford, 2006). CBM fostered appraisal habits that influenced automatic appraisal of future encounters.

2. *Response-focused regulation*—Two approaches to *response-focused regulation* are *re-appraisal* (effortful processing of the automatic appraisal to revise the link between the schema and the appraisal) and *expressive suppression* (which involves inhibiting the overt expression of emotion), both of which entail challenges. Expressive suppression (appearing cool when experiencing inner turmoil) does not alter the experience, changing only its visibility to others, and comes at a social cost such as sacrificing social support and interpersonal

(continued)

closeness (e.g., Srivastava, Tamir, McGonigal, John, & Gross, 2009). Deliberate re-appraisal of an initially unconscious appraisal may be difficult, requiring the individual to become aware of the automatic appraisal processes and shift to a controlled processing mode, which is not easily accomplished. Two approaches discussed earlier are pertinent. Telling one's story from a different perspective (how another person might feel) seems to expand the narrator's scope, directing awareness to features of a distressing situation beyond the immediate, thereby mitigating the emotional response (Libby & Eibach, 2002). Opportunities to re-appraise situations without disputing the initial appraisal tendencies (such as CBM) provide alternative mindsets that preempt uncomfortable states. Expressive suppression may be necessary at times but, if overused, it taxes the individual's resources, siphoning energy away from other meaningful pursuits, and creates distance in social relationships.

COPING

The term *coping* is defined as "regulation under stress" and involves dual processes that parallel those previously discussed, such as automatic or effortful information processing and antecedent- or response-focused emotion regulation. The dual-process models distinguish between the *stress reaction* as the immediate and automatic response to stressful conditions and *action regulation* as the mobilization of effort to manage the stress response (for a review, see Skinner & Zimmer-Gembeck, 2007). The elicitation of the stress reaction is viewed as being automatically linked to appraisal, and the management of the stress response is conceptualized as a more deliberate process of action regulation (Compas and colleagues, 1997, 2001). Stress may be preempted or minimized by automatic appraisals (antecedent focused) or mitigated by action regulation (response focused) to deal with the stress once it is experienced. Automatic appraisals that avert the stress reaction are advantageous because they reduce effortful coping requirements.

Two types of response-focused coping mechanisms include emotion-focused and problem-focused coping (see Compas et al., 2001; Eisenberg et al., 1997; Lazarus & Folkman, 1984). *Emotion-focused* coping, aimed at the stress reaction itself, requires the individual to deal with the emotional experience, its expression, and accompanying physiological reactions. *Problem-focused* coping, aimed at resolving the causes of the emotion, requires the individual to engage in action regulation to deal with the evoking situation. Various regulatory subsystems jointly contribute to coping responses (Holodynski & Friedlmeier, 2006; Skinner, 1999), including emotion regulation, behavioral regulation, and the deployment of attention.

Schemas as regulators of emotion are central to antecedent- and response-focused coping, giving rise to automatic situational appraisals that moderate or avert the tensions and housing potential action plans (Cole, Martin, & Dennis, 2004; Holodynski & Friedlmeier, 2006). Schema-based coping depends on individualistic conceptualizations about the sources of tensions and coping avenues. Distinct layers of clinically relevant cognitions have been identified, including content of immediate awareness, automatic schemas, deliberate explanations, and the dynamics among them (see Rapid Reference 5.6). These cognitive layers combine both automatic and controlled modes of information processing. Conceptualizations of defense mechanisms fit with the idea of preemptive regulation to avert the experience of distressing emotions such as anxiety. Recent formulations have described strategies individuals use to cope with their schemas (see Rapid Reference 5.7).

≡ *Rapid Reference 5.6*

Interrelated Layers of Emotion-Relevant Cognition

In line with the above review and consistent with clinical cognitive theory, individuals experience reality at multiple levels of awareness, including (a) moment-by-moment states and thoughts, (b) appraisals and explanations of the meaning of those states, and (c) schemas or prior knowledge structures that inform both. Clinical cognitive theory deals with each of these levels and the interplay among them.

1. **Awareness of moment-to-moment states and thoughts:** This level is the most specific and accessible, comprising the automatic thoughts and appraisals that constitute the immediate "facts" of awareness. These facts are irrefutable (subjective reality) and closely linked to mood and behavioral response tendencies. These automatic appraisals may be accurate and adaptive or may reflect errors in processing information (Beck, 2002;,1963). Although accessible to awareness, cognitions at this level may not be readily controllable.

2. **Prior knowledge structures:** What has been consolidated from previous experiences in the form of schemas informs both automatic appraisal and deliberate explanations of the content of awareness. The schemas operate at the most general and least accessible level. The schemas, like theories, organize information outside of awareness, pointing to what is relevant and what is to be discounted (Dowd & Courchaine, 2002; Dowd, 2006; Fiske & Taylor, 1991). The schemas shape real-time appraisals generating ongoing affectively charged automatic judgments (see Cervone, 2004; Lazarus, 1991a,b) and also influencing the more controlled processing to reflect on the automatic evaluations (re-appraise, explain, or sometimes correct). How individuals conceptualize their affective states hinges on the knowledge structures or schemas housing the categories used to judge their experiences.

(continued)

3. **Explanations of what enters awareness:** Whereas automatic appraisals comprise affectively charged beliefs about the relevance of the current circumstance to one's well-being, subsequent reflection or re-appraisal may put the moment-to-moment "facts" of experience in context of the "bigger picture" or provide an explanation. If the appraisal changes, the emotion also changes.

4. **Interplay among immediate content of awareness, appraisals, explanations, and schemas:** The dynamic interplay between facts of experience and explanations relates to how individuals adapt existing schemas ("theories") to new circumstances, allowing new data to modify existing knowledge structures, or, conversely, to how individuals maintain schemas in light of contradictory information that may be misperceived or ignored. The ongoing dynamic across these three layers has relevance for adjustment and is often targeted for intervention (see Beck, 2002; Clark, Beck, & Alford, 1999; Guidano, 1995; Young, Klosko, & Weishaar, 2003; Riso, Maddux, & Turini-Santorelli, 2007).

≡ *Rapid Reference 5.7*
....

Coping with Schemas (Young, Klosko, & Weishaar, 2003)

- Schema avoidance—arranging one's life so that painful schemas do not come to awareness by avoiding encounters as well as thoughts, feelings, and behaviors that activate the schema.

- Schema surrender—giving into the schema by altering perceptions, cognitions, and behaviors to confirm the preexisting mind set (e.g., selection of life styles that are in keeping with a sense of low self-efficacy). Those with depleted self-regulation are more likely to devalue schema-inconsistent information because they are less able to deal with negative emotions generated (Fischer, Greitemeyer, & Frey, 2008; Schmeichel, Vohs, & Baumeister, 2003).

- Schema compensation—negating the impact of the schema by acting in ways that oppose or disconfirm it. (For example, to counter feelings of ineptitude the individual may become a perfectionist or work relentlessly, but these efforts are often counterproductive, only serving to confirm the schema.)

How individuals mediate between the content of immediate awareness and schema-driven explanations (e.g., distinguish their emotional reaction from the "objective" characteristics of the situation) depends on the organization and complexity of their schemas. Intense negative affect along with difficulty with selective attention, or limitations in symbolizing and organizing experiences, disrupt schema development because they alter the "facts" of experience and complicate the task of making logical connections among ideas to derive meaningful lessons from daily encounters. Moreover, any severe and recurring emotional experience such as trauma, stress, or abuse can adversely affect the individual's sense of self in the world. Finally, previously organized schemas may be temporarily disrupted for various reasons such as extreme anxiety, stress, or trauma. The assessment of schemas with thematic apperception techniques is possible because constructing a "story" to standard stimuli reveals what ideas come to awareness and how they "go together."

The emotional impact of a distressing event is intensified by ruminating about the particulars of the experience and mitigated by re-appraising that event in light of a broader perspective (see Rapid Reference 5.8). Study participants (see Ray, Wilhelm, & Gross, 2008) who were instructed to ruminate about a recent unresolved anger episode (think repeatedly about the situation and how they felt) reported greater anger and had increased autonomic nervous system activation relative to participants given instructions encouraging re-appraisal (focus on how another person would feel). Recasting ruminative, emotion-laden thoughts about a stressful experience into a cohesive narrative makes the emotional impact of that experience more manageable (Gergen & Gergen, 1988; Pennebaker,

≡ Rapid Reference 5.8

Rumination, Reappraisal, and Cognitive Complexity

Rumination comprises repetitive thoughts around a common theme, without immediate environmental pulls for those thoughts (Martin & Tesser, 1996). Cognitive reappraisal is a process of active reflection on the emotion-eliciting event to formulate alternate interpretations of the meaning or relevance of the event to the self (Garnefski & Kraaij, 2006; Gross, 2001; Gross & John, 2003). Reappraisal is an emotion-regulation strategy by which an individual changes an initial interpretation to manage the emotional impact of the elicitor (Lazarus, 1991a,b) by taking into consideration additional information or adopting a different perspective on how the situation affects one's goals. Instructions that encourage persons to encode self-relevant information conditionally (I am... when...) rather than globally (I am...) reduced the impact of (imagined) negative self-ideation and yielded more nuanced, less stereotyped social perception (Mendoza-Denton, Ayduk, Mischel, Shoda, & Testa, 2001).

Mehl, & Niederhoffer, 2003). Research on the effects of emotional venting (Lewis & Bucher, 1992) or visualizing increased physical distance from the stressor (Kross, Ayduk, & Mischel, 2005) does not support the value of emotional expression or of avoidance in the absence of cognitive processing. This function of narrative as an organizer of experience, enabling the integration of feelings and thoughts, has been considered an active ingredient in psychotherapy that reduces physical and psychological symptoms (Pennebaker, 1997; Pennebaker & Seagal, 1999). In reference to the construct of cognitive complexity (reviewed in Chapter 1), rumination may increase *elaborative complexity*, whereas giving an organized account of the experience (in story form or from another perspective) enables consideration of multiple dimensions, thereby enhancing *conceptual complexity*.

EMOTIONS AND TAT STORIES

The TAT task presents scenes with tensions for the narrator to identify and gives instructions that invite the narrator to place the tension into a cognitive context that includes sequences of causal events (what happened before, what is happening) and to transcend those tensions (how the story ends). To move beyond the negativity of the scene, the narrator imbues characters with resources to cope with the challenges set before them in accord with their goals and intentions (what they are thinking and how they are feeling). The appraisal of the sources of the negative affect displayed in TAT stimuli and the mechanisms for coping are brought together in the "emotion story." Although coping is conceptually distinct from appraisal, both simultaneously influence emotions because individuals' automatic evaluations of the relevance of changing circumstances to the self take into account how well they expect to cope with them (see Lazarus, 1999; Scherer, Schorr, & Johnstone, 2001). An individual who views a potentially stressful event as manageable is likely to appraise that event as harmless, thereby dampening the stress reaction. Accordingly, the experience of anxiety involves the appraisal that a situation is threatening and the perception of being unable to manage the situation (Beck & Weishaar, 1989). Individuals typically do not pause to deliberate on their coping abilities but act spontaneously on the basis of schemas connecting actions and expected outcomes. For this reason, the regulation of emotions (including stress) occurs prior to as well as subsequent to its onset. For instance, an individual hearing a loud and unexpected noise is likely to be startled. However, the startle response is mitigated if the individual understands that the noise is harmless by seeing a large book dropping.

Problems with coping may be confined to specific situations and represented in situation-specific schemas. Accordingly, self-defeating causal attributions of socially anxious and shy college students are restricted to situations such as meeting new people where being shy is most troublesome (Teglasi & Fagin, 1984; Teglasi & Hoffman, 1982). Indeed, coping behaviors are more accurately described as responses to specific stressors than as generalized coping styles (Folkman & Lazarus, 1980, 1986, 1988). The coding procedures, described below, for evaluating the coping responses from TAT stories consider both the narrator's identification of the problem/tensions and their resolution (i.e., depending on the nature of the problem, a given coping strategy may be unrealistic).

Source of Affect

As reviewed earlier, translating "core" affect into an emotion involves linking it to its elicitors and to action plans by situating it into a story. The regulation of distressing emotions depends on whether the individual attributes the feeling to specific external sources, to internally organized psychological processes, or to some combination. Logically, if affect is explained entirely by external sources, then the only way to alter the feeling is to change the situation. In contrast, the internal organization of feelings would lend itself to internal regulation and allow important distinctions such as: a) between the impact of a person's action and its intent; and b) between the feelings and the qualities of the target of that feeling. Nevertheless, attributing feelings to internal sources does not guarantee constructive responses. For instance, depressed individuals judge their negative emotions as stemming from within but tend to rely on others to change them. The reluctance of depressed individuals to initiate behavior to alter their negative feelings may be due to a sense of hopelessness, lack of energy, or perceived inefficacy.

In a TAT story, differentiating between internally and externally organized emotions relies on the salience of intentions and purposes in the emotion-action-outcome connections. The basic question pertains to whether emotions are tied to a cohesive network of inner (intentions, shared psychological context) and outer (circumstances, consequences) considerations or pegged to external realities with possibly a rudimentary or stereotyped awareness of the inner world. Consider the following story to TAT Card 3: "He's sad because he was punished for doing something bad. [E: Ending.] He forgets about it." The affect is tied to the punishment, an external source, and not to the "meaning" or intent of the "bad" behavior or to the purposes of the punisher.

Stories told to TAT Card 2 by two sixth-grade students participating in a study (Locraft & Teglasi, 1997) demonstrate a contrast between internal and external organization of feelings that were associated with low and high levels of empathy, respectively.

Low Empathy: Card 2. A girl is walking to school and she's thinking she doesn't like living on a farm. She wants to be a great writer of books and write books about other countries like South America, Australia, and France. And maybe give speeches and maybe get invited to the White House. [E: Turns out?] Her dreams come true. It all happens like she thought and dreamed it would. [E: Feeling?] Wonderful.

The "girl" dreams of abandoning farm life for fame and glamour but only considers the external trappings. The narrator (rated by her teacher as low in empathy) pays no heed to the people in the background, associating positive emotions with an imagined "life style" but without a realistic process.

High Empathy: Card 2. It looks like she, the woman with the books, is going somewhere but she's watching her father work and she sees her mother relaxing before she works some more. She looks like she's upset about something . . . maybe they're poor and don't have enough money to send her to college. She thinks about it and it makes her sad. It turns out that she helps them with the work. They work well together because each of them has something they're good at doing and they enjoy working together. She helps them for a couple years and business gets better and they put away some money each month and after a few years she is able to go to college.

The "woman" in this story also sets goals that involve leaving the farm. However, unlike the "girl" in the previous story, she is grounded in the connection to her family and understands the reality of having to work toward her goal. More importantly, her emotions are assets that enable her to "enjoy" working with her family. In keeping with the general trend among the highly empathic children, this narrator's emotions are internally organized and woven together with cognitions into a rich and nuanced schema.

Internally organized emotions are grounded in the understanding that feelings endure beyond the precipitating event because they are sustained by memories (historical context) and intensified by prior feelings (the "last straw" phenomenon). In contrast, externally organized emotions are directly attributed to the situation without delving into the psychological world of motivation, intentions, principles, or relatedness.

Stories are coded according to sources of affect by choosing one of the categories listed below:

- *Unrecognized.* The tension depicted in the scene is not incorporated into the story.
- *Descriptive.* Emotion is tied directly to the cues in the picture (e.g., "this boy looks sad"). The feeling exists as an isolated reality tied to the stimulus without causal connection to thoughts or circumstances beyond what is pictured

in the scene. The sole basis for the identification of the emotion is the posture or facial expression of the characters portrayed or an association to the stimulus such as "this picture reminds me . . ." The word "because" may still indicate a descriptive conceptualization of affect as illustrated by the following excerpt from a story to Card 8BM: ". . . the boy [in front] is looking mad or angry, and the two men that have the knife are looking happy because they are killing someone." The response is based primarily on perception without interpretation (emphasis on what is seen versus what is known). Descriptive accounting of feelings also indicates assigning affect to external sources but relies more directly on the pictured cues than on the category below.

- *External.* The individual detects patterns and regularities between feelings and circumstances (and possibly actions) but is not aware of purposes and intentions. Feeling is virtually isomorphic with the circumstances (e.g., provoked by the situation or someone's action) without accompanying psychological process (e.g., goal, intention). The feeling is attributable to external source (e.g., blaming others) with a sense that the feeling would disappear with a change in the external conditions (e.g., "sad because someone yelled at him"). Internal states appear less salient than actual events or actions. Externally organized feelings are portrayed as (a) being tied concretely to the stimuli, (b) being tied directly to specific events or provocations, (c) being borrowed directly from "canned" stories (movies, TV, novels), (d) constituting vague or stereotypic notions about how one should feel, or (e) pertaining to the moment rather than organized into a cohesive framework of thoughts, actions, and outcomes.

- *Internal.* The source of feeling is internal if the emotions are cognitively organized inner states (e.g., "meaning," goals, ideals, values, standards) that are tied to eliciting circumstances (e.g., "sad because he can't play the violin nicely"). Thus, inner and outer worlds are balanced (conviction along with long-term meaning versus specific events). Feelings are implicitly understood as psychological processes associated with other dimensions of experience, such as thoughts and actions, as well as external circumstances. The key to locating the emotion as internal is the characters' "owning" the feeling. In contrast, the locus of the feeling is external if it is directly attributable to external sources.

Cognitions about emotions are organized in two basic ways. One is more oriented to the external world, focusing on events, actions, and outcomes as sources of affect. The other is more oriented to the psychological world, where affect is tied to connection between the inner and outer worlds. Figure 5.1 is a checklist for coding sources of affect and additional coding guidelines (see also Rapid Reference 5.9, adapted from Teglasi et al., 2008a).

(Check as many as apply for each story) **Cards →**	1	2										
Unrecognized (tension depicted is not recognized).												
External Descriptive (refers to stimulus).												
External Provoked (by context in narrative).												
Internal (coordination of inner sources of tension with those in the external world).												

Figure 5.1 Checklist for sources of affect

≡ *Rapid Reference 5.9*

Differentiating Between External and Internal Sources of Affect

Responses are coded external descriptive if:

- Feelings do not depart from the pictured stimuli.

Responses are coded external provoked if:

- Feelings are triggered exclusively by an external concern, situation, or provocation (including the way someone looks in the picture, without attributing inner qualities).
- Actions stem from desire for external rewards with no inner purpose or genuine concerns.
- Rudimentary or stereotyped awareness of the inner world.
- Concerns focus on external event, outcome, possessions.

Responses are coded internal if:

- Internal and external sources of affect are coordinated and cohesive (emotions are tied to a network of inner concerns such as intentions, plans, prior experience, and external considerations such as circumstances or consequences).
- Actions stem from inner purpose.

- Intentions for decisions or actions are considered important.
- Concern about a principle, standards, process, or valuing the common good (such as the relationship, or the feelings, intentions, or goals of others).

To check the coding decision, consider:

- What makes this individual happy? External sources of happiness include material goods, fun activities, fame, winning, approval, becoming a hero; whereas internal sources of happiness include meeting standards or following principles (commitment to autonomy of self and others, meeting an intrinsic goal, interpersonal connection such as sharing enjoyment or pride in accomplishment).
- What drives the individual's responses? Are emotions or actions discussed in terms of individual's inner world or in terms of external triggers? Does immediate emotion or action have longer-term meaning (e.g., distinction between the immediate emotional impact and the intent)? Does the individual anticipate events that are associated with emotions (hence relying on anticipatory schemas for problem solving) or is he or she surprised by events, reactions, or consequences (and hence responds to these external outcomes).
- How does this individual resolve tensions? Emotions that are exclusively rooted in the external world (reactive) are likely to be similarly resolved (change in external world elicits a different emotion without any responsibility taken for the emotion or for changing the event).

Coping with Affective Tensions

Individuals cope with tensions and contend with problems on an ongoing basis as they face daily routines or novel encounters. As reviewed earlier, when a *stress reaction* is elicited, individuals employ *action control* strategies to engage in some combination of *problem-focused* or *emotion-focused* coping strategies. The former subsumes efforts to solve specific problems, whereas the latter centers on behaviors and thoughts to overcome negative moods associated with an event. Problem-focused coping is an effective way to ameliorate negative affect (Folkman, 1984), provided that the adverse situation can be changed or avoided. Otherwise, there is little choice but to undertake strategies aimed at moderating the feeling (Folkman & Moskowitz, 2004). In those circumstances, emotion-focused coping may be the most appropriate strategy. Normal variations in emotional reactions and in sensitivity to stimuli according to temperamental dispositions (e.g., Watson & Clark, 1992) have implications for the appraisal of life events and the manner of coping with unpleasant emotions (see Carver, Scheier, & Weintraub, 1989). Individuals experiencing intense negative reactivity face greater difficulties regulating their emotions (see Rothbart & Jones, 1998).

TAT stories demonstrate three categories of coping: noncoping, immediate or partial coping, and long-term or problem-focused coping. For the purpose of coding, one of the three categories is designated first, followed by the selection of the specific subcategories.

1. *Noncoping or Unrealistic Coping*
The emotion remains unregulated either because (a) tensions are unrecognized, do not change, or become more extreme; or (b) coping strategies are nonexistent, magical, or highly unrealistic.

- Unaware. Negative emotions are not recognized. The narrator's failure to register tensions precludes the need to describe coping efforts by the characters.
- Lacking change in affect. The character is left in the original negative state without self-awareness or resolution. The final affect state may be explained by the picture.
- Overwhelmed. Extreme states of misery prevail, or negative affect escalates. Story character or narrator may engage in self-doubting or other negative ruminations or display angry outbursts that serve no constructive purpose. Emotions may disrupt problem-solving efforts of characters or the narrator's attempts to develop the story. Character remains helpless, bereft of self-directed strategies to seek assistance or to resolve the feelings or adverse circumstances.
- Reactive or impulsive. The story character or narrator may be reactive to feelings without a realistic strategy to deal with the emotion or the situation. For instance, characters lack perspective, are lost in feelings, or jump to premature conclusions. They may do or say things that aggravate the problem. Thus, characters are provoked to act without purpose or strategy.
- Detached, resigned, or hopeless. Despite registering the affective tensions, characters fail to produce any purposeful responses to regulate feelings because of a sense of futility or resignation.
- Guilty, regretful. The character wallows in unresolved guilt or regret.

- Substantially unrealistic. The tension is resolved without a realistic intervening process. Thus, affect changes without adequate transition. For example, characters may be content with unconvincing reassurance or may succeed as a result of a magical or improbable turn of events. The feeling is resolved through an unlikely turn of events (e.g., wins the war single-handedly; unrealistic demand is granted) or through dreaming or hoping (when action or request for help is warranted).

2. *Immediate or Partial Coping*

In contrast to long-term coping, which addresses the source of the feeling or problem, this immediate style is more oriented to doing whatever is expedient to manage the current feeling (minimize negative affect or enhance positive affect) than to attaining an enduring resolution. The emphasis may be either on changing the emotion without addressing its causes or on short-term actions to change the momentary situation provoking the feeling without addressing the big picture. If a feeling pertains to short-term issues, then short-term resolutions are warranted; however, short-term resolutions to durable feelings or problems constitute partial coping.

- Short-sighted tension reduction. The primary aim is to alleviate the immediate emotional discomfort rather than to address enduring issues or causes. Examples include reducing anxiety by cognitive or behavioral avoidance, relying blindly on others for help or momentary reassurance, eradicating the negative affect through a change of circumstance that does not entail an instrumental or deliberate mediating process, and naively expecting that mistakes will be accepted by others upon less-than-convincing apologies.
- Short-sighted increase in positive affect. The primary aim is need gratification or reward seeking, particularly through unlikely means analogous to a gambler who might overlook realistic probability and relish the possibility of winning the jackpot. Thus, stories may be overly optimistic with happy endings that are unlikely but not magical or highly implausible (noncoping). The narrator may tell a simplified story, overlooking some important issues. Positive feelings may prevail through a change in the external circumstance without an internally mediated process.
- Excessive dependence on others. Characters rely on others when it would be appropriate (given character's age and circumstances) to take actions themselves or use other strategies.

- Excessive independence from others. Excessive independence is indicated when the strategy is not likely to resolve the problem in the long run without cooperation or communication with others.

3. Long-Term or Problem-Focused Coping

Characters expend realistic efforts to address the source of the negative feeling or to promote durable positive states. Change is due to characters' initiative to address the source of the tension by planning ahead, altering circumstances, becoming self-aware, or realistically accepting or reframing the feeling. In other words, the narrator is capable of taking responsibility for the regulation of emotional tensions or enhancing emotional well-being in ways that balance long- and short-term considerations. Realistic coping involves the anticipation of problems and the ability to remain goal directed in the face of distress as well as resources to take initiative to seek new information or support, to negotiate different possibilities, and to restructure one's views.

- Realistic decrease in negative affect. Coping strategies address the source of the feeling as external (the actual situation) or internal (interpretation). Effective problem solving resolves tensions realistically for the long term—not just for the moment—and for all relevant characters. However, sometimes the only realistic strategy is to accept the situation and deal with the feeling constructively, find meaning, or reframe it.
- Realistic increase or maintenance of positive affect. The character uses problem solving, goal setting, or another strategy to promote positive experiences (e.g., goal attainment; relationship enhancement).
- Realistic resolution of tension without seeking/receiving help or support. Given the character's age and the dilemma posed, it is appropriate to resolve tensions without seeking or receiving help.
- Realistic resolution of tensions with appropriate request for help or support (not passive, blind dependence). The character does whatever is possible before seeking help.
- Appropriate help, advice, or reassurance provided without specific request. Natural and appropriate responsiveness of others enables the character to resolve the dilemma. Such help does not appear magically (others seem to "read" the character's mind or appear from nowhere) but occurs within a context of a mutually caring relationship.

1. Noncoping or Unrealistic Coping	Card →	1	2								
Unaware (negative emotion is not recognized).											
No changes in emotions, self-awareness, or understanding.											
Overwhelmed (misery prevails or negative affect escalates).											
Reactive/Impulsive (provoked to act without purpose or plan).											
Detached, resigned, hopeless (fails to act or react, withdraws, gives in).											
Wallowing in self-blame (shame, regret).											
Substantially unrealistic. Magical external intervention or unlikely turn of events (e.g., wins the war single-handedly; unrealistic demand is granted); dreaming or hoping (when action is warranted).											
2. Immediate or Partial Coping		1	2								
Short-sighted (temporary) decrease of negative affect or reduction of adverse impact of presenting dilemma but without fully addressing the sources of the tension (e.g., avoidance, temporary reassurance, resolving to do something, compliance with legitimate authority).											

Figure 5.2 Checklist: Coping with Affective Tensions

2. Immediate or Partial Coping	1	2					
Short-sighted (temporary) increase or maintenance of positive affect or improvement of the situation but without recognizing important issues.							
Excessive dependence on others, seeking, or getting help when independent action is warranted (blind dependence or prematurely seeking help).							
Excessive independence from others, managing situations that typically require help (such as a young child building a violin).							
3. Long-Term or Problem-Focused Coping	1	2					
Decreasing negative affect by effective problem solving (e.g., addressing the source of the feeling).							
Increasing or maintaining positive affect through effective problem solving.							
Appropriate help, advice, or reassurance provided, with or without specific request, enables the character to effectively resolve the dilemma.							

Figure 5.2 (Continued)

EMOTIONAL MATURITY AND TAT

The concept of emotional maturity refers to the cognitive interpretation of affective experience. Certain ways of thinking about emotion are conducive to better reality testing and more effective emotion management. With increasing representational and cognitive development, global, vague, or polarized affects such as happiness or sadness become differentiated into more specific emotions such as pride, guilt, gratitude, worry, or relief (Holinger, 2008). As emotions become more nuanced and organized, the connection between eliciting circumstances and feelings becomes more complex (e.g., a child is unhappy when a friend "shows off" but doesn't dislike her in general). When emotions are not embedded in an organized network of cognitions, the individual lacks the tools to reflect on the causes of the feelings and strategies for their regulation. Thompson's (1986) application of the concept of affect maturity to the interpretation of TAT stories emphasizes two characteristics as the hallmarks of maturity: (a) The feeling is specific to a situation, person, or event rather than globally experienced (everything about a person is aversive versus one habit); and (b) the feeling is embedded in a cognitive network that includes specific understandings about feelings and ways to cope with or reframe them. These essential aspects of affect maturity are tied to two related concepts: the reality testing of emotions and the understanding that emotions are internal and separate from, though related to, the external circumstance (as discussed in the previous section).

Reality Testing of Emotions

The key to reality testing emotions is in separating the individual's affective experience from the "objective" characteristics of the person or circumstance evoking the feeling. Without separating feelings from the actual characteristics of the persons or circumstances evoking them, the perceiver will judge others negatively when experiencing discomfort and positively when feeling happy. However, separation of the feeling as the property of the perceiver rather than as inherent to the target makes it possible to question the appropriateness of the feeling or to conceptualize alternative interpretations of an event or action (Thompson, 1986). It is the conceptualization of emotion as an internal process in relation to the eliciting context that permits the distinction between the psychological impact of actions and the intention of the actor. For example, the acknowledgment, "When I feel vulnerable and you are preoccupied, I feel as if you are rejecting me," suggests such a separation. Otherwise, an individual who connects feelings only to external provocations might simply feel rejected without awareness of complexities such as psychological processes (preexisting feeling) and intent of others.

Causal understanding of emotions is not only important to the testing of reality but also to the regulation of the emotion. The conceptualization of affect as mediated by internal processes, including memories and preexisting feelings (Harris, Olthof, & Terwogt, 1981; Nannis, 1988), permits internally organized efforts to regulate the feeling. Otherwise, the individual "gripped" by the feeling state looks to a change in external events, remains helpless, or vacillates between opposite emotions (Thompson, 1986). Even when feelings or reactions are internally attributed, they are difficult to resolve if they are not adequately tested against reality. Feelings that are disconnected from or vaguely linked to causes or circumstances are not amenable to reformulation or constructive problem-centered resolution primarily because they are not sufficiently understood. Vague or impressionistic processing of emotional information (described earlier as low "granularity") impedes reality testing as important details are overlooked and affect is globally attributed. Alternatively, emphasis on detail without considering the broader perspective also impedes reality testing, as does difficulty with differentiating durable emotions from transient reactions, which limits the process of self-reflection.

Reality testing may be distorted in the service of controlling affect through the use of defense mechanisms such as denial, projection, and intellectualization (for coding these defense mechanisms in TAT stories, see Cramer, 1991, and Rapid References 5.10 and 5.11). Defensive strategies that reduce distress often do so at the cost of diminished accuracy in processing information about the self and the world. Within a schema framework, defense mechanisms constitute information processing styles that conserve preexisting schemas by distorting, discounting, or restricting the information that comes to awareness. To avoid becoming overwhelmed or disorganized, individuals may curtail cognitive activities in defensive ways or limit their engagement with tasks and activities to moderate the intensity of their emotions. Because defenses can distort perceptions of reality, they may hinder the development of accurate schemas about the self and the world. However, other defense mechanisms may be adaptive and may contribute to building a well-differentiated set of representations of the self in the world (Vaillant, 1977, 1992). In turn, complex and well-differentiated schematic structures permit the individual to respond to an event effectively even while experiencing unpleasant affect. For instance, an individual may tolerate higher levels of frustration if the unpleasant activity serves a larger purpose.

≡ *Rapid Reference 5.10*

Defense Mechanisms in Children

Children use defense mechanisms to protect themselves from anxiety and from threats to self-esteem, and the defenses change and mature with age (see Cramer, 2007). *Denial* functions by the individual's ignoring or misrepresenting thoughts, feelings, and experiences that, if accurately perceived, would arouse anxiety. Denial has been correlated with undercontrol (see Cramer, 2009) but, since denial involves distorted perception of reality, it would seem logical that self-regulation based on mistaken perceptions would not be modulated to the reality of the situation. *Projection* is the attribution of what is unacceptable to the self onto others. What this means is that others in the world (or the self) are threatening and that protection is needed. Social cognition researchers have studied biases in attributing intent (tendency to impute hostile intent to neutral acts correlating with aggression; Crick and Dodge, 1994) as well as other justifications for aggression (see Frost, Ko, and James, 2007). *Identification*, a more mature defense, does not call for a change in perception of reality but involves changing the self to become more like someone who is admired by taking on their qualities or attributes.

≡ *Rapid Reference 5.11*

Coding Defense Mechanisms from Children's Stories (Cramer, 1991)

Denial: omission of major characters or objects; misperception; reversal; statements of negation; denial of reality; overly maximizing the positive and minimizing the negative; unexpected goodness, positiveness, optimism, or gentleness
Projection: attribution of hostile feelings or intentions or other normatively unusual feelings or intentions to a character; addition of ominous people, animals, objects, or qualities; magical or autistic thinking; concerns for protection from external threat; apprehensiveness of injury, death, or assault; themes of pursuit, entrapment, and escape; bizarre story theme
Identification: emulation of skills; emulation of characteristics, qualities; regulation of motives or behavior; self-esteem through affiliation; work, delay of gratification; role differentiation; moralism

Disruption of cognitive processing of affect-laden information may be chronic or temporary due to the impact of intense emotions on previously organized cognitive networks (see Rapid Reference 5.12). Reality testing may improve when the intensity of the emotion subsides and the individual reflects on the emotion (applying previously organized schemas) or seeks out others' perspectives. Although maladaptive schemas are viewed as stable structures, they are inert until activated, and then they bias attention, memory, and perception. For instance, the diathesis-stress model (of depression) posits that dysfunctional schemas are activated by certain life events, particularly when the individual is experiencing negative affect (see Beck, 2002).

≡ *Rapid Reference 5.12*

Emotions and Reality Testing

Negative emotions, particularly if intense, may interfere with reality testing by altering cognitions (Epstein, 1994; Thompson, 1986):

1. In the extreme, strong negative affect may promote inflexible or dichotomous thinking or even the loss of fundamental cognitive distinctions, thus making it difficult to evaluate the appropriateness of the feeling to the circumstance.

2. Affect may seem all-consuming and lead to the evaluation of others on the basis of the feeling without further processing. Such simplified processing makes it difficult to judge the target of the affect apart from the feeling itself.

3. Affect may disrupt information processing about intentions or circumstances, resulting in the attribution of feeling to an entire person, group, or situation without making relevant cognitive distinctions.

4. Affect may lead to the perception of minor obstacles as insurmountable barriers to accomplishment as witnessed by the association of anxiety with avoidance, defensiveness, and lowering of aspirations.

5. Affect such as boredom and low arousal may lead to disinterest in processing subtle, interpersonal information, resulting in more simplistic, wishful, or stereotyped views (such as unfounded optimism in the face of failure or adversity).

Failure to make nuanced distinctions may lead to impulsive expression of feelings such as anger or blame or to the experience of threatening or painful global expectations (e.g., general expectations of being rebuffed or criticized rather than situation-specific determinations). Behaving inappropriately during testing constitutes a direct translation of feelings into action rather than managing the emotion or expressing it verbally.

The distinction between the role of schema complexity and schema activation may explain the difference between two types of depression distinguished from TAT stories as "empty" and "guilty" (Wilson, 1988). The empty form is characterized by lack of inner resources to sustain interest (energy) in activities or relationships, or to cope with challenges that would seem to be a function of impoverished schemas. The guilty form of depression may be related to ready activation of self-reproaching schemas by negative affect or social cues (see Rapid Reference 5.13). The empty form of depression develops early and is associated with more severe pathology than the later-appearing guilty form of depression (Kernberg, 1975a, 1975b). Schema qualities play a more prominent role in chronic than nonchronic forms of depression.

≡ Rapid Reference 5.13

Chronic Forms of Depression

- Dysfunctional schemas are more relevant to chronic than to nonchronic forms of depression.
- Chronically depressed individuals were characterized by (see Riso et al., 2003) impaired autonomy (low coping efficacy and view of environment as challenging) and hypervigilance (to one's mistakes and departure from rigid performance expectations).
- Those with chronic depression rarely report clear-cut problems to be resolved but refer to a general malaise and dissatisfaction with multiple life areas (McBride, Farvolden, & Swallow, 2007). It is difficult for interventionists to deal in piecemeal fashion with each of the problem areas and it is helpful to conceptualize the variety of complaints under a common theme of generalized maladaptive schemas (see Riso, Maddux, & Turini-Santorelli, 2007).

TAT Indices of the Empty Forms of Depression

The empty form of depression, marked by insufficient internal structures to guide self-regulatory activity, manifests in TAT stories as (Wilson, 1988):

- Themes of emptiness, unworthiness, loss, or loneliness. If the picture portrays a single character, the narrator's inability to introduce other characters leads to a focus on the person's isolation or loneliness.
- Harsh criticism of the self or others rather than appropriate remorse or guilt.
- Description of characters as bored, apathetic, or feeling nothing.

(continued)

- Explosive affect or impulsive action.
- Others characterized in relation to need gratification.

The sense of "emptiness" is compatible with the inability to represent the support needed or with problems relying on these representations (inner resources) spontaneously (by introducing a helpful character not depicted in the scene or taking initiative to resolve the dilemma). Without resources of self-regulation that have been internally organized and represented, an individual may experience attempts by others to impose external sources of self-regulation as harsh and critical. The distinction between the "empty" and "guilty" forms of depression is an example of the usefulness of narrative techniques to examine schemas as adjuncts to the DSM criteria.

Levels of Emotional Maturity in TAT Stories

At higher levels of emotional maturity, the tensions depicted in the scenes are identified in ways that are coherent within individuals, coordinated across individuals, and specific rather than global or vague. These characteristics, described below, are organized into five levels of emotional maturity. These five levels in the conceptualization of emotion build on the concept of cognitive-experiential integration described in Chapter 4, but with a focus on emotions.

1. Complexity and Coherence of Emotions (within one individual).
   - Emotion pertains to characters' long-term interests or convictions rather than exclusively to immediate needs or provocations. The emotions embody durable inner motives and convictions (standard, goal, harmonious relationships) rather than reactions to the moment or to the stimulus or expressions of nonspecific distress.
   - The conceptualization of the emotional experiences distinguishes between the impact of actions and their intent. This distinction may be implicit rather than directly stated.
   - Emotions, thoughts, actions, and outcomes are congruous with each other, in tune with social causality, and fit the stimulus configuration. Thus, the emotion is attuned to the overall "message" of the scene (rather than being tied to a discrete part of the stimulus, isolated event, or preceding story detail), is meaningfully woven into the unfolding narrative, and changes as appropriate.
   - Emotions appear drawn from the meaningful synthesis of the narrator's experience rather than being stereotypic, superficial, feigned, borrowed, or associative verbiage.

Figure 5.3 Checklist: Emotional Maturity

A. Complexity and Coherence of Emotions (Within One Individual)

(Check as many as apply for each story) Cards →	1	2										
Affects pertain to durable, inner motives, long-term interests, or convictions (standard, goal, harmonious relationship versus reactions to momentary needs, immediate situational provocation, or nonspecific distress).												
Affective impact of actions is distinct from its intent.												
Emotions, thoughts, actions, and outcomes are congruous with each other, meaningfully woven into the unfolding narrative, and in tune with social causality and the stimulus.												
Feelings appear to be drawn from meaningful synthesis of narrator's experience (versus scripted, superficial, feigned, or associative verbiage).												

B. Integration and Coordination of Emotions (Across Individuals)

(Check as many as apply for each story) Cards →	1	2										
In *defining* the dilemma, feelings of all relevant characters are coordinated into a shared context.												
In *resolving* the dilemma, viewpoints and needs of all relevant characters are reconciled (with understanding of social causality).												
Separation of internal and external reality and differentiation of inner states from external provocation (i.e., the emotion of the perceiver is distinct from characteristics of the target or source of the feeling).												
Feeling is appropriate (in nature and intensity) to the circumstances described in the story and is based on accurate reading of the stimulus.												

(continued)

Figure 5.3 (Continued)

C. Clarity and Specificity in the Identification of Emotions

(Check as many as apply for each story) Cards →	1	2										
Clear and specific identification of the circumstances vis-a-vis a character's feelings.												
Clear delineation of the relationships of characters to each other vis-a-vis the feelings described.*												
Clear distinctions of different characters' feelings according to evoking circumstance or differences in personality or viewpoint.												

*If only one person is described (assuming only one is pictured), the above category applies.

2. Coordination of Emotions (across individuals).
   - In defining the dilemma, the narrator coordinates the emotions of all relevant characters into a shared context. The internal states of various characters are coordinated (explicitly or implicitly) rather than each being entrenched in self-centered preoccupations. The professional may infer such coordination, even if there is only one character, by the degree to which that character's activities are congruent with an implicit sense of consideration for others or commitment to standards or principles.
   - In resolving the dilemma, the narrator reconciles viewpoints and needs of all relevant characters. The resolution reflects adequate understanding of causes and their effects.
   - Internal and external realities are distinct. The narrator differentiates inner states from external provocation (e.g., distinguishes the emotion of the perceiver from the target or source of the feeling).
   - The characters' emotions are appropriate (in nature and intensity) to the evoking circumstances described in the story and based on accurate reading of the stimulus configuration.

3. Clarity and Specificity in the Identification of Emotions.
   - The narrator identifies events (evoking circumstances, broader context) and their relationship to a character's inner world (feelings, intentions) clearly and specifically instead of making vague connections, such as "feels sad because something bad happened."

- The narrator makes clear distinctions of different characters' emotions according to evoking circumstances or difference in personality or viewpoint. (If only one person is described, the above category applies.)
- The narrator clearly delineates the relationships of characters to each other vis-à-vis the feelings described.

Levels of Maturity in the Conceptualization and Resolution of Emotional Tensions

A comprehensive understanding of emotion involves the joint consideration of two related components: how it is conceptualized (internally organized versus externally provoked) and how it is resolved (immediate to long-term coping). The conceptualization of emotion may be more sophisticated than the resolution but not the other way around. Emotions that are poorly understood spawn coping efforts that are similarly unrealistic, vague, or short-sighted.

The five levels of emotional maturity include both the conceptualization (as described above) and resolution of tensions (as described in the coping section).

Level 1

Conceptualization: *disjointed.* Various indicators suggest that emotion is tied in a disjointed way to stimuli or story events: (a) Feelings or circumstances are discrepant from the stimulus; (b) emotions, motives, or purposes do not reflect inner attributes but are specific descriptions of the stimuli, global reactions to the feeling state in the stimulus, vague impressions, or unmodulated and inappropriate reactions to perceived provocations; and (c) intent is not separated from impact or circumstances associated with feelings are implausible.

Resolution: *noncoping or immediate/partial coping.* Emotions conceptualized at this level are not conducive to realistic resolutions nor amenable to constructive actions because they are neither internally organized nor realistically tied to events. The story concludes with a resolution that is inappropriate, highly maladaptive, or nonexistent (story ends without resolution of tensions). The emotion may be arbitrarily changed to its opposite, or the new emotion may contradict the preceding story premises. The story ending may not resolve the problem posed but constitutes a superimposed happy (just rode her bike and watched TV) or unhappy (he died) closure to the narrative process. Another possibility is that negative emotional experiences (fear/hostility/helplessness) intensify as the situation deteriorates. Characters may remain in extreme states of deprivation, fear, confusion, or abandonment with no resolution or may manifest clearly antisocial actions or poor judgment.

Let's return to Aaron, age 8-3, with a Full Scale IQ score of 119 on the WISC, who was in a therapeutic program for children identified with an "emotional disability."

Card 1. The guy that is, the kid that wanted to draw a picture with stuff that he didn't have. [E: What happened before?] He needed some ink and a pencil, but there was a crack in the paper and he didn't have any tape. [E: So what was he thinking?] He's thinking of drawing. [E: And how is he feeling?] Umm, umm, concerned because he thinks he'll mess up on the picture and everyone will laugh at him. [E: And how does it turn out in the end?] He got the tape and finished his picture.

In response to the examiner's query, the initial dilemma of not having the materials needed to carry out his intended activity escalates to a new concern that is left unresolved (messing up and being laughed at). The story concludes when the boy suddenly, without an explanation, gets only one of the needed objects ("tape" but not "ink and a pencil") and finishes the picture. Thus, the coping strategies are as fragmented as the conceptualization of the tensions.

Level 2

Conceptualization: *provoked.* Emotions pertain primarily to momentary considerations (e.g., provocation, need, desire) and involve simplistic reasoning. For example, the emotion may be triggered by a preceding event or immediate need or taken out of context rather than being embedded in a series of events (cohesive historical frame) or encompassing a long-term view (principles, ethics, goals, relatedness). Emotions may be reactions to perceived threats to one's physical or psychological well-being that would normally be anticipated, or they may stem from either getting and doing or not getting and doing what one wants in the moment. Emotions may also be overly justified by the stimulus or immediate external circumstance.

Resolution: *noncoping or immediate/partial coping.* There are several possibilities such as: (a) emotions remain the same; (b) change is not adequately explained; (c) the resolution addresses only part of the problem; or (d) one of the characters is not considered in the resolution. In other words, emotions or events change without out a clear and reasonable intervening process (e.g., change of mood or activity is the outcome; tensions are ignored or the problem simply disappears). Actions are vague, do not constructively address the problem, or overlook the distinction between short- and long-term resolutions to tensions.

This level is illustrated by a kindergarten girl's story. Her teacher described her as low in empathy and as having limited social competence.

Card 1. He's feeling sad. He lost his mommy. He thinks she's sick, that's why he's sad. [E: Then what?] He's thinking what he's gonna do with his mommy. [E: Ending?] He does something. [E: What?] Don't know.

The feeling of concern for the well-being of the character's mother is tied to his sense of loss and immediate desire to do "something" with his mother. Likewise, the vague resolution ("does something") is not pegged to the mother's recovery (a longer term concern). The child does not have an internal representation of the relationship with her mother that can "stand in" for the times that she is not physically present.

Level 3

Conceptualization: *externally organized.* Emotions are recognized as internal to the characters but are elicited by external sources such as evaluation of others (e.g., success, approval, criticism) or from self-evaluations that are referenced to perceived evaluation of others or tied to pressure to conform to external standards, obligations, or rules (but not to arbitrary or capricious demands). The distinction between intent and impact of others' actions and demands is at least superficially understood.

Resolution: *noncoping or immediate/partial coping.* Shifts in emotion are tied realistically to external change in circumstances or intervention by others but do not demonstrate durable convictions or initiative to seek long-term solutions. Given conceptualization at this level, failure to resolve tension due to inaction (noncoping) may be interpreted as a need for an external agent. If the character takes constructive action to meet perceived external demand, the motive is either to obtain approval or reward or to avert short-term consequences. Thus, the external source creates the change in emotion (e.g., wrongdoing is regretted only because of external consequences; emotion changes because others provide rewards or reassurance). Resolution of inner tensions and expenditure of effort are tied to the reactions of others. Some incompatibility or ambivalence may remain between short- and long-term resolutions or in dealing with internal and external sources of tension.

This level is illustrated by Jaime, a first grader.

Card 1. The boy lost his bow to his violin, and his mother came in and said, "Why aren't you fiddling?" "Because I lost the bow to my violin." She said, "You look for it and if you don't find it, you'll be in big trouble." Then the end. He found it, and his mother said, "Good, before you finish fiddling, I'm going to give you a treat." [E: Feeling? Thinking?] In the beginning, he's thinking, "Boy, I lost my bow, wait 'till my mom finds out." He's sad. At the end, he's thinking, "Oh goody, I'm getting a treat." End.

The boy takes no initiative to search for the missing bow until prompted by his mother. Thoughts and feelings, both positive and negative, center on external pressures or incentives.

Level 4

Conceptualization: *internally organized*. Problem definition or tension is in tune with the circumstances described in the story, and emotional experiences are organized according to rules, values, or goals that are socially sanctioned and internalized. Thus, concerns are not trivial and reveal a balance between immediate and long-term perspectives and external and internal frames of reference. Moreover, emotions are assets that motivate and guide principled, deliberate, purposeful actions or decisions.

Resolution: *long-term coping*. Characters take responsibility for regulating their feelings and actions. Negative emotions serve as cues to identify the sources of tension, anticipate potential obstacles to coping, and realistic strategies to manage the emotions or address the circumstances. Coping strategies give appropriate weight to both external factors and inner states of characters who coordinate purposeful thought, planning, and action (where possible) to resolve tensions or promote positive states. If such proactive efforts are not possible, characters seek appropriate help and accept logical consequences or inevitable events. When little else can be done, characters resolve tensions by reframing them. Outcomes are appropriate to the problem set and effort expended. Moreover, the resolution reflects initiative in responding to both internal and external sources of tension.

This level is illustrated by a kindergarten girl's story. The girl was participating in a study and was rated by her teacher as high in empathy.

Card 1. A boy is looking at his violin. He's going to play. He doesn't like it. His mother told him to play it. He tells her he doesn't want to play. She says he can play it later. He puts it away. He plays it after dinner. Then he likes it. His mother likes it.

The story reconciles internal and external sources of tension. Initially, the boy doesn't want to play the violin as requested by his mother. After the boy informs his mother, they come to a mutually satisfactory compromise ("play it later") that encompasses a longer term perspective. The final touch, indicating sensitivity to the feelings for both characters ("... he likes it, his mother likes it"), demonstrates appreciation of the importance of feelings (not merely outward compliance). If the narrator had elaborated on the boy's goals or commitment to playing the violin, this story would be coded at the highest level.

Level 5

Conceptualization: *principled*. Emotions stem from prosocial, self-defined standards and goals coupled with self-awareness and acceptance of appropriate boundaries and limitations without feeling pressured. The narrator resourcefully incorporates nuances of the stimuli into the narrative.

Resolution: *long-term coping*. The abstract and mature conceptualization of the problem is linked with coping that is geared to "meaning," principles, or values (e.g., acting with integrity or courage; making thoughtful decisions) and is not exclusively directed toward attaining a desired outcome (e.g., maintaining or repairing a relationship, overcoming obstacles, achieving success) or managing distress.

Let's consider again Benjie's story.

Card 1. The boy has a violin except he can't play it very nicely. So he's kind of upset because he can't figure out how to play it well. You want to know what I think this thing is? [Points to the paper under the violin] [E: Up to you.] He's thinking whether he should keep trying or quit it because he doesn't know how to play it. [E: Turns out?] He gives up because he decides that he'll never be able to do it.

The dilemma is not framed in terms of external pressure or expectation but in terms of a boy's autonomous decision about whether to continue investment in an activity in which he falls short of his own standards. What is important here is not whether the boy chooses to play, but the process by which the decision is made. The reason the boy gives up the violin is not because of momentary frustration but because he concludes that he will "never" play well.

LEVELS OF MATURITY OF EMOTIONS

Level One: Conceptualization—Disjointed. Affect is tied in a disjointed way to stimuli or story events (e.g., situations associated with feelings are highly implausible; feelings or circumstances are poorly coordinated with the stimulus). Emotions, motives, or purposes do not reflect inner attributes but are specific descriptions of the stimuli, global reactions to the feeling state in the stimulus, vague impressions, or unmodulated and inappropriate reactions to perceived provocations. Intent is not separated from impact.

Resolution—Noncoping or Immediate Coping. Feelings as conceptualized at this level are not conducive to realistic resolutions because they are not internally organized or realistically tied to events. The story may conclude with an inappropriate, highly maladaptive resolution or no resolution. Affect may be arbitrarily changed to its opposite so the new feeling contradicts the premises of the preceding story. Outcomes may reflect extreme helplessness, fear, hostility, and/or involve clearly antisocial actions or poor judgment. Affects may become more negative or more intense as the situation keeps deteriorating; characters may remain in extreme states of deprivation, confusion, or abandonment with no resolution.

(continued)

Level Two: Conceptualization—Provoked. Emotions are poorly integrated into a larger context, pertaining primarily to immediate concerns (provocation, need, desire). Feelings are tied to events in ways that may be implausible, short-sighted, self-absorbed, simplistic, or extremely vague. Feelings may be reactions to the last event or immediate need rather than pertinent to a larger context or cohesive with a series of events. Feelings may be superficial, feigned, or overly justified by the stimulus or by immediate external circumstance. Poor understanding of psychological process or of social causality.

Resolution—Noncoping, Immediate, or Partial Coping. Affect does not change, or shifts are inadequately explained. Feelings or events change without a clear and reasonable intervening process or without considering important aspects of the stimulus or the dilemma (change of affect or activity is the outcome; affect is ignored or the problem simply disappears). Actions are vague or do not constructively address the problem. Lack of distinction between short- and long-term resolutions to affective tensions.

Level Three: Conceptualization—Externally Organized. Emotions are recognized as internal to the characters but are elicited primarily by external sources such as actions and reactions of others or by external feedback or demand but with at least a superficial distinction between intent and impact. Emotions may be tied to pressure to conform to legitimate external standards, demands, or rules (not someone's whims) or by situations that are unfamiliar or that entail being evaluated.

Resolution—Noncoping or Immediate/Partial Coping. Affect shifts are realistically tied to external change in circumstances or interventions of others but do not entail durable conviction or initiative of characters to seek long-term resolution or pursue goals. At this level, failure to resolve tensions due to inaction may be interpreted as need for an external agent. When constructive action is taken to meet legitimate external demand, the motive is to obtain approval or reward or to avert consequences. Thus, external source influences affect change (e.g., positive actions are valued because they bring reward or approval; wrongdoing brings external consequences only). Resolution of inner tensions depends on the reactions of others. Some incompatibility or ambivalence remains between short- and long-term resolutions or in dealing with internal and external sources of tension.

Level Four—Conceptualization, Internally Organized. Emotions are smoothly incorporated into the narrative in ways that are congruent with external circumstances and coordinated with motives and convictions, as well as with deliberate, purposeful actions. External and internal frames of reference are balanced; various perspectives are coordinated; characters communicate appropriately and act constructively on their feelings. Problem definition or affect is in tune with the circumstances and respects the psychological integrity of all relevant characters. Emotional reaction to the problem or task is appropriate to the stimulus and story context and described with clarity and specificity. Concerns are not trivial, but represent a balance between immediate pressures and long-term perspective.

Resolution—Long-Term Coping. Characters take responsibility for regulating feelings and actions. They engage in realistic, planned, active problem-solving efforts (where possible) or resolve their negative feelings by accepting logical consequences or inevitable events. Resolutions are appropriate to problem set and to effort expended with appropriate initiative in responding to both internal and external sources of tension. External factors along with inner states of characters guide purposeful thought, planning, and actions.

Level Five—Conceptualization, Principled. Emotions stem from prosocial self-defined standards and/or goals coupled with self-awareness and acceptance of boundaries and limitations. Nuances of the stimuli are resourcefully incorporated into the narrative.

Resolution—Long Term. The abstract and mature conceptualization of the problem is linked with coping that is geared to "meaning," principles, and values and not directed exclusively to regulation or management of feelings, maintaining or repairing a relationship, overcoming an obstacle, or achieving success.

CASE ILLUSTRATION

Jane

At the time of the evaluation, Jane, a 13-year-old, was being home-schooled because the school setting was viewed as not suited to her needs. Her psychiatrist requested a psychological evaluation to obtain more information. Levels of emotional maturity, coded from the stories below, are shown in Figure 5.4.

Card 1. This boy's mother always wanted him to take violin lessons and he was always sure that if he did start taking them, that he wouldn't live up to his mom's expectations. And so he went to take his lessons and his teacher was a lot more understanding than he thought he would be. But he had to take lessons after school and he was really tired. He's feeling right now he's about to go to his lesson and he's feeling too tired to go but he doesn't want to let his mom down, so he's going to.

Content import: If a boy is convinced he will always fall short of his mother's standards, he will try not to disappoint her and struggles against discouragement and fatigue.

This story accurately accounts for the stimulus configuration and differentiates between externally imposed standards and internally experienced pressure to meet them. Possible barriers to effective coping relate to the character's feeling discouraged (anticipation of negative events, though things turn out better than expected) and being tired (lacking drive and energy). The boy has no intrinsic desire to play the violin but is motivated by not wanting to disappoint others. In the process of trying to do what the boy thinks he should, he remains stuck in an unpleasant emotional state.

Card 2. This one girl lives on a farm and she's [long pause] she's going to school in a couple of minutes and at first it was a hard decision for her because she had a lot of work to do around her house. But her family encouraged her to try and go but she was afraid because not a lot of her friends went. Um, this is the third day that she's going to school and every time she goes she feels nervous but her classmates treat her surprisingly well and so she's kind of looking forward to it. [E: How does it turn out in the end?] In the end, she . . . she comes back and she's learned a lot and she's even made some new friends that treat her well and she wants to go back soon.

Content import: If a girl is apprehensive about going to school (without her friends), family encouragement motivates her to go, and she is surprised to find that she likes it (makes friends and learns).

Again, the character is initially apprehensive (particularly about peer social support) but finds that things work out better than expected. At first, the girl considers the possibility of not going to school but accepts the challenge with family encouragement. An underlying issue is one of making choices to tolerate or avoid situations that are expected to be uncomfortable. There seems to be a desire (also seen in Card 1) to engage in socially sanctioned activities, but doing so comes at a high price in terms of stress.

Card 3BM. I'm going to assume this lady's sleeping. Okay. Um, this this lady is at the beginning of college and that she had to get up really early and when she went to class, no one was there and then she found out it had been like a closing day but the building was still open because they had work to do on it. So she was too tired to walk back to her car, so she thought she would just take a nap. And when she wakes up I guess she'll go back to her car. That's pretty bad but I guess that's it. What was she thinking? Well, when she went to sleep she thought that she would take a quick nap but when she got up she found out that it had been like four hours. She was embarrassed but no one seemed to mind so she was okay with it.

Content import: Normal life demands are so exhausting that, if given a respite from her obligations (class cancelled), a girl opts for instant relief (can't wait to take a nap) even at the risk of feeling embarrassed.

The theme of fatigue seen in Card 1 resurfaces along with embarrassment about not having the requisite stamina to meet daily demands. In this story, the fatigue is so intense that the girl naps in the classroom before she goes home. There is an emerging sense that the narrator, experiencing nervousness and fatigue and anticipating negative events, struggles to balance her tolerance for stress with her desire to live up to social expectations. As she vacillates between accepting and avoiding difficult and burdensome expectations, she discovers that, when she meets the challenge, things often turn out better than anticipated. However, in the face of such stress, it would be difficult to sustain positive action, and avoidant behavior is likely. The protagonist gets through the day as the resolution is relatively short-term relief without dealing with the larger issues.

Card 4. When this guy got home from work he was in a bad mood because his boss is always giving him trouble . . . um . . . and he worked with computers and he felt like his boss was always being lazy because he would never do any work himself. And he . . . when he was driving home he almost got in a car accident and it made him feel even worse. And when he got home his wife didn't understand why he was upset and he was in too bad of a mood to explain it to her. But she wanted to help and he thought that maybe if he waited a little while to calm down then he'd be able to talk about it. But he was afraid that if he explained it to her now that he would be yelling at her and he didn't want to do that. So he feels he doesn't want to make his wife upset and he just wants to wait a little bit so he'll feel better about it and then he'll talk about it.

Content import: If a man is intensely upset during the course of a routine day and it is difficult to explain his feelings without upsetting others (family members who want to help), he waits until he's calm before he will talk about it.

Again, life is a hassle, and negative emotions build over the course of the day. Others, such as family members, want to help, but it may be hard for them to understand the emotional intensity. Uncomfortable emotions generated by daily hassles complicate relationships, and it is necessary to moderate emotional intensity to keep from upsetting others. Although the problem "always" occurs, the resolution takes care of a single day, focusing on how to modulate its expression (immediate/partial coping).

Card 5. This lady is a mother to a 12-year-old boy and she thought she had heard him yelling for his mom, probably for a glass of water or something about an hour after she tucked him in. And the mother was . . . ah . . . knitting some things, so she decided to just come up and see what he wanted and when she came up to look in he looked really sick. And she asked him how he felt and he said he felt like he had a fever, so she took his temperature and it wasn't that bad. But she thought that she would take him to the doctor anyway. And, and when she took him to the doctor, they said that he just had the flu and that they would give him some medicine. So she was . . . she was happy that he was okay.

Content import: When a 12-year-old boy is sick, his mother takes good care of him.

Not only does the mother respond to what the child says, but she also uses her own judgment to notice that her son "looked really sick" and copes effectively. There is a contrast between a child's being cared for when physically ill and otherwise struggling to meet demands.

Card 6BM. The man is from the police place. He's a a police officer and the lady he's standing next to is the mother of someone who died. And he was sent out to tell her, which is something he's never done before because he never likes dealing with their reactions. So he . . . he told his superior that he didn't want to go but he said that he had to. So he went to tell her . . . and when he told her that her son was dead she was really upset and couldn't believe it. But she didn't . . . like . . . she wasn't as . . . she didn't act like he would expect her to and he tried to make her feel better. And he wanted to say some things to make her feel better but didn't want to upset her more. So he just waited until she wanted to hear what he had to say.

Content import: If a person dislikes having to deliver bad news and cannot avoid this responsibility, he or she will try to minimize the pain by waiting for the right time.

This story captures the narrator's interpersonal sensitivity, the salience of emotions, and anxiety associated with doing something unfamiliar. The officer has never delivered bad news before and tries to avoid what he expects will be difficult but, when pressed, he carries out his duties with great care.

Card 7GF. This girl just turned 10 years old. And her mom always bought her a doll for her birthday and she had gotten sick of them by then but she didn't want to say anything to hurt her mom's feelings, because she appreciated that she got gifts from her parents. And . . . um . . . one of the people who worked in her kitchen noticed that she was upset and wanted to help. So she tried talking to her but the girl didn't seem to want to talk about her own feelings. So the kitchen lady read her some stories that she wrote and it calmed the girl down . . . like . . . she thought about it and she was happy that her mom got her something and the end. Yeah.

Content Process import: If someone (mother) is being nice to a girl, but the girl is not satisfied, she does not express her true feelings and comes to appreciate what others are trying to do for her.

As with the story to Cards 4 and 6BM, this story shows deliberation and sensitivity in broaching emotionally sensitive topics. Rather than risk a potential confrontation that might hurt her mother's feelings, the girl keeps her dissatisfaction to herself, but positively reframes the situation (what is important is that a person cares enough to give a gift and not whether one likes the gift). However, this is not a one-time event but one that is likely to recur ("always bought her a doll . . ."). Perhaps the intensity of the emotions (as seen in previous stories) makes it feel risky to express them.

Card 13BM. This boy's father, um, liked to work with his cattle 'cause they worked at a ranch and the boy always wanted to help him with the cattle. But his dad didn't want him getting close to them because he was afraid that because he was so little that he'd get trampled if he wasn't careful. And the boy was upset because he always felt like his dad was always leaving him out of things and not letting him participate in things that he thought he should. And so he just sat and watched his dad working and thought that maybe if he watched him for a long time he would learn how to do it, so if his dad ever let him help him he would be better at it than his dad would expect him to be. And how does it turn out? In the end he . . . he doesn't get to help his dad for several years but when he does he turns out to be a big help to his dad.

Content Process import: If a boy's father prevents him from doing grown-up things, he feels left out but waits years to earn his father's trust and finally proves himself.

The boy seems to make a prudent decision that is likely to work for the long term but remains "stuck" with his feelings of being left out. There is an understanding of short- and long-term considerations and an appreciation of the intention on the part of both characters (father and son). The son wants to help, and the father wants to protect the child from harm. However, the sense of optimism that a child can be a big help when he gets older is accompanied by the unresolved negative feelings in the present. Again, the boy waits and observes without expressing his feelings of disappointment or working toward a compromise to address the gap between short- and long-term outcomes.

Jane attributes feelings to internal sources and identifies emotions in ways that are clear, specific, and coordinated within and across characters. Although the conceptualization of emotions is relatively mature (often at Level 4), the resolutions of the negative emotions are addressed with short-term and partial coping strategies (often at Level 2). The combination of conceptualization and coping codes results in characterizing most stories at Level 3 emotional maturity (as seen in Figure 5.4).

(Choose the highest level applicable for each story)

Card	1	2	3BM	4	5	6BM	7GF	13B
Jane	3	3	2	3	4	3	3	3

Figure 5.4 Emotional Maturity: Jane's Stories

Narrative Summary

During the 8th grade (about a year prior to this evaluation), Jane had begun homeschooling due to various concerns summarized as a "poor match" between her and the school system. She was cooperative throughout the four evaluation sessions but was usually tired and lethargic, probably because the testing sessions took place in the morning, and Jane typically did not get up until mid-afternoon. When responding to the structured cognitive and achievement tasks, Jane had a tendency to get off track by giving unnecessary detail that was not pertinent to the question. Although Jane completed the academic tasks presented to her, she had a difficult time working for long periods, requiring a break after an average of 45 minutes.

Currently, Jane has poor sleeping habits and many somatic complaints. She experiences headaches and stomach aches when anticipating a stressful event, and these appear to subside after the event has taken place. Physical reactions such as stomach upset, irritability, sleep problems, and headaches have been evident from an early age. More recently, this stress cycle has become pronounced in connection to school attendance. Jane was described by her mother as a fidgety baby and as reactive to low-level stimuli such as ordinary household noises as well as to social cues. Jane's current tendency to withdraw and protect herself from stimuli that are too intense to handle (e.g., avoiding relationships with friends her own age and wanting to leave school) is traceable to a history of being highly reactive and alert to the stimuli around her. Currently, Jane's irregular sleep habits interfere with her functioning. She is extremely lethargic in the morning, and her mother reports that it is difficult to get her up by two in the afternoon. Jane indicated that she feels sick to her stomach and light-headed when she wakes up. However, as the day goes on, the build-up of nervous energy results in Jane's being so keyed up that she stays awake until two or three in the morning and sometimes all night. Jane explained that she frequently worries at night, mostly about the small, mundane details of day-to-day life.

Jane's scores on structured cognitive and achievement tasks ranged from average to high average on the Wechsler Scales and from average to very superior on the Woodcock-Johnson Test of Achievement. Jane's TAT stories are consistent with her spending so much of her energy coping with the everyday hassles of life that she is left without much energy to explore long-term goals or interests. Jane's stories indicated a coping style focused on the amelioration of immediate feelings without coming up with strategies to address more long-term issues. In accord with the daily dilemmas confronting Jane, characters in the stories struggle to deal with their intense emotions and to manage their fatigue to meet demands of daily tasks and relationships. The stories suggest a sophisticated understanding of relationships and of social causality, but problem solving often focuses on ameliorating tensions and meeting others' expectations. At this point, so much of Jane's energies are consumed with managing her anxieties that she is often occupied with immediate relief from the pressures she experiences rather than on setting priorities for the long term. She would benefit from medication that would break the cycle of anxiety that tends to escalate over the course of the day. In conjunction with the reduction of anxiety and the establishment of a consistent sleep pattern, Jane may benefit from counseling to manage her sensitivities and reactions to daily hassles and to increase her resources to tackle more long-term issues, including setting goals and pursuing interests.

DON'T FORGET

Cognitive processing difficulties that interfere with an organized accounting of the emotions portrayed, and qualities of thinking about emotionally charged situations (such as the accuracy of sizing up the tensions), were presented in previous chapters.

DON'T FORGET

In a sense, all interpretive units apply simultaneously. Emotions that are significantly out of tune with circumstances in the story or discrepant from picture stimuli (see Chapter 4) suggest impaired reality testing.

CAUTION

The examiner should not assume a one-to-one correspondence between a particular story component and its interpretation. A response such as "This picture doesn't remind me of anything" may reflect the narrator's defense against anxiety by avoidance and blaming the stimulus (see Cramer, 1996) or the narrator's inability to develop a story around the scene presented.

🐟 TEST YOURSELF 🐟

1. **What is meant by an "emotion story"?**
2. **How does emotion influence the appraisal of events?**
3. **Which characteristics of schemas are relevant for emotion regulation?**
   (a) complexity
   (b) retrieval from memory
   (c) coordination with "on-line" cognitive processes
   (d) all of the above
4. **Which of the following pairs are least related to each other?**
   (a) appraisal and coping
   (b) positive affect and internal organization of emotion
   (c) emotional maturity and reality testing
   (d) defense mechanisms and cognition
5. **Appraisals that are _____ are most likely to result in the distinction between the intent and impact of actions.**
   (a) internally organized
   (b) vague
   (c) provoked
   (d) well-intentioned
6. **Define reality testing of emotions.**

Answers: 1. The emotion is connected to a network of justifying experiences, reactions, thoughts, plans, actions, and outcomes; 2. Appraisal of a particular event is influenced by the individual's current emotions and activated schemas representing prior experience (real or vicarious) in that situation. The qualities of schemas that influence appraisals—such as their complexity, organization, and activation—are shaped by the individual's regulation of emotional and attentional processes in the given situation. Finally, because memories are encoded according to their associated feelings, positive and negative emotions facilitate selective access to mood-congruent schemas; 3. d; 4. b; 5. a; 6. Separation of one's feelings from the objective characteristics of the target of those feelings to enable the individual to question the appropriateness of the emotional reactions.

Six

ESSENTIALS OF TAT ASSESSMENT OF OBJECT RELATIONS

chema theory and object relations theory converge in their underlying assumptions that mental structures represent "...regularities in patterns of interpersonal relatedness" (Baldwin, 1992, p. 461) that serve as templates for what is to be expected in future interactions. Historically, in comparison with schema theory, the study of object relations has been more clinically rooted with more extensive documentation of its relevance to adjustment and psychopathology, as well as to treatment decisions (e.g., Bornstein & O'Neill, 1992; Leigh, Westen, Barends, & Mendel, 1992; Masling & Bornstein, 1994; Westen, 1993). However, schema theory is increasingly applied to understanding psychopathology and to designing psychotherapeutic interventions (e.g., Riso, du Toit, Stein, & Young, 2007). Much like schemas, "object relations" represent the organization of accumulated experiences that function outside of awareness as lenses for understanding interpersonal experiences. Internal images of both self and others are referred to as *objects* (Meissner, 1971, 1972). Object relations theory does not focus on the observable transactions among people but pertains to the manner in which actual interactions become subjectively represented within the individual in the process of development (Fairbairn, 1952; Klein, 1948; Winnicott, 1965). According to object relations theory, individuals relate to other people according to the internal patterning of self-other experiences. Thus, the subjective experience of relatedness is grounded in the content of memory regarding self and others and in processing current information in ways that support past perceptions.

Mirroring the developmental trends of schemas in general, internal representations (objects) become less grounded in the immediate situation, more symbolic or conceptual, and more consistent. Thus, more specific object representations transform into general principles of object relations (Greenberg & Mitchell, 1983). Object representations are tied directly to specific relationships, whereas object relations are abstract schemas embodying the principles and processes that organize the individual's conception of self and other people. Essentially, object relations (like all abstracted schemas) constitute an inner structure that enhances capacity for internal regulation by providing inner resources for organizing experiences in the absence of external support or guidance. The concept of internal objects, first postulated by Klein (1932), assumes that actual relationships become intrapsychic structures that enable individuals to feel connected to others even in their absence. These internal objects or object representations organize and direct the relationship between the inner and outer worlds. The object relations also contribute to the motivational system because the internalized psychic structures motivate the individual in ways that external relationships did previously. The creation of an "internal world" through a process of internalization (Meissner, 1981) promotes a sense of "true self," as compared to a superficial, "false," or inauthentic self that is oriented to external appearances (e.g., Guntrip, 1968; Kernberg, 1976; Kohut, 1977; Winnicott, 1965). The individual's "inner world" is the filter for understanding and orchestrating encounters with the external world.

Assessment of object relations provides a map of the inner world of relationships. The construct of "object relations" has been measured from various theoretical perspectives using diverse instruments including the Rorschach and several narrative techniques such as stories told to thematic apperceptive stimuli, as well as analysis of dreams and early memories (see Stricker & Healey, 1990; Pinsker-Aspen, Stein, & Hilsenroth, 2007). The use of stories in response to pictures seems particularly suited to assess internal representations of relationships because the stories given ". . . provide considerable access to cognitive and affective-motivational patterns related to interpersonal functioning in intimate relationships" (Westen, 1991, p. 56). Bellak's scoring system for the TAT and CAT (Bellak, 1993; Bellak & Abrams, 1997) subsumes object relations under the general rubric of integration of the ego because object relations permit the ego to perform the self-regulatory functions previously provided by caregivers.

DEVELOPMENT OF OBJECT RELATIONS

The object relations model developed by Fairbairn (1954) and later elaborated by others (Guntrip, 1968, 1974; Kernberg, 1976; Kohut, 1977) attempts to correct some of the deficiencies of classical psychoanalytic theory by emphasizing interpersonal relatedness in understanding development and behavior. The development of self-representation and representation of others occurs in tandem (Sandler, 1992), and distinctions within the self are prerequisites to the differentiation of self from other (Meissner, 1981). As discussed in earlier chapters, the infant's attributing intentionality to others hinges on awareness that his or her own behaviors are intentional. Infants as young as 18 months have been shown to imitate others' intended rather than their actual behaviors (Meltzoff, 1995). The general developmental course of object representation is paralleled by an increasing differentiation of self-representation. Consistent with schema development in general, the representation of self and others becomes more complex as a function of maturation and experience.

The development of object relations (see Rapid Reference 6.1) proceeds through increasing articulation of a sense of self as distinct from others through the separation-individuation process (Mahler, 1966; Mahler, Pine, & Bergman, 1975), delineating the growth of cognitive-affective mechanisms relating to the mental representations of self and other. The earliest representations of others correspond to the need satisfaction of the perceiver. But, as schemas about others are created apart from the individual's own needs, the characteristics of the inner and outer worlds become independently conceptualized. Nevertheless, the distinctions that are made among others depend on cognitions and emotions of the perceiver. As discussed in earlier chapters, feelings influence judgments and guide attention to what is relevant or meaningful, and, in concert with cognitions, emotions direct the structural organization of object representations.

≡ Rapid Reference 6.1

Development of Object Relations

The internalized images of self and other develop together through a progression that ranges from perception of objects as global or diffuse or as disconnected fragments to greater organization and coherence, resulting in more stable and consistent representation of self and others (Kernberg, 1976). At the highest developmental stage (ego identity), past experience has been consolidated into a system of values and abstract principles of conduct that transcend the specific objects to which they were previously attached. Failure of self-object differentiation and lack of self-cohesion make it impossible to appreciate characteristics of others apart from the needs of the self. The mechanism of splitting refers to dichotomously classifying experiences as either all good or all bad rather than integrating them into a more complex or abstract conceptualization (e.g., ambivalence). Such dichotomous thinking may occur in reaction to overwhelmingly intense emotions or because of difficulty integrating experience due to cognitive/attentional limitations. However, without coordinating various facets of experience, including pleasant and unpleasant encounters, the individual is confined to live in the present and to appreciate only what others provide in the moment. The individual remains trapped in the one-dimensional immediacy of the current experience without the capacity to coordinate self with other or "now" with "later."

≡ Rapid Reference 6.2

Moral Emotions: Guilt and Shame
(see Tangney, Stuewig, & Mashek, 2007)

A number of emotions have been implicated in moral conduct, including (but not limited to) guilt, empathy, shame, and even anger. Although both guilt and shame are negative emotions arising from violation of moral or social norms, there are important distinctions that influence the likelihood of taking moral action. When feeling guilt, the individual focuses on the specific action or inaction and the individual is motivated to make amends. However, when feeling shame the individual focuses on the self as being inadequate and hence may be inclined to save face (avoid, withdraw) rather than repair the situation. Nevertheless, shame may contribute to moral action where the individual would avoid violation of standards to avoid feeling badly about the self.

The development of increasingly complex self and other representations and the acquisition of adaptive behavioral patterns through reinforcement follow different principles (e.g., Meissner, 1974; Raynor & McFarlin, 1986; Sandler & Rosenblatt, 1962). The continuing growth of inner structure increases the capacity to sustain constructive behavior without extrinsic reinforcement and the capacity to tolerate separation from others. Such development depends not so much on the acquisition of a repertoire of functional skills but on the quality of relationships in terms of stability and affective involvement. Accordingly, the learning paradigm in terms of specific reinforcements is subsumed by a larger framework of the object relation (Meissner, 1981). Internalization is a form of learning that makes it possible to shift from contingency-based to self-directed behavior based on conscience and internal standards (Kochanska and Thompson, 1997). However, actual moral conduct involves complex and multifaceted sources of internal regulation (see Kochanska and Aksan, 2006), including the activation of moral emotions (such as guilt, shame, or empathy) and behavioral standards as well as the self-regulatory capacity to implement those standards. Guilt and shame have been studied together as moral emotions but differ in important ways (see Rapid Reference 6.2).

OBJECT RELATIONS AND ADJUSTMENT

Many psychoanalytic investigators link problems with object representation to the severity and type of psychopathology (e.g., Blatt, Brenneis, Schimek, & Glick, 1976; Blatt & Lerner, 1983; Bornstein & O'Neill, 1992; Mayman, 1967;

≣ Rapid Reference 6.3

Pathological Modes of Relating

1. Self-object relations: a conceptualization of others only in terms of how the individual wishes or needs them to be. The attributes of others that do not pertain to the self are not valued or, perhaps, not even noticed. Such a solipsistic view has a distorting influence on the perception of others and precludes the possibility of appreciating their individuality. At the extreme, lack of self-cohesion and absence of self-other differentiation is associated with delusional distortion, fragmentation, or loss of cohesion of the self.

2. Transitional-object relations (Winnicott, 1971): objects that are intermediate between an actual person and the internal representation of that person. Transitional objects serve an anxiety-reducing function much like a special blanket or teddy bear at bedtime provides comfort that comes from outside the self, though not directly from another human being. Rather than assuming the self-soothing or self-regulating functions through internal means, persons use other individuals the way a normal child uses transitional objects. Such individuals externalize responsibility from the self onto others, and this process detracts from stability in both self- and object representation.

3. Part-object relations (see Klein, 1948; Sullivan, 1953; Mahler et al., 1975; Kernberg, 1976): a view of others that is restricted to the function they provide. Accordingly, attributes of individuals that are not pertinent to carrying out specific functions remain unnoticed or unappreciated. The individual is evaluated only in terms of how he or she carries out specific functions. This type of interpersonal orientation could be due to a variety of factors such as inability to make the distinction, lack of interest, or fearful avoidance.

Procidano & Guinta, 1989; Spear & Lapidus, 1981; Stuart, Westen, Lohr, & Benjamin, 1990). Such a connection seems logical for two related reasons. First, difficulty organizing experience limits the capacity to engage in the complex integrative task of internalization. Second, problems with internalization curtail the development of inner structures needed for self-regulation. Three pathological modes of relating (see Rapid Reference 6.3) have been described within the object relations framework (e.g., Kernberg, 1975; 1976; Kohut, 1971): (a) relating to others as "self-objects," (b) relating to others as "transitional objects," and (c) relating to others as "part objects." All three modes of relating are appropriate during specific developmental moments but are pathological if they persist (Klein, 1948; Mahler et al., 1975; Winnicott, 1971).

The actual qualities of others combine with individualistic styles of processing information to determine whether encounters are seen as damaging or harmful (versus rewarding, satisfying, or inspiring). The primary cognitive underpinning of object relations development is the complexity of information processing to differentiate nuances in self and others and to integrate these elements cohesively (also see Chapters 4 and 5). *Differentiation* refers to noticing moods, values, preferences, points of view, and other qualities of the self and the other. *Integration* is the formation of linkages among the multiple dimensions that have been differentiated (Baker-Brown et al., 1992; Suedfeld, Tetlock, & Streufert, 1992). Complex mental representations permit a nuanced understanding of psychological processes (such as the relationship between enduring personality dispositions and transient states, conscious and unconscious) and of other influences on the current interpretation of events (such as prior history or personal meanings).

Information processing is more complex when the content is personally engaging or relevant (e.g., McArthur & Baron, 1983; Woike & Aronoff, 1992). Empathy and positive emotions are thought to sustain interest in processing the nuances of interpersonal information, thereby increasing the cognitive complexity of representations of persons and relationships. By definition, empathy requires the accurate understanding of another's experience as different from one's own (Hoffman, 1982, 2000), enabled by accurately processing interpersonal information. Among children in kindergarten to sixth grade, the complexity of representations measured by the TAT was much more closely related to children's empathy than chronological age (Locraft & Teglasi, 1997). When the same data were recoded according to the five levels of mutuality of autonomy described in this chapter, the TAT measure was substantially linked to grouping by empathy and modestly linked to grouping by age (Teglasi, Locraft, & Felgenhauer, 2008a).

The regulation of emotion has emerged as an influential variable in empathy-related responding (for a review, see Eisenberg, Wentzel, & Harris, 1998). Depending on emotion regulation, empathy produces *other-focused* emotions such as sympathy (concern or sorrow) or *self-focused* emotions such as personal distress (or a combination). *Other-focused* emotions direct individuals to discern and appreciate qualities of others apart from their own needs. However, individuals experiencing problems regulating negative emotions respond to the suffering of others with personal distress rather than sympathy or empathy. In turn, personal distress promotes behavior aimed at ameliorating one's own discomfort rather than helping the other. Thus, intense affect results in temporary loss of complex distinctions as well as increased concern for one's own state.

Individuals experiencing higher empathic emotions are more open to processing interpersonal nuances, thereby promoting increased understanding of the others' (and likely one's own) mental and emotional states. In turn, self-regulatory resources enable the individual to translate what is discerned into constructive prosocial acts. Self-regulation enables both autonomy in the sense of agency to act purposefully when discerning another's distress and also mutuality of autonomy in valuing others on their own ground apart from the perceiver's self-regulatory concerns. The attribution of feelings to internal or external sources (detailed in Chapter 5) is also pertinent. An external perspective is compatible with an exchange orientation in relationships where the focus is not on shared understanding but on the pattern of behavioral give-and-take. Such an orientation may be a function of limited insight into behavior or of limited emotional engagement.

DON'T FORGET

A "relationship" is distinct from an "interaction." There are numerous situations where cooperative interactions, such as among members of a committee, need not involve a relationship. Nevertheless, the nature of the exchanges may be influenced by individuals' capacity to appreciate the contributions of the others, balanced with their own. In more routine or scripted interactions such as an encounter with a receptionist, value is placed on the quality of the service (the interaction) and not the relationship.

MUTUALITY OF AUTONOMY

Mutuality of autonomy refers to interdependence and mutual respect among individuals who understand (on a continuum of complexity) and value each other's unique qualities. Only when autonomy is experienced within the self can it be granted to others. Thus, two important dimensions of the personality, the definition of the self and relatedness to others (Blatt, 1990), are developmentally linked to the concept of mutuality of autonomy. Individuals may emphasize one over the other such as by sacrificing self-definition to maintain relatedness or by being preoccupied by issues of self-definition (e.g., guilt, self-reproach). Both limit the capacity to experience mutuality of autonomy. If the self-definition is disconnected from lived experience, the sense of autonomy suffers, and relatedness with others seems inauthentic.

The assessment of mutuality of autonomy (Urist, 1977, 1980; Urist & Shill, 1982) has emphasized two separate but overlapping dimensions of object relations: (a) degree of self-object differentiation, and (b) degree of empathic relatedness. When differentiation is low, boundaries between self and others are blurred, and there is little or no sense of autonomy. When differentiation is high, definitions of self and others are clearly articulated with well-defined boundaries between separate and autonomous individuals, each with relatively stable and unique psychological processes. When empathic relatedness is low, perceptions of others are determined by one's preoccupations. In contrast, high empathic connection is associated with views of others that are realistic, mutual, and respectful of individuality (Teglasi et al., 2008a). Appreciation of individuality requires awareness that others have different values, opinions, or standards. Otherwise, principles that regulate the relationship between self and other may not stem from empathic understanding but from rigid reliance on duty or normative expectations. As Westen (1985) noted, a need-gratifying form of relatedness is difficult to separate from a need-gratifying view of morality. Thus, empathic relatedness and information processing are intricately tied to morality and concerns for others.

Westen and colleagues, arguing for the necessity to understand current and future interpersonal transactions to inform the psychotherapeutic process, constructed a procedure for interpreting TAT stories to assess various developmental levels of object relations in adults and children (Westen, Klepser, Ruffins, Silverman, Lifton, & Boekamp, 1991). These levels (see Rapid Reference 6.4), which incorporate object relations theory, social cognition, and clinical observation, have been shown to relate to social adjustment and to predict criterion groups (Leigh et al., 1992; Westen, 1993).

Previous chapters in this volume explicate the cognitive and affective processes of differentiation and integration generally applied to social information processing and schema development. Biases or gaps in processing information noted earlier interfere with systematic development of object relations, depriving the individual of a valuable inner resource for self-regulation. The cognitive organization of emotions described in Chapter 5 plays a key role in the development of self and other representations. The "emotion story" expresses individual differences in the connections between the inner world of emotions, intentions, or goals and the outer world of reactions, actions, and consequences. Positive or negative emotions experienced as stemming from internal sources provide the foundation for intrinsic motivation, empathy, commitment to standards, and valuing others apart from one's needs. Alternatively, emotions experienced as prompted directly by external sources lay the groundwork for a focus on rewards or punishments and on need-gratifying relationships. Another dimension of the "emotion story" comprises the connections among intentions, means, and ends, which are, in turn, the cornerstones of autonomy defined as the individual's acting purposefully on intentions to attain goals.

The construct of mutuality of autonomy captures the essence of object relations because it combines the intra- and interpersonal worlds. Autonomy focuses on the intrapersonal world of intentions, goals, feelings, thoughts, and connections between actions and expectations (i.e., outcomes or reactions from others),

≡ Rapid Reference 6.4

Social Cognition and Object Relations Scales (SCORS; Westen et al., 1991; Westen, 1993)

Five levels are used to rate each of four dimensions of social cognition and object relations (see also Kelly, 1996, 1997):

1. Complexity of representations of people. This construct subsumes three developmental phenomena: (a) the capacity to differentiate between self and others, (b) the perception that self and others have stable, multidimensional dispositions, and (c) the awareness of complex motives and subjective experiences in self and others. The most mature level encompasses an understanding of the interplay between transient and enduring psychological experience. At the most primitive level, people and perspectives are not clearly differentiated.

2. Affect tone of relationships. Unlike the other three, this dimension does not assume a developmental progression with age. The quality of the representation of people and relationships ranges from the highest level (benevolence), where relationships are expected to be safe or enriching, to the lowest level (malevolence), where relationships are expected to be destructive.

3. Capacity for emotional investment in relationships or moral standards. This scale was designed to evaluate sources of moral concern such as orientation to reward or punishment versus guilt or meeting others' expectations. At the highest level, relationships are based on mutual care, appreciation of each other's attributes, and commitment to moral standards. At the lowest level, relationships are based on need gratification.

4. Understanding social causality. This dimension focuses on causal attributions about interpersonal behavior ranging from the highest level, where the multiply interacting dimensions of experience are well understood as explanations for social interactions, to the lowest level where causes are poorly understood with explanations being illogical, inappropriate, unlikely, or absent.

whereas mutuality of autonomy acknowledges the complementary relationship between the intra- and interpersonal worlds of interacting individuals. Thus, the basis of mutuality of autonomy is the recognition that each person brings his or her representation of prior experience and current frame of mind to a given interpersonal encounter. Individuals relate to each other according to how they coordinate the inner and outer worlds (self in relation to the world, to generalized others, and to a specific other). Basically, object relations are interpersonal schemas that govern social information processing. A professional may apply qualities of schemas, such as their complexity, logic, and organization, to the assessment of object relations with thematic apperception techniques.

CODING OBJECT RELATIONS AS MUTUALITY OF AUTONOMY

The twin processes of differentiation and integration contribute to mutuality of autonomy. Differentiation entails the awareness of nuances of various dimensions of experience within and across individuals. Integration is the coordination of the dimensions that have been differentiated. Attributes that are differentiated occupy awareness, and the rules governing the integration of these distinctions dictate their relevance. The distinctions and connections made within the self (e.g., intention-action sequences) are amenable to generalization to others. Therefore, a nuanced awareness of one's own psychological world permits the understanding that others have their own perspectives, reasons, or motives for action. Characteristics of self and other (and world) that are salient for the individual are most prominently represented in the mental structures and stand out the most during interpersonal encounters as well as in stories told to picture stimuli. Thus, the narrative task brings to light qualities of persons and relationships that the individual is most likely to discern (e.g., inner or outer attributes) and the number of different dimensions considered (e.g., intent and impact). An individual may elaborate extensively on a given dimension of experience, such as action, without ties to other dimensions, such as thought. Moreover, an individual may offer intricate details about characters' appearance (clothing, age) or the background but downplay feelings or intentions.

Coding object relations includes several dimensions: (a) differentiation of viewpoints and attributes within and across individuals, (b) integration of feelings, thoughts, actions, and outcomes within and across individuals, and (c) mutuality of autonomy as indicated by characters' mutual respect of each other's autonomy. The next section presents these three parameters of stories in checklist fashion and then distills them into five levels of object relations. Coding of the checklists and of the levels of object relations is not based on the words per se but on the extent to which the schema conveyed by all the story details (not in the additive fashion) correspond to a particular mode of relatedness in terms of the construct of mutuality of autonomy. The coding parameters that focus on object relations incorporate the basic cognitive and affective processes described in Chapters 4 and 5 and are informed by research on object relations, including their application to the Rorschach technique (Blatt & Lerner, 1983; Urist, 1977, 1980) and TAT (DeCharms, 1992; Thompson, 1986; Westen, 1991). Using the procedures detailed below, TAT stories of children with high teacher rated empathy were coded at higher levels of mutuality of autonomy than were those of children with low empathy (Teglasi et al., 2008a). Empathy grouping substantially predicted TAT empathy scores whereas grade grouping (low = k–3; high = 4–6) was a weak

≋ *Rapid Reference 6.5*

Indicators of Differentiation

- Individuals exist as psychological beings separate from physical surroundings and from the specific events that occur (i.e., a person is not what s/he owns, where s/he lives but exists in reference to *various contexts*, not a single one).
- Subjective states differ from behavior—outward, observable aspects of a person are distinct from inward, covert aspects (i.e., a person is not how s/he looks and *intentions* may differ from the *impact* of actions or *true feelings* from *self-representation*).
- Individuals are not one dimensional (all good or all bad), but may have multiple qualities, including contradictory tendencies and complex motives.
- Individuals' long-term aspirations may conflict with momentary experiences, and discrepancies between them may need to be managed.

predictor. Mean number of words or of inquiries per story did not add to the variance beyond empathy and grade group.

Differentiation of Viewpoints and Attributes

Differentiation focuses on what the narrator notices about individual characters (outward attributes versus inner concerns) and on clarity (specific versus vague) in communicating these distinctions. (See Rapid Reference 6.5.)

Integration of Viewpoints and Attributes

Integration focuses on how individuals' attributes that are discerned are coordinated within and across persons. In TAT stories, integration is evident when each character is related to his or her circumstances and to other characters as pictured in the scene, with recognition of individuality in prior experience, preferences, goals, and values as influencing their current responses in accordance with prosocial or principled values and understandings of social causality. If only one character is depicted, then integration involves the cohesive coordination of intrapersonal attributes with those of external circumstances, actions, and outcomes. If more than one character is depicted, then these aspects of each character are coordinated with those of others. (See Rapid Reference 6.6.)

≋ Rapid Reference 6.6

Indicators of Integration

- **Within one individual:** coherent connections among a single character's intentions, actions, and outcomes that are motivated by prosocial aims and principles. Characters take actions that are motivated by purpose, principles in line with understanding of social causality.
- **Across individuals:** coordination of intentions, actions, and outcomes of all parties involved where interactions are reciprocally respectful and no one is at the mercy of the other or is left to wallow in misery.
- **Across and within individuals:** continuity of relatedness is conveyed by reconciliation of characters' negative and positive attributes or commitment to genuine connections rather than focusing on isolated traits or a series of action-oriented interactions. Continuity of time perspective is conveyed by realistic resolution of the tensions in ways that coordinate present, past, and future interests of the parties.

DON'T FORGET

Intrapersonal schemas pertain to coordination of various dimensions of the inner and outer worlds of one individual.

Interpersonal schemas pertain to coordination of intrapersonal schemas across individuals.

- Individuals who reason simplistically about their own feelings in connection to external events reason similarly about others' feelings, motives, or life conditions (unless temporarily disrupted by intense emotion).
- Expectations about others are reflected in intrapersonal schemas; therefore, even if the story is about a single character, it is possible to infer how that person relates to others.
- Full coordination of perspectives of different individuals would require an implicit understanding that each person brings a unique set of experiences and viewpoints (unique intra- and interpersonal schemas).

Aspects of TAT stories pertaining to differentiation and integration have been organized into five levels of object relations in a scale called mutuality of autonomy. Mutuality of autonomy levels coded according to procedures described in this chapter differentiated between high and low empathy groups (Teglasi et al., 2008a, b). However, it is important to keep in mind that the groupings are more likely reflective of *sympathy* than of *empathy* because classification relied on teacher ratings, based on their observations of children's expression of sympathy and not the children's experienced empathy. Much of the research linking moral emotions with prosocial behavior in children, adolescents, and adults has focused on *sympathy* (for a review, see Eisenberg, 2006).

1. Differentiation of viewpoints and attributes within and across individuals.
   - Viewpoints of each character remain fuzzy. The views or needs of a single character are vague or virtually no distinction is evident between characters. The narrator does not recognize individuality within or across persons. Characters are not distinguishable in terms of their intentions, goals, actions, feelings, thoughts, or outcomes. (This is particularly problematic if their depiction in the stimulus warrants such distinctions.) The narrator may describe characters in ways that are too global (e.g., diffuse negative affect; pervasive sense of upset) or too specific (e.g., has an eyebrow; feeling the table).
   - The narrator bases distinctions among characters on superficial, outward attributes (appearance, wealth), or how they look in the stimulus.
   - The narrator bases distinctions on a simple, event-feeling connection or a vague intention without grasping the psychological process (e.g., "crying because he fell" or "wants to find out what something is").
   - The narrator bases distinctions on stereotypes or duty, such as carrying out a role as mother, husband, or friend.
   - The narrator uses dichotomous distinctions (e.g., good versus bad, weak versus strong, threatening versus safe, special versus ordinary).
   - Characters' attributes are seen only in relation to another's needs, desires, or preoccupations (e.g., emotions are misperceived; reasoning about interpersonal events is based on wishes, fears, preoccupations, or associations of the perceiver rather than realistic understanding of social causality).
   - Characters differ in their needs, views, and actions in line with their depiction in the stimulus, and these differences are seen as legitimate in a mutually respectful relationship.
   - The narrator makes distinctions based on elaboration of characters' values, goals, principles, long-term investment, or purposeful, constructive actions.

2. Integration of feelings and perspectives within and across individuals.
   - The narrator incorporates feelings, tensions, and conflicts into a meaningful context that relates perspectives across individuals (e.g., shared understanding, common goals) or within individuals (e.g., when only one character is portrayed, there are prosocial connections among intentions, actions, and outcomes).
   - The narrator conveys a sense of continuity of inner life by reconciling positive and negative facets of characters or genuine connections among individuals (rather than focusing on isolated attributes or momentary concerns).
   - The narrator differentiates the perspectives and needs of all characters and balances them by coordinating past, present, and future interests of all concerned.
   - Individuals are not left to wallow in painful insight or an upsetting circumstance, nor is there a magical solution. Rather, characters communicate their ideas to others or engage in constructive actions motivated by purpose and principles, as well as mutual respect and understanding.

3. Mutuality of autonomy.
   - The narrator gives characters autonomy, sense of initiative, conviction, and deliberate pursuit of realistic, goal-directed activities.
   - All characters (in the picture or introduced in the story) are balanced in their respective sense of autonomy. Each is autonomous and appreciates the other's individuality apart from his or her own needs or feelings.
   - Characters respond to an immediate situation, action, or demand without prior history or personal conviction (or investment), fail to act, or act without deliberate intention.
   - The narrator evaluates people only in terms of what they provide. Characters relate in terms of what they do for or want from each other without recognition of one another's autonomy.
   - The narrator presents an imbalance of autonomy where one character is competent, heroic, or intrusive while others are incompetent, helpless, or ignored. This code also applies when a character portrayed in the stimulus is left out of the story.
   - The narrator evaluates people as obstacles or hindrances without mutual respect.

(Check as many as apply for each story) Cards ➡	1	2	3BM	4	5	6BM	8BM	13MF	17BM	
Fuzzy distinction of viewpoints as characters portrayed differently in the picture being described as doing, feeling, or thinking the same thing.										
Superficial, outward attributes are distinguished (lifestyle, possessions, or how characters look or what they are doing in the stimulus).									✓	
Global distinctions, depicting characters in terms of diffuse negative affect or pervasive sense of upset.					✓					
Distinctions based on **immediate needs, desires, or wants** (not realistic goals or durable intentions).	✓	✓	✓	✓			✓	✓		
Distinctions are based on **simple event-feeling connections** (crying because he fell; feels good because she got out of her punishment) or **vague intentions** (find out what something is; solve the problem) without grasping the psychological process (not recognizing the **functions of feelings and thoughts** as distinct from events).						✓				

Figure 6.1 Checklist: Differentiation, Integration, and Mutuality of Autonomy Characteristics of Differentiation Within and Across Individuals

(Check as many as apply for each story) Cards →	1	2	3BM	4	5	6BM	8BM	13MF	17BM		
Emphasis on the function served by a character, such as **stereotypical role or duty** as parent, spouse, child, or friend.											
Distinctions are **dichotomous** (good-bad; weak-strong; threatening vs. safe; special vs. ordinary).											
Distinctions of characters' values, goals, principles, long-term investment.											
Characters have legitimate differences in their needs, feelings, views, and actions **(psychologically distinct from one another)**.											
Different individuals are **viewed on their own ground** and not simply as serving others' immediate needs.											
Persons balance **durable investment** in relationships or in prosocial **goal-directed** activities (not just wanting an outcome) with immediate concerns.											

Figure 6.1 (Continued)

Integration within and across individuals

(Check as many as apply for each story) Cards →	1	2	3BM	4	5	6BM	8BM	13B	13MF	17BM	
Autonomy, sense of initiative, conviction, deliberate pursuit of realistic, prosocial, or goal-directed activities in any character.											
All characters are accorded autonomy, each respecting and appreciating others' individuality (e.g., intentions, feelings, thoughts, actions, outcomes), and each retaining that individuality while interacting cooperatively.											
Relationships among characters are well-defined rather than vague or stereotypic.											
Characters relate to the moral dimension of experience rather than respond exclusively to the immediate situation.											
Characters bring prior history, conviction, or investment and act on the basis of deliberate intention rather than momentary provocation.											
Legitimate differences in feelings, tensions, and goals are appreciated and addressed respectfully											

Figure 6.1 (Continued)

(Check as many as apply for each story) Cards →	1	2	3BM	4	5	6BM	8BM	13B	13MF	17BM	
Outward aspects of a person are connected with inner psychological processes (the impact of actions vs. intent and true feelings vs self-presentation).											
Stable, enduring dispositions as well as momentary experiences of a single individual are reconciled.											
Positive and negative facets of a single character are reconciled.											
The connections among individuals are valued (versus isolated attributes, momentary concerns, material gain, honors, or recognitions).											
Views and needs of all characters depicted in the stimulus or story are considered in the resolution rather than centering on only one character.											
Characters communicate their ideas to others and/or their actions are based on mutual understanding and respect.											

Note: The above qualities may be implicit, particularly when only one character is depicted.

Figure 6.1 (Continued)

Limited **Differentiation and Integration**

(Check as many as apply for each story) Cards →	1	2	3BM	4	5	6BM	8BM	13B	13MF	17BM		
Imbalance of autonomy where one person is competent, heroic, or intrusive, while others are incompetent, helpless, or ignored.				✓	✓		✓		✓			
People are viewed as obstacles or as harmful and act with no remorse or consequence.					✓		✓					
Characters react to isolated experience without the perspective of a bigger picture (considerations that should inform appraisal and reactions).	✓	✓	✓	✓	✓	✓	✓	✓	✓	✓		
People are evaluated only in terms of what they provide. Characters relate in terms of what they do for or want from each other without recognition of one another's autonomy.	✓	✓	✓				✓		✓			

Figure 6.1 (Continued)

Levels of Object Relations: Mutuality of Autonomy (choose the one that fits best)

Although thematic apperceptive narratives reveal the individual's typical style of social information processing, they may not apply to all situations or types of relationships. Individuals who are capable of more nuanced awareness of relationships may choose to behave at lower levels. Some relationships are scripted encounters or functional by design. For example, neighbors who arrange a carpool to transport their children may have no interest in relating to one another except for carrying out their agreed-upon functions. Under stress, individuals may tune out the nuances of others' experiences (by choice or necessity) as they focus on their own concerns. Rather than being general, blind spots in perceiving self and others may be limited to specific relationships or specific times when the individual feels jealous or threatened. The point of assessing levels of object relations is not to predict behavior in all relationships but to evaluate the distinctions within and connections among individuals that the narrator characteristically discerns.

1. *Disorganized or Detached Experience of Relatedness*
The individual is devoid of resources to understand relationships and, therefore, experiences a severe imbalance of mutuality (e.g., helpless against the whims of controlling and powerful others), poor reality testing, or serious restrictions in autonomy. An impaired cognitive-emotional process (disorganized or highly simplified) disrupts the differentiation and integration of various perspectives (mutuality) and the sense of self-cohesion (autonomy). The individual's inner life is chaotic or globally diffuse, or he or she does not perceive individuality among others, resulting in undifferentiated or unclear boundaries between the inner (self) and outer (others) worlds. The individual may not distinguish thoughts, feelings, and actions among characters ("both feel same way") when their postures and facial expressions in the picture are different. Autonomy is so limited, and disparity of power is so severe, that characters exploit, malign, or overpower others or feel similarly victimized. Characters show no remorse for hurtful actions or make unrealistic or unreasonable demands on one another. The narrative suggests impaired social reasoning stemming from problems integrating affect and thought or differentiating between wishes and realistic considerations (e.g., implausible sequence of events).

Three stories illustrating this level were told by Slade, age 15, with a Full Scale IQ score of 113. Slade was undergoing a psychological evaluation in connection with his arrest for a seemingly premeditated murder. The entire protocol is presented later in this chapter.

Card 1. You want a story about this? Okay. I think the school's gonna have a concert, and he wants to be in it. He goes home gets Dad's old violin, looks at it, and tries to figure it out. Gets Dad to help him play it and learns how and gets in the concert. [E: Thinking?] That he doesn't know how to play and thinking how to learn. [E: Feeling?] Feels anxious, confused.

The premise of the story is unrealistic. The boy wants to attain something instantly (playing in a concert) that ordinarily takes months or years of preparation. Through a succession of unlikely events, he simply "gets" what he wants (Dad's old violin, Dad's help, and the opportunity to play in the concert) without considering the context (history with music) or purpose beyond participating in one concert. Analogously, the narrator's schema engenders quick solutions to complex and long-term problems.

Card 4. I think guy getting ready to go somewhere. Woman doesn't want him to go. Turns out he leaves. Man's feeling determined to leave. Woman feels alone 'cause he's leaving.

The narrator appears to construct the story in a rote fashion according to each component of the instructions and according to the characters' appearance in the picture. The story does not capture the intensity of the man's emotion or the connection between the man and the woman (i.e., prior history or context). There is no concern about the inner world of intentions or motives. The harsh reality of Slade's schema is that people simply do as they desire without justification (beyond wanting to) and regardless of the feelings of others.

Card 8BM. Uh, think this boy's shot somebody . . . gun there. Looks like he did it on purpose . . . not a sorrowful look on his face. Imagining the guy getting surgery. [E: Future?] Guy's gonna live and he's gonna get charged with attempted murder. [E: Feeling?] Look like pretty mean.

This depiction of a boy who shot someone on purpose is cold and factual. The story is tied to the pictured cues and centers around social consequences ("gonna get charged with attempted murder"). However, there is no attempt to explain the motives or mitigating circumstances and no remorse. Throughout Slade's protocol, there is a marked absence of a moral rudder or empathic relatedness to steer his behavior.

2. Momentary Experience of Relatedness

A rudimentary sense of autonomy or limited mutuality exists in the moment and coincides with a self-absorbed or self-serving style of relatedness. The narrator notices characteristics of others as they pertain to immediate need states, so that perception of self and others shifts according to circumstances and without insight or reflection. Emotions are tied to immediate external considerations, and remorse is tied to consequences. Inner attributes are ill-defined (e.g., diffuse negative affect or global sense of upset) or are based on stereotypes (e.g., unconvincing verbalization about duty or blind obligation) without experiencing the personality as a continuous, cohesive whole. Interactions entail significant imbalance in mutuality of autonomy (e.g., emphasis on one perspective or disparity of status or of power) where individuals need others to foster self-cohesion. The narrator differentiates characters on the basis of momentary need or immediate gain without the sense that they are whole persons. Relatedness may be experienced only when the other is physically present (a single character feels alone, no one helps; concerns are basic, revolving around needs for safety, survival, or protection). The relationship per se is unimportant, not durable, and interchangeable (e.g., no reference to shared experience; no stated or implied standards or principles). Fantasy may replace actual relations (e.g., characters are unreal such as actors). Characters may be passive or reactive, taking no responsibility for actions or outcomes.

Three stories told by Jim, age 16, with average IQ, illustrate this level. Prior to the evaluation, which took place in an inpatient setting, Jim had been diagnosed with Conduct Disorder.

Card 1. He's looking at a violin. Probably bored, doesn't want to do. Somebody put it in front of him. Feeling angry and mad 'cause somebody asked him to do it. So he doesn't do it.

The boy is reactive to his immediate feelings in response to an external demand, the purpose of which is unexplained. The "somebody" who put the violin in front of him is not seen as a whole person (with intentions, reasons, or even an identity).

Card 4. Don't know. I'm not good at these things. It's a man and a woman and she's trying to talk to him. Maybe they're arguing. I don't know. He's feeling, I don't know. She's feeling, I don't know, and he's trying to leave 'cause maybe he's angry, hurt, upset. Don't know. Probably stay and listen and then he leaves.

In contrast to Slade's story at the previous level, the two individuals are engaged (arguing) in an interaction that captures their depiction in the stimulus. However, their engagement is momentary as the man will go through the motions of listening, then leaves as he originally intended.

Card 8BM. Somebody got messed up so two people have to do surgery and person is on the table. Son's in the room. He's feeling scared 'cause maybe he, Dad, might die. He deals with it and waits to see what happens.

When someone gets "messed up," it is natural for others to try to save him. However, as the father's life hangs in the balance, the son "deals with" his own feelings (in the moment) and then "waits to see what happens" to his father.

3. Functional Experience of Relatedness

Emphasis is on the duty or function served rather than the human connection. Reciprocity is recognized in the form of a rigid reliance on quid pro quo exchanges. Approval or disapproval, as well as rewards and punishments, contribute to the functional exchange. Individuals anticipate punishment for wrongdoing and feel genuine remorse. However, they do not set their own standards but attempt to conform to expectations. Obligation is not grounded in internal forces (such as ethical principles) but constitutes a give-and-take response or duty as dictated by societal mores. Thus, obligation or reciprocity is not valued as an end (i.e., a matter of principle) but as instrumental to something else (i.e., reciprocal functions).

Three stories told by Jaime, age 10-9 with Stanford-Binet IQ score of 138, illustrate this level. At the time of the evaluation, teachers described her as "very smart" but often "spacey" and "inattentive."

Card 1. Okay. This boy, he is sad because before his mother told him that he had to practice violin, otherwise he would be in trouble. Now the boy doesn't like to practice violin, and he's mad at his mother. And he wants to break the violin except it's an expensive violin and his grandfather gave it to his mother and his mother gave it to him so he knows he shouldn't break it. So he practices, but it's without heart and soul.

The narrative smoothly incorporates the directions and stimulus cues. The boy in the story is resentful of family pressure (at least two generations) to pursue an activity that he doesn't like but succumbs to this extrinsic source of motivation. He suppresses his anger and complies, playing without "heart" to avoid getting into trouble. Jaime has a longer term view than Jim and understands the intentions of others and the sentimental and monetary value of the violin. She, like her character, goes through the motions of what she is supposed to do. Difficulty with sustained attention or disinterest in the activity may be contributing to the tension ("doesn't like to practice").

Card 4. This guy is a cop, spy, and he goes to meet people, does spy work. And his wife is worried about him because this is one of his most dangerous things. He wants to go out, and she won't let him. He breaks free and tells her it is for the good of the country and he leaves. The end.

There is acknowledgment of the good intention of the other (wife is worried) and a context for the disagreement. Yet, the man's function as a "spy" is carried out with only lip service to the relationship ("tells her it's for the good of the country"). Duty to one's country could have been balanced with responsiveness to the wife's concern, for example, promising to be careful or to keep in contact. Again, we see that Jaime discerns others' good intentions and wants to stay within conventional bounds (do her duty). However, her character, similar to the boy in the previous story, acts without "heart" by not reciprocating the emotional engagement of his wife. Being a "spy" is an exciting activity that would appeal to an individual who has difficulty sustaining attention in more routine situations.

Card 8BM. This little boy is hoping that his father will come out of surgery healthy. His father had internal bleeding, and the doctor said it could be fatal. He doesn't want his father to die because his father is his only living relative besides his grandparents, who are so old and frail and wouldn't be able to take care of him. His mom was killed when she gave birth to him because the doctor made a mistake and cut something that killed her. After a few weeks, the doctors say the boy's father will be able to go home in a matter of days. The boy is extremely happy for two reasons. One, the doctors say his father will be able to go home soon and the doctors also say that he won't have another fatal sickness for a long time. The end.

The boy's concern for his father is linked to his function as the only living relative who is capable of taking care of him.

4. *Reciprocity and Standards Are Basic to Relatedness*

Autonomy and relatedness are governed by a strong sense of fair play or prosocial standards. These values promote continuity and consistency in relations with others and within the self. Reciprocity is not perceived as quid pro quo but as a natural mode of relating among individuals who care about each other. The narrator clearly differentiates the characters' internalized standards and rules of conduct that are sufficiently flexible to permit appropriate compromise.

The following three stories were told by #203, a kindergarten participant in a research study, rated by his teacher as high in empathy. (All participants had a verbal IQ of average or higher.)

Card 1. He feels sad. Then he still's sad. He can't . . . doesn't know how to play it. He tries to play it but it sounds squeaky and ugly. [E: Thinking?] How would it sound if he knew how to play it. Then he tries again and then he does it good.

The character is sad because the violin sounds squeaky and keeps working to attain an implied standard (to improve from sounding squeaky to good). The boy's effort is sufficient for the goal and outcome; trying to make a nice sound (a process goal) can be accomplished relatively easily (compared to the dilemma presented in Slade's story of getting into a concert without knowing how to play). Although no other character is introduced, there is a clear sense of internalized standards that "stand in" for external relationships. The next story, told to an interpersonal scene, reveals this generalized connection in the context of a specific interaction.

Card 4. There is a man sick and there's a woman taking care of him. He does want to do something but she won't let him because she knows he is sick. And he was almost ready to do it but she did not let him. He didn't do it because she didn't want him to. She's thinking if she had let him do it, what would have happened. He was thinking what would happen if he didn't do it. [E: Feeling?] Sorta happy because he didn't do it. Maybe at that moment he wanted to kill a snake.

A man refrains from doing something he wants because a caring woman insists that this will jeopardize his health. There is no threat of disapproval or other form of coercion, hence no major disparity of power. At the end, the man is glad he listened.

Card 8BM. The boy is having an operation. And he's asleep. He gets a big cut. [E: Before?] He got in an accident on a wedding day. That's the same boy after the operation [boy in the front of the picture]. After the operation that's what he looks like. He feels sad because he has his operation. [E: Turns out?] It turns out okay, the doctors help him, and he gets better.

This story is about a boy thinking back on his surgery that was necessitated by an accident. He recovers and goes on with his life. Despite the unsophisticated language, this narrative is a resourceful explanation of the relationship between foreground and background in the stimulus and depicts an autonomous character who recovers from adversity.

5. *Relatedness Through Mutuality of Autonomy*

This level is characterized by full appreciation of uniqueness and individuality, apart from needs or requirements of social exchange or conventional morality. The narrative conveys awareness of the relationship between transient and enduring psychological experience and of complex motives in self and others. The narrator portrays the inner lives and concerns of all characters in accord with their depiction in the stimulus and in ways that entail mutual respect for individualistic styles, together with appreciation of subtle intra- and interpersonal nuance. Characters value societal rules or obligations in the context of mutual care and commitment to moral standards. Mutuality of autonomy is far removed from the concept of rugged individuality or extricating oneself from the web of community. Indeed, the ties are so strong that they transcend the other's immediate presence. There is a fine-tuned understanding of multiply interacting dimensions of experience such that the concerns of one character seamlessly incorporate the views of the others or balance short- and long-term considerations.

Three stories told by Benjie, age 9-11, Stanford-Binet IQ score of 140, illustrate this level. Benjie was participating in a research study and was described by his teacher as being intrinsically motivated by standards rather than by grades and highly esteemed by classmates.

Card 1. The boy has a violin except he can't play it very nicely. So he's kind of upset because he can't figure out how to play it well. You want to know what I think this thing is? [Points to the paper under the violin] [E: Up to you.] He's thinking whether he should keep trying or quit it because he doesn't know how to play it. [E: Turns out?] He gives up because he decides that he'll never be able to do it.

The boy makes an autonomous decision, not in the spur of the moment or in response to frustration, but after concluding that he will never succeed at the particular activity. He does not seek help, advice, or approval because the decision is his to make. The feeling of "upset" is caused by the boy's perception of being unable to meet his own standard for playing "nicely." There is no hint of external pressure; the boy simply assumes that others would respect his (well-reasoned) decision.

Card 4. Well, there's a man that looks very mad at someone who annoyed or offended him, and his wife is trying to stop him from doing anything he'll regret such as attacking the person who was offending him. At the end, she'll restrain him and he'll stop and get over his anger.

Mutuality of autonomy is demonstrated by the wife's trying to stop the husband from doing anything "he'll regret." Therefore, she does not impose her own standards but realizes that her husband is blinded by his anger and offers a rational perspective. In turn, the husband understands the force of his anger. After he listens to his wife, he takes responsibility for his feelings and "gets over his anger." Short- and long-term psychological processes are nicely balanced in this story. The inner and outer worlds of both characters are differentiated and coordinated.

Card 8BM. A boy, yeah a boy, more like an adolescent has to have surgery, and he's dreaming about how it's going to be, and he's a little scared so he's thinking how it's going to be. So he sees what's going to happen to him, and it makes him even more scared. I don't know why there's something that looks like a rifle there. [E: Ending?] He goes through it, and he realizes he was worried about nothing because he didn't even feel it.

There is a nuanced understanding that dwelling on an anxiety-provoking event is counterproductive, particularly if nothing can be done about it. Sometimes, reality is less scary than one anticipates. Again, this is a nice portrayal of time sequence and a resourceful accounting of the stimulus.

CASE ILLUSTRATION

Slade, a 15-year-old, was evaluated to understand his frame of mind pursuant to being charged with murder. Professionals administered various assessment tools, including the TAT, the Rorschach, and Wechsler scales. Though he was generally cooperative during the evaluation, Slade was constantly drumming his fingers on the table and, at times, laughed inappropriately. Figures 6.1 and 6.2 display the coding of Slade's protocol on the variables introduced in this chapter. The applicable categories are marked.

LEVELS OF OBJECT RELATIONS

Level One: Disorganized or detached level of relatedness. At this level, disorganized or highly simplified cognitive processing (poor reality testing) may disrupt the differentiation and integration of various perspectives (mutuality) and interferes with the sense of self-cohesion (autonomy). Impaired social reasoning may stem from problems coordinating affect, intention, and thought within or across individuals, from problems differentiating wishes from realistic considerations, and from serious problems with understanding social causality. This level is evident in TAT stories characterized by any of the following:

- A severe imbalance of autonomy with helplessness in the face of the whims of controlling and powerful others.
- Severe restrictions on a character's autonomy (extreme helplessness).
- Individuality is not perceived (characters feel the same way despite postures or facial expressions that are clearly different).
- Severe limitations in autonomy and disparity of power is evident in characters who exploit, malign, or overpower others or feel similarly victimized.
- Absence of remorse for actions that are substantially hurtful.
- Characters make highly unreasonable or unrealistic demands on one another.

Level Two: Momentary experience of relatedness. At this level, a rudimentary sense of autonomy or limited mutuality coincides with a self-absorbed and self-serving mode of relatedness that pertains to the moment. Individuals are differentiated on the basis of momentary need or immediate gain without the sense that they are whole persons. Characteristics of others are noticed only if they pertain to the observer's immediate need states so that perceptions of self and others shift according to circumstances without insight or reflection. This level is shown in TAT stories that are characterized by any of the following:

- A character's evaluation of persons as obstacles or hindrances without considering any other attributes or reciprocity.

(continued)

- Emotions are tied to immediate external considerations, such that remorse is linked to immediate consequences.
- Inner attributes are ill defined (diffuse negative affect) or based on stereotypes (unconvincing verbalization about duty or blind obligation) without a sense that the personality is a continuous, cohesive whole.
- Significant imbalance in mutuality of autonomy where one character may be competent, heroic, or intrusive and others are incompetent, helpless, or ignored (also when a person in the scene is left out of the story).
- Characters experience relatedness only if another person is physically present and, when single characters are portrayed, they are unable to cope with their misery but no one is introduced to help.
- Concerns of characters are basic, revolving around safety, survival, or protection.
- The relationship per se is neither important nor durable and others who meet needs are interchangeable.
- Characters take no responsibility for their feelings or actions. (Fantasy may replace actual relationships—characters are actors or characters easily abandon their intentions, convictions, or intense feelings.)

Level Three: Functional experience of relatedness. At this level, individuals notice attributes that pertain to reciprocity in the form of *rigid quid pro quo exchanges* where the emphasis is on duty or function served (including duty and obligation) rather than on the human connection. Responsibilities are not internally rooted or valued as ends (matter of principle) but constitute give-and-take responses in relationships that are valued for mutual exchanges. Approval or disapproval, as well as rewards and consequences, may be salient in these exchanges. Individuals anticipate punishment for wrongdoing and express genuine remorse for transgressions or for perceived failure to meet expectations. However, they do not set their own standards. Attributes of others that are noted and appreciated are those that contribute to their expected functions. At this level, what is salient in others is no longer dependent on the perceivers' immediate needs and feelings but on a longer term view of the functional exchanges with recognition of reciprocity. This level is shown in TAT stories when characters:

- Are differentiated according to what they can provide and relate in terms of what they do for or want from one another without recognition of one another's autonomy;
- Respond without consideration of one another's prior history, personal conviction, or investment. What matters is the quid pro quo exchange;
- Fail to act or act without deliberate intention; or
- Take turns as givers and takers, although in a rigid or stereotypic manner.

Level Four: Reciprocity and standards as basic to relatedness.
Autonomy and relatedness at this level are governed by a sense of fair play or
prosocial standards that promote continuity and consistency in relationships
with others and within the self (commitment to standards, pursuit of self-
directed purposeful action). Reciprocity is not perceived as quid pro quo but
as a natural mode of relating among individuals who care about each other.
Thus, the range of attributes of others that are salient and appreciated is
wider and more independent of the perceiver's needs or preoccupations.
Individuals accord one another the freedom to have their own views and to
pursue self-directed and purposeful activities. Individuals may be disappointed
if they don't meet their own standards but persist. At this level, TAT stories
portray characters who are:

- Clearly differentiated in terms of internalized standards and rules of conduct
  that are sufficiently flexible to permit appropriate compromise;

- Autonomous, having a sense of goals or principles, and able to take self-
  determined actions that are prosocial; if only a single character is included,
  the autonomy implies appreciation of the other's individuality;

- Balanced in their respective sense of autonomy (intentions, actions,
  outcomes are distinct but coordinated); characters' initiative, purpose,
  conviction, and deliberate pursuit of goal-directed activities do not
  diminish others.

Level Five: Relatedness through mutuality of autonomy. At this level,
the individual's sense of autonomy encompasses a balanced appreciation of
uniqueness and individuality of self and others, apart from needs or requirements of social exchange or social convention. The narrative conveys a fine-
tuned understanding of multiply interacting dimensions of experience through
awareness of both transient and enduring psychological experiences and of
complex motives in self and others by any of the following:

- Inner lives and concerns of all characters are portrayed in line with their
  depictions in the stimulus and entail mutual respect for individualistic
  styles together with appreciation of subtle intra- and interpersonal
  nuance.

- Characters value societal conventions and obligations in the context of
  mutual care and commitment to moral standards and have the flexibility to
  interact in ways that enhance the autonomy of all parties.

- Interpersonal ties are strong enough to transcend the threat of consequences or disapproval.

- The narrative coordinates the concerns of characters in ways that balance
  short- and long-term considerations and their respective autonomy.

(Choose one level for each story)

Card	1	2	3BM	4	5	6BM	8BM	13B	13MF	17BM
Slade	1	1	1	1	1	1	1	1	1	1

Figure 6.2 Levels of Object Relations for Slade's Stories

Card 1. You want a story about this? Okay. I think the school's gonna have a concert and he wants to be in it. He goes home, gets Dad's old violin, looks at it, and tries to figure it out. Gets dad to help him play it and learns how and gets in the concert. [E: Thinking?] That he doesn't know how to play and thinking how to learn. [E: Feeling?] Feels anxious, confused.

Import: A person can get what he wants even if it is unrealistic if he can get his parent to help (to play in the concert without going through the normally time-consuming process).

In this story, the narrator expresses the conviction that quick and easy solutions are attainable for complex and long-term problems. The story shows a lack of understanding of "how" things happen and simplistic reasoning with unrealistic expectations about parental support. First, wanting and getting to be in a school concert without a prior history of playing or practicing with the band violates basic tenets of social causality. The expectation that a boy would learn a complex skill (by getting his father's violin and help) in the time between the announcement of a concert and the actual performance indicates a failure to grasp the process involved. There is a sense that the narrator's judgment disregards the constraints of social reality. Second, there is no explanation for why the boy wants to be in the concert (e.g., interest in music, being with friends). In fact, when asked how the boy feels, Slade focuses on the stimulus (negative emotion) without connecting the feeling to the happy events in the story.

Card 2. I draw a blank. All right. I think her father wants her to do work. [E: What kind?] On farm. She wants to go to school and learn something good. Family wants her to work on farm. She's trying to decide. Looks like she goes to school, walkin' away. [E: Feeling?] Concerned, little worried, unsure.

Import: If a girl's family wants something different from what she wants, she will do as she pleases without considering their reasons or intentions and without any communication.

Simplified reasoning and either/or thinking are evident in the girl's decision-making process. In delineating the central problem as a dichotomy between what is wanted by the family and the girl, there is a sense of detachment as though each encounter is split from the others (no intent, no relationship, no historical context). The central character does what she wants without heeding the needs of others or recognizing her place in the family. The girl's decision also fails to include implications for the future and is only vaguely connected to her own intentions or goals ("learn something good"). One wonders what this girl did yesterday and what she will do tomorrow. As in the previous story, the emotions and actions refer back to the stimulus (girl looks as if she is walking away) rather than being incorporated meaningfully into the narrative progression.

Card 3BM. What's that by the foot? Don't know if boy or girl. [E: Doesn't matter.] This person, uh, don't know, maybe he/she drunk. Trying to decide whether to drive or not and thing by leg is keys to car. Doesn't want to drive 'cause afraid will crash car.

Import: A person who is drunk thinks about driving (without a destination) but decides against it only because he or she is afraid of crashing the car.

Again, reasoning is simplified and is restricted to the immediate considerations with no history or aim. The premise of the story (to drive or not to drive while drunk) has no tie to past events that might provide a reason to drive to a particular destination or explain why the character might be drunk. Hence, the character's dilemma has no context in external circumstances or inner psychological processes. The story ends with the character not wanting to drive for fear of crashing the car, a decision provoked by character's safety concerns without reference to the reason for wanting to drive in the first place or to legal or moral constraints. (Note: Actions such as driving or leaving one's family, as in the above story, are not reflective of autonomy. Rather, autonomy lies in taking initiative in pursuit of a purpose).

Card 4. I think guy getting ready to go somewhere. Woman doesn't want him to go. Turns out he leaves. Man's feeling determined to leave. Woman feels alone 'cause he's leaving.

Import: If a man wants to leave a woman, he will do so knowing that she will feel alone.

The interaction is understood simplistically without any sense of relatedness between the man and woman or durable intentions for actions. Characters' intentions or history of prior interactions seems irrelevant, and there is no communication, compromise, or concern for others. Likewise, a person has no larger, internal purpose for actions; the man just wants to leave. The emotions are ignored, and there is no glue that binds people together, even for a moment. The message here (as in Card 2) is that, if people want different things, they just go their separate ways without caring about each other and without any particular reason for leaving.

Card 5. Don't know. She gets home and window broken and door open. Just walkin' in to the living room looking to see what's missing. Safe been broken open and all the money's gone. [E: Feeling?] Scared all stuff stolen and don't know if burglar still in the house or not.

Import: If someone (an older woman) is a victim, she remains at the mercy of others without taking constructive action.

Following a burglary, a frightened woman, concerned about the loss of her possessions, is left vulnerable to revictimization without acting or seeking help to protect herself (e.g., calling the police, leaving her house). The narrator seems to feel no inclination to bring closure to the woman's predicament, leaving her afraid and not knowing if she is safe from the burglars who may still be lurking. The character's emotion fails to spur appropriate action, and the narrator is too detached to provide an ending to tie up loose ends and remove the woman from danger.

Card 6BM. I think man just told mother he's going off to war. She looking out window contemplating what's going to happen. Turns out he goes to war and comes home safely. Got to tell one that's different.

Import: When a man tells his mother that he's going off to war, he gets no response, but he does return safely.

This is no ordinary good-bye scene as mother and son seem disconnected emotionally. The son brings seemingly distressing news about having to go off to war, yet the emotional impact of this information is lost (the mother distantly contemplates what will happen in the future but does not communicate with her son). The story is bound to a stilted and literal reading of the picture without any hint of relatedness between mother and son.

Card 8BM. Uh, think this boy's shot somebody . . . gun there. Looks like he did it on purpose . . . not a sorrowful look on his face. Imagining the guy getting surgery. [E: What happens in the future?] Guy's gonna live and he's gonna get charged with attempted murder. [E: Feeling?] Look like pretty mean.

Import: When a person shoots someone on purpose, he doesn't regret it, and because the "guy" lives, he only gets charged with attempted murder.

Taking his cues from the picture, Slade describes a shooting done on purpose without remorse because "not a sorrowful look on his face." The act of shooting someone would normally beg for an explanation rather than being accepted as a routine occurrence. However, Slade does not provide a socially acceptable reason for the shooting. He matter-of-factly concludes the story with the boy's being charged with attempted murder. Again, the reasoning is simplified; the presence of the gun and the boy's facial expression automatically "add up" to a shooting done on purpose, without prior history, reason, or moral feelings. Analogously, Slade is likely to act on the basis of highly simplified reasoning that is detached from moral emotions, interpersonal connections, or durable intentions. Even his awareness of possible consequences seems detached from its implications.

Card 13B. Think he's living on a farm and growing up farm life. He's just sittin' in the sun. [E: In the future?] Grows up, becomes a farmer. [E: Thinking? Feeling?] Seems concerned about something, looks a little troubled, maybe he's worried about the livestock.

Import: If a boy lives on a farm, he grows up to be a farmer (without his own thoughts or feelings).

Like the other stories, this one is a product of simplistic reasoning. Slade uses the pictured cues to construct a simple storyline that ignores the boy's inner life and does not introduce any other characters. Rather than dealing with the boy's current thoughts and feelings, the narrator takes a big jump in time (boy grows up to be a farmer). In response to inquiry, Slade describes the boy as concerned with livestock, a vague and seemingly associative connection to farm life that is not quite appropriate to the child's age.

Card 13MF. Think they're both drunk. At a party and had sex. He wake up not knowing who she was. He's kind of in a stupor. [E: Thinking?] Worried, unsure of surroundings.

Import: After getting drunk at a party and having sex with a woman, a man is disoriented, not knowing the woman, and unsure of his surroundings.

In a matter-of-fact way, Slade describes a man thinking only of himself and of his situation in the moment. Again, intentions, prior events, relatedness, or future consequences do not factor into Slade's thinking.

Card 17BM. Uh, looks like he's climbing a rope. Maybe a construction dude, but not wearing shoes, pants. Happy, naked guy climbing a rope. [E: Thinking?] Climb rope. [he laughs] Being a monkey. [E: In the future?] He ends up here [referring to the institution in which he is confined].

Import: If a man enjoys an activity (as depicted in the picture), he ends up in a psychiatric institution.

Process import: Without understanding emotions or intentions, a person cannot explain this situation so he laughs it off.

Unable to delve into motives or intentions, Slade cannot explain what is happening in the scene and basically describes the stimulus. Though he recognizes consequences, he fails to experience their emotional impact.

Narrative Summary

The simplified process of reasoning and concrete thinking reflected in Slade's stories contrast with his performance on more structured tests (IQ and achievement). Focusing on external appearances, Slade describes what is happening in the pictured scenes without tying the current situation to past or future events or to an inner world of emotions or durable intentions. His characters are frozen according to their portrayals in the stimulus, without meaningful relationships to one another and without emotional engagement in long-term pursuits. When prompted to include feelings (because he does not do so spontaneously), Slade's tendency is to refer back to how the characters looked in the stimulus, thus divorcing the characters' experiences (story events) and their actions from their feelings. Although Slade is able to provide a label for the feelings portrayed in the picture, he does not grasp their psychological significance in sustaining relationships or formulating intentions. Actions and reactions are based on momentary considerations that do not have a realistic link to the past or future and are not meaningfully integrated with feelings or intentions. Slade's judgments and expectations fail to incorporate a realistic understanding of social causality or consideration for others. When responding to situations, he is not guided by interpersonal connections, long-term goals, or durable intentions. Rather, he is preoccupied with what he wants in the moment and does not grasp any links between the current circumstances, prior history, and implications for later. Moreover, on an emotional level, he sees no connection between himself and others, nor is he invested in concerns beyond the moment. His focus on isolated events that are disconnected from the multiple dimensions of human experience is consistent with the detached demeanor he exhibited during the evaluation and with the general impressions that he lacks remorse.

DON'T FORGET

In addition to content, structural attributes of the story, such as the appropriate match to the stimulus and logical sequence of events, are important in determining the level of object relations.

CAUTION

Those with severe intellectual disability often cannot tell stories, but provide concrete descriptions and many of the indicators of object relations described in this chapter are not applicable. Nevertheless, responses show individuality in identifying and dealing with the emotions and relationships depicted in the scenes.

TEST YOURSELF

1. **Object relations theory**
   (a) focuses on observable transactions among people.
   (b) focuses on early memories.
   (c) overlaps with schema theory.
   (d) all of the above.

2. **Explain why object relations is to object representations as abstract is to concrete.**

3. **The process by which individuals learn skills for daily functioning is essentially the same as the process of "internalization" that leads to the development of psychic structure.**

   True or False?

4. **Define each of the following three pathological modes of relating described within the object relations framework: (a) self-object, (b) transitional object, (c) part-object.**

5. **How are autonomy and mutuality of autonomy pertinent to object relations?**

6. **How are positive emotions, empathy, and emotion regulation pertinent to level of object relations?**

Answers: 1. c; 2. Object relations and abstract schemas embody principles that organize conceptions of self and other, whereas object representation is directly tied to a specific relationship; 3. False; 4. (a) Self-object relations: failure to notice characteristics of others apart from one's own feelings or preoccupations. (b) Transitional object relations: valuing others only in terms of the comfort they provide. (c) Part-object relations: restriction of interest in others to the function they serve; 5. Autonomy refers to the connections between the inner and outer worlds within a single individual, and hence to the representation of the self in relation to external circumstances. The more autonomous an individual, the more he or she can value the autonomy of others (mutuality of autonomy) and appreciate others apart from self-interest; 6. Poor emotion regulation is associated with focus on one's own discomfort in response to others' distress and disrupts empathy. Positive emotions and empathy spur interest in characteristics of others, resulting in more complex processing of interpersonal information.

Seven

ESSENTIALS OF TAT ASSESSMENT OF MOTIVATION AND SELF-REGULATION

Motivation and self-regulation are reciprocally linked: Goals serve regulatory functions, and performance of goal-directed activities requires self-regulation. Theories of motivation and self-regulation converge on two central questions (see Johnson, Chang, & Lord, 2006): What does the person want (goal setting), and how does the person seek what is wanted (goal pursuit)? Motivational schemas include the desired goals (what) and the means to attain them (how). Once goals have been solidified, they become sources of self-regulation because they (a) selectively orient attention to information in the surroundings or in memory, (b) influence choices of tasks or activities, and (c) energize effort in the pursuit of purposeful activities (Gollwitzer & Moskowitz, 1996; McClelland, 1987; Payne, Youngcourt, & Beaubien, 2007).

To carry out the intended actions, self-regulatory processes subordinate immediate preferences to long-term commitment and maintain intentions in the face of competing motivational tendencies or distraction from external sources (Kuhl, 1984, 1992). *Implementation intentions* that are formulated to enact goal-relevant behaviors include plans for when, where, and how to enact goal-directed actions (Gollwitzer, 1999; Gollwitzer & Sheeran, 2006). Once an implementation intention is associated with a situation (the when and where), it automatically activates the goals (what) and action plans (how). In other words, a situation, by association with a set of action plans, may activate complex motive-relevant behaviors without the individual becoming aware of having that goal (see review, Chartrand & Bargh, 2002). Thus, motivated behavior entails not only the setting of goals but also includes the plans for their implementation and resources to maintain intentions over time or in the face of external or internal barriers. Indeed, the field of motivation highlights the self-regulatory functions of goals and the self-regulatory processes needed to pursue goals.

Self-regulation itself is an important goal that influences other goals. The disciplines of temperament and personality acknowledge the centrality of self-regulation but differ in their emphases about what is being regulated and how it is being regulated. The field of temperament focuses on regulation of basic processes, such as maintaining optimal levels of stimulation or emotional intensity, that are grounded in neurobiological systems (Rothbart, Derryberry, & Posner, 1994; Posner & Rothbart, 2007; Strelau, 1994). The study of personality emphasizes structures or processes (i.e., an "executive" or "ego") that perform self-regulatory functions by orchestrating and balancing the individual's various tendencies to meet adaptive demands or attain specific purposes (see Karoly, 1993, for a review). In a sense, temperamental self-regulation is a building block of regulation studied in the field of personality (see Teglasi, 2006). On a daily basis, individuals make decisions (with or without awareness) to balance temperamental inclinations with social expectations in the formulation and pursuit of goals. Individuals who expend a great deal of energy to keep from being overcome by negative affect may be limited in focusing on long-term interests and may favor coping strategies geared to immediate relief. Those who often engage in activities that are at odds with temperamental predispositions may pay a heavy price in stress (Strelau, 1983).

Individuals with greater temperamental reactivity face greater self-regulatory challenges to allay fears, control their irritability, put their negative and positive emotions in perspective, and keep unwelcome, ruminative thoughts at bay (e.g., Henderson & Fox, 1998; Rothbart & Bates, 2006). Preoccupation with efforts to control emotion, attention, or behavior diverts resources from long-term strivings. Individuals are more likely to make errors in judgment when effortful control is depleted but nonconscious processes continue to operate effectively regardless of depletion (i.e., retrieval from long-term memory; Hasher & Zacks, 1979; automatic goal-directed activity; Bargh, Gollwitzer, Lee-Chai, Barndollar, & Troetschel, 2001; automatic evaluation of novel stimuli; Duckworth, Bargh, Garcia, & Chaiken, 2002). Following mental exertion (Fischer, Greitemeyer, & Frey, 2008) or to conserve mental energy in anticipation of an arduous task (Muraven, Shmueli, & Burkley, 2006), individuals reduce mental effort (such as avoiding belief-inconsistent information). Individuals may strategically use implementation intentions to automate the regulation of desired goal-relevant behaviors (see, Gallo, Keil, McCulloch, Rockstroh, & Gollwitzer, 2009).

Any given behavior may be the product of flexible compromises between effortful and automatic sources of regulation and between short-term self-regulatory demands and long-term goals. Behavior may also be a product of aimless reactions to external stimuli or short-sighted efforts to reduce negative emotions (e.g., anxiety, boredom, tension, emptiness). For instance, those with high reactivity in novel situations may haphazardly avoid unfamiliar situations or may have developed effective strategies to deal with the feelings such situations elicit (plan ahead, prepare, practice). Thus, the aims of motivation may range from attempts to cope with immediate preoccupations and temperamental exigencies (including depletion) to the pursuit of well-articulated goals and principles. In other words, the goal-directed behaviors may range from decisions and actions that are reactive and haphazard or planned and organized. A comprehensive theory of motivation would identify the psychological processes, both automatic and effortful, that influence goal setting and shape goal-directed actions, as well as the reciprocal influences among goals, cognition, emotion, and behavior (see Cantor & Sanderson, 1999).

TAT AND MOTIVATION

Motive-relevant constructs exist in both explicit and implicit versions (see Chapter 1), measured respectively with self-report and with performance measures such as the TAT. Implicit motives, expressed in TAT stories, are embedded in schemas that delineate the type of goals, the contexts in which they are salient, the means to pursue them, and expectations for their attainment. Individuals vary in the nature and strength of the linkages among goals, actions, and expected outcomes (Kruglanski et al., 2002) that are housed in the schemas. The coding procedures in this chapter characterize motivational concerns in terms of the connections among goals/intentions, actions, and outcomes regardless of the specific motive (e.g., individualistic achievement, interpersonal relationships, moral decision making, and coping with adverse circumstances). Although various motives such as achievement, power, or affiliation are typically studied separately with TAT stories (see Smith, 1992), persons often balance individualistic aspirations and interpersonal goals with concerns for the welfare of others, and their relative emphases may differ according to culture (Suarez-Orozco, 1989).

The linkages among four motive-relevant constructs prominent in the literature have been incorporated into coding TAT stories as described below: (a) goal formulation, or manner in which the problem, goal, or dilemma is delineated; (b) goal maintenance, or reaction to the goal, which includes emotions or complications engendered by the goal; and (c) goal-directed decisions, plans, and actions; and (d) expected outcomes in reference to goals and the means to pursue them.

Goal Formulation

The types of goals set by individuals establish what they value about outcomes and about their performance. Goals motivate behavior regardless of whether they focus on self-development (e.g., seeking fulfillment, overcoming feelings of inferiority through work), lifestyle (e.g., earning a living, overcoming poverty, being like everyone else), relationships (e.g., avoiding rejection, gaining friendship, earning freedom from control of others), feeling good (e.g., avoiding fear or anxiety, seeking enjoyable activities), or striving for accomplishment. *Goal theory* relates the nature of goals in academic settings to the individual's self-evaluation as being based either on social comparison or self-development (Pintrich & Schunk, 2002). Mastery goals are set by those who are motivated by their own self-evaluation and who prefer to undertake challenges aimed at self-improvement and who seek realistic feedback. Performance goals are set by those who are more concerned with demonstrating their competence and gaining favorable judgment of others (see Rapid Reference 7.1). Another perspective, *self-determination theory* (Kasser & Ryan, 1993, 1996), focuses on whether the individual values a particular goal as an outcome that is *extrinsic* to relevant activities or because of the *intrinsic* appeal of the activities themselves (see Rapid Reference 7.2). The essential contrast is between *intrinsic goals* (such as growth, relationships, and community) and *extrinsic goals* (wealth, fame, and image). Individual differences in goals held are relevant to learning, achievement, and persistence (Vansteenkiste, Simons, Lens, Sheldon, & Deci, 2004).

≡ *Rapid Reference 7.1*

Mastery and Performance Goals

- *Mastery versus performance goals*: At its core, the distinction between mastery and performance goals is the *standard* used by the individual to evaluate performance (Elliot & McGregor, 2001; Pintrich & Schunk, 2002). Mastery goals orient persons to strive for self-improvement and to derive satisfaction from mastering the task. Performance goals point persons to strive to outperform peers or to surpass normative performance standards and to derive satisfaction from social comparison. A focus on competitive self-evaluations may detract from mastery goals (see Brophy, 2005, for a review). In educational settings, mastery goals promote the use of learning strategies that enhance conceptual understanding and recall (Grant & Dweck, 2003; Wolters, 2004), whereas performance goals are linked with surface-level learning strategies such as memorizing and rehearsing rather than conceptual understanding (Elliot & Harackiewicz, 1996).

- *Approach or avoidance mastery and performance goals*: Mastery-approach goals (consistent with the definition of mastery goals) focus individuals on what they want to learn, master, and truly understand. Mastery-avoidance

(continued)

goals focus individuals on avoidance of misunderstanding or on preventing the prospects of not being able to learn from a specific task (Elliot & McGregor, 2001; Moller & Elliot, 2006). Performance-approach goals prompt individuals to attain favorable judgments of competence by out-performing others, whereas performance-avoidance goals orient individuals to avoid unfavorable judgments of competence, relative to others (Elliot & Harackiewicz, 1996). The approaching and avoiding versions of goals have been associated with emotions (Pekrun, Elliot, & Maier, 2006). Mastery goals are positively linked with enjoyment of learning and negatively with boredom and anger. Performance-approach goals are associated with pride, and performance-avoidance goals are associated with anxiety, hopelessness, and shame.

- *Combined mastery and performance orientations*: Although often examined as separate goal orientations, individuals often hold both mastery and performance goals (Midgley, Kaplan, & Middleton, 2001; Regner, Escribe, & Dupeyrat, 2007).

- *Goal structure of the learning environment*: How students fare in a particular classroom is influenced by the goodness of fit between a student's endorsement of mastery and performance goals and the goals emphasized (see Meece, Anderman, & Anderman, 2006; Lau, Liem, & Nie, 2008).

Goals influence the nature of feedback sought, persistence in the face of challenges, and the conditions under which the goal is salient. Generally, TAT pictures suggest a dilemma to be identified and resolved, in line with the characters' implicit goals and action plans that are incorporated into the narrative. Provided that a goal has been set, and regardless of whether it is imposed or self-initiated, both narrative structure and content sheds light on the nature of the goal.

≋ *Rapid Reference 7.2*

Self-Controlled and Self-Regulated (Autonomous) Sources of Motivation

(Self-determination theory: Deci & Ryan, 1985, 2000; Ryan & Connell, 1989; Vansteenkiste, Lens, & Deci, 2006)

Motivation in educational settings has been classified as to whether learning is driven *intrinsically* (interest or enjoyment) or *extrinsically* (extraneous factors such as outcomes). Motivation was further differentiated into two types according to the relative degree of *autonomy*, captured by the terms self-control and self-regulation, applied to goal-directed behaviors (Kuhl & Fuhrmann, 1998).

Self-control refers to the pursuit of goal-directed activities that are imposed by significant others or assumed by the adoption of cultural values but are not supported by the individual's preferences. The self-control mode of pursuing goals involves a great deal of effort to overcome personal proclivities in a struggle to keep going against one's grain. In contrast, *self-regulation* refers to the pursuit of goal-directed activities that are in accord with the person's short- and long-term inclinations and are congruent with an integrated sense of self. *Autonomous* motivations (i.e., *self-regulation*) have advantages over controlled motivations for less superficial information processing (Vansteenkiste, Simons, Lens, Sheldon, et al., 2004), higher achievement (Soenens & Vansteenkiste, 2005), and enhanced well-being (Black & Deci, 2000; Levesque, Zuehlke, Stanek, & Ryan, 2004). These advantages (see Reeve, Deci, & Ryan, 2004) have been replicated outside the United States (Chirkov & Ryan, 2001; Vansteenkiste, Zhou, Lens, & Soenens, 2005).

- *External regulation* is the least autonomous form of motivation (extrinsic) as the individual undertakes actions only because of external contingencies such as rewards, punishments, or deadlines. The impetus for action is entirely external (student studies to get parental reward).

- *Introjection* is a process of "taking in" rules for actions by referencing external authority (approval or disapproval) that involves the underlying subjective experience of being controlled by rules and expectations of others (punishment) or by inner forces acting on the individual (threat of guilt, promise of self-approval, pressure based on self-esteem). The individual has internalized the desire to follow rules and meet expectations but experiences pressure to carry out the necessary activities (studying to avoid feeling guilty).

- *Identification* is a process by which a person identifies with and values an activity, accepting full responsibility for the behavior and its outcome. The subjective experience entails a greater sense of consistency and coherence between the person's behavior and inner states. Identified regulation is still somewhat extrinsic in nature, but it is relatively volitional (studies for the bar exam because it is important to practice in chosen field). The person sees the relevance of the activity, engages voluntarily, and experiences the source of control as emanating from the self (e.g., Black & Deci, 2000).

- *Internalization* is a process that serves human psychological needs for competence, autonomy, and relatedness (Grolnick, Deci, & Ryan, 1997) as drivers of tendencies to take on the values, beliefs, and behaviors endorsed by family and community.

Narrative Structure and Process in Goal Formulation

Does the narrator:

- Offer clear and appropriate definition of the central problem, tension, or dilemma, given the stimulus that implies cause-effect understanding rather than a vague, nonspecific intention or tension?

(continued)

- Produce a story that is logical, unfolding without irrelevant or contradictory details, and involving reasoning that is realistic and sequences of events that are plausible?

Do characters:

- Face a realistic, prosocial goal, either imposed by others but accepted willingly or set by the character? In other words, do characters face goals that are in accord with socially accepted roles and responsibilities that they accept and are not coerced by others' whims?
- Face realistic, prosocial goals or seek to resolve a conflict or dilemma rather than react to the provocation or desire of the moment (such as wanting to get a toy or to play) or engage in routine activities?
- Exhibit interest, curiosity, pride, concern, empathy, and a commitment to standards or ideals that foster achievement or prosocial activity?

Characteristics of Goals (Indicate for each story):

absent – vague – clear	self-initiated – imposed	realistic – unrealistic
long term – short term	prosocial – antisocial	interpersonal – task
process – outcome	idealistic – materialistic	meet inner standards – meet demands or expectations
substantial – trivial	attain positive – avert negative	

Goal Maintenance

To sustain goal-directed activities, individuals must maintain intentions in the face of competing motivational tendencies or distraction from external sources (action control) and possess the competencies to carry out the intended actions (performance control). Assuming that the person can effectively manage goal-relevant behavior, willingness to do so becomes salient. In part, sustaining goal-directed activities depends on the reasons they are undertaken, such as compliance with others' expectations, importance of the goal or the activity to one's identity, or interest in the activities (see Burton, Lydon, Alessandro, & Koestner, 2006; Deci & Ryan, 1985; Reeve, Deci, & Ryan, 2004; Sheldon, Ryan, Deci, & Kasser, 2004). Goal-directed activities are difficult to sustain to the extent that they are viewed as imposed by others, requiring inordinate effort, likely to be ineffective, or uninteresting. Individuals balance multiple considerations in goal pursuit, setting subgoals toward larger purposes, revising goals, and pacing their efforts to minimize the impact of stress or temporary loss of interest or conserving mental energy in anticipation of an arduous task (e.g., Muraven, Shmueli, & Burkley, 2006).

In TAT stories, complications in the plot, perceived competency to attain the goal, external barriers, or changing conditions flesh out the narrator's motive-related schemas. Characters' reactions may reveal problems sustaining the goal (e.g., abandoning the goal, changing the goal, facing conflicting goals, viewing activities as taxing), anticipating obstacles or supports from the environment, difficulties implementing goal-related activities (e.g., experiencing boredom or lack of confidence), or other complexities.

The following characteristics of narrative pertain to the maintenance of goals:

Narrative Structure and Process of Goal Maintenance
Does the narrator:
- Construct the story according to a plan rather than generate ideas detail by detail?
- Incorporate all parts of the instructions with or without inquiry? If prompted, the response enhances the story rather than being minimal or repetitive.
- Integrate emotions with the unfolding story rather than merely describing how the character looks in the picture?

Content of Goal Maintenance
Do characters:
- Coordinate between the inner world (what is wanted) and external realities (of the identified problem, stimulus pull, and the means to desired ends)? If so, characters would display foresight, plan ahead, set priorities, or anticipate consequences for self, others, or both. Characters would also realistically appraise external or internal barriers to goal attainment (not ruminative preoccupation) without abandonment of the goal or may choose a realistic alternative rather than opt for an "easy" goal.
- Perceive the goal (not as a vague wish or to meet immediate need or want) as interesting, desirable, enjoyable, or relevant rather than feel pressured or rely on external incentives? If so, they desire to engage in goal-related activity rather than procrastinate or avoid the demand or responsibility.

Goal Pursuit

Goal directed actions are more likely to be sustained if (a) the individual possesses cognitive, attentional, and emotional resources to do so, and (b) the individual relies less on effortful self-control strategies and maximizes the use of the

≡ Rapid Reference 7.3

Factors Influencing Pursuit and Attainment of Goals

1. To meet long-term goals, it is necessary to manage conflicting goals and resist distraction from environmental sources (Cantor & Blanton, 1996). Self-regulation involves *proactive* (downplay immediate pulls in favor of long-term perspectives) and *reactive modes* (modulate immediate behavior according to input from external sources) of control (Bandura, 1988, 1989). Reactive control is is necessary for the execution of a skill or application of knowledge to changing cues and circumstances and proactive control is needed to maintain focus on the long term.

2. Excessive reliance on self-control is associated with the subjective experience of stress and may jeopardize the individual's physical and psychological well-being (Deci & Ryan, 1991). Conflict between implicit sources of motivation (what one wants) and explicit sources (what is important to others or to one's own self-definition) may be a "hidden" source of stress that disrupts well-being (Baumann, Kaschel, & Kuhl, 2005). Still, self-control is necessary when short-term inclinations are likely to result in adverse future consequences. Ideally, self-control is temporary until the activity in question becomes self-sustaining or emotionally satisfying.

3. Schemas bridge the gap between effortful and automatic control over goal-directed actions. The transition from conscious and effortful control over goal-directed behavior to reliance on schemas is facilitated if the individual can become automatically guided by selected environmental cues. This shift occurs when the individual formulates *implementation intentions* that specify when, where, and how to engage in goal-directed behavior (Gollwitzer, 1996). Eventually, the initiation of sequences of goal-directed behavior is placed under the control of situational cues rather than each requiring an act of will (i.e., a college student establishes a morning routine that automatically cues a sequence of actions leading to class attendance--alarm, shower, breakfast, and class). Individuals are more likely to reach goals with specified implementation intentions than when goals remain vague (Locke & Latham, 1990).

automatic, self-regulatory mode, thereby freeing up resources for complex and long-term endeavors (see Rapid Reference 7.3). In any given situation, the sense of competence to pursue intentions is undermined when the individual cannot meet the information processing, emotional, or behavioral demands. Individuals who tune out information that is relevant to daily decision making will err in judgment, and individuals who cannot sustain action based on long-term investment will abandon their goals. The struggle to meet temperamental self-regulatory demands may deplete the individual's resources, and stress or frustration may temporarily restrict the ability to initiate or sustain goal-directed behavior.

Efforts to pursue intentions involve some combination of actions, plans, or decisions. Actions may emphasize control over the external world or changing the inner world to exert more effective control over the outer world or adjust to the inevitable. In TAT stories, three characteristics of actions are relevant: (a) deliberateness of the actions, such as actions directed toward a goal versus aimless, haphazard, unplanned, or provoked behaviors; (b) intent of the actions, such as a routine action or an action taken solely to satisfy a need (eat, shower, go to bed) versus instrumental action; and (c) breadth of perspective of the action, such as reaction to immediate need, provocation, or stimuli versus a broader perspective, including a longer timeframe that includes the interests of self and other. Also relevant is the quality of goal-directed mental effort, such as deliberate planning and thought versus ruminative mental process. Actively making a decision to resolve the story tensions or to meet one's goals in a thoughtful, self-directed way may be considered independently from the actual decision.

Several characteristics of narratives pertain to the narrator's schemas for active pursuit of intentions including means-ends and cause-effect connections.

Narrative Structure and Process of Goal Pursuit

Does the narrator:
- Include appropriate transitional events or means-ends connections, suggesting sufficient resources to maintain self-directed activity and follow through on intentions?

Content

Do characters:
- Take actions or make decisions that are prosocial, realistic, and sufficient for the expected outcome?
- Value responsible, goal-directed actions or decisions as distinct from outcomes? If so, characters are aware of the implications of their actions for others and assume appropriate responsibility for self-regulation and principled choices.
- Realistically balance inner motives and external constraints with regard to the connections between means and ends? If so, characters anticipate and deal with potential barriers to actions and are sensible in their outcome expectations.

Characteristics of Actions (Indicate for each Story):

present – absent	planned – haphazard	realistic – unrealistic
prosocial – antisocial	proactive (planned) – reactive (haphazard)	seeking positive – avoiding negative
goal directed – aimless	reliance on self – reliance on externals	enjoyable – burdensome

Outcome Expectations

The TAT story conveys the narrator's implicit expectations about how desired or undesired outcomes come about. The moral of the story (its import, as described in Chapter 3) is derived by answering the question: What are the conditions under which favorable and unfavorable outcomes are attained? The "motive story" connects the goal (what the person wants or intends in a given context) and the means (plans, decisions, plans for coping with a dilemma, or actions) with the actual outcome, thereby expressing the narrator's expectations about paths to various ends. Characteristics of narrative structure and content discussed above are summarized in Figure 7.1. The next section details approaches to delineating levels of motivation.

LEVEL OF MOTIVATION

Narratives provide a vehicle for understanding the integration of human action with intention in reference to anticipated outcomes. Although each of the components of motivation (goal formulation, goal maintenance, instrumental action and outcome) may be examined separately, the narrator's schemas about the conditions for happy or unhappy outcomes (imports) are inferred from their coherence within the "motive story." Therefore, the four levels of motivation are keyed to the import of the story (see Chapter 3) rather than to the sum of the discrete components such as goals or actions identified above as pertinent to motivation.

Levels of motivation are determined not by happy or unhappy endings but according to the convictions expressed primarily through the intentions-means-ends connections. Thus, happy outcomes represent constructive convictions only when they are realistic and result from appropriate actions or attitudes. Unhappy outcomes also represent constructive convictions when the import is prosocial and realistic (e.g., "crime does not pay" or "lack of effort leads to failure"). For example, if the narrator offers a negative outcome in a story about a theft, he or she communicates the moral that one should not steal, and this conviction is beneficial for the long-term interest of the individual and of society. The four levels of motivation described next are pegged to the import representing the narrator's schema and not to the immediate outcome for the story characters.

A Task performance—narrative structure and process

	Cards →	1	2									
Clear and appropriate definition of central problem, tension, or dilemma given the stimulus (versus vague, nonspecific intention or tension).												
Story is logical and proceeds without irrelevant or contradictory detail; reasoning is realistic; and sequence of events is plausible.												
Story proceeds according to a plan rather than made up detail by detail.												
Narrator incorporates all parts of the instructions with or without inquiry. Prompted responses enhance the story (versus minimal or repetitious).												
There are clear and logical connections between actions and outcomes and congruence among the narrative components.												
Appropriate means-ends connections (or other transitional events) suggest that the narrator can maintain self-directed activity and follow through on intentions.												

B Nature of goals or aspirations

	Cards →	1	2		
A realistic, prosocial goal or dilemma is imposed by others but accepted by a character (not wish or desire).					
Characters set a realistic, prosocial goal, conflict, or dilemma.					
Characters exhibit interest, curiosity, pride, concern, empathy, and commitment to standards, ideals, task, or prosocial activity.					

Figure 7.1 Checklist of motivation-relevant qualities of TAT stories

229

C Implementation resources

(Check as many as apply for each story)	Cards →	1	2							
Characters acknowledge possible external obstacles or internal limitations, without being stymied; they set priorities, display foresight, plan ahead, and anticipate consequences.										
Characters perceive the goal-related activities as interesting, desirable, or relevant, rather than feeling pressured, relying on external incentives, or avoiding the demand or responsibility.										
Characters maintain their commitment to the goal or make a reasonable decision that the goal is not the right one for them at this time (choose a more self-directed goal).										

D Means-ends connections

(Check as many as apply for each story)	Cards →	1	2							
Actions are prosocial, realistic, and sufficient for the expected outcome.										
Responsible, goal-directed actions or principled decisions are valued as distinct from outcomes.										
Characters' inner motives and external constraints are realistically balanced in the intention–action–outcome set.										

Figure 7.1 (Continued)

Characteristics of goals			1	2							
absent – vague – clear											
long term – short term											
process – outcome											
substantial – trivial											
self-initiated – imposed											
prosocial – antisocial											
idealistic – materialistic											
attain positive – avert negative											
realistic – unrealistic											
interpersonal – task											
meet inner standards – meet demands or expectations											

Characteristics of actions			1	2							
present – absent											
prosocial – antisocial											
goal directed – aimless											
planned – haphazard											
proactive – reactive											
reliance on self – reliance on externals											
realistic – unrealistic											
seeking positive – avoiding negative											
enjoyable – burdensome											

Figure 7.1 (Continued)

1. *Extremely Poor Motivation*

This level is characterized by unrealistic or illogical connections among goals, actions, and outcomes, or a lack of coordination among these components. For example, "success occurs without goals or efforts" or "failure follows hard work."

Positive Outcome:
- Intentions/goals are vague, ill-intended, unrealistic, unstated, inadequately defined, trivial, or extremely lofty.
- Dynamics include boredom, obvious lack of interest or inability to withstand setback or frustration, or negative attitudes toward effort or success.
- Actions by the character who owns the problem are unrealistic, nonexistent, or not constructive: absence of response or effort; aimless or reactive activity; blind dependence on, rebellious defiance of, or humiliation by others; unlikely or antisocial means; or wishful thinking with no realistic basis.

Import: One can attain success or happiness without clear or realistic goals, long-term investment or interest, or active effort, or one can attain it through unrealistic (impossible turn of events, magic, being rescued) or antisocial means.

Negative Outcome (or no change in the tensions):
- Intentions/goals are unclear, unstated, inappropriate, or unrealistic (no positive intent is stated or implied).
- Dynamics include expectation of failure, in spite of active effort or self-determined choices (or the narrator cannot meet the storytelling task demands or reasons without connecting causes and effects or means with ends); blaming failure on others or the sense that genuine efforts are misunderstood; failure or adversity cannot be overcome but leads to despair, frustration, inaction, confusion, feelings of inadequacy, hopelessness, pretense, deceit, escape, fantasy, dream, or sleep.
- Actions include positive effort that may be misunderstood or thwarted by circumstances, or absence of constructive action due to discouragement, lack of goals, or confusion.

Import: A person should expect negative outcomes in spite of good intentions, realistic goals, and active effort, or because of confusion or disorganization. Challenges or setbacks may lead to despair, frustration, impulsive action, or inaction.

Illustration

Anthony, age 14-6, below average Wechsler IQ score, identified in the school with emotional disability, depression, and need for structure.

Card 1. He reading a book, I mean, he made something, he looks bored and he going to sleep. He don't have no ideas, that's it. [What do you think happened before that?] I don't know. [*I gave him additional prompts and reassurances.*] He was outside. [How do you think the story ends?] He still sad. [What do you think he is thinking?] He trying to come up with something. [*He was flipping the picture over and pushing it away, indicating that he doesn't want to do this, so I had to redirect and reassure him.*] He was playing a game. Then he went outside… with his um… project and he hit somebody and killed him. [Go on.] That's all I know. [Okay, well how does it turn out?] Still sad. I'm done with that one. [*He flips and pushes the card away.*]

2. *Poor Motivation*

At this level, the narrator displays some understanding of what is needed to produce desired outcomes but has not incorporated the self-reliance needed for independent achievement. Characters attain success with easier goals that are whimsically substituted or success follows upon reluctant or insufficient actions. Failure is due to barriers that are not clearly understood.

Positive Outcome:

- Intentions/goals may be clearly stated and prosocial or remain vague. Even in the absence of a well-formulated goal, some positive intent is articulated or implicit in the story.
- Dynamics include optimism without adequate reasons—a character simply forgets a problem, makes the best of it, or is happy having tried—and the feeling that success is empty or unrewarding and leads to tension.
- Actions are not directly pertinent to the task at hand or taken reluctantly; means to goals are vague or the character expends less effort than is required; actions are undertaken for approval, recognition, conformity, or self-centered motives; the character hopes for success or thinks about the problem; actions taken without commitment or interest; the character displays passive dependence on help or advice.

Import: A person can attain success despite actions that are reluctant, not directly pertinent to the goal, not fully adequate, or by setting "easy" goals.

Negative Outcome:

- Intentions/goals may be clearly stated and prosocial or remain vague. Even in the absence of a well-formulated goal, some positive intent is articulated or implicit in the story.
- Dynamics include frustration, boredom, or anger; external barriers preclude sufficient action or interfere with engaging in expected behaviors.

- Actions include thinking and planning but no direct effort; inter-
ference of extraneous factors; and tolerance of adversity or failure,
though action is possible.

Import: A person fails or is unhappy (when goals are prosocial) because of inadequately defined goals, internal or external barriers, or insufficient action, despite planning and thinking. The causes for failure or unhappiness are not clearly
understood by the character or narrator (rather, the story comprises associations
based on experiential regularities that have not been synthesized into useful convictions).

Illustration

Jason, age 12, average IQ score, was referred by parents who describe him as getting "stuck" when facing challenges and "shutting down."

Card 1. A little boy gets a violin for his birthday. He then wants to learn how
to play the violin. His grandfather plays the violin when he was young. His grandfather teaches him how to play the violin. And now he plays for a very famous
orchestra. [E: Tell me more.] He loves to play the violin and wants to teach his
kids how to play it. [E: What do you think he's thinking?] Learning how to play the
violin. [How do you think he's feeling?] A little depressed, a little confused.

3. Mildly Positive Motivation

At this level, the narrator appropriately recognizes difficulties involved in goal
attainment and the need for compensatory action, revision of goals, or seeking
of assistance. If barriers or adverse conditions cannot be overcome by sustained
effort or other appropriate means, the result is failure or unhappiness (with appropriate responsibility taken). If there are realistic compensatory strategies to
overcome obstacles, then success may follow. The linkages among the motivational
elements reflect adequate understanding of causality. Success is proportionate to
the goals set and strategies used (becoming world famous requires extraordinary
commitment). The motivational and volitional aspects of intentions or schemas
are present or strongly implied. The goals are evident, but reaction to the goal
may be mixed. The need for planning and instrumental activity is recognized, but
implementation of the intention poses difficulties.

Positive Outcome:
- Intentions/goals are prosocial and adequately articulated but involve
mixed feelings, are difficult to achieve, or are modest.
- Dynamics involve mixed or ambivalent reactions or the character
actively seeks extra help or advice before doing everything possible.
However, the character does not show blind dependence and judges

advice on its merits; others provide adequate support or inspiration. Some temporary tension or loss is associated with success.

- Action is maintained despite obstacles or initial discouragement; the character expends effort, but the outcome may be uncertain, conditional, or viewed as a possibility; the character continues constructive action despite disapproval or temporary setback.

Import: A person attains success or happiness (possibly conditionally or after initial discouragement) with goals that are modest or with help from others prior to doing everything possible but still through realistic means.

Negative Outcome:
- Intentions/goals are prosocial, realistic, and adequately stated.
- Dynamics include a grasping of the implications of characters' lack of planning, mistakes, procrastination, negative attitudes, or poor organization as well as of excessive independence or refusal to heed sound advice.
- Actions include insufficient strategic effort (though planning may have taken place).

Import: Insufficient planning or effort leads to appropriate negative consequences and the character learns the lesson. The story is well-constructed, conveying the sense that the narrator both possesses and can use this insight.

Illustration

Mathew, age 11-8, Wechsler IQ score in the superior range.

Card 1. A boy wanted a violin, wanted it a lot so he asked his parents to get him one and they said no. He kept asking them, and, finally they thought he really wanted it so finally they got him one. Now that he has one, he doesn't know what to do with it. He's thinking about maybe he didn't really want it after all. Eventually, he learns how to play and he feels good about himself and becomes a famous violinist.

4. High Motivation

At this level, the narrator operates from a framework of personal and social responsibility and articulates a realistic understanding of connections among circumstances (pictured stimuli and story events), goals, intentions, actions, and outcomes. The narrator's schema clearly and cohesively represents the various elements needed to sustain long-term, motivated action.

Positive Outcome:
- Intentions/goals are realistic, clearly articulated, and reflect long-term purpose.

- Dynamics reflect interest, principles, standards, and realistic self-confidence. Characters display self-determination but are able to seek advice after doing everything possible and accept legitimate demands. They exhibit a positive attitude toward work and show preference for values that are abstract, ethical, and altruistic rather than materialistic or expedient.
- Actions are autonomous, prosocial, respectful of others, sufficient for stated goals and outcomes, and reflect principles.

Import: Realistic goals or self-determined, principled actions lead to success, satisfaction, happiness, or harmonious relationships.

Negative Outcome:
- Intentions/goals include ill intent, self-glorification, self-centered goals, or mistaken action.
- Dynamics include recognizing the inappropriateness of blaming failure on others and understanding the negative implications of boredom, disinterest, inadequate means, or impulsive action. The narrator recognizes other factors such as blind dependence, defiance, and refusal to seek or accept reasonable help or advice as contributing to negative outcomes.
- Actions are cohesive with outcomes, and intention-action-outcome sequences are compatible with each other and with the outcome. Thus, inaction, unreasonable action, or ill-intended action is associated with negative outcomes, thereby representing a prosocial conviction and cohesion of motivational elements.

Import: Ill-intended actions or inadequate means (e.g., "too little, too late") lead to failure, unhappiness, or disrupted relationships. Ill-intended actions, even if accompanied by success, are punished. Again, there is a sense that the narrator possesses and can use this insight.

Illustration
Robert, age 9–7, above average Wechsler IQ score.

Card 1. What's that thing right there? Hmmm. Ah, this boy wants to take an instrument lesson. He wants to take piano, and his mom wants him to take violin. So she signed him up for violin lessons. So he's looking at the violin feeling sad. [E: Turns out?] Then on his first violin lesson it turned out that he liked it.

Table 7.1 Levels of Motivation in Relation to Outcome—The Coherence of the Connections Between Means and Outcomes in Reference to the Goal or Intention

	Positive Story Outcome	Negative Story Outcome
Level One: Extremely Poor Motivation Unrealistic, illogical, or no connections among goals, actions, and outcomes ("success without goals or efforts" or "failure follows hard work").	**Intentions/Goals**—Vague desire, unstated, ill intended, unrealistic, trivial, inadequately defined, or extremely lofty. **Dynamics**—Boredom, obvious lack of interest or inability to withstand setback or frustration; negative attitude toward effort or success. **Actions**—Absence of effort, aimless activity, blind dependence on, rebellious defiance of, or extreme pressure by others. Unlikely, antisocial, or nonconstructive actions. Wishful thinking with no realistic basis. **Conviction**—Success or happiness can be attained without clear/realistic goals, long-term investment, or interest, or active effort, or through unrealistic or antisocial means.	**Intentions/Goals**—Unclear, unstated, inappropriate, or realistic and socially appropriate. **Dynamics**—Expecting failure despite active effort or self-determined choices or because of difficulty with understanding or meeting demands. Failure or adversity cannot be overcome, is blamed on others, or leads to despair, frustration, inaction, hopelessness, pretense, deceit, escape, fantasy, dream, sleep, inadequacy, or confusion. **Actions**—Positive effort that may be misunderstood or thwarted by circumstance or absence of constructive action due to discouragement, lack of goals, or confusion. **Conviction**—Negative outcomes are expected despite good intentions, realistic goals, and prosocial actions or active effort or because of confusion or extreme disorganization.

(continued)

Table 7.1 (Continued)

	Positive Story Outcome	Negative Story Outcome
Level Two: Poor Motivation Some understanding of means to ends but absence of self-reliance needed for independent achievement (success with easier goals, whimsically substituted; success follows reluctant or insufficient actions; barriers to failure not clearly understood).	**Intentions/Goals**—Clearly stated and prosocial or vague. **Dynamics**—Optimism without adequate reasons; character forgets, makes the best of it, is happy having tried; success is empty or unrewarding and leads to tension. **Actions**—Not directly pertinent to the task at hand; taken reluctantly; means to goals are vague or less than required effort is expended. Actions are undertaken for approval, recognition, conformity, or self-centered motives; hoping for success or thinking about the problem; actions taken without commitment or interest; passive dependence on help or advice. **Conviction**—Success or happiness can be attained despite actions that are reluctant, or not directly pertinent to the goal nor fully adequate or by setting "easy" goals.	**Intentions/Goals**—Clearly stated and prosocial or vague. **Dynamics**—Frustration, boredom, anger, or external barriers preclude sufficient action or expected behavior. **Actions**—Thinking and planning have occurred, but no action is taken; extraneous factors have interfered; adversity or failure is tolerated, though action is possible. **Conviction**—Failure or unhappiness (when goals are prosocial) may be due to internal or external barriers or insufficient action—despite planning and thinking or wanting to act differently. (The causes for failure or unhappiness are not clearly understood by the character or narrator.)
Level Three: Mildly Positive Motivation The goals are evident and need for planning and action is recognized, but implementation of the intention poses difficulties. Outcomes are in tune with means and social causality and are proportionate to the goals set and strategies used.	**Intentions/Goals**—Prosocial and adequately defined but modest, very difficult, and/or involving mixed feelings. **Dynamics**—Mixed or ambivalent; character actively seeks extra help or advice before doing everything possible. Dependence on others who provide adequate support or inspiration, but dependence is not blind as advice is judged on its own merits; some temporary tension or loss is associated with success. **Actions**—Maintained despite obstacles or initial discouragement; effort is expended but the outcome may be uncertain, conditional, or viewed as a possibility. **Conviction**—Success or happiness are attained (possibly conditionally) or after initial discouragement or with help from others prior to doing everything possible through realistic means.	**Intentions/Goals**—Prosocial and adequately defined. **Dynamics**—Narrator grasps implications of character's lack of planning, mistakes, procrastination, negative attitudes, or poor organization as well as excessive independence, refusal to heed sound advice. **Actions**—Insufficient strategic effort (though planning may have occurred). **Conviction**—Insufficient planning or effort leads to appropriate negative consequences and lesson learned. (The story is well-constructed conveying a sense that the narrator possesses and can utilize this insight.)

Table 7.1 (Continued)

	Positive Story Outcome	Negative Story Outcome
Level Four: **High** **Motivation** Connections among circumstances (pictured stimuli and story events), goals, intentions, actions, and outcomes are clear, specific, and realistic, congruent with sustained independent, socially responsible goal pursuit.	**Intentions/Goals**—Realistic, clearly articulated, and reflect long-term purpose. **Dynamics**—Interest, principles, standards, and realistic self-confidence. Self-determination, but able to seek advice after doing everything possible; acceptance of legitimate pressure. Positive attitude toward work; preference for values that are abstract, ethical, altruistic rather than materialistic or expedient. **Actions**—Autonomous, prosocial, respectful of others, sufficient for stated goals and outcomes and in keeping with principles. **Conviction**—Realistic goals, self-determined, principled actions lead to success, happiness, or harmonious relationships.	**Intentions/Goals**—Ill intent, self-glorification, self-centered goals, or mistaken action. **Dynamics**—The narrator recognizes inappropriateness of characters' intentions or prior action (e.g., inadequate or impulsive). **Actions**—Actions and outcomes are cohesive and convey prosocial principled conviction. **Conviction**—Ill-intended actions or inadequate means (e.g., "too little, too late") lead to failure, unhappiness, or disrupted relationships. Ill-intended actions, even if accompanied by success, are punished. (Again, there is a sense that the narrator possesses and can utilize this insight.)

TAT AND SELF-REGULATION

Self-regulation is an overarching construct, subsuming motivation, because it incorporates multiple processes, controlled and automatic, involved in setting/maintaining goals and pursuing intended courses of action (see Rapid Reference 7.4). As noted previously, effortful regulation is easily depleted and themes of depletion in TAT stories should be carefully reviewed as possibly suggesting that effortful self-regulatory processes may be difficult to sustain.

Self-regulation to organize and prioritize goal-relevant activities involves balancing individualistic strivings with relational goals (Andersen & Chen, 2002; Baldwin, 1992; Markus & Kitayama, 1991) and the capacity to override distractions or other short-term pulls to engage in actions that serve broader purposes. Self-regulation of behavior within socially appropriate bounds is facilitated

≋ Rapid Reference 7.4

Automatic and Controlled Processes

Automatic processes: Automatic processes that do not require active guidance by the individual often influence behaviors. These processes include mental associations, habits, feelings, and action tendencies that are activated automatically and may be difficult to control.

Controlled processes: Deliberate regulation termed *executive function and effortful control* entails the control of prepotent response tendencies and substituting an alternative, more appropriate response. Both types of controlled processes are enabled by the capacity for initiation, planning, and anticipation. However, the term *executive* function has been used in the context of controlling cognitive responses such as attention shifting and working memory in structured tasks, whereas the term *effortful control* has been used in socioaffective contexts as measured with informant or self-report (Blair & Razza, 2007; Rothbart, Ahadi, & Evans, 2000; MacDonald, 2008; Zelazo & Cunningham, 2007).

Multiple processes: Self-regulation at any given time is not purely a function of automatic or controlled processes but of their combinations (Sherman, Gawronski, Gonsalkorale, Hugenberg, Allen, & Groom, 2008). Controlled processing may prevent prepotent response tendencies from becoming enacted into behaviors. Using deliberate thought to correct "errors" in automatic (schema-driven) information processing, hence overriding automatic control, is important to social regulation (Richeson & Shelton, 2003). However, use of such cognitive controls requires the individual to recognize the relevance of information in the surroundings to the activated schemas.

by resources to moderate emotional reactivity and to deploy attention flexibly (Eisenberg & Fabes, 1992; Kochanska & Aksan, 1995; Rothbart & Bates, 2006). Executive self-regulation allows individuals to judge whether or not an automatic schema-based response tendency is appropriate to a situation and to substitute another response if necessary(e.g., MacDonald, 2008).

A full accounting of self-regulatory dynamics considers the ongoing interplay of automatic and controlled processing as individuals calibrate and re-calibrate their decisions and actions based on changing situational cues, temperamental exigencies, and intentions housed in the schemas.

Self-regulation is context dependent because tasks and settings differ in their self-regulatory demands. As noted in Chapter 1, the TAT task makes self-regulatory demands that are analogous to those of settings that are ill-defined with respect to what is "the correct" response. Accordingly, assessment of any psychological construct such as executive functioning using highly structured tasks may not predict its expression in a less structured setting (Chaytor & Schmitter-Edgecombe, 2003). Real-world problem solving involves planning and implementing hierarchically arranged goals and subgoals, but highly structured tasks minimize the role of these processes. To navigate the complexities of day-to-day encounters, individuals balance among numerous self-regulatory demands to enable *self-monitoring* to calibrate responses in the moment, *self-direction* to channel activities in line with a specific goal, and *self-determination* to bring harmony and balance among various priorities. These three increasingly complex self-regulatory mechanisms manifest themselves in storytelling. Typically, individuals juggle multiple goals, short and long term, that are served by a hierarchy of self-regulatory processes that operate as the individual composes stories to pictured stimuli.

Self-Monitoring

The modulation and calibration of responses to changing cues in the current situation comprises a basic adaptive repertoire that enables the individual to function in the moment. Self-monitoring to keep behavior in line with the demands of the immediate situation requires cognitive control mechanisms to allocate attention to what is most relevant and behavioral regulation to suppress inappropriate behaviors (Nigg & Casey, 2005). The individual relies on mental models of what is expected in the situation and on working memory to keep track of changing cues in order to adjust behavior on an ongoing basis. An individual may monitor actions to be appropriate in the immediate context but may not necessarily gear behavior to a purpose beyond the short term. General indicators of adequate self-monitoring of ideas, of affective expression, and of other behaviors to the requirements of the immediate situation include (a) exhibiting appropriate behavior during the evaluation, such as attempting to modulate speed of telling the story with the examiner's writing pace, maintaining eye contact, and engaging in reciprocal conversation with the examiner; and (b) demonstrating basic narrative competencies, such as accurately interpreting the pictured stimulus and staying within the bounds of basic logic and social acceptability of story content.

Behavior During the Evaluation

When self-presentation is inappropriate, either in terms of behavior during the assessment (irrelevant conversation, unacceptable or unusual behavior) or in content of the story (gruesome, hostile, sadistic, bizarre), the individual is not using organized schemas to monitor thought processing or actions to social expectations.

Use of the Stimulus

Self-monitoring requires the individual to size up the relevant information in the surroundings. This awareness is indicated by the narrator's grasping the "gist" of the pictured scene.

Internal Logic of the Story

A narrative that is socially appropriate, free from contradictory details, perseverations, or clearly illogical ideas suggests that the narrator has listened to and remembered the unfolding story details.

Basically, self-monitoring entails the essential skills to gear actions and reactions to situational expectations. Going beyond self-monitoring requires not only continuous evaluation of the individual's activities over time but also increasing differentiation and integration of schemas to organize the immediately available environmental cues from lessons drawn from the past and according to implications for the future.

Self-Direction

Self-direction involves shifting attention and effort away from current situational pulls to more distant concerns. The internal organization of behavior permits individuals to extricate themselves from the draw of the immediate situation when necessary to pursue long-term adaptive demands. Self-direction entails prioritizing, sustaining, and monitoring behavior over time to resolve problems or deal with adverse situations, generate strategies and maintain efforts to accomplish tasks and to carry out complex sequences of behaviors, and meet long-term social expectations rather than attending only to current external presses. Self-monitoring is reactive to the immediate environment, whereas self-direction is more proactive and requires greater internal control of behavior. Various levels of difficulty maintaining intentionally controlled behavior are implicated in most DSM disorders such as

Attention-Deficit/Hyperactivity Disorder (ADHD), Mood Disorder, and Schizophrenia, as well as various conduct and character disorders (Frick & Lahey, 1991). For example, attentional deficits have been described as the control over attention by external contingencies rather than by the individual's goals (Barkley, 1997).

In the storytelling task self-monitoring in the absence of self-direction is reflected in stories that are organized around stimulus features, directions, external demands, or stereotypes. Self-direction is demonstrated by the portrayal of characters whose actions are directed toward a prosocial purpose, goal, or expectation beyond the provocation of the immediate circumstance depicted in the picture or described in the narrative. Furthermore, the narrative construction is monitored for cohesion, is constructed according to a plan, transcends the stimulus pull, and smoothly incorporates storytelling directions.

Self-Determination

The field of motivation has postulated various constructs to distinguish between goal-directed activities that are intrinsically valued from those that are socially promoted. Self-determination involves decisions, goals, or actions that balance the inner and outer aspects of experience, such as self-presentation with feelings; actions with intrinsic satisfaction, values or standards; and immediate demands with long-term aspirations. A subjective sense of self-determination is linked with higher levels of motivation and self-regulation (Deci, Eghrari, Patrick, & Leone, 1994; Deci & Ryan, 1985; Reeve, Deci, & Ryan, 2004).

In the storytelling task, self-determination requires resources needed for self-monitoring and self-direction as well as other assets, including: (a) integrative information processing, based on accurate grasp of social causality, in which decisions and behaviors are predicated on multiple considerations (e.g., self and others, now and later, outcome and process, expedience, principles); (b) investment in standards and prizing instrumental behaviors, not only outcomes; (c) realistic and flexible coping to rebound from failure or disappointment. Self-determination is evident in the depiction of characters whose actions are deliberate, purposeful, and organized, based on an integrated, well-elaborated inner life and reliance on internal standards or motives beyond successful outcomes.

LEVELS OF SELF-REGULATION

Self-regulatory processes are characterized along a continuum of complexity, proceeding from the very basic level of reacting to the incoming stimulation to the strategic pursuit of long-term goals or ideals in ways that simultaneously serve immediate and long-term functions for self and community. Increasing complexity of information processing permits multiple considerations to guide self-regulation, and well-developed schemas reduce the effort of processing information by providing templates that automatically and adaptively organize the cues in the surroundings in relation to the individual's goals, standards, or principles. The five levels of self-regulation presented in this section are derived from a synthesis of all the previously described coding dimensions (see Rapid Reference 7.5).

≡ Rapid Reference 7.5

Self-Regulation: Convergence of Cognition, Emotions, Relationships, and Motivation

(see Blankman, Teglasi, & Lawser, 2002; Bassan-Diamond, Teglasi, & Schmidt, 1995; Teglasi, 1993; Lohr, Teglasi, & French, 2004).

- Cognition. Higher levels of self-regulation entail increasingly accurate and nuanced awareness of self, others, and the world as well as increased organization of what is perceived, in line with dictates of logic and of social causality. Higher levels are characterized by applying greater synthesis to the organization of experience, whereas lower levels entail grasping reality by stringing together islands of experience that are not cohesively related to the past or future or to convictions or principles. Serious problems with self-regulation are evident when the narrator has difficulty keeping track of ideas (contradictions, excessive repetition, logical fallacies) or keeping content within the bounds of social acceptability (extreme violence, morbid helplessness).

- Organization of emotions and relationships. At higher levels of self-regulation, increased organization of inner life governs actions and standards for evaluation of self and others versus being reactive to external events or anticipated consequences. Increasingly well-integrated information processing enables modulation of short-term reactions or overreactions and nuanced problem-solving (i.e., that balances self-other interests and compromises among conflicting goals or motives).

- Motivation. Higher levels of self-regulation involve increased emphasis on well-organized concerns, goals, or principles that are planned and pursued proactively. Reactive, haphazard, or unplanned actions or decisions prompted by immediate needs, wishes, or provocations represent lower levels of self-regulation than those that involve more distant goals, foresight, or commitment to principles or values.

Given that schemas are activated by external cues, internal states (motives, feelings), or both, different schemas may be salient in different circumstances. A person who functions well under some conditions (e.g., structured or low risk or when in a better mood) may become indecisive and disorganized in others. It is not unusual for individuals to function below customary levels under the influence of intense emotions or during times of stress or transition. At such times, the individual may be less responsive to the needs of others and more focused on the immediate pressures. In the face of stress or other negative emotions, integrated schemas about the self and the world may not be activated (Gray, 1987; Kuhl, 1996).

1. *Dysregulation*

Form and content of stories reflect fragmentation in processing life experience associated with impairment in thought organization or affect modulation. These impairments are reflected in problems with reality testing, with formulation of intentions, and with establishing relationships. The individual reacts to faulty perceptions and cognitions such as a focus on minute, irrelevant considerations or is driven by intense emotions such as fear, panic, terror, or rage. The individual does not integrate relevant components of the immediate situation, and he or she has difficulty monitoring routine behavior without clear guidelines. Narratives may focus on isolated aspects of experiences (e.g., centering narrowly on elements of the picture without capturing the meaning of the stimulus) or global impressions (e.g., expressing global reactions to the scene as a whole). Five story characteristics, in addition to highly inappropriate behavior during the evaluation, suggest this level:

1. The narrator perseverates or overelaborates certain feelings and details or includes fragments of ideas that are not pertinent to the story as a whole.
2. The narrator shows faulty logic or contradictory or grossly incompatible ideas (e.g., juxtaposing different levels of abstraction).
3. The narrator shows faulty interpretation of the pictured scene.
4. The story contains implausible, socially inappropriate, or bizarre content.
5. A character acts or reacts on the basis of highly idiosyncratic views of causes and effects (e.g., remains in an extreme state of helplessness or deprivation).

At this level, the narrator's schemas fail to provide an accurate map to size up how the various cues in the immediate surroundings "go together." Because the need for well-organized schemas is minimized in highly structured situations (that do not require the appraisal of ambiguous information), individuals who tell stories at this level may perform within the highest ranges on some achievement and intellectual tests, yet function with little awareness of the implications of actions for others and for the self, even in familiar situations.

This level of self-regulation is illustrated by the following stories told to Cards 1 and 2 by Aaron, age 8-3, who is receiving special educational services for an emotional disability and who scored in the above average range of intelligence on the Wechsler Scale.

Card 1. The guy that is, the kid that wanted to draw a picture with stuff that he didn't have. [E: What happened before?] He needed some ink and a pencil, but there was a crack in the paper and he didn't have any tape. [E: Thinking?] He's thinking of drawing. [E: Feeling?] Umm, umm, concerned because he thinks he'll mess up on the picture and everyone will laugh at him. [E: Turns out?] He got the tape and finished his picture.

Aside from being discrepant from the contextual cues depicted in the stimulus, the story lacks cohesion due to arbitrary shifts in perspective (e.g., from being preoccupied with lack of tools for drawing to concern about being laughed at) and the introduction of ideas that don't fit well together (e.g., the boy needed some "ink and a pencil"). The initial premise of not having the materials with which to draw is rather trivial, especially in comparison to the more serious issue of the boy's concern about messing up the picture and being laughed at (i.e., juxtaposition of ideas at incompatible levels of conceptualization). This seemingly more serious twist in the story is casually introduced and then abandoned (i.e., introduction of ideas left incomplete), as if the narrator did not understand its significance. At the end, the boy "got the tape and finished the picture" but the narrator offers no explanation as to how "ink and pencil" are still missing.

Card 2. The old barn that had a big plowing field [short pause]. The, the farm didn't have any money, so they couldn't buy any tools but they did have a plow and a horse too. The man who had a horse, the horse was 50 years old and the girl, she always carries a book in her hand, and she wraps her hand around it, and she always wears her same clothes every day, and she wears her hair down really great, and she likes plowing the field, and she lives in the field farm with all the hay and animals, and she lived happily ever after. [E: Thinking?] They are thinking and having a great time with lots of money, and they can buy anything they want. [E: Feeling?] They feel, well, they got some money and they feel very, very happy.

A shift in perspective from the personification of the farm ("the farm didn't have any money") to the people in the scene ("so they couldn't buy any tools . . .") gives the story an "odd" quality. Eventually, thoughts about being rich make the characters happy; however, this is an unrealistic connection between means and ends. The description of the scene is unusual because it weaves together details that are at different levels of conceptualization ("the girl, she always carries books in her hand and she wraps her hand around it"). "Carrying books" is a more meaningful description than the trivial observation of "wrapping her hand around it." Other details, such as the age of the horse or the girl's wearing the same dress every day, are irrelevant to the story as a whole. The narrator ignores more substantial considerations such as the feelings or intentions of the people portrayed in the scene and the relationships among them.

2. *Immediacy*

Information processing and behavior center on the feelings or concerns of the moment without adequate reflection on prior events, future consequences, or implications for others. Judgments and actions are based on what immediately dominates awareness without relating salient aspects of the current situation to the past or future. Therefore, actions are reactive to the situation and are aimed at seeking immediate gain or relief without adequate reflection on future consequences or implications for self or others. Interpersonal information processing is distorted by selective attention to characteristics of others that serve the individual's wants or needs in the moment without attending to other pertinent considerations. The individual's self-presentation may pass muster in the moment, but over time behavioral inconsistencies become obvious to others, and the individual's lack of enduring commitments hampers adjustment. Long-term self-regulation is constrained by the individual's inability to sustain interest in situations that do not contribute to the immediate sense of well-being.

Emotions, intentions, thoughts, actions, and outcomes simply do not "add up" with respect to time perspective or intra- and interpersonal context but are not as jarringly incompatible or illogical as the previous level. Thus, content is not bizarre or socially inappropriate, but the narrator demonstrates poor understanding of cause-effect relationships vis-à-vis the long term. Lack of specificity in the description of inner states such as thoughts, feelings, or intentions may contribute to the impression of poor understanding of social causality. Five story characteristics pertain to this level:

1. The narrator relies exclusively on external or concrete cues to read emotion because of difficulty reading internal states; emotions are generated by a stimulus, unexpected event, or provocation (lack of anticipation) that is not clearly tied to the unfolding sequences of events.
2. Characters relate to each other based on their momentary affective impact without considering their intentions or circumstances. Thus, intent is not separated from impact.

3. Information processing is determined by what the individual desires without taking into account realistic considerations.

4. Goals emphasize short-term relief from unpleasant affective states or avoidance of conflict, or characters act or react without having anticipated the problem or with no plan.

5. Problem conceptualization is limited by focusing on the immediate.

Jim, age 16 and diagnosed with Conduct Disorder, illustrates this level in his stories about TAT cards 1 and 2.

Card 1. He's looking at a violin. Probably bored . . . doesn't want to do. Somebody put it in front of him. Feeling angry and mad 'cause somebody asked him to do it. So he doesn't do it.

The entire story occurs in the "moment" as captured by the picture without meaningful consideration of preceding context ("somebody puts it in front of him") and without regard to intention or rationale behind the vague request "to do it." Thus, understanding of social causality and separation of intent and impact are minimal. Poor understanding of social causality is also suggested by the seeming absence of consequence for noncompliance ("so he doesn't do it"). The boy's (and narrator's) awareness is dominated by immediate cues and feelings, and this style guides behavior that is reactive to the moment.

Card 2. Okay. This is a farm. Hmm, girl's coming home from school. Her mother and father is on the farm doing work. She has to do homework. She acts like she's going to do it but doesn't do it. . . . What I do? [E: Feeling?] Probably mad 'cause has to do homework but she's not going to do it.

There is an effort to avoid the burdens of work by pretending to do it. Again, pretending may work for the moment but does not serve longer purposes. In this story and the one above, the character is angry, and information processing and behavior are reactive to this feeling to the exclusion of other considerations.

3. External Direction

Various elements of the current situation, including relationships, are more realistically appraised, but information processing and behavior are externally guided, governed by others' standards and directed by feedback. At this level, the story content revolves around more long-term expectations and more general, less narrow concerns, such as conformity to more complex external demands (grades, rules, stereotyped social expectation), rather than the momentary provocation, whim, or avoidance of socially expected activity (e.g., going to school) characterizing the previous level. Nevertheless, perceptions of self and others are not differentiated, and flexibility is limited by reliance on rigid quid pro quo reciprocity. Emotions attributed to characters have a superficial, stereotypic flavor. Thus, characters suffer the consequences of ill-advised action but do not dwell on the intentions or on feelings of remorse.

At this level, the individual needs external feedback or bolstering to initiate or sustain independent, instrumental behavior, even when the tasks and goals are accepted as legitimate or self-imposed. The individual may be aware of the struggle to meet expectations or of problems prioritizing seemingly conflicting demands, which results in a sense of pressure to conform to acknowledged standards of conduct. Emotional and cognitive impediments to self-regulation may contribute to difficulty giving inner direction to sustained efforts without external validation or sources of motivation. The need for external sources of regulation may be rooted in mild problems with sustaining attention, regulating emotion, or organizing ideas. The individual may perceive day-to-day expectations as legitimate but burdensome, and self-direction is vulnerable to derailment. Six characteristics of stories apply to this level:

1. The narrator is aware of inner motives and separation of impact from intent but places emphasis on external events rather than insight or inner direction.

2. Perceived norms or consequences guide behavior rather than personal commitment. Characters do the right thing due to external pressure, approval, duty, or reward or to avert potential negative consequences.

3. Characters may have problems carrying out intentions or acting constructively on insight.

4. Limited intrinsic motivation places burdensome demands on characters to meet legitimate external demands or attain goals and aspirations without external incentive.

5. The narrator may emphasize the details of the picture to bolster judgment but is able to get beyond the cues provided.

6. Characters may need external support due to affective sensitivity (e.g., tendency to experience anxiety and/or frustration) in response to performance demands.

Stories told by Jaime, age 10-9, with a very superior IQ score, illustrate this level. Her teacher describes her as doing very well academically but experiencing some difficulty with interpersonal relationships.

Card 1. Okay. This boy, he is sad because his mother told him that he had to practice violin otherwise he would be in trouble. Now, this boy doesn't like to practice violin, and he's mad at his mother. And he wants to break the violin except it's an expensive violin and his grandfather gave it to his mother and his mother gave it to him so he knows he shouldn't break it. But he practices but without heart and soul.

The boy is aware of the meaning that the violin has for his family but does not share this connection with the family tradition. He feels stuck with his resentment and plays "without heart and soul." The boy regulates behaviors to the demands of the family but he requires the threat of external consequences to do so. The source of motivation and regulation is extrinsic.

Card 2. Can I study the picture for a little? Okay, this will be funny. In the picture there is a big farm and no civilization around for 20 miles. The girl's mother is pregnant and the girl's mother has some books on how to give birth and the little girl has to study it so she could help her mother give birth. The man is her brother, and he wants a boy except the girl wants a sister and they fight about it. A few weeks later the mother gives birth to twins, a boy and a girl. So both kids are satisfied. Oh, I forgot to say that the reason the man couldn't help the mother give birth is that he had to attend to the farmwork.

The narrator resourcefully pulled together the apparent pregnancy of the woman with the girl carrying the books. In contrast to the solitary activity needed to comply with family expectations in Card 1, Jaime is more comfortable and resourceful when called on to assume an important helping role. Jaime's external orientation is evident in the nature of the conflict between the brother and sister and its external resolution (birth of twins). The reason given for the man's inability to help was possibly based on an inflexible adherence to the stimulus ("had to attend to the farmwork") or difficulty balancing activities or collaborating. It would not be unreasonable to temporarily set aside farmwork to attend to a pressing need. However, external demands seem to take priority over internally organized actions, cooperation, or compromise.

4. *Internal Direction*

Information processing and behavior are guided by internal representations of standards and values. Action at this level is proactive, modulated, and internally organized, but it emphasizes cultural values or standards rather than personal commitment to principles. Characters' actions and reactions are set in a reasonable context that is consistent with but transcends the immediate environmental pull or provocation. A greater sense of competence than at the previous level imparts more initiative and persistence of goal-directed behavior as appropriate for desired ends. Task engagement and interpersonal reciprocity no longer have the demanding flavor of the previous level. Nevertheless, the thoughts, feelings, and behaviors, though cohesive and oriented to the long term, are organized around meeting adaptive demands or goals rather than emphasizing investment in a standard or commitment to principles. Persons operating at this level may be vulnerable to experiencing a relatively mild duality between their behaviors spurred by self-attributed motives (internalized standards not fully supported by temperamentally-based preferences) and implicit motives.

The individual displays more self-reliance in the pursuit of long-term interests and maintains more durable interpersonal connections than at the previous level. Despite some specific blind spots, individuals functioning at this level are able to balance specific goals with concerns for family and friends and coordinate long- and short-term considerations. The narrative is well-organized, and characters anticipate, plan, and gear their efforts toward prosocial ends.

This level is illustrated by #203, a student in kindergarten participating in a research study.

Card 1. He feels sad. Then he still's sad. He can't . . . doesn't know how to play it. He tries to play it but it sounds squeaky and ugly. [E: Thinking?] How would it sound if he knew how to play it. Then he tries again and then he does it good.

The boy begins the process of playing the instrument by taking initiative to change the "squeaky" sound, and then "he does it good." The language is simplistic, as appropriate for a 5-year-old, but the schema is sophisticated.

Card 2. What's happening here is this girl has her books in her hands. There's a farm, too. There's a boy with his horse. There is a lady by a tree. They are sad because they don't have food. They try to grow food. All of them work together and they make the food grow and they are happy.

At first, the narrator merely described stimulus elements then tells a simple story about a family that works together to meet a common goal. At the end, the family is happy having resolved the problem by growing the food that they need.

5. *Self-Determination*

A complex and well-integrated inner framework for information processing is evident in the cohesiveness among the described circumstance and characters' thoughts, feelings, actions, and outcomes. Multiple considerations are seamlessly integrated within and across perspectives. The narrator incorporates the nuances of the stimuli without glossing over the intense negative emotions depicted. Thoughts, feelings, actions, sequences of events, and views of various characters are well-coordinated in relative emphasis, context, and timeframe. Characters engage in deliberate, planned, volitional, autonomous, and purposeful action or decision with realistic outcomes. They are highly invested in the process of these activities, with outcomes being important but secondary. The combination of complex information processing and a balance between relatedness and autonomy permit the evaluation of people as they are, apart from the feelings or needs of the perceiver.

Besides having all the characteristics of the previous level, stories at this level indicate (1) inner standards for self-evaluation or conduct (explicit or implied) in the story content and structure, (2) abstract aims or principles that give coherence to the stream of events or govern behavior, and (3) a valuing of goal-related activities as intrinsically satisfying or serving a purpose distinct from the outcome. Self-determination involves an intrinsic drive to meet standards or goals that are valued beyond their connection to desired ends. The instrumental activities themselves are sustaining to the individual, sometimes even at the expense of the outcome. Even at the highest levels of self-regulation, there may be temporary or situation-specific lapses of self-monitoring or self-direction due to stress, fatigue, or intense emotion.

This level is illustrated by stories told by Benjie, age 9-11, described by his teachers as highly motivated, empathic, and respected by his peers.

Card 1. The boy has a violin except he can't play it very nicely. So he's kind of upset because he can't figure out how to play it well. You want to know what I think this thing is? [Points to the paper under the violin] [E: Up to you.] He's thinking whether he should keep trying or quit it because he doesn't know how to play it. [E: Turns out?] He gives up because he decides that he'll never be able to do it.

The boy is upset because he can't figure out how to play the violin well. This is an inner concern having to do with standards and not a reaction to external demand. Given the premise that this is a voluntary activity, the tension shifts to the process of making a decision about whether the boy should continue with the violin or quit. The autonomous decision is not a reaction to frustration but made according to a deliberate process of concluding that the boy will "never be able to do it."

Card 2. It looks like a family in the mid to late 1800s, and there's the mother who looks like she's taking a rest, and there's either one of the sons or the father who's taking the horse, and one of the girls looks like she has just read a book, and she's coming back to the house with the book she read. I'm not sure they let girls go to school at that time. Otherwise, I would have said she's coming home from school. [E: Anything going on in the family?] Just looks like they're trying to get the day's work done so they can make a living.

In describing the farm, Benjie is concerned with interpreting the stimulus in the proper historical context (the 1800s). Thus, in processing information, he goes well beyond immediate considerations, even struggling with whether "they let girls go to school at that time." The narrator is too concerned with being precise to make up just any story that seems logical by today's standards. He finally tells a simple story about a family trying to get their work done so they can make a living. Benjie's previous story also hints at his precision and high standards.

This seemingly simple story might be coded at Level 4, except for two considerations that bring it up to Level 5. First, the effort to give a historical context and the precision to keep story details compatible with the social realities of the time and pictured cues suggest a sophisticated approach to information processing and self-regulation. (Message: Whatever the historical time and place, family members work together to earn a living.) Second, the implied understanding of individuality in the context of a common goal indicates a complex and sophisticated schema. (Message: Individuals are free to pursue their interests, such as "reading books," while cooperating to "make a living.")

Table 7.2 Levels of Self-Regulation

Level One: Dysregulation—Form and content of stories reflect fragmentation in processing life experience associated with impairment in thought organization (e.g., ideas out of context; implausible sequence of events; illogical or bizarre ideas; inconsistent level of conceptualization; perseveration). The person reacts to faulty perceptions provoked by minute, irrelevant considerations or is hopelessly immobilized. The respondent may focus narrowly on elements of the picture without capturing the meaning or may express global reactions to the stimulus as a whole. Characters act and react without awareness of causes and effects, and/ or the narrator's behavior during the evaluation is clearly inappropriate. Relevant components of the immediate situation are not integrated, and the individual has difficulty monitoring routine behavior without clear guidelines.

Level Two: Immediacy—Information processing and behavior relate to the moment without adequate reflection on prior history, future consequences, or implications for others. Judgments and actions are based on what immediately dominates awareness without organization or integration of salient aspects of the current situation with important but remote implications. Self-monitoring may pass muster in the moment, but longer term self-direction is hampered by inability to maintain interest in situations that do not contribute to immediate sense of well-being. Actions are aimed at seeking immediate gain or relief. Feelings are not regulated internally but evoked by immediate external circumstances. Thus, intentions behind actions are not clearly distinct from their impact.

Level Three: External Direction—Information processing and behavior are guided by externally imposed standards, feedback, or necessity (e.g., adverse event) rather than by the provocation or whim of the moment. Various elements of the current situation and relationships are more realistically assessed than at previous levels (including a distinction between intent and impact, awareness of rules and expectations, quid pro quo reciprocity). Story content revolves around more long-term expectations, more general, less narrow, or trivial concerns, but might be mildly unrealistic or naive because perceptions of self and others are not well differentiated. There may be a sense of pressure to meet demands of others or to conform to acknowledged standards of conduct rather than being directed by inner values or standards. External sources of motivation or reassurance are needed to tolerate frustration and persist in long-term instrumental action.

(continued)

Table 7.2 (Continued)

Level Four: Internal Direction—Information processing and behavior are implicitly guided by standards and prosocial values that are internally represented and that the individual feels competent to attain. The individual can balance personal concerns with needs of family and friends and coordinate short- and long-term considerations. Task engagement and interpersonal reciprocity do not have the demanding flavor of the previous level but lack the personal conviction of the highest level. There is more initiative and greater organization of thoughts, emotions, and behaviors. Initiative and effort are appropriate for desired ends and/or for meeting adaptive demands (well-organized and long term).

Level Five: Self-Determination—Information processing is complex and responsible as indicated by stories that elaborate inner experience within or across characters in ways that are cohesive with the stimulus, described circumstance, actions, and outcomes. Thus, characters' intentions, thoughts, feelings, actions, outcomes, and story events are well-coordinated in relative emphasis, context, and timeframe. Characters are invested in autonomous, socially responsible, and purposeful action and are well planned and dedicated to enduring principles. Information processing is more complex than the previous level, incorporating multiple dimensions of experience and perspectives of relevant others over the long term. Therefore, people and events may be evaluated as they are, apart from the feelings or needs of the perceiver. Standards or goals are valued beyond their connection to desired ends; the instrumental activities themselves are sustaining to the individual.

(Choose one level for each story)

Card	1	2										

CASE ILLUSTRATIONS

Sandra

The TAT stories of Sandra, a 19-year-old college student, demonstrate that, for the purpose of intervention, it is important to understand the gap between a person's intentions and the self-regulatory resources to pursue them. Figures 7.1 and 7.2 exhibit the coding of the protocol according to the variables introduced in this chapter. Sandra was evaluated at the request of her therapist because of an impasse after 6 months of regular attendance of sessions. Sandra's participation in therapy was at the insistence of her parents who were concerned because she seemed to have "no direction in life." As part of the evaluation, the professional administered the TAT, the Wechsler Adult Intelligence Scale, and the Rorschach technique.

Card 1. . . . Don't like pictures. Not all of them . . . Umm . . . like story, like once upon a time. This is a boy . . . He's . . . okay, he . . . is it a violin? I don't know. Can I say two things? [E: Whatever you want.] He's either frustrated because he can't play it or he's sad because he's not allowed to play it anymore. He wants to play it but for some reason he can't . . . [stares at picture] [E: Turns out?] He becomes a great, did I say that was a violin?, violin player, and he's happy. [E: Okay, I think you have the idea.]

Import: Even if a person has trouble setting and pursuing goals, that person simply assumes that someday he or she will be very successful and happy.

Sandra is put off by the task and vacillates in her interpretation of the pictured scene as she does in her own intentions. The story content is appropriate to the stimulus, but Sandra cannot determine whether the boy is experiencing internal (frustration) or external (not allowed) barriers to achievement. In any case, the narrator takes no heed and describes the boy as becoming a great violinist, seemingly without effort. This lack of connection between means and outcomes parallels Sandra's own difficulties with clearly defining goals, overcoming obstacles, and taking the necessary steps to accomplish her intentions.

Card 2. God! These things are . . . Okay, there's . . . [stares] . . . this girl on her way to school, she's walking to school, and she sees this man working in the field, and that's his wife watching him. His wife's talking to him I guess, may be talking to him. He's working with his horse on the farm, and she's thinking that she doesn't want to look like that when she gets older, like the lady. She doesn't want to live on the farm. She feels sorry for that lady, for both, for the lady. So she goes to school to get an education so she's not like them.

Import: When a person sees the humdrum life of others, that person is reminded to go to school and get a good education so he or she doesn't have to be like them.

The girl goes to school to avoid becoming what she fears, not because she is interested in learning. Sandra gives lip service to the importance of education, but her implicit schema does not imbue learning or the effort involved with positive affect. In general, Sandra does not delve into the inner world of characters but relies on the stimulus or external appearances ("doesn't want to look like the lady") and social conventions (getting an education). Thus, external structure and supports guide her goal-directed actions.

Card 3BM. Don't know what this is . . . umm . . . guess it's a girl. A boy or girl, either sleeping, crying, or . . . umm . . . [frustrated] don't even know what. [Examiner repeats directions.] I guess she's crying because . . . okay, this doesn't make sense though. [stares as if answer is in the card] I think they're car keys. No idea. This is dumb. She's crying because . . . what is that thing is . . . someone stole her car. She has no way home from this place. So then she calls the police and tells them that her car is missing. Eventually they find her car, and then she's happy. Can you tell me what that is? [E: It can look like different things to different people.]

Import: Without structure, it's hard to know what's going on, but if a person looks for clues in the environment and asks for help, things will work out eventually (though he or she is stuck for the moment).

Sandra doesn't feel comfortable making decisions without clear expectations. She initially vacillates before settling on a plot. In the process, she became frustrated, stating that the task was dumb, but she responded to encouragement. This tendency to blame outside factors is consistent with her reliance on the environment to regulate her behavior. The character's calling the police is a quick and conventional reaction to the stolen car and doesn't address the other problem of having "no way home from this place." Thus, Sandra does not invest sufficient energy into the task to tie up the loose ends, and the character resolves only part of her problem. Sandra's incomplete processing of information (only dealing with part of the problem) and limited resources (no internal representation of possible sources of support, obvious frustration with the task, and unsystematic approach to narrating the story) suggest why she has difficulty regulating her behavior to accomplish long-term purposes (in the absence of supportive structures).

Card 4. Okay, . . . this is a man and a woman who . . . they either just had a fight, or he wants to go somewhere, and she doesn't want him to go. Okay, she's trying to persuade him either not to go or to forgive her. And then, I guess eventually he does it, he forgives her or he doesn't, or he might go, or he'll stay. And they live happily ever after.

Import: Even when the problem between two people remains unclear and unresolved, if they try to work things out, they can live happily ever after.

Process Import: You are determined to give this conflict a happy outcome, but you are not clear about the process.

Again, Sandra cannot commit to one story line. Her vacillation about what's going on in the picture (noted in several cards) suggests that she feels uncertain of her judgment in situations that are somewhat ambiguous and depends on external cues and supports. The story ends happily but without a resolution to the dilemma. As with previous stories, the connection between means and ends is limited.

Card 5. Okay, can you make up people who aren't there? This is a lady who is coming to tell her children it's time for their nap. So she sticks her head in and says it's dinner time, and all the kids come to dinner. Everybody eats dinner, and kids go back and play. In the library, den, I think it's supposed to be the library.

Import: If a person intends to do one thing but does something that is related, it's just as well, and things work out.

Process Import: When you are not guided by structures and lose your train of thought, things work out if you find a familiar track.

The lady is coming to tell her children it's time for their naps but calls them to dinner instead. This twist in the story suggests that Sandra is not monitoring the details (also seen in other stories) and has difficulty sustaining her own intentions in the absence of support. Her query about introducing additional characters also points to her need for external guidance.

Card 6BM. This man and his mother . . . Okay . . . [laugh] . . . he's coming to tell her he's moving away [laugh] cause of his job he was transferred somewhere, and she's upset. Doesn't want him to go. She's looking out the window wondering what she'll do without him around and . . . [asks to read story] he explains to her that he has to go. Well, then she understands his reasoning but she still doesn't want him to go, but she understands it's the best thing for him so she lets him go, not not lets him, she's not angry 'cause he can do whatever he wants. She gives him her blessing, "do you know what I mean?" But she's still upset, no hard feelings. They say goodbye. How many more?

Import: If a man explains why he must leave his mother (job transfer), she understands and, despite her sadness, "gives her blessing."

This story provides more cohesive connections among the narrative elements (circumstances, intentions, actions, and outcomes). However, no real action is required—one character simply needs to understand the other. The son explains that he has to go, and the mother understands. Still, the conventional goodbye seems a bit abrupt as no plans are made to ease the separation.

Card 8BM. Weird! I don't know what this kid's doing. Okay. Is this . . . Oh, you can't tell me. The man has been shot and two men, possibly doctors, but I doubt it. The two men are trying to remove the bullet and save his life—his son . . . daughter, don't know . . . son is praying that his father will live and survive this awful tragedy . . . and . . . okay, then it turned out, seems they're lost in the woods . . . ok, they fix him up, these men, and then they get him to a hospital, and he survives and thanks these men for saving his life.

Import: When a boy's father is shot in the woods, others will come on the scene to do what is necessary to save his life while the son prays, and later the father expresses gratitude.

After the father is shot, the two rescuers appear on the scene without any initiative on the part of the son. Sandra perceives others as helpful in playing out their conventional roles, but the characters facing the dilemma have limited resources.

Card 7GF. Oh God . . . [laughs] . . . okay. [turns it over, chews finger, makes faces] Okay, this girl . . . in with her mother or teacher . . . wait. This lady is reading to this little girl, a sad story. What else should I say? The girl doesn't look like she's paying attention, but she really is. She's amazed by the story. She's gonna drop this kid, that's how shocked she is. It's a baby doll, not real. Then she finishes the story, and the child leaves. [pauses] Hated it. Glad it's over. I don't understand how you can make anything from that.

Process Import: In a difficult situation, if you don't want to deal with the tensions, you can simply pretend that things are not the way they seem.

The narrator side-stepped the tension in this picture by describing the girl, who seems not to be paying attention, as being so engrossed that she fails to hold on to the baby who (fortunately) turns out to be a doll. Sandra's coping strategy of avoiding tension or unpleasantness is evident in other stories that conclude happily but without the necessary intervening processes. Analogously, her characters are limited in their instrumental actions to resolve the problems or dilemmas set before them. For Sandra, the TAT task was frustrating and onerous. Her discomfort with the ambiguity of the pictures and the task, coupled with her reliance on external cues rather than on her own resources, made it difficult for her to settle on one explanation of the scene.

Narrative Summary

Sandra appears to be floundering in the campus setting because she is not intrinsically invested in the learning process and because she has not developed the resources necessary to regulate her behavior in the unstructured environment of a large university. She wants to stay in school because she believes that her future well-being depends on getting an education. However, she is not able to invest herself in the process of learning and has difficulty keeping a schedule for eating, sleeping, and attending classes. She told her examiner that in high school she also experienced difficulty getting up and would miss school on the average of once a week. Moreover, she rarely studied, cheated to get by, and admitted having significant involvement with drug abuse since the fifth grade. Sandra characterized her therapist (who had requested the evaluations) as not providing direction during the sessions and indicated that she did not discuss important issues because she wasn't asked about them. As a result, she just talked about meaningless topics. Sandra was clear about her desire to succeed academically, but at the same time, she acknowledged that she found school work aversive and recognized that she was not achieving her goals.

Sandra's scores on the structured Wechsler Scales were in the high average range and were otherwise unremarkable. However, the TAT provided many clues to explain Sandra's predicament. First, though Sandra was generally able to recognize the conflict or tension in stimuli, she had difficulty sticking to one explanation, mirroring the discomfort she feels in making judgments or decisions without clear external guidelines. The task itself was frustrating and burdensome, and without additional direction from the examiner, Sandra looked to the external cues. In doing so, she had difficulty developing the themes that she introduced, placing relatively greater emphasis on explaining the stimulus (external) than on elaborating feelings, thoughts, or intentions (internal). Moreover, the stories produced positive outcomes without sufficient plans, actions, or initiatives on the part of characters facing a dilemma, suggesting these resources are not available to guide Sandra's daily behavior.

Sandra needs more directive therapeutic interventions to help her put the external structures and supports in place. Subsequent to the evaluation Sandra worked on identifying and seeking the external structures that would prompt her to engage in behaviors to meet her goals (e.g., entering a sorority so she could join peers at regular meals; planning a realistic schedule and developing routines to enable her to get ready in the morning, be on time for classes, and study by forming *implementation intentions,* discussed earlier in the chapter). Sandra responded quickly to these external structures and began to feel increased control over her life. Subsequent sessions focused on ways to make these routines automatic and to examine the factors that impeded the development of connections between intentions, actions, and outcomes. As her implementation intentions became solidified and automated, the daily routines shifted to being activated by the environment. Accordingly, when the alarm clock rang, she did not deliberate about what to do next because the alarm was her cue to jump in the shower, which then cued other elements of the morning routine.

DON'T FORGET

Story analysis seeks answers to the "what" and "how" of motivation and of self-regulation.

1. What information about self, other, and the world is of interest to the individual?

2. What makes the person happy or unhappy? What does the person want? What is valued about accomplishments (e.g., outcomes, process, standards, harmonious relationships)?

3. What does the individual seek when choosing tasks, activities, goals, and risks (e.g., immediate relief, intrinsic interest)?

4. What are the individual's priorities in balancing different goals such as short- versus long-term or intrinsic interest, obligation, or external pressure?

5. What are the individual's expectations about support or hindrance from others and about the likelihood of accomplishing goals or getting what he or she wants?

(continued)

6. How cohesive and realistic are the various elements of motivation-related intentions, feelings, thoughts, actions, and anticipated outcomes?

7. How organized and planned are the actions in the pursuit of intentions?

Card	Import of Story	Choose Level of Motivation	
		Positive Outcome	Negative Outcome
1	Even if a person has trouble setting and pursuing goals, that person simply assumes that someday he or she will be very successful and happy.	1	
2	When a person sees the humdrum lives of others, that person is reminded to go to school to get a good education to avoid that life.	2	
3BM	Without structure, it's hard to know what's going on, but if a person looks for clues and asks for help, things will work out eventually.	2	
4	Even when the problem between two people remains unclear and unresolved, if they try to work things out, they can live happily ever after.	2	
5	If a person intends to do one thing but does something that is related, things work out just as well.	2	
6BM	If a man explains why he must leave his mother (job transfer), she understands and despite her sadness she gives her blessing.	3	
7GF	In a difficult situation, if someone doesn't want to deal with the tensions, he or she can simply pretend that things are not the way they seem.	1	
8BM	When a boy's father is shot in the woods, others will come on the scene to do what is necessary to save his life while the son prays, and later the father expresses gratitude.	2	

Figure 7.2 Import and Motivational Level

Note: If a meaningful import cannot be extracted from the story content, it may be derived from formal qualities of narrative structure or process.

Card	1	2	3BM	4	5	6BM	7GF	8BM
Sandra	2	3	2	2	2	3	2	3

Figure 7.3 Self-regulation

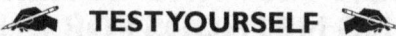

TEST YOURSELF

1. **Motivation and self-regulation are related because**
   (a) goals regulate thoughts, feelings, and behaviors.
   (b) self-regulation is an important goal that influences other goals.
   (c) both "a" and "b."
   (d) neither "a" nor "b."

2. **How is an "import" linked to motivation?**

3. **Motivation that is congruent with temperamental inclinations is associated with which of the following terms?**
   (a) introjection
   (b) integration
   (c) implementation intentions
   (d) self-control

4. **The designation of levels of motivation does not include**
   (a) goal setting.
   (b) goal maintenance.
   (c) the specific goal.
   (d) means to attain goals.

5. **How do the levels of self-regulation incorporate all previous coding dimensions?**

6. **To be rated at the highest level of motivation, a story must have a happy ending.**
   True or False?

7. **Self-regulation is characterized as optimal when the individual frequently engages in behaviors that go against the temperamental grain.**
   True or False?

Answers: 1. c; 2. incorporates the key components of motivation; 3. b; 4. c; 5. Cognitive, emotional, and motivational processes contribute to the development of broader self-regulatory schemas that guide perceptions of self, others, and the world; 6. False; 7. False.

Eight

ESSENTIALS OF THE CHILDREN'S APPERCEPTION TEST AND OTHER STORYTELLING METHODS FOR CHILDREN

All thematic apperception techniques use pictures to elicit stories, and require trained professionals to interpret the responses. The essential differences across methods reside in the specific pictures presented and the particular approaches used to analyze the stories. The development of storytelling tools subsequent to the introduction of the TAT has proceeded through the delineation and validation of various approaches for interpreting stories told about TAT pictures, the introduction of new sets of pictures without additional interpretive procedures, as exemplified by the Children's Apperception Test (CAT), and the packaging of new sets of pictures with interpretive criteria, such as the Roberts 2 (supplanting the Roberts Apperception Test for Children, RATC) and Tell-Me-A-Story (TEMAS). The term Thematic Apperception Test (TAT) is associated with the set of pictures (introduced by Murray and described in earlier chapters) across a wide range of interpretive procedures. In contrast, some picture sets are linked with a particular interpretive method. Without question, the TAT has been the most popular storytelling instrument in clinical use with adults (e.g., see Gieser & Stein, 1999) and is also useful with children and adolescents (Teglasi, 1993). This chapter describes three storytelling tests developed specifically for use with children or adolescents. In-depth coverage of every storytelling measure is unnecessary, as a solid grounding in one narrative technique should generalize to others (Russ, 1998).

CHILDREN'S APPERCEPTION TEST

The introduction of the Children's Apperception Test (CAT) was based on the premise that children between the ages of 3 and 10 would identify more with animal than with human figures (Bellak & Bellak, 1949, 1952). However, subsequent research did not support the contention that the CAT would be superior to the TAT and, where differences were found, the data pointed in favor of pictures with human figures (Holt, 1958; Light, 1954; for a review, see French, Graves,

& Levitt, 1983). Indeed, it has been suggested that the CAT pulls for regressive content (Eagle & Schwartz, 1994; Schwartz & Eagle, 1986) and may be less useful than the TAT, except possibly with the youngest children, ages 3 and 4.

In response to studies questioning the superiority of animal figures over those depicting humans, the Bellaks published the CAT-H, substituting human characters for the animal figures in the original CAT (Bellak & Bellak, 1965). In developing the human version, the authors aimed to make the two sets equivalent, but it was not possible to retain the same level of ambiguity in regard to age, gender, and cultural attributes of some of the figures. Although the Bellaks continued to prefer the original CAT, they acknowledged that the CAT-H may be more suitable with children between the ages of 7 and 10 or with highly intelligent younger children (who may find the animal figures to be "childish"). Studies comparing responses elicited by the CAT and CAT-H were not remarkably different (Gardner & Holmes, 1990; Haworth, 1966; Myler, Rosenkrantz, & Holmes, 1972; Neuringer & Livesay, 1970) and differences generally indicated that human cards were either equal or superior to the animal cards in evoking psychologically meaningful material. This conclusion held across various ages (preschool to sixth grade) and populations (well-adjusted, emotionally disturbed, intellectually retarded, or gifted). Other authors review the history of the CAT and CAT-H in greater depth (see Bellak & Abrams, 1997).

Despite the failure of research to support the superiority of CAT stimuli with children, it is important to remember that the cards (the original CAT and CAT-H) pull for specific themes (see Rapid Reference 8.1). Clinicians deal with individuals and the usefulness of specific thematic cards depends on the case. For instance, clinicians have noted the advantage of using the CAT with certain adult personality types (Kitron & Benzimen, 1990). The authors and others have considered use of the CAT animal figures to be advantageous (Kline & Svaste-Xuto, 1981) because of gender neutrality and crosscultural applicability. In an attempt to make the CAT administration more engaging for children, Hoar and Faust (1973) developed a jigsaw-puzzle version of the CAT cards. Thus, the CAT and its variations provide still another tool for the practitioner.

Each of the 10 CAT cards depicting animal figures in human-like situations was designed to clarify children's problems around various issues: eating, relating to parental figures as individuals and as a couple (primal scene, Oedipal feelings), fears of loneliness, sibling rivalry, toilet training, mastery, aggression, and acceptance by the adult world (see Rapid Reference 8.1). Whereas the authors designed the CAT stimuli to elicit content pertaining to universal issues according to a psychoanalytic view of development, they introduced a supplemental set of stimuli, the CAT-S (Bellak & Bellak, 1952), to learn about specific problems (see Rapid Reference 8.2). The examiner may select any single picture or combination from the supplemental set in addition to the CAT stimuli.

≣ *Rapid Reference 8.1*

CAT Cards

1. Chicks are seated around a table upon which a large bowl of food has been set. Off to one side is a large chicken, dimly outlined.
2. One bear pulls a rope on one side while another bear and a baby bear pull on the other side.
3. A lion with a pipe and cane sits in a chair. In the lower right corner a little mouse appears in a hole.
4. A kangaroo with a bonnet on her head carries a basket with a milk bottle. In her pouch is a baby kangaroo with a balloon. On a bicycle is a larger kangaroo child.
5. The card shows a darkened room with a large bed in the background and a crib (with two baby bears) in the foreground.
6. The card shows a darkened cave with two dimly outlined bear figures in the background and a baby bear in the foreground.
7. A tiger with bared fangs and claws leaps at a monkey that is also leaping through the air.
8. Two adult monkeys sit on a sofa drinking from tea cups. One adult monkey is in the foreground sitting on a hassock and talking to a baby monkey.
9. A darkened room is seen through an open door from a lighted room. The darkened room contains a child's bed in which a rabbit sits up looking through the door.
10. A baby dog lies across the knees of an adult dog, both figures show a minimum of expression in their features. The figures are set in the foreground of a bathroom.

≣ *Rapid Reference 8.2*

CAT Supplementary Cards

1. Four mouse-children are on a slide. One is just sliding down, one is about to start the slide, and two are climbing up the ladder. Numbers one and three suggest males; two and four suggest females (skirts, bows in hair).
2. The card shows a classroom situation with three little monkeys. Two sit at typical school desks, one stands with a book in hand while one of the seated monkeys holds his tail.

3. Mouse-children are "playing house." "Father Mouse" wears eyeglasses that are much too big for him and obviously belong to an adult and is receiving a beverage from "Mother Mouse" while toys and a baby doll in a carriage are dispersed about them.

4. A big bear sits crouched forward, holding a baby bear on its lap and in its arms.

5. A kangaroo is on crutches and has a bandaged tail and foot.

6. A group of four foxes (two male and two female) are in a race with the goal in sight, and one male is closest to it.

7. A cat stands before a mirror looking at its image.

8. A rabbit doctor is examining a rabbit child with a stethoscope; some bottles of medicine are visible in the background.

9. A grown deer is taking a shower and is half hidden by a shower curtain. A small deer is looking toward the larger figure. An enema bag hangs against the wall.

10. An obviously pregnant cat stands upright, with a large belly and apron askew.

ADMINISTRATION OF THE CAT

The administration procedures described in Chapter 2 apply to all storytelling methods. However, cards presented and the specific wording of the instructions vary across techniques. The authors of the CAT suggest that all 10 cards be administered in numerical order. However, if the child becomes restless, the clinician may present fewer cards with selections based on the themes elicited by the cards. The following instructions to the CAT differ from those of the TAT by introducing the task as a game and by not directing the narrator to tell what the characters are thinking and how they are feeling:

This is a story game. There are ten pictures altogether. When I show you each picture, the idea is for you to try to make up a make-pretend story for the picture. Tell what is happening in the picture, then what happens next, and how the story ends. Another way is you can make up what you think happened before, then tell what's happening in the picture, and then put an ending to it. We are interested in how you make up a story with a beginning, middle, and an end from your own imagination. Okay, here is the first picture. (Bellak, & Abrams, 1998, p. 3)

If the child has described the picture but is having trouble continuing, the examiner may prompt by saying, "That's a good beginning to the story. Now can you tell me what you think is going to happen next?" If the child does not put an ending to a story, the examiner may prompt with, "Now, how does the story end?" If necessary, the examiner may read the story back to the child (noting it on the transcript).

INTERPRETATION OF THE CAT

When the authors introduced the CAT stimuli and its variations, the pictures were not accompanied by new interpretive procedures, and methods for interpreting stories told to TAT cards were applied. However, others subsequently introduced interpretive units specific to CAT stimuli (e.g., Haworth, 1963) or adapted units previously used with TAT pictures (e.g., Chandler, Shermis, & Lempert, 1989). Bellak and Abrams (1997) indicate some minor differences between interpreting the TAT and CAT, noting the lack of systematic research delineating specific differences in responses of children and adults to the TAT or year-by-year changes in responses of children. Haworth (1966) provides some examples of normal CAT stories at various ages and reviews some developmental trends from preschool to age 10 (see Rapid Reference 8.3).

Bellak's (revised, 1992) Short Form for analyzing stories is intended for use with both the TAT and the CAT stimuli. The examiner who is familiar with the theoretical underpinnings of the Form uses it to organize the narrator's responses by scrutinizing each story according to the 10 variables listed: the main theme, the main hero, the main needs of the hero, conception of the environment, interpersonal object relations, significant conflicts, nature of anxieties, main defenses against conflicts and fears, adequacy of superego, and integration of the ego.

≡ Rapid Reference 8.3

Age-Related Shifts in Perceptions Noted in CAT Stimuli*

1. At younger ages (6 and below) children may not be aware of small details such as the mouse in Card 3 or the pouch and baby in Card 4. Therefore, expectations for eliciting content such as father/child relations in Card 3 cannot be met if the narrator does not take note of the much smaller mouse figure. In the human version of this stimulus, the child is much more prominent and difficult to ignore.

2. By age 7, there are few omissions (mean = 1.4) of pictured characters.

3. The figures that are omitted, particularly at ages 5 and below, are very small, vague, or blurred.

*See Haworth (1966).

The interpreter pulls the variables considered for each story into a summary analysis based on the interpreter's familiarity with and endorsement of the psychoanalytic perspective for content interpretation. Bellak's suggestion that clinicians analyze the 10 variables to find patterns and trends rather than judge from a single isolated story is shown in the case example below. The form also includes a section for rating each of 14 ego functions (see Rapid Reference 8.4).

≡ *Rapid Reference 8.4*

Ego Functions Assessed with CAT and TAT

1. Reality testing—distinction between inner and outer stimuli; accuracy of perception; reflective awareness.

2. Judgment—anticipation of consequences and the emotional appropriateness of this anticipation.

3. Sense of reality—extent of derealization or depersonalization; clarity of boundaries between the self and the world.

4. Regulation and control—regulation of drives, affects, and impulses; directness of impulse expression; effectiveness of delay mechanisms.

5. Object relations—degree and kind of relatedness (e.g., extent to which objects are perceived independently of oneself; primitiveness of the perception).

6. Thought process—memory, concentration, attention, and conceptualization; primary and secondary process.

7. Adaptive regression in the service of the ego—creativity such as formation of new cognitive configurations.

8. Defensive functioning—adaptiveness or maladaptiveness of defenses.

9. Stimulus barrier—threshold for reacting to stimuli and effectiveness of strategies for managing excessive stimulus input.

10. Autonomous functioning—freedom from impairment in managing everyday life tasks.

11. Synthetic-integrative functioning—extent to which the narrator actively relates events to each other or reconciles incongruities.

12. Mastery-competence—effectiveness in mastering the environment.

13. Superego—strength and adaptiveness of conscience (e.g., too strong, too weak, inconsistent).

14. Drive—strength and adaptiveness of drives (e.g., too strong, too weak, inappropriate, too aggressive or impulsive).

Other interpretive procedures for stories told to CAT stimuli were developed specifically for use with the CAT pictures or were adapted from the TAT. The Schedule for the Analysis of the CAT (Haworth, 1963), intended primarily as an aid for the qualitative evaluation of the stories and secondarily as a rough quantitative index for within-subject

CAUTION

The units for CAT interpretation have not been normed, and inter-rater reliability for various scoring systems has been sketchy. Therefore, the instrument has been described as theoretically, but not psychometrically, valid (Hatt, 1985).

and group comparison, includes three broad categories: (a) defense mechanisms such as reaction formation, undoing and ambivalence, isolation, repression and denial, deception, symbolization, and projection and introjection; (b) phobic, immature, or disorganized responses indicating fear or anxiety, regression, or weak or absent controls; and (c) gender identification rated as adequate (same gender) versus confused or opposite gender. Critical "scores" calculated for each category have been found to differentiate between clinical and school samples. More recently, Cramer (1991; 2007) extensively studied three mechanisms of denial, projection, and identification with both the TAT and the CAT.

Byrd and Witherspoon's (1954) classification of CAT responses as enumerative (naming of objects), descriptive (qualities of objective stimulus features), and apperceptive (interpretation beyond the objective features of the picture) gave credit to the highest level. In Picture 1, "chicks" are seen as enumerative, "sitting" is rated as descriptive, and "eating something, mother hen is feeding them" is apperceptive. Apperceptive responses may be further classified according to the underlying dynamic such as sibling rivalry, fear, or aggression (Bellak & Bellak, 1952).

Associative Elaboration and Integration Scales (Slemon, Holzwarth, Lewis, & Sitko, 1976) introduced for use with TAT pictures have been applied to the CAT (Schroth, 1977). The Associative Elaboration Scale, intended to measure the tendency to embellish stories with details beyond what is suggested by the card, is scored on a 10-point scale based on the number of interpretive comments. The Integration Scale, intended to measure the degree to which the narrator brings together the story details into a cohesive plot, is scored on a 6-point scale, ranging from no theme or pure description to a complete and integrated story with no irrelevancies. In applying these scales to the CAT, Schroth found interrater correlations sufficiently high for clinical settings. Children 8 to 10 years of age had significantly higher Associative Elaboration and Integration scores than those aged 6 and 7. The correlation between IQ scores and Associative Elaboration (.13) and Integration (.03) were not significant.

The Transcendence Index, originally devised for use with the TAT (Weisskopf, 1950), has been applied to the CAT (Armstrong, 1954; Budoff, 1960; Haworth, 1963; Weisskopf-Joelson & Lyn, 1953; Weisskopf-Joelson & Foster, 1962). The Transcendence Index is the number of statements that either go beyond pure description of the stimulus or are independent of what is actually shown in the picture. Despite the fact that any frequency count is subject to the undue influence of story length, this index has been popular as a measure of productivity because it includes elaborations of the characters' inner worlds (emotions, thoughts) and events that occur prior or subsequent to the pictured scene. However, the Transcendence Index does not take into account either the cohesiveness among these components or their compatibility with the stimuli.

COMPARING TAT AND CAT STORIES

This section presents DM's TAT stories at chronological age 6-4, followed by conclusions based on coding of the cognitive variables included in Chapter 4 (see Rapid Reference 8.5). The section then moves on to DM's CAT stories told 5 months later, along with conclusions based on Bellak's 10 variables (see Rapid Reference 8.6). As the reader will note from the complete report that follows, the major conclusions from the two procedures are virtually identical.

TAT Stories

Card 1. Him thinkin' of that... the fiddle, and he's lookin' at it... [E: Before?] I think it's broken. [E: Feeling?] Sad... [E: Happens?] He'll cry... [E: And in the end?] Nothin'.

Import: When someone is sad that something is broken, he or she cries and nothing happens.

Notes: External events (broken violin) evoke sadness and crying without initiative to act or seek assistance. The story departs minimally from the moment depicted in the scene and does not include previous events, intentions, or another character to give relief.

Card 2. She's holdin' the bible. And that man up there is carrying a horse, holding the horse. And the lady is standing by the tree, and she's lookin' at the lady... [E: Thinking?] She's thinkin' about Jesus... [E: Feeling?] Happy, 'cause she's thinkin' about Jesus. [E: Happens next?] That she will say Alelulia! [E: End?] She get, gives some money to them people that's poor. We have all them pages to do? All them?

Import: When you don't understand the whole picture, you focus on something safe to feel happy but you are still overwhelmed.

Notes: Difficulty pulling together the parts of this relatively complex stimulus is not unusual at this age. However, DM's poor reality testing of the perceptual cues (e.g., the man is "carrying a horse" corrected to "holding the horse") is unexpected. Given the difficulty of the task for DM, an expression of anxiety about having to produce more stories is understandable.

Card 3BM. He's cryin', she's crying. I mean she looks like she's dead, 'cause the knife is right there. [points] [E: Happened before?] Somebody put a knife in her. . . . [E: Why?] I don't know. That's why she's crying. That's number 3.

Process Import: If it is hard to figure out what is going on, you react to isolated cues and are left scared and confused.

Notes: DM's inflexibility and problems with causal understanding (e.g., inability to consider intentions) leads to reliance on simplistic associations (e.g., one-to-one correspondence between objects such as knife and events). Again, his uncertainty and anxiety about this task prompts him to check the numbers of the cards.

Card 4. She's lookin' at that man. That's her husband. And she hug him. [E: Feeling?] Happy. [E: Which one?] She's happy . . . [E: Him?] He's sad. [E: Why?] I don't know . . . [Examiner encourages him to make up the story.] . . . Somebody killed his grandmother. [E: Thinking?] Nothing. [E: End?] Them hug. She gives him a hug. That's one, two, three, four. . . . [counts cards in stack].

Process Import: If you don't understand emotions and relationships, you react to parts of what you see without grasping how the parts go together.

Notes: At first, DM focuses on one character, ignoring the feelings of the other, in keeping with his tendency to react to parts of the information without connecting the pieces. When specifically asked, he recognizes that the husband feels differently than his wife. However, describing the wife as happy and the husband as sad is discrepant from the pictured scene.

Card 5. She lookin' at the lamp, and she's lookin' at the flower that is broke. It needs some water. And she needs something to drink. [E: Thinking?] She's thinking about the different colors. [E: Where?] Right here . . . the books. [E: Feeling?] Happy. [E: End?] Don't know . . . don't know. [Examiner reads his story.] She puts water in there.

Process Import: A situation or task is hard to understand because you consider only what you see without bringing an organized base of understandings that connect what you see in the moment with what you know from prior experience.

Notes: The woman has no particular goals or intentions but feels happy looking at the various objects portrayed in the scene or thinking about the different colors (which are actually variations in shades of black and white). Her need for a drink seems on par with the flower's needing a drink. It appears that, in the absence of specific cues that elicit unhappy emotions, when characters are engaged in routine activities, DM associates happy emotions.

Card 6BM. He's lookin' over there, and the woman is lookin' over there to see if her car is . . . is . . . um is . . . fixed. And then he hugs her. [E: Feeling?] Happy,

happy . . . [points] Both are happy. What's that number? [points to story number in examiner's notes].

Import: It is hard to understand feelings and relationships, but hugs bring happiness.

Notes: DM superimposes affection and happiness on a tense scene without a logical explanation.

Card 7GF. She is carryin' the baby and her mom says, "Don't hold it down 'cause she can fall!" And then she, the daughter, punched her in the mouth, [E: Punched who?] Her mother . . . and the baby. [E: Feeling?] They're feelin' happy. What's that spell, F G? That's six! [looks on back of previous card turned down].

Import: If a parent admonishes her daughter, the child will lash out by punching everyone around but they all end up happy.

Notes: The story is consistent with DM's tendency to overreact to information that is not well understood with externalizing behavior. Being corrected seems to set him off.

Card 8BM. Oh, she's stickin' a knife at him, putting it in him, stick a knife in him. . . . But the boy is not doin' nothin'. The boy is just happy. And the boy killed that man, them [points to men in back], them that's putting the knife in his father. And then him lived happily ever after . . . and the father too, and the boy.

Process Import: You react to information literally without understanding it.

Notes: DM superimposes the familiar story structure where everyone lives happily ever after but without the logical ties to story events. DM is not able to synthesize experiences and grasps at fragments of information without connections.

Card 13B. That's number what? He's thinkin' about his mom, but his mom died. And his grandma's takin' care of him, and he's thinkin' about his friends. [E: Feeling?] Happy. [E: Happens?] He gets somethin' to drink, and then his school bus came and then he went on the school bus.

Import: As long as a person has someone to take care of him or her and he or she is participating in the familiar daily routine, that person is happy.

Notes: Concerns center on maintaining sources of need satisfaction and salience of the routine activities.

Summary of Imports

Overall, there is a sense that DM is very reactive to faulty perceptions about the world and needs a highly structured and predictable environment. Without access to organized schemas for understanding social causality, he has difficulty sizing up situations and either feels helpless or acts in a rote and inflexible manner. Because he has no goals or plans that would organize an enduring set of responses, DM's actions are guided by external triggers. He is particularly vulnerable to lashing out or behaving inappropriately when he feels confused or provoked (e.g., admonished).

CAT Stories

Card 1. Looks like they're eating soup . . . [E: Feeling?] Happy . . . [E: Thinking?] Don't know . . . maybe about them mom. [E: Thinking about her?] Don't know . . . [E: Turns out?] Good, good, good . . . [E: What happens?] Them play.

Import: When children in a family are eating, they are happy and play later.

Notes: The narrative style is similar to that of stories told to the TAT pictures. Specifically, DM needed prompting for each component of the story and had difficulty describing the inner world of intentions, emotions, and thoughts. Because the TAT cards show negative emotions, the narrator is expected to introduce some tension and to resolve the dilemma prior to concluding that the characters are happy. In contrast, happy emotions are not out of tune with this stimulus.

Card 2. Them pullin' a rope . . . And he's fallin' down. [points to figure on left] He's scared . . . And he's tired [points to middle], and he's pullin' it [points to right] . . . [E: Why's he scared?] Scared him bump his head. [E: Happens?] Don't know . . . mmm . . . bump his head and lay down.

Import: When pulling a rope with others, a person is scared that he or she may get hurt and then does get hurt.

Notes: The depiction of characters as "pulling a rope" rather than engaged in a purposeful activity is a literal translation of the picture, reminiscent of TAT responses. Moreover, each character is entrenched in his own feeling or activity unrelated to the others.

Card 3. He's sittin' down. He's an old lion . . . And that's a mouse. And that's his cave . . . and this is a board. [points to background] This is his pipe . . . and this is flowers. [points to floor] [E: Feeling?] Sad. [E: Why?] 'Cause he don't . . . really don't have no friends . . . [E: End?] And then he had friends.

Import: If one feels sad without friends, one gets a friend without understanding how.

Notes: In response to inquiry after enumerating the characters and objects in the stimulus, DM describes the lion as sad because he has no friends. When pressed for an ending, the lion magically has friends. Though the mouse is noticed, there is no attempt to relate the mouse to the lion. This lack of coordination among characters is common in DM's responses to both the CAT and TAT stimuli. In both sets of stories, DM also lists external attributes of characters or labels objects without a priority in emphasis.

Card 4. That's the baby kangaroo [points to one on bike], and this is the wheel and the other wheel, and they drivin' a bike . . . No, this is the, the big baby and that's the little one, the little baby. [points to one in pouch] Them goin' to a picnic.

And she's wearin' a hat. And this is a tree and another tree, and smoke . . . [E: Feeling?] Happy. [E: Happens?] They sit down and have them picnic.

Import: It is difficult to distinguish what is important from what is not, but when a family has a picnic they are happy.

Notes: An inability to prioritize elements of the pictured scene (i.e., the inanimate objects and characters are not differentiated in relative importance) and to develop ideas apart from associations with the immediate surroundings (also evident in TAT stories) suggests that DM does not use an organized set of schemas to interpret the cues in his environment.

Card 5. The bears is layin' down. And this is a bed and this is a . . . uhm . . . crib. This is a window and the blinds. And this is the light and this is the floor. [E: That's a good description. Now tell me a story] I don't know . . . from being tired and pulling a rope. [E: End?] Them get up.

Process Import: You notice what is around you on a literal level but can't interpret what is happening.

Notes: When pressed to tell a story after providing a description, DM explains that two bears are lying down because they are tired "from pulling a rope" (an association to a previous story). Unable to use previously organized schemas to understand the current situation, DM grasps at isolated ideas from the immediate surroundings.

Card 6. This is the big bear. This is the little bear . . . And this is the rock and this is a tree and stuff. [E: Bears thinking?] Sad. [E: Why?] They probably, the family got killed. [E: Turn out?] Don't know . . . them cryin'.

Process Import: When the situation is hard to understand, you helplessly assume the worst (i.e., family killed).

Notes: DM has problems organizing this stimulus, and a sense of uncertainty evokes fears of being left alone.

Card 7. Ugh!!! I don't like that one. It's too scary. I don't like this one. [E: Just look at it for a minute. Take your time.] Them tryin' to eat the gorilla . . . for his dinner, and the gorilla climbin' up and that's the tree. And him stripes. [E: Turn out?] He got ate up! And the family was sad.

Import: If a smaller animal gets eaten by a bigger one, his family is sad.

Notes: The narrator's fear of this picture is stylistically similar to his reactivity to the knife in the TAT cards. Furthermore, DM's failure to give priority to different levels of detail ("climbing up" and "him stripes") shows evidence of problems with conceptual organization.

Card 8. I don't like that one! . . . [E: Just look at it for a minute.] . . . It's funny! That's the mother and that's the Dad . . . other mom and the boy. This is the chair and couch. That's the baby [points to picture in background], and that's the door. . . . [E: Happening?] Them happy. . . . [E: Doing?] Them's talkin' to each other . . . in secrets. [E: Turn out?] Good. [E: What happens?] Don't know. . . . Climb trees.

Import: When people are talking together, they are happy.

Notes: Again, DM notices minute features of the scene, equating major and minor aspects of the stimuli (inanimate objects such as the chair and couch are enumerated along with characters; the picture of the baby in the background is listed along with the prominent figures). As with the other cards, DM can't "explain" what is happening in the picture or predict what might happen later (other than "happy").

Card 9. The baby carrot... [E: Baby what?] ... carrot. No, baby rabbit. Sittin' in his bed. That's the mirror, the light, window, shade ... This the door ... the floor. And then he gets up from his nap. [E: Feeling?] Sad. [E: Why?] 'Cause he can't go out yet. [E: When?] After his nap.

Import: If a baby rabbit gets up from his nap, he's sad because he can't go out yet.

Notes: When the narrator is asked when the rabbit can go out, the response is when he gets up from his nap. Just as DM lives in the moment, the character reacts emotionally (sad) to his immediate situation rather than anticipating that he can go out soon.

Card 10. This is a dog, and that's the little dog, and that's his mother givin' him a bath. And his mother is on a chair. This is a bathroom, and the toilet, and that's the towel, and that's the garbage can, and that's the wall. He's happy, the baby. [E: Mom doing?] Petting him. [E: End?] Then he, um, makes food for his mom.

Import: The baby is happy being bathed and petted by his mother and later makes his mother something to eat.

Notes: DM tends to tell happy stories when the activity is familiar (eating, picnic). However, he has no resources to deal with novel, complex, or unhappy pictures.

≡ *Rapid Reference 8.5*

Conclusions from the TAT, Organized According to Variables in Chapter 4

- Perceptual Integration. DM responds to isolated stimulus features interpreted literally rather than conceptually. About half of the stories are significantly discrepant from the emotions and relationships depicted.

- Level of Abstraction. Stories are characterized by descriptions that are enumerative (naming or describing isolated or irrelevant stimulus detail) or concrete (no inner world or simplistic tie between events and feelings).

- Planning and Monitoring. Poor understanding of social causality leads to difficulty anticipating the outcomes of his actions or the reactions of others, resulting in a tendency to act or react without defining goals or purposes. DM's inability to figure things out or consider alternatives further limits goal-directed thoughts or actions.

- Time Perspective. DM's thought processes, feelings, and actions are rooted in the immediacy of the moment.
- Process of Reasoning/Coherence of Story Structure. Narratives provide numerous examples of disorganized thinking, faulty logic, and poor understanding of how ideas "go together."
- Coordination of Inner and Outer Elements of Experience. DM doesn't imbue his characters with intentions, standards, or psychological processes. Lack of cohesion between the inner and outer worlds makes it difficult for DM to reflect on his behaviors to separate fantasy from reality. Without a durable or cohesive sense of self in relation to others, DM needs routines, clear expectations, and direct signals of acceptance. Otherwise, he reacts to isolated cues or provocations with confusion, fear, or anger.
- Coordination of Perspectives of Different Individuals. Not understanding the inner world of thoughts, feelings, or intentions, DM has difficulty organizing the postures, facial expressions, and relationships portrayed in the pictures. He notices aspects of outward appearance according to their implications for basic needs for routine, safety, and acceptance. (Coding object relations, not shown here, indicates problems with relatedness influenced by difficulties with information processing and affect regulation.)
- Level of Cognitive-Experiential Integration. Numerous instances signaling disorganized processing of information and poor reality testing (including difficulty sizing up emotions as well as situational and interpersonal cues) characterize DM's functioning (Level 1).
- Level of Associative Thinking. The progression of DM's ideas is tangential or linear, with minimal causal connections (Levels 1 and 2). Ideas are evoked as reactions to the stimuli or to his emotions and show no apparent organization.

≣ *Rapid Reference 8.6*

. . . .

Conclusions from the CAT, Organized According to Bellak's Short Form

- Unconscious Structure and Drives (based on main themes, main hero, and main needs and drives of hero). DM sees familiar situations, such as a family eating dinner, talking, or bathing routines, as happy. Otherwise, DM feels helpless and confused, afraid, and needing but unable to seek reassurance and security.

(continued)

- Conception of Environment. DM has difficulty understanding the nuances of the environment, leading him to a dichotomous construction of the world with familiar, routine situations associated with happy feelings and other situations eliciting feelings of vulnerability and confusion. DM is highly reactive to what he perceives as threatening, frightening, or provoking aspects of the environment.
- Interpersonal Object Relations. DM construes parental or family figures as supportive and reassuring and other figures as neutral or overpowering. DM does not infer relatedness when it is not directly portrayed in the stimulus.
- Significant Conflicts. No inner conflicts are apparent.
- Nature of Anxieties. DM's primary fears are of being left alone to suffer physical harm and of being helpless against powerful others.
- Main Defenses Against Conflicts and Fears. Few defenses are apparent (mostly denial).
- Adequacy of Superego. Descriptive stories are not sufficiently elaborated to note expectations about being punished for wrongdoing.
- Integration of the Ego. Concrete thinking and unrealistically happy outcomes, along with hero's inability to deal with adverse situations, suggests impaired ego functioning and difficulty meeting age-appropriate expectations for autonomous behavior.

PSYCHOLOGICAL EVALUATION

Name: DM

School: G. Center

Age: 6-4

Tests Administered

Wechsler Intelligence Scale for Children

Bender Visual Motor Gestalt Test (Bender-Gestalt)

Child Behavior Checklist (CBCL), Parent and Teacher Report Forms

Thematic Apperception Test (TAT)

Rorschach Inkblot Technique

Sentence Completion Task

Projective Drawings

Reason for Referral and Background Information

DM, a first-grade male student age 6-4, was recently transferred from out of state to a center serving children diagnosed with emotional disabilities, and this is where the current evaluation was conducted. From his first day at G. Center, DM demonstrated overactivity, impulsivity, defiance, and aggressive behavior, which the staff could not successfully handle even in this structured setting. He regularly shouted obscenities, verbally threatened staff, sexually touched and grabbed adults, and displayed physical aggression by kicking, biting, and spitting. On 9/27, DM verbalized self-degrading remarks and suicidal thoughts, at which time staff members alerted his mother and made a referral to the S. Mental Health Center. As an outcome of that outpatient mental health evaluation, DM started taking Ritalin on 10/19 to address symptoms of previously diagnosed ADHD, and he has been participating in therapeutic counseling. DM's behavior as charted by his teachers during the period from 10/13 through 12/6, in relation to the implementation of various interventions, showed that negative behavior decreased over time. Teachers discontinued recording after significant improvements in behavior. As a result of more positive behaviors, DM started successfully mainstreaming into a language arts class for 45 to 50 minutes per day, 3 days each week. When DM returned from winter break on or about 1/6, the negative behaviors resurfaced for approximately 2 weeks despite all interventions remaining in place. The individualized education program (IEP) team agreed that a thorough psychological and educational evaluation, as well as a comprehensive social history (Social/Cultural Report, not included), would assist in better understanding and educationally serving this child.

Background information on DM is incomplete despite brief reports on file from the School District of P and Family Resources, Therapeutic Parents and Children's Center. DM and his mother had recently moved to this area from P, where DM had an IEP for special education services as a student with emotional disabilities. According to the evaluation by the School District of P, although DM refused to attempt most of the tasks, those portions he did complete suggested average learning ability, vocabulary, quantitative reasoning, and short-term memory. That evaluation refers to a diagnosis of ADHD and Oppositional Defiant Disorder; although the primary source of this diagnosis is not available, it does concur with two of the provisional diagnoses suggested in the Mental Health evaluation (4 months ago).

Behavior Observations

DM was pleased to participate in testing and to receive special attention from an adult. He enjoyed social conversation and participated in an age-appropriate manner, except for his inability to inhibit some sexual content. He worked to the best of his abilities on most tasks, for example, persevering for nearly 11 minutes on one puzzle until he completed it correctly. At the same time, on other tasks he did not enjoy or found extremely difficult, he would start to whine, fuss, cry, and seek distractions to avoid the work.

DM had been taking Ritalin for approximately 1 month when testing was started. This medication clearly improved his availability for testing, because with frequent redirection he was able to work in this optimal one-on-one situation for up to 1 hour per session. At the same time, there were still extreme indications of attentional difficulties. His responses were consistently impulsive and associative, lacking evidence of planning and flexible thought. He often started tasks before instructed and had difficulty following directions. He required frequent directions to watch and listen to the examiner and additional training or examples to teach a task before he could perform correctly. Similar patterns in both verbal and nonverbal tasks suggested that this is an attentional problem more than possible deficits in the auditory channel. For example, on a verbal item, when asked to name three coins, his immediate association was to the pictures of presidents on U.S. coins, and he named "Abraham, Lincoln, and George Washington." While it was clear that he understood the question and had significant knowledge of coins, his impulsive response was not correct. Furthermore, he was unable to reflect upon or monitor his response and had no conception that he had made a mistake. He was usually unable to change his strategy if his initial impression was incorrect, and this pattern, observed throughout testing, is an indication of cognitive inflexibility.

Discussion of Test Results

DM's impulsive response style, which resulted in many incorrect answers despite apparent knowledge, suggests that he has not learned how to take time to think (i.e., to ponder the meaning of a question, consider alternatives, and plan his best response). His attentional problems clearly affected his performance on the cognitive measure. Although these results are a fair indication of his present level of functioning, they are likely an underestimate of his true ability.

On the WISC, DM obtained a Full Scale IQ of 82, suggestive of cognitive ability in the low average range, at the 12th percentile compared with children his age. Significant scatter among the subtest scores, particularly within the verbal domain, suggests learning difficulties. His performance on the verbal tasks, at the 10th percentile compared to his peers, was strongly affected by his associative thinking and impulsive responding. His relatively strong skill in vocabulary (solidly average) is readily apparent to any observer. Hence, he comes across as a much more capable child than his present overall level of functioning. DM struggled with verbal tasks that required concentration and working memory, performing well below average.

DM enjoyed the nonverbal tasks more than the verbal and was able to concentrate fairly well without as much external structure. On these tasks of visual processing, organizing, planning, nonverbal learning, and memory, he scored in the 18th percentile compared with other children his age. On many of these activities, the examiner noticed a pattern where DM tended to focus on one detail or clue, such that his attention was "stuck," and he failed to explore all information provided. This is an example of the cognitive inflexibility mentioned earlier. He had difficulty differentiating essential from nonessential details, impulsively and inflexibly focusing on that which first caught his attention.

When asked to copy geometric designs of the Bender Visual Motor Gestalt Test, DM approached the task impulsively, without planning or monitoring his work. He filled three pages with his large and, at times, perseverative drawings, clearly using the edge of the paper for structure and boundaries. This approach is often associated with impulsiveness, low frustration tolerance, and acting out behavior in children. DM completed the task in 4 minutes, 30 seconds—quicker than most children his age. It was not surprising that the quality of his drawings suffered, and his score translated to a standard score of 75. It cannot be stated that all of his errors were due to his impulsive style, for some of the rotation and distortion errors were quite significant indicators of developmental delay. His fine motor skills should be closely monitored and reassessed, should these not improve along with his attention, concentration, and behavior as a result of ADHD medication. His recall of the figures (incidental visual memory) was in the average range. Again, he expanded his effort onto three sheets of paper.

DM's mother and classroom teacher completed the Child Behavior Checklist (CBCL; Achenbach). Mrs. M answered this questionnaire twice, according to her perception of his behavior both before and after he started medication for ADHD. His teacher completed the questionnaire after DM began medication and before his negative behaviors resumed early in January. Results are reported in T scores with a mean of 50. Scores below 67 are considered to be within the normal range. Scores followed by an asterisk (*) are in the borderline clinical range, and scores followed by a double asterisk (**) are in the clinically significant range (i.e., they represent a high level of maladjustment).

	Before Meds (mother's responses)	After Meds (mother's responses)	After Meds (teacher's responses)
Total Score			
Internalizing Behavior	77**	53	48
Withdrawn Behavior	66	51	43
Somatic Complaints	58	50	50
Anxiety/Depression	50	50	50
Externalizing Behavior	72**	57	50
Delinquent Behavior/ Aggressive Behavior	82**	53	46
Social Problems	85**	51	50
Thought Problems	73**	64	51
Attention Problems	67*	50	50
Sex Problems	88**	70**	50

The difference in DM's behavior before and after ADHD medication is striking. Before medication, Mrs. M endorsed items such as "Argues a lot," "Can't concentrate," "Can't pay attention for long," "Can't get his mind off certain thoughts: sexual obsessions," "Destroys things," "Disobedient at home and school," "Doesn't seem to feel guilty after misbehavior," "Impulsive acts without thinking," "Lying and cheating," and "Stealing." After medication, Mrs. M did not see most of these behaviors, or she at least did not observe them to the same degree. However, DM's sexual obsessions remained an issue. The teacher's views are similar. With medication she observed normal classroom behavior. When commenting on DM's behavior before medication, her narrative stated, "frequently refuses to do work, needs one-on-one attention to complete any task, physical aggression (hitting, kicking), inappropriate language, sexual verbalizations, and sexual touching."

DM's social-emotional functioning was further evaluated through personality performance techniques. On all of these unstructured tasks DM experienced great difficulty, suggesting a need for clear task expectations and supports to keep him on track and set boundaries/limits for appropriate behavior. DM's

TAT responses are characterized as concrete, often at odds with the stimulus, and lacking logical progression, with numerous examples of faulty thinking. His poor understanding of social causality leaves him feeling vulnerable and helpless without the resources to assess accurately and to respond to situations that depart from the familiar routine. For example, in two of his TAT stories, after seeing a knife, DM assumed that someone would "put" or "stick" the knife into one of the characters without a specific purpose or intention. DM's disorganized ideation is often confusing to him and others. He has difficulty separating reality from fantasy, and he therefore clings rigidly to the limited schemas he has, even when they do not fit the circumstances. His schemas for understanding himself and others do not include intentions or psychological processes and fail to connect causes and effects. This extent of impaired cognitive functioning is likely the culmination of severe attentional problems as well as intrusive ideation from affective concerns.

Similar to his responses to the TAT, DM's responses to the Rorschach show that he tends to get lost in perseveration and tangential details and inappropriate integration of ideas. Moreover, the content of the Rorschach percepts suggests that he is unusually preoccupied with his body and bodily functions. At home this manifests in unusual urination and bowel habits. Both at home and at school DM is obsessed with sexual innuendo and language. This bodily preoccupation appears to stem from an image of himself as a fragile and vulnerable person. In his TAT stories, when DM perceives a negative stimulus (e.g., a knife or a gun) he assumes that someone controlling or powerful will use it against someone who is helpless or defenseless. His sentence completions also support this feeling of vulnerability (e.g., "What I want to happen most is . . . be a superhero and save all the kids"). When children experience such imbalance of autonomy (such that some people are intrusive and overpowering, while others are helpless and controlled), many cope through distance and detachment in relationships. The characters in DM's stories relate like robots, without individuality or emotion. For example, in one story, "somebody put a knife in her," and in another, "She punched her mother in the mouth . . . and the baby. They're feelin' happy." He is confused even about the concept of family, for when asked to draw a picture of his family (examiner confirmed "family" as DM began), he drew himself, a friend, and a girl, "I don't know her name." He appears devoid of inner resources to understand relationships and guide social behavior. He is lacking age-appropriate schemas that are built upon a child's subjective experiences, suggesting that he either has not been exposed to these experiences or he has not been cognitively and emotionally available to learn from them.

Summary and Recommendations

DM is a 6-year-old, first-grade student at G. Center, having transferred into F. County Public Schools as an emotionally disabled student from the School District of P. Due to the difficulty he was having in his adjustment to school this year, and due to limited information regarding prior evaluations, the IEP team decided to proceed with a full evaluation at this time. Testing suggests cognitive functioning in the low average range, a possible underestimate of his true ability. Struggling with ADHD in these early years of development has likely limited his availability to observe, process, and store knowledge typically held by other children his age. Additionally, although he recently started medication to improve his attention and decrease impulsivity, behavior during testing suggested that cognitive processing patterns related to attention deficit (e.g., associative thinking) have not yet changed, and this has further depressed scores. Difficulty in visual-motor integration was noted; however, impulsivity confounds the issue of a developmental delay in processing. Further evaluation for learning disabilities is recommended in approximately 1 year.

Although DM's behavior has clearly improved since he started taking medication for ADHD symptoms, there remain issues of disorganized ideation that preclude his ability to size up a situation accurately (e.g., confusing reality with fantasy) and plan or solve simple social encounters (faulty judgment). Testing, interview, and observation further suggest that significant problems with relationships underlie DM's behavioral concerns. He anticipates victimization by controlling and powerful others, which results in his feelings of helplessness (regarding realistic resolution) and detachment. The combination of impaired information processing and poor relational development begins to explain DM's acting out behavior. He has not developed a sufficient (age-appropriate) schematic framework from which he can accurately interpret and understand his surroundings and by which he can guide his own behavior. He is presently in need of external structure and clear guidelines set by others to maintain his behavior. Continued therapeutic counseling to address underlying relationship concerns is strongly recommended.

Test results will be used along with all other current assessment data to determine the most appropriate educational plan for DM at this time.

Lauren B. Lohr, MA
NCSP School Psychologist
Examiner

Mila French, PhD
NCSP School Psychologist
Supervisor

TELL-ME-A-STORY (TEMAS)

In an effort to develop a thematic apperception test that is useful for minority children, the authors of the Tell-Me-A-Story (TEMAS) designed two parallel sets of pictures depicting minority and nonminority children interacting in urban settings and provided population-specific norms for designated scoring criteria (Constantino, Malgady, & Rogler, 1988; Constantino, Malgady, Rogler, & Tsui, 1988); Constantino, Dana, & Malgady, 2007; Constantino & Malgady, 2008). The authors reasoned that the context depicted in the pictured scene should be closer to the experience of the narrator (see Rapid References 8.8). Otherwise, interest and responsiveness to the stimuli are minimal, and the resulting data are insufficient and unreliable.

Stimuli

The authors contend that the pictures in the TEMAS set are particularly relevant to poor, urban, Black, and Hispanic children, but are also useful with White and middle-class children. The test includes two parallel sets of pictures, one for minorities and another for nonminorities, with normative data for both populations. The TEMAS pictures, like the TAT, depict conflictual interpersonal situations but, unlike the TAT, these stimuli present two sides of a conflict, with most pictures resembling a split screen that represents opposite sides of an antithetical situation or inner dilemma (e.g., ice cream now or a bicycle later). Thus, the TEMAS stimuli are highly structured and familiar, and presentation of both sides of a conflict provides clear expectations of what narrators should include in the story. The scoring identifies adaptive and maladaptive responses to these conflict situations.

Each version of the TEMAS, designed to elicit identical themes, includes 23 pictures, with the minority set featuring predominantly Hispanic and African American characters in urban environments and the nonminority set depicting predominantly nonminority characters in an urban environment. Both versions have a short form composed of nine cards. Of the short form, four cards are given to both genders and five are specific to gender. Of the 23 in the long form, 12 are used for both genders and 11 are specific to gender. Only one is age-specific (Card 22, adolescent girls or boys). The set includes four that depict pluralistic characters that can be used for either minority or nonminority groups. The cards for the short form are described in Rapid Reference 8.8, and the reader is invited to consult the Manual (Constantino, Malgady, & Rogler, 1988) for further detail.

≡ *Rapid Reference 8.7*

Picture Content, Race, and Culture

1. Situation may be unfamiliar to the child due to cultural influences.
2. A child may not identify strongly with individuals from another cultural or racial background.
3. The same stimulus situation may be interpreted differently due to cultural experiences or norms.
4. Presenting all White figures may interfere with rapport when administering the test to minority children.

≡ *Rapid Reference 8.8*

TEMAS Stimuli Included in the Short Form

Card 1B. A mother is giving a command to her son. A father is in the background. Friends are urging the boy to play basketball with them. (Theme: interpersonal relations and delay of gratification.)

Card 1G. A mother is giving a command to her daughter. A father is in the background. Friends are urging the girl to jump rope with them. (Theme: interpersonal relations and delay of gratification.)

Card 7. An angry mother is watching her son and daughter argue over a broken lamp. (Theme: interpersonal relations, aggression, and moral judgment.)

Card 10B. A boy is standing in front of a piggy bank and holding money while imagining himself looking at a bicycle in a shop window and buying an ice cream cone. (Theme: delay of gratification.)

Card 10G. A girl is standing in front of a piggy bank and holding money while imagining herself looking at a bicycle in a shop window and buying an ice cream cone. (Theme: delay of gratification.)

Card 14B. A boy is studying in his room. A group of boys and girls is listening to music in the living room. (Theme: interpersonal relations, achievement motivation, and delay of gratification.)

Card 14G. A girl is studying in her room. A group of boys and girls is listening to music in the living room. (Theme: interpersonal relations, achievement motivation, and delay of gratification.)

Card 15 (minority version). A policeman is giving an award to a group of Police Athletic League (PAL) baseball players. A policeman is arresting a group of three boys and one girl who have broken a window and stolen merchandise. (Theme: interpersonal relations, aggression, achievement motivation, and moral judgment.)

Card 15 (nonminority version). A policeman is giving an award to a group of soccer players. A policeman is arresting a group of three boys and one girl who have broken a window and stolen merchandise. (Theme: interpersonal relations, aggression, achievement motivation, and moral judgment.)

Card 17B. A boy is studying and daydreaming about receiving an A from his teacher and receiving an F from his teacher. (Theme: anxiety/depression, achievement motivation, and self-concept.)

Card 17G. A girl is studying and daydreaming about receiving an A from her teacher and receiving an F from her teacher. (Theme: anxiety/depression, achievement motivation, and self-concept.)

Card 20. A youngster is in bed dreaming of a scene showing a horse on a hill, a river, and a path leading to a castle. (Theme: anxiety or depression.)

Card 21. A youngster is in bed dreaming of a monster eating something and of a monster making threats. (Theme: aggression, anxiety/depression, and reality testing.)

Card 22B. A boy is standing in front of a bathroom mirror, imagining his face reflected in the mirror with attributes of both sexes. (Theme: anxiety/ depression, sexual identity, and reality testing.)

Card 22G. A girl is standing in front of a bathroom mirror, imagining her face reflected in the mirror with attributes of both sexes. (Theme: anxiety/depression, sexual identity, and reality testing.)

Administration

The entire protocol of 23 cards or a subset of 9 cards may be administered to any given child. The clinician chooses the set of cards (minority or nonminority) that corresponds to the racial or cultural identification of the child. The manual provides detailed instructions: "Initially, the examiner says: 'I'd like you to tell me a story. I have a lot of interesting pictures that I'm going to show you. Please look carefully at the people and the places in the pictures and then tell me a complete story about each picture—a story that has a beginning and an end'" (p. 19).

After showing the first picture to the child, the examiner provides a temporal sequence to structure events in the story by saying, "Please tell me a complete story about this picture and all the other pictures I will show you. The story should answer three questions: (1) What is happening in the picture now? (2) What happened before? (3) What will happen in the future?" These instructions may be repeated for each card.

After giving the instructions for temporal sequencing, the examinee is given the opportunity to tell the story spontaneously. The story is considered complete, and no further inquiry is necessary, if it includes the temporal sequence and addresses the six areas listed in Rapid Reference 8.9. Because the requested story elements are scored, the respondent may be unduly penalized if the examiner fails to inquire. At the completion of each story, the examiner first addresses the temporal sequence of the events as needed, followed by the remaining six story elements. Generally, the examiner should encourage the child to complete ideas (or sentences) and to clarify and explain characters' motives and behaviors. The examiner may ask such clarifying questions as the story is being narrated and should indicate them parenthetically, such as "(?)." Clarifying questions are not analyzed in the scoring system but may be clinically useful. The examiner makes structured inquiries after the story has been told and records these inquiries parenthetically by the number used (e.g., "1a").

Examiners use a stopwatch to record both the reaction time and the total time. The examiner starts the stopwatch when handing the picture to the child and stops it the moment the child begins to respond. This latency time is the reaction time recorded at the beginning of each story. If the story is complete the examiner stops timing. If not, the stopwatch remains running until the inquiry has been completed. The examiner encourages the child to speak for at least 2 minutes per story by using prompts such as, "Tell me what is happening in this picture," or, "Tell me what you see." The test allots a maximum time of 5 minutes for each story and, if the respondent is overly verbose, he or she is prompted to complete the story after 4 minutes (e.g., "How does your story end?").

≡ Rapid Reference 8.9

Six Areas to Be Queried

1. (a) Who are these people? Do they know each other?
   (b) Who is this person?
2. (a) Where are these people?
   (b) Where is this person?
3. (a) What are these people doing and saying?
   (b) What is this person doing and saying?
4. (a) What were these people doing before?
   (b) What was this person doing before?
5. (a) What will these people do next?
   (b) What will this person do next?
6. (a) What is this person (main character) thinking?
   (b) What is this person (main character) feeling?

Interpretation

The TEMAS measures 18 cognitive functions, 9 personality functions, and 7 affective functions, and includes three qualitative indicators (see Rapid References 8.10 to 8.13). The authors indicate that the test can be interpreted normatively and clinically for children aged 5 to 13 and clinically for children aged 14 to 18. The norms provided are to be used with children who are cooperative and understand the requirements of the task, and who are able to communicate a sequence of events. Interpretations are based on a dynamic cognitive model incorporating the theoretical frameworks of ego psychology, interpersonal psychology, social learning theory, cognitive psychology, and motivational psychology (see the Manual).

Rapid Reference 8.10

Cognitive Functions

1. Reaction Time*—elapsed time between presentation of the picture and start of the narration.
2. Total Time*—elapsed time between start of story and conclusion of the inquiry.
3. Fluency*—number of words in the story.
4. Total Omissions*—number of characters, events, and settings depicted but not mentioned in the story.
5. Main Character Omissions***—failure to mention principal character or characters in the story.
6. Secondary Character Omissions***—failure to mention figures other than main character or characters in the story.
7. Event Omissions***—failure to identify what is happening in the picture.
8. Setting Omissions***—failure to identify the location of the event.
9. Total Transformations**—the number of perceptual distortions of characters, events, and settings depicted.
10. Main Character Transformations***—incorrect identifications of main figures.
11. Secondary Character Transformations***—incorrect identifications of secondary figures.
12. Event Transformations***—incorrect identification of what is happening in the picture.
13. Setting Transformations***—incorrect identification of location.

(continued)

14. Inquiries**—number of questions, including clarifications and structured inquiry.
15. Relationships**—identification of the characters and their relationships to each other.
16. Imagination**—content that goes beyond descriptive details about characters, events, and settings.
17. Sequencing**—relation of past, present, and future events.
18. Conflict**—recognition of the conflict depicted as polarities.

*Quantitative scale
**Qualitative scale
***Optional scale

≡ Rapid Reference 8.11

Personality Functions

The nine personality functions are assessed along an adaptive–maladaptive continuum that is defined according to psychosocial criteria.

1. Interpersonal relations—ability to synthesize the polarities of dependence/individuation, respect/disrespect, and nurturance/rejection.
2. Aggression—direct verbal or physical expression of intent to harm self, other, or property.
3. Anxiety/depression—irrational fears or worries about the current situation or about the future or pervasive unhappiness, psychosomatic symptoms, suicidal thoughts, feelings of worthlessness, and a tendency to cry or feel shy and withdrawn.
4. Achievement motivation—the desire to attain a goal or to succeed in an endeavor that is related to some standard of excellence.
5. Delay of gratification—the foregoing of an immediate reward in favor of delayed but more substantial reward or gratification.
6. Self-concept—realistic self-perception of intellectual, social, physical, and vocational abilities and mastery over the environment.
7. Sexual identity—realistic perception of roles appropriate to gender.
8. Moral judgment—ability to tell right from wrong and to act accordingly, to accept responsibility for wrongdoing, and to experience appropriate guilt for improper action.
9. Reality testing—ability to distinguish between fantasy and reality, to recognize problematic situations, and to anticipate the personal and social consequences of behavior.

≡ Rapid Reference 8.12

Affective Functions

Seven distinct moods or affects are attributed to the main character or characters following the resolution of the tensions depicted in the scene:

1. Happy*—contentment following a satisfactory resolution of the dilemma depicted in the scene.
2. Sad*—discontent associated with resolution of the conflict.
3. Angry*—strong displeasure associated with the conflict.
4. Fearful*—feeling of impending danger associated with the resolution of the conflict.
5. Neutral—emotional indifference to the resolution of the conflict.
6. Ambivalent—emotional indecision associated with the resolution of the conflict.
7. Inappropriate affect—incongruence between mood state of main character or characters at the resolution of the conflict and earlier behavior in the story.

*Quantitative scales

≡ Rapid Reference 8.13

Unscored Qualitative Indicators

1. Observed Test Behavior.
2. Rejection of Cards.
3. Content Analysis of Stories.

As a first step, the interpreter follows a systematic sequential analysis of the scores on the cognitive, personality, and affective functions. Raw scores are converted to normalized T-scores (M = 50; SD = 10), and each function is examined in terms of high and low scores (one standard

CAUTION

The limitations of the TEMAS include geographically narrow standardization samples and little research other than studies conducted by the authors (Flanagan & DiGiuseppe, 1999).

deviation above or below the mean). The authors caution against interpreting functions in isolation, advocating for establishing meaningful patterns of quantitative and qualitative data across and within the cognitive, affective, and personality functions.

CAUTION

The standardization sample includes a small number of children per age group.

All nine personality functions are qualitatively scored on a scale of 1 (most maladaptive) to 4 (most adaptive). In addition, if a personality function is not pulled (N) as part of the content of a TEMAS story, it signifies a serious omission, denoting maladaptive selective attention to the specific function. The N cut-off is at or above the 15th percentile. Due to limited variability, 14 cognitive functions and 3 affective functions were not converted into T-scores. Cut-off scores were designated at the 90th percentile.

ROBERTS–2

The Roberts–2 (Roberts & Gruber, 2005) replaces the Roberts Apperception Test for Children (RATC; McArthur & Roberts, 1982). The name change was intended to delete any reference to apperception and to disavow any connection to the enterprise of projective testing. The authors explain that neither the Roberts–2 nor its predecessor (Roberts Apperception Test for Chidren) fits into the rubric of projective test. Whereas a projective test presents ambiguous stimuli, subject to various interpretations, the Roberts pictures portray commonly occurring real-life events that are easily recognized. The Roberts is intended for use with children and adolescents referred to mental health or special educational settings or to serve research purposes by providing an index of social cognitive understanding.

The argument that more structure and less ambiguity enable greater fluency in responses was also the basis for increased structure in the TEMAS pictures (see Constantino and Malgady, 2008). Nevertheless, the question of optimal structure and ambiguity is still open. Cards that differ in structure may yield different information and there is no basis to assume that ease of responding to a particular storytelling task determines the interpretive usefulness of the response.

The initial rationale for developing the Roberts Apperception Test for Children (RATC; McArthur & Roberts, 1982) was based on dissatisfaction with the available stimuli for use with children and the absence of an agreed-upon scoring system. The authors noted that the use of animal figures in human situations was not appropriate for most school-age children. Moreover, though they

≡ Rapid Reference 8.14

Features of the Roberts–2 (see Manual, Roberts & Gruber, 2005).

- The pictures (16) were designed for use with children and adolescents between the ages of 6 and 18 to assess perceptions of common interpersonal situations as an aid to general personality description and clinical decision making. The stimuli have been updated to depict more contemporary clothing and hair styles.

- The authors state that the framework for projective testing does not apply because the stimuli in the set are not ambiguous but depict recognizable real-life events.

- The pictures pull for themes of parent-child relationships, sibling relationships, aggression, mastery, parental disagreement, parental affection, observation of nudity, and school and peer relationships. Four of the cards depict aggressive situations and require the demonstration of strategies for coping with aggressive provocation.

- The Roberts–2 uses children's expressive language as an index of cogitive social skills. Scoring criteria are objective and yield high interrater agreement.

- The standardization sample (N = 1,060) includes a nationally representative sample of children ages 6 to 18 years, encompassing the school-aged population (grades 1 to 12) and an additional sample of clinical cases (N = 467).

- Validation evidence comprises developmental progression of social cognitive skill and differences between a national representative sample and a clinical sample.

acknowledged that the TAT was designed for use with children and adults, with more than half the cards deemed appropriate for use with children (Murray, 1943), the authors observed that few cards actually depict children. In the absence of an agreed-upon system for scoring the content and structure of stories, the authors proposed an interpretive approach along with a new set of stimuli. The revised version of this test described in the Manual (Roberts & Gruber, 2005) is supplemented by a Casebook (Roberts, 2007) and higlighted in Rapid Reference 8.14.

Administration

On an individual basis, all 16 cards are administered in numerical order using the version appropriate to the subject's gender and following the instructions in the standardization procedures:

> I have a number of pictures I am going to show you one at a time. I want you to make up a story about each picture. Please tell me what is happening

in the picture, what led up to this scene, and how the story ends. Tell me what the people are talking about and feeling. Use your imagination and remember that there are no right or wrong answers for making up stories to the pictures." If necessary, the examiner may add, "I want you to tell me a story about the picture with a beginning, middle, and end. Tell me what's happening in the picture. Tell me what the people are doing, feeling, thinking, and talking about. I will help you get started with the first two stories. (p. 11)

During the administration of the first two cards, the examiner provides sufficient structure to assure that the instructions are understood, presenting the following queries: (a) What is happening? (b) How is he or she feeling or how are they feeling? (c) What is he or she doing or talking about or what are they doing or talking about? (d) What happened before? (e) How does the story end, or what happens next? These questions may be used freely during the stories told to the first two cards but should be used sparingly thereafter. The child's consistent omission of certain story elements requested by the instructions is relevant information. The examiner may inquire as needed to clarify responses. Examples include asking the child to identify who is meant by "he" when a pronoun may refer to more than one character. The examiner should indicate the point in the story where an inquiry was used to distinguish spontaneous responses from those that were cued. A child who is unable to tell a story may be encouraged to start by describing the picture.

Stimuli

The examiners select the most appropriate set of cards for the individual being examined from among three distinct sets (depicting persons who are White, Black, or Hispanic). The stimulus cards depict common situations, conflicts, and stresses in children's lives. Of the 27 cards in each set, 11 have parallel male and female versions, indicated by the letter "B" and "G" on the back of the card, and 5 are used for both. Therefore, only 16 of the cards may be administered to each child (see Rapid Reference 8.15).

Interpretation

The measures include indices of *developmental adaptive function*, documenting change in social understanding with maturity and experience, and *clinical function*, documenting differences between children and adolescents experiencing social or emotional difficulties and normative peers. Normative data and clinical comparisons are available for seven scales and their subscales (Rapid Reference 8.16).

≡ *Rapid Reference 8.15*

The Roberts–2 Stimuli Were Designed to Elicit the Following Themes:

Card 1B/G: Family interaction

Card 2B/G: Maternal support

Card 3B/G: Schoolwork

Card 4: Peer support

Card 5B/G: Parental affection

Card 6B/G: Peer/racial interaction

Card 7B/G: Anxiety/illness

Card 8: Family interaction

Card 9: Physical aggression

Card 10B/G: Sibling rivalry

Card 11: Fear

Card 12B/G: Maternal depression/illness

Card 13B/G: Aggression release

Card 14B/G: Maternal limit-setting

Card 15: Nudity/sexuality

Card 16B/G: Parental support

≡ *Rapid Reference 8.16*

Roberts–2 Scales and Subscales

The Roberts–2 includes seven groups of scales, each encompassing two to six subscales:

Theme overview:* popular pull; complete meaning of the scene.

Available resources: Five categories include: 1. support self-feeling; 2. support self-advocacy; 3. support other-feelings; 4. support other-help; 5. reliance on other; 6. limit setting.

Problem identification:* Five hierarchical levels of problem identification are: recognition, description, clarification, definition, explanation.

Resolution:* Five hierarchical levels of problem resolution are: simple closure, easy and realistically positive outcome, process described in constructive resolution, process described in realistic outcome with feelings and situations, and elaborated process with possible insight.

Emotion: Four categories of emotions are included: anxiety, aggression, depression, rejection.

Outcome:** Include four types: unresolved, nonadaptive, maladaptive, unrealistic.

(continued)

Unusual or atypical responses: Categories are: refusal (no scorable responses or antisocial content) and atypical responses (content or structure that significantly deviates from the usual in five categories: illogical, cognitive distortion, loose thought; misidentification of theme; violence or excessive aggression; abuse or deprivation; imaginary content such as monsters or ghosts; death of main figure in the card; sexual content or other clinically significant content).

*differentiates both developmental and clinical status;
**differentiates best between clinic and nonclinic groups.

COMPARISON OF ROBERTS AND TAT

To use the Roberts–2 as it was intended, the reader is referred to the Manual. To illustrate the role of the stimulus pull, stories told about Roberts–2 cards 3F and 10F are compared with stories told about TAT cards 1 and 7GF. The stories were selected from the protocol obtained from January, a 10-year-old girl in sixth grade, who was evaluated to clarify her parents' concerns that their daughter is not completing schoolwork in a timely manner and seems troubled by worries and self-doubts about her ability to finish and perform well on tests, especially when they are timed and seem important. According to her parents, January requires much more time to complete academic work than a typical student would require. Despite her currently good grades, her parents are concerned about her ability to complete high-stakes tests in the future and her ability to finish work on her own without extensive support from parents or teachers. Scores on the Wechsler scales (shown in Rapid Reference 8.17) were in the average range, with the exception of a below average score in processing speed. The Roberts stories were coded according to selected variables from the Roberts Manual, and TAT stories were coded according to selected variables described in earlier chapters of this book.

≡ Rapid Reference 8.17

January's Wechsler Intelligence Scale for Children–Fourth Edition (WISC-IV)

Mean = 100, SD = 15

	Index	Score 95% CI	Percentile Rank	Classification
Verbal Comprehension	102	[95–109]	55th	Average Range
Perceptual Reasoning	108	[100–115]	70th	Average Range
Working Memory	110	[102–117]	75th	Average Range
Processing Speed	83	[76–94]	13th	Below Average
FSIQ	103	[98–108]	58th	Average Range

Roberts Card 3F:

The card depicts a student sitting at a desk with books unopened. The most common theme, hence the *popular pull*, is school-related difficulty. The Roberts–2 Manual indicates that nonreferred children tend to demonstrate a positive attitude toward the task and to *resolve the problem successfully*, whereas clinic-referred children express negative attitudes toward school and *do not resolve the problem*. Often, clinic-referred children describe the character as being punished, not completing schoolwork, or as angry at parent or teacher for demanding the work.

"Once upon a time there was a girl who liked to study but also to have fun. She was very intelligent. She had many books that she liked to read. She had a perfect handwriting and a perfect cooperation in class. One day for some reason she felt sad and her handwriting started to look sloppy, and as if she doesn't like to study any more. She felt very tired. She didn't understand why. Last night she had a big party, up till 2 AM, that was probably why she was tired because usually she sleeps at 8:30 PM. So she figured out that she has to try her best to cooperate in the classroom. And that she decided that I can work harder than this, even though I'm tired, because I really like to learn. And that's her final decision, to learn even though she's tired. The end."

Popular pull: Yes, the story is about a child having difficulty with schoolwork.

Problem identification: Levels are *recognition, description, clarification, definition,* and *explanation.* The highest of these levels, Problem Identification 5 (explanation), applies as the preceding factors and reasons for the problem situation and resulting internal conflict are well articulated.

Problem resolution: The five levels include simple closure or easy outcome, easy and realistic positive outcome, process described in constructive resolution, process described in constructive resolution of feelings and situations, and elaborated process with possible insight. The applicable level is Resolution 5 (where the process is fully described in a constructive resolution that addresses the problem and the feelings).

TAT Card 1: Boy is sitting at desk with violin in front of him. Although common themes relate to achievement, playing the violin is not mandatory and the impetus to play often comes from the family, hence not necessarily related to the school context. Nevertheless, January links playing this instrument with school outcomes.

"Once upon a time there was a boy who liked, who didn't like to play the violin. But he was obligated to play the violin. When, now he is looking around and thinking if he should play it to get a good grade in school or if he shouldn't cuz he doesn't like to do it. And at the end he says I'd rather not play it because I don't like it. The end. [Feeling?] He's feeling like the fact that he is not playing the violin. He feels quite satisfied that he doesn't have to do it because he doesn't really care about it."

Perceptual Integration: Refers to the extent to which the narrative coordinates the *perceptual* (details of the scene) and *conceptual* (meaning of the scene) processes (includes the *accuracy* of the story in accounting for the nuances of the stimulus; narrator's understanding of *social causality*, and narrator's *psychological mindedness* in coordinating the inner and outer world). The perceptual details are well accounted for but social causality is not as well incorporated. In giving up the obligation and the good grades because of not liking the activity, the character does not anticipate any consequences. Of five levels, this story is coded at level 3 (superficial).

Level of coping with the negative affect: Coping is coded at three levels—*noncoping or unrealistic coping with negative emotions, immediate or short-term coping,* and *long-term realistic coping* with the feeling and the problem. In this story, coping level 2 is coded, indicating that the tensions are addressed with an immediate, short-term strategy that ignores the long-term issues.

Level of self-regulation: Five levels include: *dysregulation, immediacy, external direction, internal direction,* and *self-determination.* If the violin was a hobby and not linked to the child's future education, then deciding not to play would be compatible with a high level of self-regulation, depending on the decision-making process. However, to get a high score on self-regulation in this story, the problem resolution would have to address not only the immediate feelings but also the long-term issues raised by the conflict. The level of self-regulation is *immediacy* (level 2).

In the more structured context of the Roberts stimulus, the resolution reveals January's self-attributed motive or commitment to be a good student (despite being tired), whereas the less structured TAT stimulus reveals her implicit desire to be free of burdensome obligations. The imports of the two stories capture January's explicit and implicit motives, respectively.

Import Roberts: If you take pride in being smart and cooperative, when your work starts to slip and you are no longer interested, you decide you have to try harder.

Import TAT: If you feel obliged to engage in a disliked activity, you are satisfied with your decision to abandon that activity, even if it means getting bad grades.

Roberts10F: This card, depicting a mother caring for a baby with an older child observing the interactions, often elicits feelings of being jealous or being ignored. Both clinic-referred and nonreferred children describe the older child as having negative feelings about the mother's attention toward the baby. However, nonreferred children, in contrast to referred children, tend to generate positive resolutions.

"Once upon a time there was a girl and her mother. The mother had, the girl had a baby brother which the mother gave birth to. But for some reason the girl didn't like the new baby. She felt it cries too much and it takes her mother away from her. Now her mother is too occupied with taking care of the baby. She thinks that her mother doesn't like her any more though. The mother is very happy about the baby, that she has gave birth to a healthy baby. And the baby is showing that the baby likes her. So it turns out that the mother understands that her other daughter is not very happy about her, so she explains to her how it's important to take care of the baby and she still likes her, but she also has to take care of the baby, but she will always love her. And so it turns out that the girl's not that mad anymore even though she sees the baby occupying her mother at all times. Except the time when the mother got to take 2 minutes to talk to her. And they both understand each other and the three people find out to like each other, even the baby who likes the mom. And it turns out that the baby also likes the sister. The end."

Popular pull: Yes, the story is about a mother taking care of an infant with older sibling observing (and feeling jealous or ignored).

Problem identification: The highest level, *explanation*, applies. The preceding factors and reasons for the problem situation are well articulated and the resulting internal conflict is adequately described.

Problem resolution: The highest level, Resolution 5, is coded (where the process is fully described in a constructive resolution that addresses the problem and the feelings).

TAT 7GF: This card depicts an older woman sitting on the sofa, reading or speaking to a girl close beside her who is holding a doll in her lap and looking away.

"Once upon a time there was a little girl with her mom who was begging her to go to school. But her mom just gave birth to a baby and told the girl now, you must take care of the baby for her mom because her mom is busy studying or reading a book. The girl is now looking outside, wishing she could go to school while she's watching the other kids playing outside a game, and now going to the classroom and learning how to read. She also likes to read. So she wishes very much that she can go to school. She feels sad and lonely without her friends but at the same time, warm, that at least she is helping her mother. For taking care of the baby. The end. [Turn out?] That she figured out that it's better to take care of her mom and maybe when the baby will grow up and probably be a student and she doesn't have to watch over it any more, and she could probably go to school and from there, she might proceed and be successful. So it turns out that, she was ok because she knew she was actually helping her mom. The end."

Perceptual integration: The narrator relies on the perceptual details at the expense of conceptual process (understanding social causality is amiss as mother and daughter switch roles, mom reading and daughter giving up her education). Of five levels, this story is coded at level 3 (superficial).

Level of coping with the negative affect: This story is coded at level one of three—noncoping as the tensions are not addressed realistically.

Level of self-regulation: The level of self-regulation is external direction (level 3) as the story resolution is stuck in the pictured cues and the character's decisions are based on meeting others' expectations (without balancing external demands with one's own needs).

Stories about Roberts card 10F and TAT card 7GF share the general theme of the birth of a sibling and the reaction of the older sister. However, the TAT story provides a less clear-cut positive resolution in which a significant sacrifice is required of the sibling to put her education on hold until the baby grows up so the mother can busy herself reading (as portrayed in the picture). This unlikely resolution to the story appears to be influenced by the perceptual features of the card (where the mom is reading and the girl is holding the baby). The outcome did not transcend the scene as portrayed, underscoring January's reliance on the immediate stimulus cues to resolve the dilemma at the expense of incorporating realistic social causality in her reasoning. On the familiar Roberts pictures, she was able to rely on available social schemas (scripts).

Roberts Import: If a new baby takes mother's attention away, the older sibling feels rejected but with reassurance of being loved she accepts the situation and understands that they all love each other.

TAT Import: If upon the birth of a new sibling the older sister complies with the request to delay going to school (indefinitely) to help raise the baby (while her mother is busy reading), she feels lonely and deprived, but thinking about helping her mom makes her feel okay.

To clarify functioning across tasks and situations requiring different competencies, more research is needed to compare cognitive-emotional processes applied to storytelling in response to stimuli that vary in degree of structure, novelty, and complexity (Teglasi, 1998).

 **TEST YOURSELF**

1. **Subsequent to the introduction of the TAT, innovations in storytelling assessment involved**

   (a) introducing new stimuli without additional interpretive procedures.

   (b) developing new ways to interpret existing picture sets.

   (c) proposing new sets of stimuli along with interpretive criteria.

   (d) all of the above.

2. **What was the rationale for introducing the CAT, CAT-H, and CAT-S?**

3. **CAT administration differs from TAT administration because the CAT**

   (a) does not request the inclusion of thoughts and feelings.

   (b) introduces the task as a game.

   (c) both "a" and "b."

   (d) neither "a" nor "b."

4. **What was the rationale for developing the TEMAS?**

5. **What was the rationale for developing the Roberts-2?**

Answers: 1. d; 2. The rationale behind CAT was that young children would identify more with animal than with human figures; furthermore, there was a perceived need for a set of stimuli designed to study specific developmental issues. The rationale for CAT-H was the need for a parallel set with human figures because research did not support the superiority of animal figures. Also, some children age 7 and older thought that the animal stimuli were "childish." The rationale for the supplemental stimuli in CAT-S was to learn about specific clinically relevant problems; 3. c; 4. TEMAS stimuli were introduced in an effort to make the storytelling technique more suitable for minority children by depicting urban settings, parallel sets showing minority and nonminority characters, and population-specific norms; 5. Roberts-2 stimuli were designed to portray children in contrast to the TAT set, which contains few cards depicting children. Moreover, in the absence of an agreed-upon scoring system, the authors proposed an interpretive approach along with new stimuli.

Nine

STRENGTHS AND WEAKNESSES OF
STORYTELLING ASSESSMENT TECHNIQUES

Storytelling makes a unique contribution to a comprehensive assessment. The dilemma for the field is that the technique's versatility and richness, which constitute its greatest assets, are also the sources of its greatest liability. A chief advantage of storytelling is its capacity to go beyond the content of cognitions, such as a tally of anxiety-related thoughts, to reveal the process of thinking, reasoning, and developing ideas. Reducing rich and complex narrative data to simple units that are normatively and psychometrically evaluated may undermine the strength of the method. As with any other assessment procedure, storytelling must be used in accord with its purpose and with acknowledgment of its strengths and limitations. Strengths or weaknesses that apply broadly to storytelling methods may vary across specific approaches to eliciting, coding, or interpreting the stories. Narratives may be elicited with different stimuli, coded in multiple ways, and interpreted in light of multiple perspectives. Interpretive procedures abound (see Jenkins, 2008), with no consensus on a single approach that is sufficiently comprehensive for clinical use. Perhaps the strengths and weaknesses of storytelling methods are most evident in comparison to other types of measures in a comprehensive assessment battery.

UNIQUE CONTRIBUTION OF STORYTELLING
TO A COMPREHENSIVE ASSESSMENT

Storytelling techniques have been described as performance tests of personality to differentiate between what is self-reported and what is gleaned from task performance (Teglasi, 1998). The unique contribution of storytelling methods in the assessment of psychological functioning is based on two fundamental distinctions. One is between what individuals report and what they actually experience and the other is between how individuals perform under conditions that are maximal and typical. As a personality performance measure, storytelling reveals the narrators' thought processes and problem-solving strategies in managing the task in ways that differ from self-report. Moreover, the task demands of storytelling techniques (typical performance conditions) may be compared with those of the more structured performance tests used to assess ability or achievement (maximal performance conditions). Whereas items on tests of cognitive ability and knowledge require a single correct solution, personality performance tests permit a wide range of "correct" approaches. These variations reveal individual differences in the schemas for organizing information about the self, others, and the world that may be outside conscious awareness and not amenable to self-report. In an assessment battery, personality performance measures such as storytelling are unique among performance tasks in that they predict resources for organizing responses to situations without clear performance standards, whereas performance on the more structured tests predict competence in similarly structured situations (see Teglasi, 1993, 1998).

DON'T FORGET

The storytelling task demands may vary according to the characteristics of the cards presented (such as ambiguity or complexity, see Chapter 2), instructions given (including prompts), and the method for evaluating responses.

Comparison with Other Performance Tests in the Battery

Similar to life situations, performance tests vary in terms of the amount of structure, cues, or prompts provided to support responses and in the amount of organization required for adequate performance. Generally, cognitive measures, such as tasks on the Wechsler scales, provide more structure than do conditions encountered in everyday situations. For example, verbally communicated problems tend to contain words that act as cues for accessing relevant knowledge, whereas daily judgments and decisions require spontaneous use of prior knowledge. The presence of cues, instructions, feedback, or external incentives to bolster responses defines *maximal* performance conditions, whereas the absence of such external guides characterizes *typical* conditions. Typical and maximal performances are weakly correlated (Sackett, Zedek, & Fogli, 1988). Structured standardized tests predict important academic and professional outcomes (see Sackett, Borneman, & Connelly, 2008). However, fluid intelligence as measured with structured tests does not correspond well with intellectual efforts expended day to day (Ackerman & Heggestad, 1997). Typically, correlations between cognitive test scores and real-life accomplishments are no better than about .30 (e.g., Deary & Stough, 1996; Hunt, 1980).

Knowledge that is available when prompted by specific questions (maximal conditions) but is not sufficiently organized to be used in problem-solving situations (typical conditions) has been described as "inert" (Bransford, Franks, Vye, & Sherwood, 1989). Limitations on generalizing from responses to structured tasks to real-life conditions are understandable in terms of the attributes that these measures do not assess, including: being aware that a problem exists or that a task needs to be done; recognizing and responding to implicit or subtle cues; setting priorities and planning toward their implementation; taking necessary initiative to pursue intentions; organizing, pacing, and monitoring responses; seeking or utilizing feedback; and sustaining long-term investment in relationships and independent activities. These competencies, traditionally viewed as pertaining to the personality domain, are needed for everyday functioning. Yet, they are not assessed when tasks are highly structured (see Rapid Reference 9.1).

To characterize day-to-day functioning, the essential distinction is not between "cognitive" and "noncognitive" processes. If the term *noncognitive* refers to a process not related to thinking or reasoning, it is a misnomer when applied to responses to personality performance measures or to life challenges. All human responses are based on some form of perception and encoding of stimuli as well as interpretation of such stimuli in light of prior experiences. Therefore, the relevant contrast between performance tasks of cognition and of personality is the type of information processing or reasoning that is required and the type of life tasks or circumstances to which such processing is germane.

Whereas the *ability* to reason is evaluated with tasks providing maximal conditions, the *disposition* to reason in various real-life conditions is evaluated under typical performance conditions. The disposition to reason is influenced by the individual's *sensitivity* to recognize the moments that call for reasoning and the *inclination* to invest the necessary energy (Perkins and Ritchhart, 2004). Individuals may be more or less inclined to scrutinize the available cues, to seek new information, and to think about or act on the information that is available. A dispositional view of thinking focuses on how the person *typically* reasons in real-life conditions, not on whether the person is *able* to reason under maximal performance conditions that elicit solutions to clear problems (Ritchhart, 2002). This maximal-typical distinction applies regardless of whether performance pertains to content under the purview of personality (social emotional) or

≡ Rapid Reference 9.1

Contrast Between Structured Performance Measures and Storytelling

Structured Performance Measures	Storytelling
Provides the verbal cues to access specific information or models that guide problem solving, thereby revealing performance under *maximal conditions* (Sackett et al., 1988)	Entails spontaneous use of schemas to interpret the scene, recognize that a problem exists, and formulate a resolution, thereby revealing performance under *typical conditions*
Elicits knowledge in piecemeal fashion without revealing the process involved in learning or using it (Spitz, 1988)	Reveals the synthesis of ideas in accord with characteristic style of organizing experiences
Specifies a single correct solution	Sets general performance criteria, such as coherence, logic, and match-with-stimulus, in line with many acceptable ways to accomplish the task
Predicts performance in familiar, scripted situations	Predicts adjustment in novel, stressful, or complex situations
If complex, the task may require planning multiple steps	Reveals planning over time to anticipate likely outcomes and pursue intentions
Is the product of logical learning and analysis	Is the product of reciprocal encounters with the world and reflection

cognition/achievement (nonsocial and nonemotional). For instance, a construct such as *emotion understanding* may be measured with highly structured tasks as *ability* (e.g., emotion identification from facial expressions or selecting emotions to match common situations) or under ambiguous conditions as *disposition* (e.g., telling a story that involves accurate interpretation of emotions and relationships depicted in TAT cards).

Comparison to Self-Report

Despite their many advantages, self-report inventories have significant limitations (for a review, see Glass & Arnkoff, 1997), and there is an increasing awareness of the need to combine self-report measures with other approaches to assess personality. Paper-and-pencil measures, open-ended interviews, and other procedures for obtaining verbal self-descriptions all require respondents to give a conscious accounting of their concepts of self, others, and the world. However, considerable research indicates that people are not aware of many of their own cognitive processes (e.g., Kihlstrom, 1987). For instance, self-judgments of emotional intelligence (e.g., Brackett et al., 2006; "do you usually clearly perceive the emotional state you are in?") are not closely related to performance measures. To the extent that schemas operate outside awareness, they are not amenable to assessment via self-report, but are inferred by others. Storytelling brings to light the cognitive-emotional contents and structures comprising schemas that operate outside awareness, whereas self-report questionnaire methods clarify the characteristics that are attributed to the self (see Rapid Reference 9.2).

In the assessment of motives, a convincing body of evidence (see Burton, Lydon, Alessandro, & Koestner, 2006) indicates that questionnaires measure *self-attributed* motives (important to an individual's identity or self-presentation) and TAT-type tasks measure *implicit motives* (derived from enjoyment and intrinsic interest). The independence of self-attributed and implicit psychological constructs holds up even when the method of measurement is comparable in the specific situational cues and themes sampled (Schultheiss, Yankova, Dirlikov, & Schad, 2009). Schultheiss and colleagues measured implicit motives using a picture story exercise where individuals freely told stories about pictures of everyday scenes in response to standard instructions. They measured the analogous explicit motive by presenting respondents with the same pictures (about which they just told stories) and provided self-descriptive statements that were matched with the themes used to code the free response stories. The instructions for the explicit motive measure were: "imagine for each picture that you would be one of the people in the situation and then answer 14 questions about what you would think, feel, want or try to do in that situation" (p. 74). Each of the questions was posed in true–false format. In essence, the ideas spontaneously expressed in response to stimuli differed from those chosen from among various options.

Because self-attributed and implicit motives predict behavior under different conditions, low agreement between motives measured with narrative and with

⬟ *Rapid Reference 9.2*

Contrast Between Self-Report and Storytelling

Self-Report	Storytelling
Provides information that the individual has verbally organized (*self-attributed, explicit*) and wishes to share.	Reveals understandings that may not be incorporated into the individual's conscious self-concept (*implicit*) and that thus are not amenable to assessment with self-report.
Is amenable to defensive distortion and faking to present a socially desirable account of oneself.	Works around the problem of faking by assessing schemas that operate outside awareness.
Predicts immediate choices, particularly if cued by the situation.	Predicts spontaneous and sustained preferences (Spangler, 1992).
Does not capture the idiosyncratic nature of thoughts, because concerns are not tied to information processing or coping.	Reveals the content of thoughts and manner of processing information (problem identification, reasoning, resolving the problem).
Reveals controlled reflections that may not be sensitive to automatic cognitive processing. Such cognitions may change with intervention (e.g., cognitive therapy) but may not mediate other changes (Hollon & Kendall, 1980; Hollon, Kendall, & Lumry, 1986).	Reveals functional structures that organize ideas and connect intentions, actions, outcomes, and other aspects of information processing.

self-report (e.g., Brunstein & Maier, 2005; Pang & Schultheiss, 2005; Schultheiss & Brunstein, 2001; Spangler, 1992) may be viewed as advantageous. Recent work has focused on their joint influences where individuals might channel implicit motives in ways that are congruent with their preferences for self-presentation. For instance, persons who are high on implicit aggression but endorse a prosocial self-image would likely espouse cognitions to justify aggression or favor indirect over direct ways to express aggression (see Frost, Ko, & James, 2007). Moreover, implicit motives may be amenable to observation and report by well-known others (e.g., Daugherty, Kurtz, & Phebus, 2009).

Versatility as Both a Strength and a Liability

Storytelling provides rich and complex information that is difficult to obtain in other ways and is particularly useful in assessing individuals' resources in unfamiliar, complex, or stressful situations. Systematic use of the technique requires labor-intensive interpretation by highly trained professionals. However, training generalizes to other interactions, such as interviews, where clinicians make judgments about communication, speech patterns, and the reality base of clients' thought processes. Given the inherent drawbacks of reducing multifaceted data into "scores," professionals have different opinions as to the need for precise psychometric documentation in contrast to continued reliance on general interpretive guidelines and performance standards for storytelling. Other sources of information compensate for gaps left by storytelling and vice versa. The storytelling task has the advantage of going beyond the content of cognitions by establishing functional interpretive units that combine structure, process, and content of responses. Indeed, counting specific cognitions apart from their contexts would violate narrative assumptions. As Cramer (1996) put it, "Scoring schemas that rely on checklists to characterize what the storyteller did and did not say overlook the important qualities that make one story different from another—different, not because of using different words but because the words are arranged in different ways to convey different meanings" (p. 33). The problem is not with the use of checklists per se but with how they are used. Checklists that segment words from the whole distort the psychological process of the narrator. Some authors advocate that raters stay close to the actual words to minimize inference and increase rater agreement. However, increasing consistency among coders by relying on the words ignores the implicit understandings conveyed by the juxtaposition of ideas and runs the risk of sacrificing validity (see Rapid Reference 9.3). Tallying the frequency of ideas that are consistent with certain emotions such as anxiety, depression, or anger, even comparing them to norms, may engender high reliability but does not provide information about how the narrator understands those emotions. It has been said that "The aim of science is to seek the simplest explanation of complex facts. We are apt to fall into the error of thinking that the facts are simple because simplicity is the goal of our quest. The guiding motto in the life of every natural philosopher should be 'seek simplicity and distrust it'" (Alfred North Whitehead (1861–1947) English mathematician and philosopher. Concepts of Nature, p. 163). In the interest of science, it is better to provide coders of narratives with adequate training than to obtain consistency across raters by sacrificing the meaning of the response.

CAUTION

Because reliability, validity, and norms for storytelling are established for a particular set of stimuli, method of administration, and interpretive procedure, it would be unwise to undertake large-scale, normative studies prior to arriving at some consensus about clinically valid units of interpretation and a set of agreed-upon stimuli.

≡ Rapid Reference 9.3

Cautions About Validation

1. Validity must be demonstrated separately for each set of stimuli, interpretive system, and procedure for administration.
2. Validity must be documented for each professional, and each professional must have intensive training. The quantification of rich qualitative data is possible but requires trained inferences.
3. Units of content in isolation, particularly if coded directly from the words, has not been clinically useful. More promising approaches consider clusters (of content, structure, and narrative process) pertaining to a particular psychological construct.
4. Validation studies are often conducted through group comparison, yet clinical decisions are made for individuals.
5. Although consulting norms or comparisons with clinical samples is informative for the interpretation, the TAT is best used to clarify individuality within clinical diagnoses rather than to verify that diagnosis.
6. The selection of external criteria for validation should be guided by considering the match between the constructs as assessed by the TAT task and by indicators in real-life settings (i.e., coping, self-regulation, or meeting task demands under typical conditions).

Self-report about emotions does not reveal how the individual thinks about emotions. For instance, individuals who are high in the "granularity" of their emotional experiences make finer distinctions such as between anger, annoyance, humiliation, or frustration, whereas those with low granularity are less precise in categorizing emotions. More granular representations of emotions increase coping resources, partly because they provide more nuanced connections of the experienced state with potential causes and response options (Barrett & Gross, 2001).

The following two stories, told to TAT card 3BM by two teens with above average IQ scores, portray unpleasant states with different degrees of emotional "granularity."

Brian (age 14): (Laughs) Suzie's 18 years old. She just went into college at University of Maryland and she went to her first Frat party. She got way too drunk, crashed her car into a trash can and fell asleep like this. The next morning she had a really bad hangover and she couldn't find where she put her keys. /T/ She's dreaming. /F/ Drunk. (laughs)

Gail (age 15): Um, [SP] a little boy is walking his dog and he decides to let the dog off the leash for a while so that it can run around by itself. And the dog runs away and he looks over and he calls his name and he can't find him. He is getting more and more upset and he realizes that he probably won't find the dog because he lives in a big city and the dog could be anywhere. So he sits down by a bench and puts his head on the bench and begins to cry. He feels really guilty because he knows it's his fault that the dog ran away; he doesn't know what to do. He is trying to think of places he could look. And then he looks up and the dog is next to him.

Gail's story is consistent with high granularity, which involves associations of rich mental content with emotional valence (upset, guilty, at fault), and Brian's story is consistent with low granularity (no emotion words at all, but physical states of being drunk, hungover, asleep). Both narrators recognize the negative affect tone of the stimulus but Gail conceptualizes the negative emotions as internally organized responses to one's actions and events, whereas Brian views negative states as exclusively a function of external events.

The clinical value of the TAT is not in the prediction of specific actions but in the explanation of the behaviors that are of concern by clarifying how the individual thinks about the self, others, and the world. Thus, although the TAT may suggest that an individual has the resources to plan, anticipate, and cope with challenges, actual adjustment in a particular context will depend on how that environment responds to the individual's initiative and on other characteristics of the individual. Temperamental qualities also play an important role. An individual who misreads social cues in the TAT pictures but has an easygoing temperament will behave differently than an individual who similarly misreads social cues but is highly reactive and easily provoked. Predicting behavior from TAT responses is a complex endeavor (see Rapid Reference 9.4).

≡ Rapid Reference 9.4

Pitfalls of Predicting Aggressive Behavior from Story Content

1. Individuals who exhibit aggressive behavior do not necessarily express aggressive content in stories. Hence, simple frequency counts are not only misleading but also fail to capitalize on the capacity of storytelling to assess social information processing that may explain aggressive behavior.

2. Interpretation must take into account the nature of stimuli, such as their ambiguity and presentation of aggressive cues. Pictures that pull for aggression bring to light factors that mitigate its expression, whereas aggressive themes told to nonaggressive stimuli signal problems inhibiting aggressive thoughts and/or actions (Salz & Epstein, 1963). Aggressive children assume hostile intent in ambiguous situations (Crick & Dodge, 1996); hence the importance of stimulus ambiguity.

3. Interpretation of aggressive content must take into account the

- pull of the stimulus.
- justification for the aggression.
- perceived benefits and consequences of aggressive behavior.
- factors that inhibit aggressive actions, such as anxiety about aggression, anticipation of consequences, reasoning about the intent of actions (not just their impact), social information processing, and empathy.
- level at which aggression, such as thoughts, feelings, actions, or some combination of these, is expressed. When making predictions, thoughts correspond to thoughts, feelings foretell emotions, and behaviors forecast actions (Tomkins, 1947).
- what is important to the individual's identity or self-presentation. Accordingly, in the prediction of how implicit aggression is likely to be expressed, it is helpful to consider self-attributed aggression and cognitions to justify aggression (see Frost, Ko, & James, 2007).

Future Directions

Two general trends regarding assessment with storytelling techniques that will inform future directions are (a) the broadening of theoretical perspectives to include emerging constructs from across various psychology subfields, and (b) the increasing call for standard scoring criteria with documented reliability, validity, and normative data.

Theoretical perspectives. Previous chapters have reviewed the relevance to storytelling of conceptual distinctions between (a) self-attributed and implicit versions of psychological constructs; and (b) maximal and typical conditions of performance. Current evidence documenting implicit and explicit versions of psychological constructs calls for evaluating both in an assessment battery by including self-report and personality performance measures. As individuals face various life situations, they bring a combination of implicit and explicit components of psychological processes. Implicit and explicit versions of psychological constructs explain responses under different conditions. Moreover, through their joint influences on behavior, cognition, and emotion, implicit and self-attributed

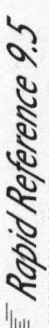

Rapid Reference 9.5

Template to Organize Information in a Comprehensive Evaluation

	Current Contexts	Prior History	Current Evaluation
Functional Resources: Implicit and explicit processes that are automatic or effortful, measured via self-report or performance tasks with social and nonsocial content under maximal or typical performance conditions			Measures: Self-attributed or implicit; maximal or typical
Affect self-regulation *Resources for affect regulation reside in temperamental dispositions and in the schemas that guide the interpretation of available information to appraise implications.*	Performance Conditions: SOCIAL • Maximal • Typical NONSOCIAL • Maximal • Typical	Performance Conditions: SOCIAL • Maximal • Typical NONSOCIAL • Maximal • Typical	Self-report scales Interview Personality performance Parent report Teacher report Peer report Observation
Attention self-regulation *Resources to regulate attention include detecting relevant information (vigilance), shifting focus as needed, and maintaining attention. Executive attention, such as flexibility in shifting focus, contributes to planning and anticipation along with prior knowledge or schemas that point to what is salient as the focus of attention.*	TASK • Maximal • Typical SOCIAL • Maximal • Typical	TASK • Maximal • Typical SOCIAL • Maximal • Typical	Self-report scales Personality performance Performance tests of attention Parent report Teacher report Peer report Observations

Behavior self-regulation *Behavior may be reactive to the moment or may be governed by rules, standards, or long-term purposes. Reactive regulation is unplanned, responsive to isolated, momentary provocations, immediate feelings, or situational presses (immediate consequences). More deliberate behavioral regulation, guided by goals and purposes, requires resources to implement the intended responses including plans, perseverance, and stamina.*	TASK • Maximal • Typical SOCIAL • Maximal • Typical	TASK • Maximal • Typical SOCIAL • Maximal • Typical	Self-report Interview Parent report Teacher report Peer report Personality performance Observations
Cognition *This construct includes reasoning, abstraction, working memory, executive functions, insight, and problem-solving resources.*	TASK • Maximal • Typical SOCIAL • Maximal • Typical	TASK • Maximal • Typical SOCIAL • Maximal • Typical	Structured tasks Personality performance
Attainment/Achievement/Knowledge *Prior knowledge informs performance and beliefs in multiple domains depending on how that knowledge is organized (ranging from rote or piecemeal to flexibly structured).*	TASK • Maximal • Typical SOCIAL • Maximal • Typical	TASK • Maximal • Typical SOCIAL • Maximal • Typical	Structured tasks, including standardized achievement tests Personality performance Grades Self-reports Parent reports Teacher or supervisor reports

(continued)

	Current Contexts	Prior History	Current Evaluation
Functional Resources: Implicit and explicit processes that are automatic or effortful, measured via self-report or performance tasks with social and nonsocial content under maximal or typical performance conditions			Measures: Self-attributed or implicit; maximal or typical
Motivation *Goals, intentions, standards, and ideas about sources of happiness or unhappiness direct action in concert with self-regulatory resources (attention, emotion, cognition, energy, stamina) and prior knowledge or skill to accomplish aims.*	TASK • Maximal • Typical SOCIAL • Maximal • Typical	TASK • Maximal • Typical SOCIAL • Maximal • Typical	Self-report Personality performance Parent report Teacher report Observation
Relationships *Connectedness, empathy, mutuality, and autonomy.*	Family Peer Authorities	Family Peer Authorities	Self-report Parent report Teacher report Peer report Personality performance

motives promote selective attention and information processing as well as patterns of approach and avoidance that shape individuals' experiences of exposure to contexts.

Rapid Reference 9.5 provides a template for organizing information about selected variables obtained in the course of a comprehensive evaluation by distinguishing between self-report and performance measures and between performance tasks providing maximal and typical conditions, regardless of whether the content is social or nonsocial. The variables included in this template (self-regulation of emotion, attention, and behavior; cognition; motivation; relationships) were selected because they are broadly applicable to real-life functioning and amenable to measurement with different methods and under various conditions. Conceptual clarity within each of these variables is crucial to a systematic assessment.

Psychometric perspectives: A clinically useful scoring system would have to focus on structural characteristics of narratives and principles abstracted from content (such as levels of problem solving implicit in connections between means and desired ends) rather than on coding content from words out of context. In clinical use, formal or structural variables have greater empirical support than tallies of content (e.g., McGrew & Teglasi, 1990). Moreover, certain formal characteristics of narrative come up in many studies with variations only in name or slightly different coding criteria. The field would benefit from a systematic synthesis of these structural qualities and the establishment of agreed-upon general criteria. However, to capture the unique concerns of the individual, these formal components will still have to be integrated with qualitative analysis of content. Even when norms are available, they are not sufficient for an adequate "interpretation," which entails a recursive, multistep process (see Rapid Reference 9.6).

≡ *Rapid Reference 9.6*

Steps in Clinical Use of Storytelling

1. Use a system to organize relevant information conceptually. This step may or may not include the consideration of formal normative data but does require familiarity with the specific storytelling method and knowledge of the conceptual and empirical underpinnings of assessed variables. In the absence of documented norms, the examiner must be aware of the types of responses expected, given the respondent's age, other characteristics, and circumstances.

(continued)

2. Synthesize conclusions drawn from storytelling with other sources of information. This step requires knowledge of how the various tests in the battery measure relevant constructs and an understanding of the client's circumstances and sociocultural context.

3. Translate the synthesized conclusions to the presenting concerns and circumstances of the examinee using relevant conceptual frameworks about development, psychopathology, and personality.

4. Plan interventions based on an understanding of the complexities of the presenting problem (with or without a formal diagnosis) and of the process of change and development.

🖎 TEST YOURSELF 🖎

1. **The richness and versatility of storytelling assessment methods have complicated the process of documenting its psychometric properties.**
   True or False?

2. **Storytelling differs from performance tasks such as the Wechsler scales by setting general performance criteria rather than designating a single correct solution.**
   True or False?

3. **Self-report differs from storytelling in all but one of the following:**
   (a) Self-report is easier to fake.
   (b) Self-report may not be sensitive to automatic cognitive processing.
   (c) Self-report usually captures the idiosyncratic nature of thought processes.
   (d) Self-report may change with intervention but may not mediate other changes.

4. **For clinical purposes, methods of coding stories that stay close to the words to minimize inference tend to be**
   (a) more reliable.
   (b) less valid.
   (c) both "a" and "b."
   (d) neither "a" nor "b."

5. **When predicting aggressive behavior from story content, which of the following statements is not a pitfall?**
   (a) Simple frequency counts of aggressive content fail to consider information that may mitigate against its expression.

(b) Depending on the stimulus, aggressive individuals are reportedly less likely to include aggressive content.

(c) Prediction is complicated by the expression of aggressive content through thoughts, feelings, or actions.

(d) All of the above are pitfalls.

Answers: 1. True; 2. True; 3. c; 4. c; 5. d.

Ten

STORYTELLING IN THE ASSESSMENT BATTERY

The template introduced in Chapter 9 for organizing information obtained in the context of a comprehensive evaluation distinguishes each psychological construct according to whether it applies to: (a) maximal or typical performance conditions; (b) procedures that pull for implicit or explicit versions of the construct; and (c) contexts that are primarily social or nonsocial. According to the template, each variable to be assessed is examined in light of patterns of consistencies or variations across maximal and typical conditions of performance, social and nonsocial contexts, self-attributed and implicit versions of constructs, and across various informants (see Rapid Reference 10.1).

Kyle, a 17-year-old high school junior, was evaluated to address his concerns about distractibility and lack of focus and the implications of these difficulties for his transition to college. Background information was given by his parents prior to the assessment and by Kyle during the course of the evaluation. Currently, Kyle's distractibiliy interferes with many aspects of his academic work (completing homework, remembering to hand in assignments, finishing tests) and with day-to-day activities (losing focus when playing team sports, driving a car, or performing on the keyboard). At the time of the evaluation Kyle was enrolled in a large public high school, taking some AP courses. Despite his admittedly minimal effort, Kyle observed that he was getting decent grades. Although Kyle first expressed concerns about difficulty concentrating in the ninth grade, his parents recall a history of "goofing off" going back to the second grade. Other aspects of his developmental history, including peer relationships and alcohol or other substance use, appeared normal. Kyle was recently diagnosed with ADHD by a psychiatrist and has begun to take medication on a regular basis, reporting that it helps his focus. He did not take the medication during the evaluation sessions.

DON'T FORGET

With questionnaires used in clinic settings, low agreement is common across informant pairs (e.g., parent-teacher; parent-child; child-teacher; mother-father; De Los Reyes, & Kazdin, 2005).

≋ Rapid Reference 10.1

Functioning in Social and Nonsocial Contexts Under Maximal and Typical Performance Conditions

Nonsocial Maximal	**Social Maximal**
Performance measures—examples are structured tasks of ability, achievement, attention, memory, or executive functioning.	*Performance measures*—examples are structured tasks to evaluate social cognitions or socioemotional understanding (contrived situations or vignettes).
Informant reports—about functioning or interest in conditions that provide structure and support (such as when receiving help with homework).	*Informant reports*—about functioning or interest in structured social settings such as how one would respond to a hypothetical situation or preferences for routine/structure.
Performance history—records of scores on structured tests, completion of structured class assignments, engagement, preferences to seek and persist in such situations.	*Performance history*—school record of social-emotional behaviors in the classroom or other structured social encounters; approach of such conditions.
Nonsocial Typical	**Social Typical**
Performance measures—examples are more open-ended measures (of knowledge, reasoning, attention) that call for planning, information seeking, autonomy to define the task or problem, or generating new ways to use prior knowledge (e.g., Rorschach).	*Performance measures*—examples are open-ended responses that involve intra- and interpersonal situations and require attention to relevant cues, self-regulation of emotions and behaviors, and schemas to set priorities and govern actions (e.g. TAT); observations in open-ended interactions.
Informant reports—about open-ended tasks requiring independent effort not guided by immediate feedback.	*Informant reports*—about functioning under open-ended social conditions as well as preferences, interest, enjoyment.
Performance history—records of task performance where independent effort and planning are required.	*Performance history*—records of disciplinary incidents kept in the schools or other settings; observations of behavior, nonverbal expressions, engagement, or proxy measures such as being accepted by peers as reflecting social responses under typical conditions.

 *Rapid Reference 10.2*

Template to Organize Assessment Information for Kyle

Functional Resources:	Maximal and Explicit (social and nonsocial)	Typical and Implicit (social and nonsocial)
Cognition	Performance on structured cognitive tasks (Wechsler Adult Intelligence Scale–Fourth Edition, WAIS-IV). K's scores ranged from average to high average.	In less defined problem-solving situations, K's reasoning was simplified (all or none) and inflexible (inability to see alternatives). Historical information and current adjustment reported by family and by K was consistent with inflexible thinking shown in the TAT stories. Paralleling the characters in his stories, K's reactions to daily challenges are often extreme, with little middle ground. In TAT stories, when people disagree or want different things, their relationship permanently ends with no attempt to compromise or understand each other. Dichotomous thinking, such as viewing people as either worthless or worthwhile, was evident in the TAT and in his self-report.
Affect self-regulation	Under structured conditions, K tries to portray a calm image and refrain from expressing his negative emotions. However, his frustration and impatience were evident in behavioral observations during structured tasks and in his self-reports of resentment when teachers and parents insist	Under the less structured performance condition of the TAT task, K did not demonstrate constructive strategies to cope with emotional tensions. In the face of negative emotions or burdensome expectations of others, characters in K's stories do not act to address the problem or to resolve the

	on his doing work that he views as meaningless (such as a report or homework). K talked about being troubled by pervasive feelings of anger and frustration and by not being able to concentrate. He describes a negative cycle where he cannot sleep and cannot concentrate, reporting that it takes extraordinary will power for him to do his schoolwork and that much of the time he feels like giving up. K reported that, when he feels worried or unhappy, he pushes those negative thoughts aside. K did not verbalize any other coping strategies to deal with issues that bother him, describing himself as passive.	sources of his distress, engaging instead in avoidance or unrealistic ways to make the problem disappear. K's tendency to make all-or-none judgments, evident in the TAT, often leads him to appraise situations simplistically, in ways that fuel his anger and prompt extreme responses. For instance, his interpretation of many of his parents' decisions as manifestations of their wrong-headed values, hypocrisy, and disrespect leaves him feeling enraged when they set limits or impose demands.
Attention self-regulation	Scores on selected subtests of the NEPSY (Attention & Executive Functioning) ranged from well below average (scaled scores of 2) to average (scaled scores of 9 and 10). The lowest score (2) was due to K's not having processed the instructions (shown by testing limits). Generally, K's performance was in the average range on easier tasks, requiring simple naming, but fell to well below average on items that required learning of new rules and working quickly. Difficulties with attention were also evident in his relatively low performance on tasks requiring concentration on the Woodcock-Johnson achievement test (following directions and story recall). K's relatively low	Both K and his parents expressed concerns about K's wandering mind and difficulty with concentration. Problems regulating attention are evident in struggles to complete and remember to turn in homework as well as in a tendency to "zone out" during some important daily activities. There are no reported concerns that distractibility impedes social adjustment. K's self-report placed him in the clinical range (Conners-Wells Adolescent Self-Report Scale) for Cognitive Problems/Inattention, Hyperactivity, and ADHD Index. These elevations are consistent with presenting concerns, task performance, and prior history, described by his parents. K's history of frustration due to

(continued)

Functional Resources:	Maximal and Explicit (social and nonsocial)	Typical and Implicit (social and nonsocial)
	performance on the recall portion of the Bender-Gestalt suggests that insufficient attention may be influencing incidental short-term memory.	undiagnosed attentional problems may have impacted his schemas. For example, difficulties with attention and concentration may have contributed to his view of others' expectations as burdens that he cannot meet (from TAT stories). In turn, his simplified reasoning in less structured contexts limits his flexibility to generate alternative paths to meet challenges or solve problems.
Behavior Self-Regulation	Though cooperative, K often seemed tired during the evaluation, frequently yawning and slouching in his chair. On most structured test items, K responded quickly and without reflection, often seeming to say what first came to mind without carefully crafting an answer. When writing sentences, he rushed and often did not use proper punctuation (such as periods at end of sentence). K was friendly and engaging during small-talk discussions with the examiner and appeared comfortable talking about his struggles at school and at home. He openly shared his frustrations and anger about school and the limits set by his family. According to examiner observations, self-, and parent reports, in most structured situations, K's behavior is socially appropriate. In structured contexts, if he thinks the work is sufficiently important, he complies by doing the bare minimum.	In less well-defined situations where immediate cues or social conventions are not salient, K has a tendency to react without planning. His schemas for self-regulation assessed with the TAT, along with difficulties regulating attention and affect, promote short-sighted, reactive behavior regulation. K seems caught in a vicious cycle of distractibility, sleeplessness, anger, and feelings of failure. He does not take stock of the bigger perspective but responds to the immediate preoccupations and external prompts.

Attainment Achievement Knowledge	Scores on structured achievement testing vary from above-average to average. Fluency with academic tasks was in the average range, indicating that his level of automaticity with basic skills is slightly less developed than the skills themselves. Oral language was lower than other areas of language achievement, (95% CI, [87–104], 38th percentile), lowered by difficulty recalling information from passages. K seemed to remember the gist of the stories, but not the details.	In typical contexts, K's achievement on difficult tasks is hindered by his lack of persistence, distractibility, frustration, and limited resources to organize long-term assignments and to set priorities. He devalues work that he finds onerous as not relevant to his goals. His attentional difficulties, undiagnosed until recently, probably constrained the development of schemas that connect constructive means to desired ends and contributed to his contempt for achievement strivings. These schemas, in combination with his difficulties concentrating and lack of interest in most academic subjects, present considerable obstacles to self-directed learning and performance.
Motivation	Observations of K's responses on structured tasks suggest that he is satisfied with doing the bare minimum and he did not take much pride in the work he did during the assessment. On the incomplete sentences task, K finished many of the stems with a single word rather than a complete idea. In general, on structured tasks (WAIS, Woodcock-Johnson, NEPSY, Bender-Gestalt), K persisted as long as it was easy for him but, when items became more difficult, he would give up rather than increase his effort.	Observations of his behaviors and response styles during administration of the various tasks, both structured and unstructured, are consistent with K's own reports and those of his parents. K's difficulty concentrating and low investment beyond doing the bare minimum to get by are consistent with his own report that much of his schoolwork is burdensome, boring, not worth doing, and irrelevant to his goal of becoming a musician and of getting into college. He characterized school as stupid and pointless. He expects life to improve in college, anticipating relief from work that holds no interest or meaning for him. Yet, K admitted concerns about sometimes losing his concentration

(continued)

Functional Resources:	Maximal and Explicit (social and nonsocial)	Typical and Implicit (social and nonsocial)
		even during preferred activities such as driving or playing the keyboard in his band. His lack of persistence is general across activities that call for effortful concentration, regardless of whether it is of his own choosing. TAT stories suggested low levels of motivation due to the virtual absence of instrumental actions of the characters to deal with the tensions or dilemmas they face. The stories were remarkable in the absence of initiative on the part of characters to set goals, to actively pursue intentions, or to cope with tensions. Lacking interest in his schoolwork, K stated that it takes an extraordinary amount of will power to focus on his work and that he often feels like giving up.
Relationships	According to self-reports (clinical interview and sentence completions), family interactions often make K feel angry and misunderstood. Despite his acknowledgment that his parents love and want to help him, K experiences their actions and decisions as working against his desires for independence, freedom, and responsibility for himself. He sees no rationale for their wanting to protect him and to help him structure his time to promote school success. K talks about friends as a source of support and happiness, describing himself as a reliable and caring friend. He also noted that he does not like most people and that a lot of people (peers and adults) get on his nerves (they are ignorant and have wrong values).	K's TAT stories indicate some uncertainty about the durability and importance of interpersonal relationships. Attributes of persons that pertain to momentary feelings were salient and relationships ended in rejection when characters experienced conflict or felt burdened by demands. There were no instances of understanding or compromising when characters had different views.

Rapid Reference 10.2 organizes information obtained from Kyle's assessment according to the template presented in Chapter 9. The TAT stories (Rapid Reference 10.3) and the coded worksheets are also provided (Rapid Reference 10.4). The intent is not to present a comprehensive report but to illustrate the use of the TAT within an assessment battery.

Procedures Used:

Bender-Gestalt Test of Visual-Motor Integration (copy and recall)
Wechsler Adult Intelligence Scale–Fourth Edition (WAIS-IV)
Woodcock-Johnson Tests of Achievement–Third Edition (WJ III Ach)
Developmental Neuropsychological Assessment (NEPSY), Second Edition, selected tests
Conners-Wells Adolescent Self-Report Scale: Long Version
Incomplete Sentences Structured Interview
Thematic Apperception Test
Clinical Interview

≣ Rapid Reference 10.3

Kyle's TAT stories

1. Johnny got a violin for his birthday. He tried to play it but he couldn't so he got really sad. He feels bad about himself and now he is crying so he put the violin on the table. The end. *Before?* He always wanted to play violin so he asked for one. *Thinking?* That he failed.

2. People live on a farm. The man has to stay home and plow the fields and the woman/girl goes off to school. They have to earn money because the woman in the corner is pregnant and is having a baby. *Before?* The man and the woman got married and then her sister came to live with them. *Feeling?* Worry, worrisome that they don't have enough money to feed the baby. *End?* Baby dies so they don't need money anymore.

3. BM. There was a man who wanted to be a painter but then he wasn't good enough so he shot himself and died. And after he died his paintings got famous but he didn't know about it because he was dead. *Feeling?* Not feeling. He is dead. *Before?* He was extraordinarily depressed.

4. They were childhood friends. She fell in love with him but he is gay. So she is sad. So he went and ran off with another man and she died alone. *Feeling?* She is depressed. He is confused. *Thinking?* He wants her to go away. She wants him to love her.

5. This woman's husband is always doing work in his study and never comes out. She comes in, tries to get him to come out, but he won't, so she leaves him. *She feeling?* Angry. *Before?* He was being reclusive all the time.

(continued)

7. GF. The little girl doesn't want to learn, but her mom is making her. She wants to go outside and play with her doll but her mother won't let her so she runs away. *End?* They never see each other again. *Feeling?* Angry at each other.

8. BM. The little boy is getting operated on. He gets killed during the operation and his brother's depressed. He's got...so his brother ran away. *Tell me more.* He got hit by a car so he had to go to the hospital.

13. The little kid doesn't want to work on the farm, so he sits playing the harmonica all day. *Tell me more.* So he becomes a famous harmonica player and makes millions of dollars. *Feeling?* Happy.

≡ *Rapid Reference 10.4*

Worksheets and Coding of Kyle's TAT Stories

COGNITION

Level of Abstraction

Card	1	2	3	4	5	7GF	8BM	13B						
Level	3	2	3	3	3	3	3	3						

Level of Perceptual Integration

Card	1	2	3	4	5	7GF	8BM	13B						
Level	3	3	3	2	3	3	3	3						

Notes: K incorporates the tensions depicted in the scenes as he identifies the problem or dilemma facing the characters. However, he does not generate appropriate resolutions or fully grasp the psychological processes. The tensions identified in the pictures often refer to frustration about inadequate performance, unwanted or burdensome obligations, or not getting what is wanted from a relationship.

Planning and Monitoring: Checklist of impediments

I. Narrator behavior

(Check as many as apply for each story)	Cards →	1	2	3	4	5	7GF	8BM	13B		
Resists task by making silly or irrelevant responses while narrating the story, such as making fun of or blaming the cards.											

(Check as many as apply for each story) Cards →	1	2	3	4	5	7GF	8BM	13B		
Negative reaction to the stimuli where the narrator is uncomfortable looking at the cards or is frightened or has an extreme emotional reaction to the scene.										
Significant discomfort, boredom, or frustration with the task (wants to stop, keeps asking how many more).										
Off task by chatting in a friendly manner while receiving instructions or narrating the story.										
Unusual behaviors such as throwing the cards or making noises.										

2. Narrator's plan for telling the story

(Check as many as apply for each story) Cards →	1	2	3	4	5	7GF	8BM	13B		
Associative or reactive generation of ideas (each idea relates to a previous one but none connect to an overall theme).										
Personal reactions (he's looking at me, this is scary) or first person stories suggesting difficulty distancing self from objective demands of the task.										
Narrator loses the set for telling the story (drawn away from initial focus by Examiner's inquiry or personal associations; switches sets from initial premises without transition; arbitrary shifts in perspective, abrupt changes from third to first person).										
Inconsistencies or contradictory details in the story.										

(continued)

(Check as many as apply for each story) Cards →	1	2	3	4	5	7GF	8BM	13B		
Narrative implies poor understanding of social causality (motives, intentions, means-ends connections).	✓	✓	✓	✓	✓	✓	✓	✓		
No tension and/or no outcome. (If checked, ignore the two items below.)										
Outcome or change occurs without adequate transition.								✓		
Outcome does not adequately address the central conflict, tension, or dilemma as posed by the narrator.	✓	✓	✓	✓	✓	✓	✓	✓		

3. Characters' feelings, thoughts, intentions, and behaviors

(Check as many as apply for each story)* Cards →	1	2	3	4	5	7GF	8BM	13B		
Characters don't care, are unable to overcome boredom, bored, engage in wishful thinking or short-term solutions.										
Characters preoccupied with immediate gratification or material gain without sufficient effort to attain them.										
Characters act or react without clearly defining the problem or goal; actions occur in response to a previous event or previous action without planning or anticipation.	✓	✓	✓	✓	✓	✓	✓	✓		
Characters take actions that are haphazard, unplanned, or without having anticipated outcome (consequences of their actions or inactions).	✓	✓	✓	✓	✓	✓	✓	✓		
Characters face challenges or situations that are ordinarily anticipated.	✓	✓	✓	✓	✓	✓		✓		

(Check as many as apply for each story)*	Cards →	1	2	3	4	5	7GF	8BM	13B		
Characters jump to inappropriate or premature conclusions; can't figure things out; fail to consider reasonable alternatives or overreact.		✓	✓	✓	✓	✓	✓	✓	✓		
Characters desire to avoid/escape legitimate, age-appropriate restrictions/ responsibilities considered unfair or incomprehensible.							✓		✓		
Characters continue to behave in ways that contradict how they think they "should" act.											

*Content may be too limited for any to apply

Notes: The above checklist highlights K's difficulties with planning and monitoring actions to pursue goals. Responses to external events or to frustrations are reactive and short-sighted. Although these extreme reactions are often hurtful, they are not ill-willed. Rather, the potential of adverse impact of the actions is not considered.

Time perspective

(Check as many as apply for each story)	Cards →	1	2	3	4	5	7GF	8BM	13B		
Immediate timeframe that does not transcend the stimulus cues or short-term emphasis on the "here-and-now."		✓									
Unrealistic or vague timeframe.			✓	✓	✓	✓	✓	✓	✓		
Appropriate timeframe for the problem set in the story.											

Process of reasoning/coherence of story structure

(Check as many as apply for each story)	Cards →	1	2	3	4	5	7GF	8BM	13B		
Disorganized narration, including level one PI, unfocused progression of ideas (personalized thoughts, perseveration, or emotional reactivity to the picture).											

(continued)

(Check as many as apply for each story) Cards ➡	1	2	3	4	5	7GF	8BM	13B		
Socially unacceptable content or conviction (e.g., bizarre; extreme helplessness, hostility, or violence).										
Incompatible levels of conceptual-ization (ideas don't "go together," seem bizarre).										
Faulty logic; major contradictions; magical thinking; confusion; frag-ments of ideas left incomplete; implausible sequences of events.										

Note: None of the above indicators of major thought problems is checked.

(Level of Associative Thinking)

Card	1	2	3	4	5	7GF	8BM	13B					
	2	2	3	3	3	2	2	3					

Note: K rarely comes up with ideas that tie story elements together such as posit-ing instrumental actions to address the dilemma posed or attain desired ends. Actions, reactions, and events are prompted by previous idea or story event, often constrained by the stimulus where the outcome does not transcend the negative scene (1, 8), happy endings follow unrealistically from a turn of events or irresponsible action (2, 3,13), or relationships end when people's expectations are not met (4, 5, 7). When characters don't get what they want, they see no alternatives that are outside the stimulus, consistent with linear reasoning (frustration with not playing well results in just sitting there and feeling like a failure, as shown in the stimulus; baby creates financial obligation and baby's death removes the obligation) or stereotypic narratives where a wished-for turn of events solves the problem.

Coordination of inner and outer experiences

A. Limitations in coordinating inner and outer experiences

(Check as many as apply for each story) Cards ➡	1	2	3	4	5	7GF	8BM	13B		
Exclusive external impetus—char-acters' concerns and actions respond to demand, greed, wishes, rebellion, or to previous story event rather than prompted by inner purpose or realis-tic attempt at problem resolution.	✓	✓	✓	✓	✓	✓	✓	✓		

(Check as many as apply for each story)	Cards →	1	2	3	4	5	7GF	8BM	13B		
Exclusive internal impetus— characters' concerns and actions are ruminative associations or reactions that are not coherently connected with circumstances in the external world; emotions drive story events with little regard to the circumstances or to solving the problem at hand.											
Absence of moral dimension of experience—characters or narrator lack concern for consequences of actions, do not take responsibility for their actions, or disregard the welfare of others; irresponsible acts do not have appropriate consequences.		✓	✓	✓	✓	✓			✓		
Socially inappropriate behavior— narrator behavior strains acceptable bounds in relating to the examiner or characters' actions are out of tune with social conventions (antisocial, morbidly helpless).											

B. Assets in coordinating inner and outer experiences within and across individuals

(Check as many as apply for each story)	Cards →	1	2	3	4	5	7GF	8BM	13B		
Wishes and fantasies are distinct from realistic appraisal (external demands, rules).											
Intent of an action is distinct from its impact.											
Actions and outcomes are clearly and specifically linked with motives and intentions, in line with realistic social causality.											

(continued)

(Check as many as apply for each story) Cards →	1	2	3	4	5	7GF	8BM	13B		
Characters are meaningfully and reciprocally related to one another (not entrenched in separate concerns or insights that are not relevant or not communicated).										
Resolutions of the "problem" coordinate views and needs of all characters.										
Characters retain their individuality (intentions, goals) while interacting cooperatively.										

Note: Actions are not antisocial or ill-willed but simply fail to consider the moral dimensions of experiences.

Level of Cognitive Experiential Integration

Card	1	2	3	4	5	7GF	8BM	13B					
Level	2	2	2	2	2	2	2	2					

Note: Simplified reasoning, including absence of constructive purposeful actions, wishful resolutions, and insufficient transitions, is compatible with level 2 of cognitive experiential integration. Outcomes are often vague and fail to resolve the dilemma posed. The inner world (intentions, thoughts, and feelings) is not well coordinated with the outer world (plans, decisions, actions, and outcomes), and past, present, and future timeframes are not well delineated. The narrator's thinking and problem solving is highly inflexible, prompting extreme reactions to frustrations with actions that are poorly planned and fail to anticipate realistic consequences.

I. EMOTION

Sources of affect: Checklist

(Check as many as apply for each story) Cards →	1	2	3	4	5	7GF	8BM	13B		
Unrecognized (tension depicted is not recognized)										
External Descriptive (refers to stimulus)										
External Provoked (by context in narrative)	✓	✓	✓	✓	✓	✓	✓	✓		
Internal (coordination of inner sources of tension with those in the external world)										

Coping with Affective Tensions (For each story choose one from among three levels: non-coping, immediate-coping, or long-term coping. Then check the most appropriate subcategories within each coping style.)

1. Noncoping or Unrealistic Coping — Cards →	1	2	3	4	5	7GF	8BM	13B		
Unaware (negative emotion is not recognized)										
No changes in emotions, self-awareness, or understanding	✓	✓	✓	✓	✓	✓	✓	✓		
Overwhelmed (misery prevails or negative affect escalates)	✓			✓	✓	✓	✓			
Reactive/Impulsive (provoked to act without purpose or plan)	✓	✓	✓	✓	✓	✓	✓	✓		
Detached, resigned, hopeless (fails to act or react, withdraws, gives in)										
Wallowing in self-blame (shame, regret)										
Substantially unrealistic. Magical external intervention or unlikely turn of events (e.g., wins the war single-handedly; unrealistic demand is granted); dreaming or hoping (when action is warranted)		✓	✓					✓		
2. Immediate or Partial Coping										
Short-sighted (temporary) decrease of negative affect or reduction of adverse impact of presenting dilemma but without fully addressing the sources of the tension (e.g., avoidance, temporary reassurance, resolving to do something, compliance with legitimate authority)										
Short-sighted (temporary) increase or maintenance of positive affect or improvement of the situation but without recognizing important issues										

(continued)

Cards →	1	2	3	4	5	7GF	8BM	13B		
Excessive dependence on others, seeking or getting help when independent action is warranted (blind dependence or prematurely seeking help)										
Excessive independence from others, managing situations that typically require help (such as a young child building a violin)										
3. Long-Term or Problem-Focused Coping										
Decreasing negative affect by effective problem solving (e.g., addressing the source of the feeling)										
Increasing or maintaining positive affect through effective problem solving										
Appropriate help, advice, or reassurance provided, with or without specific request, enables the character to effectively resolve the dilemma										

Note: Every story is characterized by level 1 coping style (noncoping or unrealistic coping). Although K formulates dilemmas in keeping with the tensions depicted in the card, the resolutions are not effective, even in the short-term, in ameliorating those tensions. Stories end with characters feeling as if they are a failure (1), receiving recognition of their talent only after their death (3), being rejected, alone, angry, or in pain (4, 7, 8). When tensions are alleviated, there is no instrumental action but an unlikely turn of events (2, 13). Emotions are externally evoked and externally regulated.

Emotional maturity: Checklist of assets

A. Complexity and Coherence of Emotions (Within One Individual)

(Check as many as apply for each story) Cards →	1	2								
Affects pertain to durable, inner motives, long-term interests or convictions (standard, goal, harmonious relationship versus reactions to momentary needs, immediate situational provocation, or nonspecific distress).										

(Check as many as apply for each story)	Cards →	1	2							
Affective impact of actions is distinct from its intent.										
Emotions, thoughts, actions, and outcomes are congruous with each other, meaningfully woven into the unfolding narrative and in tune with social causality and the stimulus.										
Feelings appear to be drawn from meaningful synthesis of narrator's experience (versus scripted, superficial, feigned, or associative verbiage).										

B. Integration and Coordination of Emotions (Across Individuals)

(Check as many as apply for each story)	Cards →	1	2							
In defining the dilemma, feelings of all relevant characters are coordinated into a shared context.										
In resolving the dilemma, viewpoints and needs of all relevant characters are reconciled (with understanding of social causality).										
Separation of internal and external reality and differentiation of inner states from external provocation (i.e., the emotion of the perceiver is distinct from characteristics of the target or source of the feeling).										
Feeling is appropriate (in nature and intensity) to the circumstances described in the story and is based on accurate reading of the stimulus.										

C. Clarity and Specificity in the Identification of Emotions

(Check as many as apply for each story)	Cards →	1	2							
Clear and specific identification of the circumstances vis a vis a character's feelings.										

(continued)

(Check as many as apply for each story) **Cards →**	1	2								
Clear delineation of the relationships of characters to each other vis a vis the feelings described.*										
Clear distinctions of different characters' feelings according to evoking circumstance or differences in personality or viewpoint.										

* *If only one person is described (assuming only one is pictured), the above category applies.*

Note: None of the assets characterizing emotional maturity are checked in K's protocol.

Level of Maturity of Emotions

Card	1	2	3	4	5	7GF	8BM	13B						
Level	2	2	2	2	2	2	2	2						

Note: Emotions are provoked by perceived failure (1), a burdensome obligation (2, 7), wanting effortless fame or fortune (3, 13), another person withholding what is wanted (4, 5), or adverse event (8). Emotions do not prompt constructive, deliberate actions but drive reactions with little foresight or insight and absence of principled long-term purposes or genuine concern for others.

II. RELATIONSHIPS

Differentiation and integration
A. Differentiation within and across individuals

(Check as many as apply for each story)* **Cards →**	1	2	3BM	4	5	7GF	8BM	13B		
Fuzzy distinction of viewpoints with characters portrayed differently in the picture being described as doing, feeling, or thinking the same thing.										
Superficial, outward attributes are distinguished (lifestyle, possessions, or how characters look or what they are doing in the stimulus).							✓	✓		

(Check as many as apply for each story)*	1	2	3BM	4	5	7GF	8BM	13B		
Global distinctions, depicting characters in terms of diffuse negative affect or pervasive sense of upset.	✓		✓	✓	✓	✓	✓			
Distinctions based on **immediate needs**, desires, or wants (not realistic goals or durable intentions).	✓	✓	✓		✓	✓		✓		
Distinctions are based on **simple event-feeling connections** (crying because he fell; feels good because she got out of her punishment) or **vague intentions** (find out what something is; solve the problem) without grasping the psychological process (not recognizing the **functions of feelings and thoughts** as distinct from events).	✓	✓	✓	✓	✓	✓	✓	✓		
Emphasis on the function served by a character, such as **stereotypical role or duty** as parent, spouse, child, or friend.										
Distinctions are **dichotomous** (good-bad; weak-strong; threatening vs. safe; special vs. ordinary).	✓		✓	✓	✓	✓				
Distinctions of characters' values, goals, principles, long-term investment.										
Characters have legitimate differences in their needs, feelings, views, and actions **(psychologically distinct from one another)**.										
Different individuals are **viewed on their own ground** and not simply as serving others' immediate needs.										
Persons balance **durable investment** in relationships or in prosocial **goal-directed** activities (not just wanting an outcome) with immediate concerns.										

(continued)

B. Integration within and across individuals

(Check as many as apply for each story) **Cards →**	1	2	3BM	4	5	7GF	8BM	13B		
Autonomy, sense of initiative, conviction, deliberate pursuit of realistic, prosocial, or goal-directed activities in any character.										
All characters are accorded autonomy, each respecting and appreciating others' individuality (e.g., intentions, feelings, thoughts, actions, outcomes) and each retaining that individuality while interacting cooperatively.										
Relationships among characters are well-defined rather than vague or stereotypic.										
Characters relate to the moral dimension of experience rather than respond exclusively to the immediate situation.										
Characters bring prior history, conviction, or investment and act on the basis of deliberate intention rather than momentary provocation.										
Legitimate differences in feelings, tensions, goals are appreciated and addressed respectfully.										
Outward aspects of a person are connected with inner psychological processes (the impact of actions vs. intent and true feelings vs self-presentation).										

(Check as many as apply for each story) Cards ➞	1	2	3BM	4	5	7GF	8BM	13B		
Stable, enduring dispositions as well as momentary experiences of a single individual are reconciled.										
Positive and negative facets of a single character are reconciled.										
The connections among individuals are valued (versus isolated attributes, momentary concerns, material gain, honors, or recognitions).										
Views and needs of all characters depicted in the stimulus or story are considered in the resolution rather than centering on only one character.										
Characters communicate their ideas to others and/or their actions are based on mutual understanding and respect.										

Note: The above qualities may be implicit, particularly when only one character is depicted.

C. Limited differentiation and integration

(Check as many as apply for each story) Cards ➞	1	2	3BM	4	5	7GF	8BM	13B		
Imbalance of autonomy where one person is competent, heroic, or intrusive, while others are incompetent, helpless, or ignored.	✓	✓	✓	✓	✓	✓		✓		
People are viewed as obstacles or as harmful and act with no remorse or consequence.		✓		✓						
Characters react to isolated experience without the perspective of a bigger picture (considerations that should inform appraisal and reactions).		✓	✓	✓	✓	✓	✓	✓		

(continued)

(Check as many as apply for each story) **Cards →**	1	2	3BM	4	5	7GF	8BM	13B			
People are evaluated only in terms of what they provide. Characters relate in terms of what they do for or want from each other without recognition of one another's autonomy.	✓	✓	✓	✓	✓	✓	✓				

(Level of object relations)

Card	1	2	3BM	4	5	7GF	8BM	13B						
Level	2	2	2	2	2	2	2	2						

Note: Even close relationships (childhood friends, husband and wife, parent and child) are abandoned when the other person makes burdensome demands or fails to meet one's needs. There is insufficient commitment or valuing of another person outside of their contribution to immediate well-being and little flexibility to compromise in the face of differences in expectations. Often, relationships are imbued with burdensome obligations and lack of support. The narrator distinguishes individuality dichotomously, in an all-or-none fashion that makes it difficult to compromise. Individuals are often viewed in terms of their immediate impact such as whether or not they provide what is wanted or make unwanted demands. Other qualities are not discerned.

IV. MOTIVATION AND SELF-REGULATION

Motivation relevant assets (check all that apply to a story)

A Task performance -narrative structure and process **Cards →**	1	2									
Clear and appropriate definition of central problem, tension, or dilemma given the stimulus (versus vague, non-specific intention or tension).											
Story is logical and proceeds without irrelevant or contradictory detail; reasoning is realistic, and sequence of events is plausible.											
Story proceeds according to a plan rather than made up detail by detail.											

A Task performance -narrative structure and process	Cards →	1	2							
Narrator incorporates all parts of the instructions with or without inquiry. Prompted responses enhance the story (versus minimal or repetitious).										
There are clear and logical connections between actions and outcomes and congruence among the narrative components.										
Appropriate means-ends connections (or other transitional events) suggest that the narrator can maintain self-directed activity and follow through on intentions.										

B Nature of goals or aspirations	Cards →	1	2							
A realistic, prosocial goal or dilemma is imposed by others but accepted by a character (not wish or desire).										
Characters set a realistic, prosocial goal, conflict, or dilemma.										
Characters exhibit interest, curiosity, pride, concern, empathy, and commitment to standards, ideals, task, or prosocial activity.										

C Implementation resources	Cards →	1	2							
Characters acknowledge possible external obstacles or internal limitations, without being stymied; they set priorities, display foresight, plan ahead, and anticipate consequences.										
Characters perceive the goal-related activities as interesting, desirable, or relevant, rather than feeling pressured, relying on external incentives, or avoiding the demand or responsibility.										

(continued)

C Implementation resources	Cards →	1	2								
Characters maintain their commitment to the goal or make a reasonable decision that the goal is not the right one for them at this time (choose a more self-directed goal).											

D Means-ends connections	Cards →	1	2								
Actions are prosocial, realistic, and sufficient for the expected outcome.											
Responsible, goal-directed actions or principled decisions are valued as distinct from outcomes.											
Characters' inner motives and external constraints are realistically balanced in the intention-action-outcome set.											

Note: None of the positive motivation sustaining assets are checked in K's protocol.

Summary of Characteristics of Goals and Actions

Characteristics of actions*
absent – **vague** – clear: Individuals mostly respond to the tension in the scene and don't set durable goals as bases for instrumental acts. Rather, characters operate on the basis of vague desires or react to their frustrations or adverse events.
long term – **short term**: Immediate wishes, which at times are for future fame or fortune.
process – **outcome**: Emphasis on the end result or what is wanted and not the path of getting there.
substantial – trivial.
self-initiated – **imposed**: Mostly reactive to an adverse event, obligation, or failure.
prosocial – **antisocial**: Wishes or desires are primarily prosocial but actions are often hurtful; the impact of actions does not enter into consideration.
idealistic – materialistic.
attain positive – **avert negative**: Primarily to avoid discomfort in the moment, including the pressure of obligations.

realistic – **unrealistic**: Not taking into consideration likely cause-effect relations.
interpersonal - task: Both are common.
meet inner standards – **meet demands or expectations**: There are no implications of standards other than success.
Characteristics of actions*
present – absent: Sometimes characters fail to act and remain unhappy. None of the actions are instrumental to a goal but are reactive and lacking purpose.
prosocial – antisocial - both: Actions are not ill willed but consequences are under the radar.
goal directed – **aimless**.
planned – **haphazard**.
proactive – **reactive**.
reliance on self – **reliance on externals:** There are no purposeful self-directed actions, only reactions.
realistic – **unrealistic**: Actions are not specifically geared to resolve the problem.
seeking positive – **avoiding negative**.
enjoyable – **burdensome**.

*Bold if applicable

Imports and Motivation Level

Card	Import of Story	Choose Level of Motivation	
		Positive Outcome	Negative Outcome
1	If a task of your own choosing is difficult, you set it aside feeling sad and thinking that you are a failure.		1
2	If a husband and wife worry about having the means to support their expected baby, their worries vanish when the baby dies.	1	
3BM	If you are dismayed by not being talented enough to become a famous artist, you shoot yourself to get your work recognized posthumously.	1	

(continued)

Card	Import of Story	Choose Level of Motivation	
		Positive Outcome	Negative Outcome
4	If a woman falls in love with a man who cannot reciprocate, the man moves on but she becomes depressed and dies alone.		1
5	If a woman cannot get her husband to do what she wants, she leaves him.		1
7GF	If a girl is required by her mother to learn when she'd rather play, the daughter runs away and they remain forever angry, never seeing each other again.		1
8BM	If you are depressed because of a loss, you run away only to get hurt physically (no escape from the pain).		1
13B	If a boy opts to do what he wants rather than work, he grows up to be rich and famous.	1	

Note: If a meaningful import cannot be extracted from the story content, it may be derived from formal qualities of narrative structure or process.

Motivation Level

Card	1	2	3	4	5	7GF	8BM	13B						
Level	N1*	P1**	P1	N1	N1	N1	N1	P1						

*N1 = negative outcome, level I motivation; **P1 = positive outcome, level I motivation

Note: All of the story imports are characterized by level I (extremely low) motivation because of: (a) **How the problem, dilemma or tension in the scene is defined and addressed:** The "If" in the above imports characterize the dilemma as: unwanted or burdensome obligation to work, not getting or doing what one wants, and another person failing to provide what is wanted. No constructive actions are taken to directly address the problem as defined; (b) **How goals and intentions are formulated:** Characters are reactive to wishes or provocations rather than purpose driven; and (c) **How anticipated outcomes relate to the problem, goals, and actions:** Solutions do not realistically deal with the dilemma or resolve the tensions.

Level of Self-Regulation

Card	1	2	3	4	5	7GF	8BM	13B						
Level	3	3	2	3	2	2	2	2						

Note: Stories convey characters' extreme reactions to everyday problems, likely
related to inflexibility to see alternatives and ongoing feelings of frustration
viewed as being caused by burdens imposed by family and society. The following metaimports (synthesis of imports) capture K's experiential schemas: Day to day, one is faced with inordinately burdensome expectations
of society and its agents (authorities, parents, and teachers) that hold little
meaning or relevance. The daily struggles are frustrating (and one may feel
disappointed at not meeting them) so one simplifies demands by doing the
bare minimum and devalues others' expectations and values. It is difficult to
see how daily hassles can be minimized to improve life, so one looks forward
to the freedom of making one's own decisions and choices without others'
restrictions (such as expected in college and in adult life). Not seeing alternatives, one is left to take immediate, drastic action when feeling provoked or to
remain passive.

STORY INTERPRETATION IN THE CONTEXT OF OTHER DATA

As discussed in earlier chapters, the story is the language of experience and TAT
narratives convey implicit subjective sets for coordinating experiences in the inner
and outer worlds. Therefore, theoretical perspectives and empirical evidence that
apply to representation of human experiences also apply to the interpretation of
TAT stories. Professionals may draw conclusions from TAT stories by relating
major themes (imports) with specific coding units detailed in the worksheets and
compare these conclusions to those derived from other data obtained during a
comprehensive assessment in light of the psychological literature and the referral
questions (see Rapid Reference 10.5).

≋ Rapid Reference 10.5

Integrating the TAT with Other Sources of Information

COGNITION

Major themes in TAT stories (imports/schemas) may be understood in reference to other coded variables in TAT stories, the psychological literature, and to
other measures in a comprehensive evaluation as illustrated below with respect
to the central theme of Kyle's TAT stories that *society places inordinately burdensome obligations*. However, other themes may be treated similarly and various
themes may be related to one another.

1. **In reference to other coded TAT variables:** The experience of feeling
   put upon and burdened conveyed by many of the stories is consistent with a
   number of other coding dimensions that appear on the worksheets including

(continued)

difficulties with planning, organizing, and monitoring responses, a sense of helplessness to respond to challenges (noncoping), cognitive inflexibility suggested by dichotomous thinking and linear or scripted generation of sequences of ideas, self-regulation that is reactive to the moment, and tendency to wishful thinking rather than setting goals that are pursued with instrumental acts. The dearth of coping resources is consistent with the feeling of being burdened by expectations, particularly in the context of his high achievement-oriented family.

2. **In reference to theory and research:** Kyle's anger and frustration associated with his sense of being burdened by inordinate demands is further fueled by his appraisal of parental limit setting (imposing schedules for doing homework) as indicative that they don't trust or respect him. According to appraisal theory, the schemas (from the TAT) are the distal causes of emotions whereas appraisals are the proximal causes. Although individual differences in appraisal accounted for the lion's share of the variance in anger emotions (Kuppens, Van Mechelen, & Rijmen, 2008; Mauss, Cook, Cheng, & Gross, 2007), other influences include inborn temperamental negative emotional reactivity and sociocultural contexts. In Kyle's case, difficulties with attentional regulation likely contributed to ongoing frustration with academic demands and set the stage for the development of Kyle's schemas of being burdened by day-to-day expectations. Kyle's view of parental limits and school expectations as lacking legitimacy contributes to his anger. Research has demonstrated that emotional responses to social control depend on whether the individual views these attempts as legitimate (see Nugier, Niedenthal, Brauer, & Chekroun, 2007). Moral emotions such as shame or guilt arise when individuals consider their actions as having been contrary to internal standards or with sociocultural norms and values. In contrast, anger is evoked when individuals appraise their actions as appropriate and the social control as unwarranted, unfair, or as a sign of disrespect. Kyle does not view his behavior as being outside the norm or as deserving of disapproval and, considering parental (and to a lesser extent, teacher) attempts at social control as illegitimate, justifies his anger.

3. **In reference to other information from the evaluation:** Kyle's self-reports are consistent with the TAT theme of being burdened by inordinate obligations. Kyle shared that he is constantly angry and feels put upon by the meaningless demands of school and his achievement-oriented parents. He described his parents as misguided in their emphasis on achievement because their own high educational and occupational attainments did not bring them happiness. He also expressed considerable disdain for teachers who assign meaningless work and show poor judgment. Kyle is very angry at his parents, but recognizes their good intentions and acknowledges that he continues to benefit from their support. Kyle's approach to the various performance tasks during the assessment also contribute to an understanding

of his feeling burdened and lacking coping resources. Difficulties with self-regulation in the attentional, emotional, and behavioral domains were evident across various tasks and informants (see Rapid Reference 10.2).

4. **In reference to the referral issues:** Emerging approaches to interventions consider schemas as the underlying mechanism of psychological vulnerability (Riso et al., 2007). Maladaptive schemas, like prejudice, lead to selectively processing information, ignoring certain facts and overvaluing others. Kyle's experiential schema that society places inordinate burdens leads him to make certain judgments about others by placing them in categories without fully processing all of the relevant information. His dichotomous view of self, others, and the world deprives him of the flexibility to think of alternative approaches to distressing circumstances. In designing interventions that take into account Kyle's schema that society places undue burdens, the role of factors contributing to and maintaining this schema must be addressed. As the academic demands increased with advancing grades in school, Kyle's struggles with focus became increasingly concerning, culminating in his recent diagnosis with ADHD. In the meantime, the ongoing history of frustration has encouraged Kyle to seek relief from demands rather than to master skills that would increase his resources to cope with those demands. Eventually, Kyle came to disdain those demands and to judge situations and people in terms of the obligations they imposed. Kyle's parents understood his needs for structure to complete his homework and progress academically and, although their good intent came across to Kyle intellectually, his actual experience was one of frustration, resentment, and the sense of being burdened. In the TAT task, these implicit experiential realities come to the fore. In addition, Kyle was forthcoming in his self-report, which was consistent with the TAT. Currently, Kyle and his family are most interested in paving the way for successful transition to college and in ameliorating his difficulties with attentional focus. To address these concerns, recommendations were made to the family, based on all of the information obtained in the assessment battery.

In the interpretation of TAT stories, it is necessary to consider both what is present and what is absent. Two related themes are central in Kyle's stories. One is the presence of extreme responses to frustration often triggered by the perception of burdensome obligations or of not getting something that is wanted or expected from another person. The other is the absence of initiative, interest, motivation, or strategies to cope realistically with tensions or challenges. Similarly to the story characters, Kyle views the expectations imposed on him as extraordinarily burdensome and does not cope constructively with the ongoing frustrations. He shared with the examiner that much of the school work he has to do is meaningless, with little connection to his life goals and that it takes extraordinary will power to force himself do the work on a day-to-day basis and that he often feels like giving up. He is concerned about his difficulties staying focused on his work, particularly if it jeopardizes his getting into college. He is eager to engage his parents in the college selection process and in planning for the supports he will need to transition successfully. Kyle interprets situations and people in an all-or-none fashion (dichotomous thinking in the TAT) and has come to regard people, particularly adults, in terms of the demands they make or the comfort they provide. Although he is acutely aware of what is expected of him at school and at home, his dichotomous and inflexible thinking impedes his ability to truly compromise so he often acquiesces but seethes with resentment and frustration. Conflicts with his parents center around his interpretation that parental limits and structures (such as a schedule for doing homework, curfew) are undue impositions motivated by their distrust and disrespect. This same inflexibility in thinking also keeps him from seeing alternatives and from coping effectively with day-to-day expectations. His tendency is to react to what is salient to him in the moment without reflecting on the bigger picture. Just as the characters in his stories express wishes but exhibit no goal-directed behaviors, Kyle expresses some goals for his future but he does not have realistic plans to implement his stated intentions. Recommendations were shared with the family, based on all the data gathered during the evaluation (see Rapid Reference 10.6).

≡ Rapid Reference 10.6

Four Categories of Recommendations Discussed with Kyle and His Parents Following the Evaluation:

1. **Balancing Kyle's need for independence with his need for structure.** Although Kyle will inevitably assume more independent roles, he will continue to need structures and supports, even as he implicitly eschews them. On an explicit level, he understands why they are necessary. However, his decision making is hampered by inflexibility—where he does not readily see alternatives and potential ways to compromise. It will be difficult to negotiate rules with him. Parents will need to decide what structures are really needed and impose them kindly and consistently.

2. **Creating conditions for productive work.** Kyle struggles to keep his focus across both structured and unstructured contexts. However, he performs much better with structured settings, when he knows what is expected, and when he can meet the demands for concentrated attention. In addition to issues with attentional focus, Kyle lacks strategies for coping with

feelings of frustration and has difficulty taking initiative to prioritize, plan, and organize his learning activities. Kyle and his parents should collaborate on developing a plan that can help him organize his efforts both on particular school assignments and on the larger picture of setting goals along with plans to implement them. It may be helpful to revisit the dosage of the medication that he is currently taking. Although Kyle reports that the medicine helps him with work, he still reports considerable difficulty maintaining his focus.

3. **Preparing for college.** Kyle looks forward to the freedoms and independence of college life but may be unrealistic and idealistic about the realities of college expectations and of being on his own. The college application process will likely be difficult, requiring patience and keeping lines of communication open. Kyle could also benefit from talking to a counselor who can help him to explore his interests and strengths as he looks for colleges that will meet his needs.

4. **Transitioning to life away from home.** Currently, Kyle is feeling like he is making himself do meaningless, unpleasant things to meet expectations, and it is not clear how long he will continue to sustain these efforts on these seemingly tedious activities, especially when he is on his own. If he lives away from home when starting college, he will continue to need support and understanding to help him choose courses and fashion schedules that he can manage. Kyle may find it advantageous to access support services provided by the college.

References

Abelson, R. P. (1981). Psychological status of the script concept. *American Psychologist, 36,* 715–729.

Achenbach, T. M., & Edelbrock C. (1983). *Manual for the Child Behavior Checklist/4–18 and Revised Child Behavior Profile.* Burlington: University of Vermont.

Ackerman, P. L., & Heggestad, E. D. (1997). Intelligence, personality, and interests: Evidence for overlapping traits. *Psychological Bulletin, 121*(2), 219–245.

Alexander, J. E. (1988). Personality, psychological assessment and psychobiography. *Journal of Personality, 56,* 265–294.

Alvarado, N. (1994). Empirical validity of the Thematic Apperception Test. *Journal of Personality Assessment, 63,* 59–79.

Andersen, S. M., & Chen, S. (2002). The relational self: An interpersonal social-cognitive theory. *Psychological Review, 109,* 619–645.

Andersen, S. M., Reznik, I., & Glassman, N. S. (2005). The unconscious relational self. In R. Hassin, J. S. Uleman, & J. A. Bargh (Eds.), *The new unconscious* (pp. 421–481). New York: Oxford University Press.

Anderson, J. R., Bothell, D., Byrne, M. D., Douglass, S., Lebiere, C., & Quin, Y. (2004). An integrated theory of the individual. *Psychological Review, 111,* 1036–1060.

Applebee, A. N. (1978). *The child's concept of story; Ages two to seven.* Chicago: The University of Chicago Press.

Archer, R. P., Marnish, M., Imhof, E. A., & Piotrowski, C. (1991). Psychological test usage with adolescent clients: 1990 survey findings. *Professional Psychology: Research and Practice, 22,* 247–252.

Armstrong, M. A. (1954). Children's responses to animal and human figures in thematic pictures. *Journal of Consulting Psychology, 18,* 67–70.

Arnold, M. B. (1962). *Story sequence analysis: A new method of measuring motivation and predicting achievement.* New York: Columbia University Press.

Astington, J. W. (1991). Intention in the child's theory of mind. In D. M. Frye & C. Moore (Eds.), *Children's theories of mind: Mental states and social understanding* (pp. 157–172). Hillsdale, NJ: Erlbaum.

Astington, J. W., & Lee, E. (1991). *What do children know about intentional causality?* Presented at meeting of Society for Research in Child Development, Seattle.

Atkinson, J. W. (1992). Motivational determinants of thematic apperception. In C. P. Smith (Ed.), *Motivation and personality: Handbook of thematic content analysis* (pp. 21–48). New York: Cambridge University Press.

Atkinson, J. W., Bongort, K., & Price, L. H. (1977). Explorations using computer simulation to comprehend thematic apperceptive measurement of motivation. *Motivation & Emotion, 1,* 1–27.

Bailey, B. E., & Green, J. (1977). Black Thematic Apperception Test stimulus material. *Journal of Personality Assessment, 41,* 25–30.

Baird, J., & Astington, J. W. (2005). The development of the intention concept: From the observable world to the unobservable mind. In R. R. Hassin, J. S. Uleman, & J. A. Bargh (Eds.), *The new unconscious* (pp. 256–276). New York: Oxford University Press.

Baird, J., & Baldwin, D. A. (2001). Making sense of human behavior: Action parsing and intentional inference. In B. F. Malle, L. J. Moses, & D. A. Baldwin (Eds.), *Intentions and intentionality: Foundations of social cognition* (pp. 193–206). Cambridge, MA: MIT Press.

Baker-Brown, G., Ballard, E. J., Bluck, S., de Vries, B., Suedfeld, P., & Tetlock, P. E. (1992). The conceptual integrative complexity scoring manual. In C. P. Smith (Ed.), *Motivation and personality: Handbook of thematic content analysis* (pp. 401–418). New York: Cambridge University Press.

Baldwin, D. A., Baird, J. A., Saylor, M. M., & Clark, M. A. (2001). Infants parse dynamic action. *Child Development, 72,* 708–717.

Baldwin, M. W. (1992). Relational schemas and the processing of social information. *Psychological Bulletin, 112,* 461–484.

Bandura, A. (1988). Self-regulation of motivation and action through goal systems. In V. Hamilton, G. H. Bower, & N. H. Frijda (Eds.), *Cognitive perspectives on emotion and motivation* (pp. 37–61). Dordrecht, Netherlands: Kluwer Academic Publishers.

Bandura, A. (1989). Human agency in social cognitive theory. *American Psychologist, 44,* 1175–1184.

Bargh, J. A., Gollwitzer, P. M., Lee-Chai, A. Y., Barndollar, K., & Troetschel, R. (2001). The automated will: Nonconscious activation and pursuit of behavioral goals. *Journal of Personality and Social Psychology, 81,* 1014–1027.

Bargh, J. A., & Morsella, E. (2008). The unconscious mind. *Perspectives on Psychological Science, 3,* 73–79.

Barkley, R. A. (1997). Behavioral inhibition, sustained attention, and executive functions: Constructing a unified theory of ADHD. *Psychological Bulletin, 121,* 65–94.

Baron-Cohen, S. (1991). Do people with autism understand what causes emotion? *Child Development, 62,* 385–395.

Baron-Cohen, S. (1995). *Mindblindness: An essay on autism and theory of mind.* Cambridge, MA: MIT Press/Bradford Books.

Baron-Cohen, S. (2000). Theory of mind and autism: A fifteen year review. In Baron-Cohen, S., Tager-Flusberg, H., & Cohen, D.J. (Eds), *Understanding other minds* (pp. 3–21). New York: Oxford University Press.

Baron-Cohen, S., Leslie, A. M., & Frith, U. (1986). Mechanical, behavioral, and intentional understanding of picture stories in autistic children. *British Journal of Developmental Psychology, 4,* 113–125.

Barrett, L. F. (1998). Discrete emotions or dimensions? The role of valence focus and arousal focus. *Cognition and Emotion, 12,* 579–599.

Barrett, L. F., & Gross, J. J. (2001). Emotion representation and regulation: A process model of emotional intelligence. In T. Mayne & G. Bonnano (Eds.), *Emotion: Current issues and future directions* (pp. 286–310). New York: Guilford.

Barrett, L. F. (2004). Feelings or words? Understanding the content in self-report ratings of emotional experience. *Journal of Personality and Social Psychology, 87,* 266–281.

Barrett L.F. (2006). Solving the emotion paradox: Categorization and the experience of emotion. *Personality and Social Psychology Review 10,* 20–46.

Barrett, L. F., Mesquita, B., Ochsner, K. N., & Gross, J. J. (2007). The experience of emotion. *Annual Review of Psychology, 58,* 373–403.

Bassan-Diamond, L. E., Teglasi, H., & Schmidt, P. (1995). Temperament and a story-telling measure of self-regulation. *Journal of Research in Personality, 29,* 109–120.

Baumann, N., Kaschel, R., & Kuhl, J. (2005). Striving for unwanted goals: Stress-dependent discrepancies between explicit and implicit achievement motives reduce subjective well-being and increase psychosomatic symptoms. *Journal of Personality and Social Psychology, 89,* 781–799.

Beck, A.T. (2002). Cognitive models of depression. In R. L. Leahy & T.E. Dowd (Eds.), *Clincal advances in cognitive psychotherapy: Theory and application* (pp. 29–61).New York: Springer Publishing Company.

Beck, A. T. (1976). *Cognitive therapy and emotional disorders.* New York: International Universities Press.

Beck, A. T. (2005). The current state of cognitive therapy: A 40-year retrospective. *Archives of General Psychiatry, 62,* 953–959.

Beck, A. T. (1963). Thinking and depression: 1. Idiosyncratic content and cognitive distortions. *Archives of General Psychiatry, 9,* 324–333.

Beck, A. T., & Clark, D. A. (1997). An information processing model of anxiety: Automatic and strategic processes. *Behavior Research and Therapy, 35*(1), 49–58.

Beck, A.T., Freeman, A., & Davis, D.D. (2004) *Cognitive therapy of personality disorders* (2nd ed.) New York: Guilford Press.

Beck, A. T., & Weishaar, M. E. (1989). Cognitive therapy. In R. J. Corsini & D. Wedding (Eds.), *Current psychotherapies* (4th ed., pp. 229–261). Itasca, IL: Peacock.

Bellak, L. (1975). *The TAT, CAT, and SAT in clinical use.* New York: Grune & Stratton.

Bellak, L. (1986). *The TAT, CAT, and SAT in clinical use* (4th ed.). Orlando, FL: Grune & Stratton.

Bellak, L. (1992). *Short Form TAT, CAT, & SAT Blank.* San Antonio, TX: Psychological Corporations.

Bellak, L. (1993). *The TAT, CAT, and SAT in clinical use* (5th ed.). Boston: Allyn & Bacon.

Bellak, L., & Abrams, D. M. (1997). *The Thematic Apperception Test, the Children's Apperception Test, and the Senior Apperception Technique in clinical use* (6th ed.). Boston: Allyn & Bacon.

Bellak, L., & Abrams, D. M. (1998). *A manual for the Children's Apperception Test (animal figures).* Larchmont, NY: C.P.S., Inc.

Bellak, L., & Bellak, S. S. (1949). *Children's Apperception Test.* Larchmont, NY: C.P.S., Inc.

Bellak, L., & Bellak, S. S. (1952). *The supplement to the Children's Apperception Test (CAT–S).* Larchmont, NY: C.P.S., Inc.

Bellak, L., & Bellak, S. S. (1965). *The Children's Apperception Test.* Larchmont, NY: C.P.S., Inc.

Bellak, L., & Bellak, S. S. (1973). *Manual: Senior Apperception Test.* Larchmont, NY: C.P.S., Inc.

Berkowitz, L. (1990). On the formation and regulation of anger and aggression: A cognitive-neoassociationistic analysis. *American Psychologist, 45,* 494–503.

Biernat, M. (1989). Motives and values to achieve: Different constructs with different effects. *Journal of Personality, 57,* 69–95.

Black, A., & Deci, E. (2000). The effects of instructors' autonomy support and students' autonomous motivation on learning organic chemistry: A Self-Determination Theory perspective. *Science Education,* 84, 740–756.

Blair, C., & Razza, R. P. (2007). Relating effortful control, executive function, and false belief understanding to emerging math and literacy ability in kindergarten. *Child Development, 78,* 647–663.

Blankman, C., Teglasi, H., & Lawser, M. (2002). Thematic apperception, narrative schemas, and literacy. *Journal of Psychoeducational Assessment, 20,* 268–289.

Blatt, S. J. (1990). Interpersonal relatedness and self definition: Two personality configurations and their implications for psychopathology and psychotherapy. In J. L. Singer (Ed.), *Repression and dissociation: Implications for personality theory, psychotherapy and health* (pp. 299–335). Chicago: University of Chicago Press.

Blatt, S. J., Brenneis, C. B., Schimak, J. G., & Glick, M. (1976). Normal development and psychopathological impairment of the concept of the object on the Rorschach. *Journal of Abnormal Psychology, 85,* 364–373.

Blatt, S. J., & Lerner, H. (1983). The psychological assessment of object representations. *Journal of Personality Assessment, 47,* 7–28.

Bloome, D., Katz, L., & Champion, T. (2003). Young children's narratives and ideologies of language. *Reading and Writing Quarterly, 1,* 205–224.

Blum, G. S. (1950). *The blacky pictures.* New York: Psychological Corporation.

Bornstein, R. F. (2002). A process dissociation approach to objective-projective test score interrelationships. *Journal of Personality Assessment, 78,* 47–68.

Bornstein, R. F. (1998). Implicit and self-attributed dependency strivings: Differential relationships to laboratory and field measures of help-seeking. *Journal of Personality and Social Psychology, 75,* 778–787.

Bornstein, R. F., & O'Neill, R. M. (1992). Parental perceptions and psychopathology. *Journal of Nervous and Mental Disease, 180,* 475–483.

Borsboom, D., Mellenbergh, G. J., & Van Heerden, J. (2004). The concept of validity. *Psychological Review, 111,* 1061–1071.

Bosson, J. K., Swann, W. B., & Pennebaker, J. W. (2000). Stalking the perfect measure of self esteem: The blind men and the elephant revisited. *Journal of Personality & Social Psychology, 79,* 631–643.

Botvin, G. J., & Sutton-Smith, B. (1977). The development of structural complexity in children's fantasy narratives. *Developmental Psychology, 13,* 377–388.

Bower, G. H. (1992). How might emotions affect learning. In S. A. Christianson (Ed.), *Handbook of emotion and memory* (pp. 3–31). Hillsdale, NJ: Erlbaum.

Brackett, M. A., Rivers, S. E., Shiffman, S., Lerner, N., & Salovey, P. (2006). Relating 29 emotional abilities to social functioning: A comparison of self-report and performance measures of emotional intelligence. *Journal of Personality and Social Psychology, 91*(4), 780–795.

Bransford, J. D., Franks, J. J., Vye, N. J., & Sherwood, R. D. (1989). New approaches to instruction: Because wisdom can't be taught. In S. Vosniadou & A. Ortony (Eds.), *Similarity and analogical reasoning* (pp. 470–497). New York: Cambridge University Press.

Brophy, J. (2005). Goal theorists should move on from performance goals. *Educational Psychologist, 40,* 167–176.

Bruhn, A. (1992). The early memories procedure: A projective test of autobiographical memory, Part 2. *Journal of Personality Assessment, 58,* 326–346.

Bruner, J. (1986). *Actual minds, possible worlds.* Cambridge, MA: Harvard University Press.

Bruner, J. (1990). *Acts of meaning.* Cambridge, MA: Harvard University Press.

Brunstein, J. C., & Maier, G. W. (2005). Implicit and self-attributed motive to achieve: Two separate but interacting needs. *Journal of Personality and Social Psychology, 89,* 205–222.

Budoff, M. (1960). The relative utility of animal and human figures in a picture-story test for young children. *Journal of Projective Techniques, 24,* 347–352.

Burton, K., Lydon, J., Alessandro, D., & Koestner, R. (2006). The differential effects of intrinsic and identified motivation on well-being and performance: Prospective, experimental, and implicit approaches to Self-determination Theory. *Journal of Personality and Social Psychology, 91*(4), 750–762.

Byrd, E., & Witherspoon, R. L. (1954). Responses of preschool children to the Children's Apperception Test. *Child Development, 25,* 35–44.

Campbell, D. T., & Fiske, D. W. (1959). Convergent and discriminant validation by the multitrait-multimethod matrix. *Psychological Bulletin, 56,* 81–105.

Campos, J., Frankel, C., & Camras, L. (2004). On the nature of emotion regulation. *Child Development, 75,* 377–394.

Cantor, N., & Blanton, H. (1996). In P. M. Gollwitzer & J. A. Bargh (Eds.), *The psychology of action: Linking cognition and motivation to behavior* (pp. 338–359). New York: Guilford Press.

Cantor, N., & Sanderson, C. A. (1999). Life task participation and well-being: The importance of taking part in daily life. In D. Kahneman & E. Diener (Eds.), *Well-being: The foundations of hedonic psychology* (pp. 230–243). New York: Russell Sage Foundation.

Caplan, R. (1994). Thought disorder in childhood. *Journal of the American Academy of Child and Adolescent Psychiatry, 33*(5), 605–615.

Card, N. A., & Little, T. D. (2006). Proactive and reactive aggression in childhood and adolescence: A meta-analysis of differential relations with psychosocial adjustment. *International Journal of Behavioral Development, 30*, 466–480.

Carlson, R. (1981). Studies in script theory: I. Adult analogs of a childhood nuclear scene. *Journal of Personality and Social Psychology, 40*, 501–510.

Carver, S., Scheier, M. F., & Weintraub, J. K. (1989). Assessing coping strategies: A theoretically based approach. *Journal of Personality and Social Psychology, 56*, 267–283.

Cervone, D. (2004). The architecture of personality. *Psychological Review, 111*, 183–204.

Chandler, L. A., Shermis, M. D., & Lempert, M. E. (1989). The need threat analysis: A scoring system for the Children's Apperception Test. *Psychology in the Schools, 26*, 47–54.

Chapman, B. P. (2008). Singer and Wynne's Communication Deviance Scoring System. In S. R. Jenkins (Ed.), *Scoring manual for empathy, a handbook of clinical scoring systems for thematic apperceptive techniques* (pp. 44–476). New York: Erlbaum (Taylor and Francis Group).

Chartrand, T., & Bargh, J. A. (2002). Nonconscious motivations: Their activation, operation, and consequences. In A. Tesser, D. A. Stapel, & J. W. Wood (Eds.), *Self and motivation: Emerging psychological perspectives* (pp. 13–41). Washington, DC: American Psychological Association.

Chaytor, N., & Schmitter-Edgecombe, M. (2003). The ecological validity of neuropsychological tests: A review of the literature on everyday cognitive skills. *Neuropsychology Review,13*(4), 181–197.

Chirkov, V. I., & Ryan, R. M. (2001). Parent and teacher autonomy-support in Russian and U. S. adolescents: Common effects on well-being and academic motivation. *Journal of Cross-Cultural Psychology, 32*, 618–635.

Cicchetti, D., Ackerman, B. P., & Izard, C. E. (1995). Emotions and emotion regulation in developmental psychopathology. *Development and Psychopathology, 7*, 1–10.

Cicchetti, D., & Rogosch, F. A. (1996). Equifinality and multifinality in developmental psychopathology. *Development and Psychopathology, 8*, 597–600.

Clark, D. A., Beck, A. T., & Alford, B. A. (1999). *Scientific foundations of cognitive theory and therapy of depression*. New York: Wiley.

Cohen, H., & Weil, G. R. (1975). *Tasks of emotional development: A projective test for children and adolescents*. Boston: Tasks of Emotional Development (T.E.D.) Associates.

Cole, P. M., Martin, S. E., & Dennis, T. A. (2004). Emotion regulation as a scientific construct: Challenges and directions for child development research. *Child Development, 75*, 317–333.

Cole, P. M., Michel, M. K., & Teti, L. O. (1994). The development of emotion regulation and dysregulation: A clinical perspective. *Monographs of the Society for Research in Child Development, 59*, 73–100.

Compas, B. E., Oppedisano, G., Connor, J. K., Gerhardt, C. A., Hinden, B. R., Achenbach, T. M., & Hammen, C. (1997). Gender differences in depressive symptoms in adolescence: Comparison of national samples of clinically referred and nonreferred youths. *Journal of Consulting and Clinical Psychology, 65*(4), 617–626.

Compas, B. E., Connor-Smith, J. K., Saltzman, H., Thomsen, A. H., & Wadsworth, M. (2001). Coping with stress during childhood and adolescence: Progress, problems, and potential. *Psychological Bulletin, 127*, 87–127.

Constantino, G., Dana R. H., & Malgady, G. R. (2007). *TEMAS (tell-me-a-story) assessment in multicultural societies*. Mahwah, NJ: Lawrence Erlbaum Publishers.

Constantino, G., & Malgady, G. R. (2008). Tell-Me-A-Story (TEMAS). In S. R. Jenkins (Ed.), *Empathy, a handbook of clinical scoring systems for thematic apperceptive techniques* (pp. 547–572). New York: Erlbaum (Taylor and Francis Group).

Constantino, G., & Malgady, R. C. (1983). Verbal fluency of Hispanic, Black and White children on TAT and TEMAS, a new thematic apperception test. *Hispanic Journal of Behavioral Sciences, 5,* 199–206.

Constantino, G., Malgady, R. C., & Rogler, L. H. (1988). *Tell-Me-A-Story, Manual*. Los Angeles: Western Psychological Services.

Constantino, G., Malgady, R. C., Rogler, L. H., & Tsui, E. C. (1988). Discriminant analysis of clinical outpatients and public school children by TEMAS: A thematic apperception test for Hispanics and Blacks. *Journal of Personality Assessment, 52,* 670–678.

Conway, L. G. III, Thoemmes, F., Allison, A., Towgood, K.H., Wagner, M., Davey, K., Salcido, A. et al. (2008). Two Ways to Be Complex and Why They Matter: Implications for Attitude Strength and Lying. *Journal of Personality & Social Psychology, 95,* 1029–104.

Cooper, A. (1981). A basic TAT set for adolescent males. *Journal of Clinical Psychology, 37,* 411–415.

Corbett, B., & Glidden, H. (2000). Processing affective stimuli in children with Attention-Deficit Hyperactivity Disorder. *Child Neuropsychology, 6*(2), 144–155.

Costa P. T., Somerfield, M. R., & McRae, R. R. (1996). Personality and coping: A reconceptualization. In M. Zeidner & N. Endler (coord.), *Handbook of coping: Theory, research, applications* (pp. 44–61). New York: Wiley.

Cramer, P. (2007). Longitudinal study of defense mechanisms: Late childhood to late adolescence. *Journal of Personality, 75,* 1–23.

Cramer, P. (1987). The development of defense mechanisms. *Journal of Personality, 55,* 597–614.

Cramer, P. (1991). *The development of defense mechanisms: Theory, research, and assessment*. New York: Springer.

Cramer, P. (1996). *Storytelling, narrative and the Thematic Apperception Test*. New York: Guilford Press.

Cramer, P. (2007). Longitudinal study of defense mechanisms: Late childhood to late adolescence. *Journal of Personality, 75,* 1–24.

Cramer, P. (2009). An increase in early adolescent undercontrol is associated with the use of denial. *Journal of Personality Assessment, 91,* 331–339.

Crick, N. R., & Dodge, K. A. (1994). A review and reformulation of social information processing mechanisms in children's adjustment. *Psychological Bulletin, 115,* 74–101.

Crick, N. R., & Dodge, K. A. (1996). Social information processing mechanisms in reactive and proactive aggression. *Child Development, 67,* 993–1002.

Cronbach, L. J. (1970). *Essentials of psychological testing* (3rd ed.). New York: Harper & Row.

Dana, R. H. (1982). *A human science model for personality assessment with projective techniques*. Springfield, IL.: Charles C. Thomas.

Daugherty, J. O., Kurtz, J. E., & Phebus, J. B. (2009). Are implicit motives "visible" to well-acquainted others? *Journal of Personality Assessment, 91,* 373–380.

Deary, I. J., & Stough, C. (1996). Intelligence and inspection time: Achievements, prospects, and problems. *American Psychologist, 51,* 599–608.

DeCharms, R. (1992). Personal causation and the origin concept. In C. P. Smith (Ed.), *Motivation and personality: Handbook of thematic content analysis* (pp. 325–333). New York: Cambridge University Press.

Deci, E. L., Eghrari, H., Patrick, B. C., & Leone, D. R. (1994). Facilitating internalization: The self-determination theory perspective. *Journal of Personality, 62,* 119–142.

Deci, E. L., & Ryan, R. M. (1985). *Intrinsic motivation and self-determination in human behavior.* New York: Plenum Press.

Deci, E. L., & Ryan, R. M. (1991). A motivational approach to self: Integration in personality. In E. Dienstbier (Ed.), *Nebraska symposium on motivation* (pp. 237–288). Lincoln: University of Nebraska Press.

Deci, E. L., & Ryan, R. M. (2000). The "what" and "why" of goal pursuits: Human needs and the self-determination of behavior. *Psychological Inquiry,* 11(4), 227–268.

De Los Reyes, A. & Kazdin, A. E. (2005). Informant discrepancies in the assessment of childhood psychopathology: A critical Review, theoretical framework, and recommendations for further study. *Psychological Bulletin, 131,* 483–509.

Demorest, A. P., & Alexander, I. E. (1992). Affective scripts as organizers of personal experience. *Journal of Personality, 60,* 645–663.

Derry, S. J. (1996). Cognitive schema theory and the constructivist debate. *Educational Psychologist, 31,* 163–174.

Derryberry, D., & Reed, M. A. (1994). Temperament and attention: Orienting toward and away from positive and negative signals as components of temperament. *Journal of Personality and Social Psychology, 66,* 1128–1139.

Derryberry, D., & Rothbart, M. K. (1997). Reactive and effortful processes in the organization of temperament. *Development & Psychopathology, 9*(4), 633–652.

DeSteno, D. A., & Salovey, P. (1997). The effects of mood on the structure of the self-concept. *Cognition & Emotion, 11,* 351–372.

Doane, J. A., Miklowitz, D. J., Oranchak, E., & Flores de Apodaca, R. (1989). Parental communication deviance and schizophrenia: A cross-cultural comparison of Mexican- and Anglo-Americans. *Journal of Abnormal Psychology, 98,* 487–490.

Dodge, K. A., & Price, J. M. (1994). On the relation between social information processing and socially competent behavior in early school-aged children. *Child Development, 65,* 1385–1897.

Dowd, E. T. (2006). What changes in cognitive therapy? The role of tacit knowledge structures. *Journal of Cognitive and Behavioral Psychotherapies, 6,* 21–29.

Dowd, E. T., & Courchaine, K .E. (*2002*). Implicit learning, tacit knowledge, and implications for stasis and change in cognitive psychotherapy. In R. L. Leahy & E. T. Dowd (Eds.), *Clinical advances in cognitive psychotherapy* (pp. 325–344). New York: Springer.

Downey, G., Lebolt, A., Rincon, C., & Freitas, A. L. (1998). Rejection sensitivity and children's interpersonal difficulties. *Child Development, 69,* 1074–1091.

Duckworth, K. L., Bargh, J. A., Garcia, M., & Chaiken, S. (2002). The automatic evaluation of novel stimuli. *Psychological Science, 13,* 513–519.

Dunn, J. (1991). Young children's understanding of other people: Evidence from observations within the family. In D. Frye & C. Moore (Eds.), *Children's theory of mind: Mental states and social understanding* (pp. 97–114). Hillsdale, NJ: Erlbaum.

Eagle, C. J., & Schwartz, L. (1994). *Psychological portraits of adolescents.* New York: Lexington Books.

Egloff, B., Wilhelm, F. H., Neubauer, D. H., Mauss, I. B., & Gross, J. J. (2002). Implicit anxiety measure predicts cardiovascular reactivity to an evaluated speaking task. *Emotion, 2,* 3–11.

Ehrenreich, J. H. (1990). Quantitative studies of responses elicited by selected TAT cards. *Psychological Reports, 67,* 15–18.

Eisenberg, N. (2006) Empathy-related responding in children. In M. Killen & J. G. Smetana (Eds.), *Handbook of moral development* (pp. 517–549). London: Psychology Press.

Eisenberg, N., & Fabes, R. A. (1992). Emotion, regulation, and the development of social competence. In M. S. Clark (Ed.), *Emotion and social behavior* (pp. 119-150). Thousand Oaks, CA: Sage Publications.

Eisenberg, N., Fabes, R. A., Shepard, S. A., Murphy, B. C., Guthrie, I. K., Jones, S., Friedman, J., Poulin, R., & Maszk, P. (1997). Contemporaneous and longitudinal prediction of children's social functioning from regulation and emotionality. *Child Development, 68*(4), 642–664.

Eisenberg, N., & Morris, A. S. (2002). Children's emotion-related regulation. In H. Reese & R. Kail (Eds.), *Advances in Child Development and Behavior, 30*, 189–229.

Eisenberg, N., Smith, C. L., Sadovsky, A., & Spinrad, T. L. (2004). Effortful control: Relations with emotion regulation, adjustment, and socialization in childhood. In R. F. Baumeister (Eds.), *Handbook of self regulation: Research, theory, and applications* (pp. 259–282). New York: Guilford Press.

Eisenberg, N., Wentzel, N. M., & Harris, J. D. (1998). The role of emotionality and regulation in empathy-related responding. *School Psychology Review, 27,* 506–521.

Elias, M. J., & Tobias, S. E. (1996). *Social problem solving: Interventions in the schools.* New York: Guilford Press.

Elliot, A. J., & Harackiewicz, J. M. (1996). Approach and avoidance achievement goals and intrinsic motivation: A mediational analysis. *Journal of Personality and Social Psychology, 70*, 416–475.

Elliot, A. J., & McGregor, H. (2001). A 2 × 2 achievement goal framework. *Journal of Personality and Social Psychology, 80*(3), 501–519.

Ellsworth, P. C., & Scherer, K. R. (2003). Appraisal processes in emotion. In R. J. Davidson, H. Goldsmith, & K. R. Scherer (Eds.), *Handbook of affective sciences* (pp. 572–595). New York and Oxford: Oxford University Press.

Epstein, S. (1994). Integration of the cognitive and psychodynamic unconscious. *American Psychologist, 49,* 709–724.

Epstein, S., & Pacini, R. (1999). Some basic issues regarding dual-process theories from the perspective of cognitive-experiential self-theory. In S. Chaiken & Y. Trope (Eds.), *Dual process theories in social psychology* (pp. 462–482). New York: Guilford Press.

Evans, J. (2008). Dual processing accounts of reasoning, judgment, and social cognition. *Annual Review of Psychology, 59*, 255–278.

Fairbairn, W. R. D. (1952). *Psychoanalytic studies of the personality.* New York: Basic Books.

Fairbairn, W. R. D. (1954). *An object-relations theory of the personality.* New York: Basic Books.

Fischer, P., Greitemeyer, T., & Frey, D. (2008). Self-regulation and selective exposure: The impact of depleted self-regulation resources on confirmatory information processing. *Journal of Personality and Social Psychology, 94*, 382–395.

Fish, S., & Ritvo, E. R. (1979). Psychoses of childhood. In J. D. Noshpitz (Ed.), *Basic handbook of child psychiatry* (pp. 249–304). New York: Basic Books.

Fiske, A. P., Haslam, N., & Fiske, S. T. (1991). Confusing one person with another: What errors reveal about the elementary forms of social relations. *Journal of Personality and Social Psychology, 60,* 656–674.

Fiske, S. T., & Taylor, S. (1991). *Social cognition* (2nd ed.). New York: McGraw Hill.

Fitzgerald, B. J., Pasewark, R. A., & Fleisher, S. (1974). Responses of an aged population on the Gerontological and Thematic Apperception Tests. *Journal of Personality Assessment, 38,* 234–235.

Fivush, R., & Haden, C. (1997). Narrating and representing experience: Preschoolers' developing autobiographical recounts. In P. van den Broek, P. A. Bauer, & T. Bourg (Eds.),

Developmental spans in event comprehension and representation: Bridging fictional and actual events (pp. 169–198). Hillsdale, NJ: Lawrence Erlbaum Associates.

Flanagan, R. E., & DiGiuseppe, R. (1999). Critical review of the TEMAS: A step within the development of thematic apperception instruments. *Psychology in the Schools, 36,* 21–30.

Flavell, J. H. (1963). *The developmental psychology of Jean Piaget.* Princeton, NJ: Van Nostrand.

Flavell, J. H. (1988). The development of children's knowledge about the mind: From cognitive connections to mental representations. In J. W. Astington, P. L. Harris, & D. R. Olson (Eds.), *Developing theories of mind* (pp. 244–267). New York: Cambridge University Press.

Flavell, J. H., & Miller, P. (1998). Social cognition. In W. Damon (Series Ed.) & D. Kuhn & R. Siegler (Vol. Eds.), *Handbook of child psychology: Vol. 2. Cognition, perception, and language* (5th ed., pp. 851–898). New York: Wiley.

Foa, E. B., & Kozak, M. J. (1991). Emotional processing: Theory, research, and clinical implications for anxiety disorders. In J. D. Safran & L. S. Greenberg (Eds.), *Emotion, psychotherapy, and change* (pp. 21–49). New York: Guilford Press.

Folkman, S. (1984). Personal control and stress and coping processes: A theoretical analysis. *Journal of Personality and Social Psychology, 46,* 839–852.

Folkman, S., & Lazarus, R. S. (1980). An analysis of coping in a middle-aged community sample. *Journal of Health and Social Behavior, 21,* 219–239.

Folkman, S., & Lazarus, R. S. (1986). Stress processes and depressive symptomatology. *Journal of Abnormal Psychology, 95,* 107–113.

Folkman, S., & Lazarus, R. S. (1988). The relationship between coping and emotion: Implications for theory and research. *Social Science and Medicine, 26,* 309–317.

Folkman, S., & Moskowitz, J. T. (2004). Coping: Pitfalls and promises. *Annual Review of Psychology, 55,* 745–774.

Fonagy, P., & Target, M. (2003). Being mindful of minds: A homage to the contributions of a child-analytic genius. *The Psychoanalytic Study of the Child, 58,* 307–321.

Fosha, D. (2000). Meta-therapeutic processes and the affects of transformation: Affirmation and the healing affects. *Journal of Psychotherapy Integration, 10*(1), 71–97.

Frank, L. D. (1939). Projective methods for the study of personality. *Journal of Psychology, 8,* 389–413.

Frank, L. D. (1948). *Projective methods.* Springfield, IL: Thomas.

Frijda, N. H. (2006). *The laws of emotion.* Mahwah, NJ: Erlbaum.

French, J., Graves, P. D., & Levitt, E. E. (1983). Objective and projective testing of children. In C. E. Walker & M. C. Roberts (Eds.), *Handbook of clinical child psychology* (pp. 209–247). New York: Wiley.

Frick, P. J., & Lahey, B. B. (1991). The nature and characteristics of Attention-deficit Hyperactivity Disorder. *School Psychology Review, 20,* 163–173.

Frijda, N. H. (1986). *The emotions.* Cambridge, UK: Cambridge University Press.

Frith, U. (2000). *Autism: Explaining the enigma.* Oxford: Blackwell.

Frost, B. C., Ko, C. E., & James, L. R. (2007). Implicit and explicit personality: A test of a channeling hypothesis for aggressive behavior. *Journal of Applied Psychology, 92,* 1299–1319.

Gallo, I. S., Keil, A., McCulloch, K. C., Rockstroh, B., & Gollwitzer, P. M. (2009). Strategic automation of emotion regulation. *Journal of Personality and Social Psychology, 96,* 11–31.

Gardner, D. R., & Holmes, C. B. (1990). Comparison of the CAT and CAT-H with third grade boys and girls. *Psychological Reports, 66,* 922.

Gardner, H. (1991). *The unschooled mind: How children think and how schools should teach.* New York: Basic Books.

Garnefski, N., & Kraaij, V. (2006). Relationships between cognitive emotion regulation strategies and depressive symptoms: A comparative study of five specific samples. *Personality and Individual Differences, 40,* 1659–1669.

Geary, D. C. (2005). *The origin of mind: Evolution of brain, cognition, and general intelligence.* Washington, DC: American Psychological Association.

Gergen, K. J., & Gergen, M. M. (1988). Narrative and the self as relationship. In L. Berkowitz (Ed.), *Advances in experimental social psychology, 21* (pp. 17–56). New York: Academic.

Gieser, L., & Stein, M. I. (Eds.). (1999). *Evocative images: The Thematic Apperception Test and the art of projection.* Washington, DC: American Psychological Association.

Glass, C. R., & Arnkoff, D. B. (1997). Questionnaire methods of cognitive self-statement assessment. *Journal of Consulting and Clinical Psychology, 65,* 911–927.

Gold, J. M., & Hurt, S. W. (1990). The effects of haloperidol on thought disorder and IQ in Schizophrenia. *Journal of Personality Assessment, 54,* 390–400.

Goldfried, M. R., Greenberg, L. S., & Marmar, C. (1990). Individual psychotherapy: Process and outcome. *Annual Review of Psychology, 41,* 659–688.

Gollwitzer, P. M. (1996). The volitional benefits of planning. In P. M. Gollwitzer & J. A. Bargh (Eds.), *The psychology of action: Linking cognition and motivation to behavior* (pp. 287–312). New York: Guilford Press.

Gollwitzer, P. M. (1999). Implementation intentions: Strong effects of simple plans. *American Psychologist, 54,* 493–503.

Gollwitzer, P. M., & Moskowitz, G. B. (1996). Goal effects on action and cognition. In E. T. Higgins & A. W. Kruglanski (Eds.), *Social psychology: Handbook of basic principles* (pp. 361–399). New York: Guilford Press.

Gollwitzer, P. M., & Sheeran, P. (2006). Implementation intentions and goal achievement: A meta-analysis of effects and processes. *Advances in Experimental Social Psychology, 38,* 69–119.

Grant, H., & Dweck, C. S. (2003). Clarifying achievement goals and their impact. *Journal of Personality and Social Psychology, 85,* 541–553.

Gray, J. A. (1987). *The psychology of fear and stress* (2nd ed.). Cambridge, UK: Cambridge University Press.

Greenberg, J., & Mitchell, S. (1983). *Object relations in psychoanalytic theory.* Cambridge, MA: Harvard University Press.

Greenberg, L. S. (1993). Emotional change processes in psychotherapy. In M. Lewis & J. Haviland (Eds.), *Handbook of emotion* (pp. 499–510). New York: Guilford Press.

Greenberg, L. S., Elliott, R., & Foerster, F. S. (1991). Experiential process in the psychotherapeutic treatment of depression. In D. McCann & N. Endler (Eds.), *Depression: Development in theory, research and practice* (pp. 157–185). Toronto: Thompson.

Greenberg, L. S., Rice, L. N., & Elliott, R. (1993). *Facilitating emotional change: The moment by moment process.* New York: Guilford Press.

Greenberg, M. A., Wortman, C. B., & Stone, A.A. (1996). Emotional expression and physical health: Revising traumatic memories or fostering self-regulation? *Journal of Personality and Social Psychology, 71,* 588–602.

Greenwald, A. G., Banaji, M. R., Rudman, L. A., Farnham, S. D., Nosek, B. A., & Mellott, D. S. (2002). A unified theory of implicit attitudes, stereotypes, self-esteem, and self-concept. *Psychological Review, 109*(1), 3–25.

Grolnick, W. S., Deci, E. L., & Ryan, R. M. (1997). Internalization within the family. In J. E. Grusec & L. Kuczynski (Eds.), *Parenting and children's internalization of values: A handbook of contemporary theory* (pp. 135–161). New York: Wiley.

Grolnick, W. S., & Ryan, R. M. (1987). Autonomy in children's learning: An experimental and individual difference investigation. *Journal of Personality and Social Psychology, 52,* 890–898.

Gross, J. J. (1998). Antecedent and response-focused emotion regulation: Divergent consequences for experience, expression and physiology. *Journal of Personality and Social Psychology, 74,* 224–237.

Gross, J. J. (2001). Emotion regulation in adulthood: Timing is everything. *Current Directions in Psychological Science, 10,* 214–219.

Gross, J. J., & John, O. P. (2003). Individual differences in two emotion regulation processes: Implications for affect, relationships, and well-being. *Journal of Personality and Social Psychology, 85,* 348–362.

Guidano, V. F. (1995). Constructivist psychotherapy: A theoretical framework. In R. A. Neimeyer & M. J. Mahoney (Eds.), *Constructivism in psychotherapy* (pp. 93–110). Washington, DC: American Psychological Association.

Guntrip, H. (1968). *Schizoid phenomena, object relations and the self.* New York: International Universities Press.

Guntrip, H. (1974). Psychoanalytic object relations theory: The Fairbairn-Guntrip approach. In S. Arieti (Ed.), *American handbook of psychiatry* (Vol. 1, pp. 828–842). New York: Basic Books.

Hammer, D. (1996). Misconceptions or p-prisms: How may alternative perspectives of cognitive structure influence instructional perceptions and intentions? *Journal of the Learning Sciences, 5,* 97–127.

Harris, P. L., Olthof, T., & Terwogt, M. M. (1981). Children's knowledge of emotion. *Journal of Child Psychology and Psychiatry and Allied Disciplines, 22,* 247–261.

Hartman, A. A. (1970). A basic TAT set. *Journal of Projective Techniques and Personality Assessment, 34,* 391–396.

Hasher, L., & Zacks, R. T. (1979). Automatic and effortful processes in memory. *Journal of Experimental Psychology: General, 108,* 356–388.

Hatt, C. V. (1985). Review of the Children's Apperception Test. In J. V. Mitchell (Ed.), *The ninth mental measurements yearbook* (pp. 314–316). Lincoln, NE: Buros Institute of Mental Health.

Haworth, M. R. (1963). A schedule for the analysis of CAT responses. *Journal of Projective Techniques and Personality Assessment, 27,* 181–184.

Haworth, M. R. (1966). *The CAT: Facts about fantasy.* New York: Grune & Stratton.

Haynes, J. P., & Peltier, J. (1985). Patterns of practice with TAT in juvenile forensic settings. *Journal of Personality Assessment, 49,* 26–29.

Haynes, S. N., & O'Brien, W. H. (1990). Functional analysis in behavior therapy. *Clinical Psychology Review, 10,* 649–668.

Hemenover, S. H. (2003). Individual differences in rate of affect change: Studies in affective chronometry. *Journal of Personality and Social Psychology, 85,* 121–131.

Henderson, H. A., & Fox, N. A. (1998). Inhibited and uninhibited children: Challenges in school settings. *School Psychology Review, 27,* 492–505.

Henry, W. E. (1956). *The analysis of fantasy: The Thematic Apperception Technique in the study of personality.* New York: Wiley.

Hermans, H. J. (2003). The construction and reconstruction of a dialogical self. *Journal of Constructivist Psychology, 16,* 89–127.

Hermans, H. J., Kempen, H. J., & Van Loon, R. J. (1992). The dialogical self: Beyond individualism and rationalism. *American Psychologist, 47,* 23–33.

Higgins, E. T., King, G. A., & Mavin, G. H. (1982). Individual construct accessibility and subjective impressions and recall. *Journal of Personality and Social Psychology, 43,* 35–47.

Hoar, M. W., & Faust, W. L. (1973). The Children's Apperception Test: Puzzle and regular form. *Journal of Personality Assessment, 37,* 244–247.

Hoffman, M. L. (1982). Affect and moral development. In D. Cicchetti & P. Hesse (Eds.), *Emotional development* (pp. 83–103). San Francisco: Jossey-Bass.

Hoffman, M. L. (2000). *Empathy and moral development: Implications for caring and justice.* New York: Cambridge University Press.

Holinger, Paul C. (2008). Further issues in the psychology of affect and motivation: A developmental perspective. *Psychoanalytic Psychology, 25*, 425–442.

Hollon, S. D., & Kendall, P. C. (1980). Cognitive self-statements in depression: Development of an automatic thoughts questionnaire. *Cognitive Therapy and Research, 4*, 383–395.

Hollon, S. D., Kendall, P. C., & Lumry, A. (1986). Specificity of depressotypic cognitions in clinical depression. *Journal of Abnormal Psychology, 95*, 52–59.

Holmstrom, R. W., Silber, D. E., & Karp, S. A. (1990). Development of the Apperceptive Personality Test. *Journal of Personality Assessment, 54*, 252–264.

Holodynski, M., & Friedlmeier, W. (2006). *Development of emotions and emotion regulation*. New York: Springer.

Holt, R. R. (1958). Formal aspects of the TAT: A neglected resource. *Journal of Projective Techniques, 22*, 163–172.

Holt, R. R. (1961). The nature of TAT stories as cognitive products: A psychoanalytic approach. In J. Kagan & G. Lesser (Eds.), *Contemporary issues in thematic apperceptive methods* (pp. 3–40). Springfield, IL: Charles C. Thomas.

Holt, R. R. (1978). *Methods in clinical psychology, Vol. I: Projective assessment*. New York: Plenum Press.

Horowitz, M. J. (1991). States, schemas, and control: General theories for psychotherapy integration. *Journal of Psychotherapy Integration, 1*, 85–102.

Howard, G. S. (1991). A narrative approach to thinking, cross-cultural psychology, and psychotherapy. *American Psychologist, 46*, 187–197.

Hunt, E. (1980). Intelligence as an information-processing concept. *British Journal of Psychology, 71*, 449–474.

Hunt, E. (1998). Constructivism and cognition. In J. Carlson (Ed.), *Issues in education* (pp. 27-42). Stamford, CT: JAI Press.

Hurley, A. D., & Sovner, R. (1985). The use of Thematic Apperception Tests in mentally retarded persons. *Psychiatric Aspects of Mental Retardation Reviews, 4*, 9–12.

James, L. R. (1998). Measurement of personality via conditional reasoning. *Organizational Research Methods, 1*, 131–163.

James, W. (1890). *The principles of psychology*. New York: Henry Holt.

Jenkins, S. R. (2008). Teaching how to learn reliable scoring. In S. R. Jenkins (Ed.), *A handbook of clinical scoring systems for thematic apperceptive techniques* (pp. 39–66). New York: Erlbaum.

Johnson, R. E., Chang, C-H. D., & Lord, R. G. (2006). Moving from cognition to behavior: What the research says. *Psychological Bulletin, 132*, 381–415.

Johnston, M. H., & Holzman, P. S. (1979). *Assessing schizophrenic thinking: A clinical and research instrument for measuring thought disorder*. San Francisco: Jossey-Bass.

Karoly, P. (1993). Mechanisms of self-regulation: A systems view. *Annual Review of Psychology, 44*, 23–52.

Karon, B. P. (1981). The Thematic Apperception Test (TAT). In A. J. Rabin (Ed.), *Assessment with projective techniques: A concise introduction* (pp. 85–120). New York: Springer.

Kasser, T., & Ryan, R. M. (1993). A dark side of the American dream: Correlates of financial success as a central life aspiration. *Journal of Personality and Social Psychology, 65*, 410–422.

Kasser, T., & Ryan, R. M. (1996). Further examining the American dream: Differential correlates of intrinsic and extrinsic goals. *Personality and Social Psychology Bulletin, 22*, 280–287.

Katz, H. E., Russ, S. W., & Overholser, J. W. (1993). Sex differences, sex roles, and projection on the TAT: Matching stimulus to examinee gender. *Journal of Personality Assessment, 60*, 186–191.

Keiser, R. E., & Prather, E. N. (1990). What is the TAT? A review of ten years of research. *Journal of Personality Assessment, 55*, 800–803.

Kelly, F. D. (1996). *Object relations in younger children: Rorschach and TAT measures.* Springfield, Il: Charles C. Thomas.

Kelly, F. D. (1997). *The assessment of object relations phenomena in adolescents.* Mahwah, NJ: Erlbaum.

Kelly, G. A. (1958). The theory and technique of assessment. In P. R. Farnsworth & Q. McNemar (Eds.), *Annual review of psychology, 9* (pp. 323–352). Palo Alto, CA: Annual Reviews.

Kendall, P. C. (1993). Cognitive-behavioral therapies with youth: Guiding theory, current status, and emerging developments. *Journal of Consulting and Clinical Psychology, 61,* 235–247.

Kenny, D. T., & Bijou, S. W. (1953). Ambiguity of pictures and extent of personality factors in fantasy responses. *Journal of Consulting and Clinical Psychology, 17,* 283–288.

Kernberg, O. (1975). *Borderline conditions and pathological narcissism.* New York: Jason Aronson.

Kernberg, O. (1976). *Object relations theory and clinical psychoanalysis.* New York: Aronson.

Kernberg, O. (1984). *Object relations theory and clinical psychoanalysis.* Northvale, NJ: Jason Aronson (paper edition).

Kessler, R. C., Berglund, P., Demler, O., Jin, R., & Walters, E. E. (2005). Lifetime prevalence and age-of-onset distributions of DSM-IV disorders in the National Comorbidity Survey Replication. *Archives of General Psychiatry, 62,* 593–602.

Kihlstrom, J. F. (1987). The cognitive unconscious. *Science, 237,* 1445–1452.

Kitron, D. G., & Benzimen, H. (1990). The Children's Apperception Test: Possible applications for adults. *Israel Journal of Psychiatry and Related Services, 27,* 29–47.

Klein, M. (1932). *The psychoanalysis of children.* New York: Grove Press.

Klein, M. (1948). *Contributions to psychoanalysis. 1921–1945.* London: Hogarth Press.

Kline, P., & Svaste-Xuto, B. (1981). The responses of Thai and British children to the Children's Apperception Test. *Journal of Social Psychology, 113,* 137–138.

Knobe, J. (2003). Intentional action and side-effects in ordinary language. *Analysis, 63,* 190–193.

Kochanska, G., & Aksan, N. (1995). Mother-child mutually positive affect, quality of child compliance to requests and prohibitions, and maternal control as correlates of early internalization. *Child Development, 66,* 236–254.

Kochanska, G., & Aksan, N. (2006). Children's conscience and self-regulation. *Journal of Personality, 74,* 1587–1617.

Kochanska, G., & Thompson, R. A. (1997). The emergence and development of conscience in toddlerhood and early childhood. In J. E. Grusec & L. Kuczynski (Eds.), *Parenting and children's internalization of values: A handbook of contemporary theory* (pp. 53–77). New York: Wiley.

Koestner, R., & McClelland, D. C. (1990). Perspectives on competence motivation. In L. Pervin (Ed.), *Handbook of personality theory and research* (pp. 527–548). NY: Guilford Press.

Koestner, R., Weinberger, J., & McClelland, D. C. (1991). Task-intrinsic and social-extrinsic sources of arousal for motives assessed in fantasy and self-report. *Journal of Personality, 59,* 57–82.

Kohut, H. (1971). *The analysis of the self.* New York: International Universities Press.

Kohut, H. (1977). *The restoration of the self.* New York: International Universities Press.

Kroon, N., Goudena, P. P., & Rispens, J. (1998). Thematic Apperception Tests for child and adolescent assessment: A practitioner's guide. *Journal of Psychoeducational Assessment, 16,* 99–117.

Kross, E., Ayduk, O., & Mischel, W. (2005). When asking "*why*" doesn't hurt: Distinguishing rumination from reflective processing of negative emotions. *Psychological Science, 16,* 709–715.

Kruglanski, A. W., Shah, J. Y., Fishbach, A., Friedman, R. S., Chun, W. Y., & Sleeth-Keppler, D. (2002). A theory of goal systems: Implications for social cognition, affect, and action. In M. Zanna (Ed.), *Advances in experimental social psychology, 34* (pp. 331–376). New York: Academic Press.

Kuhl, J. (1984). Volitional aspects of achievement motivation and learned helplessness: Toward a comprehensive theory of action-control. In B. A. Maher (Ed.), *Progress in experimental personality research* (Vol. 13, pp. 99–171). New York: Academic Press.

Kuhl, J. (1992). A theory of self-regulation: Action versus state orientation, self-discrimination, and some applications. *Applied Psychology: An International Review, 41,* 97–129.

Kuhl, J. (1996). Who controls whom when "I control myself"? *Psychological Inquiry, 7,* 61–68.

Kuhl, J., & Fuhrmann, A. (1998). Decomposing self-regulation and self-control: The Volitional Components Inventory. In J. Heckhausen & C. S. Dweck (Eds.), *Motivation and self-regulation across the life span* (pp. 15–47). New York: Cambridge University Press.

Kuppens, P., Van Mechelen, I., & Rijmen, F. (2008). Towards disentangling sources of individual differences in appraisal and anger. *Journal of Personality, 76,* 969–1000.

Kuppens, P., Van Mechelen, I., Smits, D. J. M., De Boeck, P., & Ceulemans, E. (2007). Individual differences in patterns of appraisal and anger experience. *Cognition & Emotion, 21,* 689–713.

Kymalainen, J., Weisman, A., Rosales, G., & Armesto, J. (2006). Ethnicity, expressed emotion and communication deviance in familiy members of patients with Schizophrenia. *Journal of Nervous and Mental Disease, 194,* 391–396.

Lau, S., Liem, A. D., & Nie, Y. (2008). Task- and self-related pathways to deep learning: The mediating role of achievement goals, classroom attentiveness, and group participation. *British Journal of Educational Psychology, 78,* 639–662.

Lazarus, R. S. (1991a). *Emotion and adaptation.* New York: Oxford University Press.

Lazarus, R. S. (1991b). Progress on a cognitive-motivational-relational theory of emotion. *American Psychologist, 46,* 819–834.

Lazarus, R. S. (1994). Meaning and emotional development. In P. Ekman & R. J. Davidson (Eds.), *The nature of emotion: Fundamental questions* (pp. 163–171). New York: Oxford University Press.

Lazarus, R. S. (1995). Vexing research problems inherent in cognitive-mediational theories of emotion and some solutions. *Psychological Inquiry, 6,* 183–265.

Lazarus, R. S. (1999). Hope: An emotion and a vital coping resource against despair. *Social Research, 66,* 665–669.

Lazarus, R. S., & Folkman, S. (1984). *Stress, appraisal, and copying.* New York: Springer Publishing Co.

Lehmann, I. J. (1959). Responses of kindergarten children to the Children's Apperception Test. *Journal of Clinical Psychology, 15,* 60–63.

Leigh, J., Westen, D., Barends, A., & Mendel, M. J. (1992). The assessment of complexity of representations of people using TAT and interview data. *Journal of Personality, 60,* 809–837.

Leslie, A. M. (1992). Pretense, autism, and the theory of mind module. *Current Directions in Psychological Science, 1*(1), 18–21.

Levesque, C. S., Zuehlke, N., Stanek, L., & Ryan, R. M. (2004). Autonomy and competence in German and U.S. university students: A comparative study based on self-determination theory. *Journal of Educational Psychology, 96,* 68–84.

Lewicki, P., Czyzewska, M., & Hill, T. (1997). Cognitive mechanisms for acquiring "experience": The dissociation between conscious and nonconscious cognition. In J. D. Cohen and J. W. Schooler (Eds.), *Scientific approaches to the question of consciousness (Carnegie Mellon Symposium on Consciousness)* (pp. 161–177). Hillsdale, NJ: Erlbaum.

Lewicki, P., Hill, T., & Czyzewska, M. (1992). Nonconscious acquisition of information. *American Psychologist, 47,* 796–801.

Lewin, K. (1935). *A dynamic theory of personality.* New York: McGraw-Hill.

Lewis, W. A., & Bucher, A. M. (1992). Anger, catharsis, the reformulated frustration -aggression hypothesis, and health consequences. *Psychotherapy, 29,* 385–392.

Libby, L. K., & Eibach, R. P. (2002). Looking back in time: Self-concept change and visual perspective in autobiographical memory. *Journal of Personality and Social Psychology, 82,* 167–179.

Light, B. H. (1954). Comparative study of a series of TAT and CAT cards. *Journal of Clinical Psychology, 17,* 281–297.

Lilienfeld, S. O., Wood, J. M., & Garb, H. N. (2000). The scientific status of projective techniques. *Psychological Science in the Public Interest, 1,* 27–66.

Lindzey, G. (1952). Thematic Apperception Test: Interpretive assumptions and related empirical evidence. *Psychological Bulletin, 49,* 1–25.

Linehan, M. M. (1993). *Skills training manual for treating Borderline Personality Disorder.* New York: Guilford Press.

Linehan, M. M., Dimeff, L. A., Reynolds, S. K., Comtois, K. A., Shaw-Welch, S., Heagerty, P., Kivlahan, D. R. (2002). Dialectical behavior therapy versus comprehensive validation plus 12-step for the treatment of opioid-dependent women meeting criteria for Borderline Personality Disorder. *Drug and Alcohol Dependence, 67,* 13–26.

Linville, P. W. (1985). Self-complexity and affective extremity: Don't put all your eggs in one cognitive basket. *Social Cognition, 3,* 94–120.

Linville, P. W. (1987). Self-complexity as a cognitive buffer against stress-related illness and depression. *Journal of Personality and Social Psychology, 52,* 663–676.

Locke, G. P., & Latham, E. A. (1990). Self-regulation through goal setting. *Organizational Behavior and Human Decision Processes, 50,* 212–247.

Locraft, C., & Teglasi, H. (1997). Teacher rated empathic behavior and children's TAT stories. *Journal of School Psychology, 35,* 217–237.

Lohr, L., Teglasi, H., & French, M. (2004). Schemas and temperament as risk factors for emotional disability. *Personality and Individual Differences, 36,* 1637–1654.

Lundy, A. (1985). The reliability of the Thematic Apperception Test. *Journal of Personality Assessment, 49,* 141–149.

Luo, W., Watkins, D., & Lam, R. Y. (2009). Validating a new measure of self-complexity. *Journal of Personality Assessment, 91,* 381–386.

Lutz, C., & White, G. M. (1986). The anthropology of emotions. *Annual Review of Anthropology, 15,* 405–436.

MacDonald, K. (2008). Effortful control, explicit processing, and the regulation of human evolved predispositions. *Psychological Review, 115*(4), 1012–1031.

Mahler, M. S. (1966). Some preliminary notes on the development of basic moods, including depression. *Canadian Psychiatric Association Journal, 11* (Suppl.), 250–258.

Mahler, M. S., Pine, F., & Bergman, A. (1975). *The psychological birth of the human infant.* New York: Basic Books.

Malle, B. F. (2001). Attribution processes. In N. J. Smelser and P. B. Baltes (Eds.), *International encyclopedia of the social and behavioral sciences* (Vol. 14, Developmental, social, personality, and motivational psychology; section editor N. Eisenberg, pp. 913–917). Amsterdam: Pergamon/Elsevier.

Malle, B. F., & Knobe, J. (2001). The distinction between desire and intention: A folk-conceptual analysis. In B. F. Malle, L. J. Moses, & D. A. Baldwin (Eds.), *Intentions and intentionality: Foundations of social cognition* (pp. 45–67*).* Cambridge, MA: The MIT Press.

Maloney, M. P., & Ward, M. P. (1976). *Psychological assessment: A conceptual approach*. New York: Oxford.

Mancuso, J. C., & Sarbin, T. R. (1998). The narrative construction of emotional life: Developmental aspects. In M. F. Manscolo & S. Griffin (Eds.), *What develops in emotional development? Emotions, personality, and psychotherapy* (pp. 297–316). New York: Plenum Press.

Mandler, J. M. (1982). Recent research on story grammars. *Language and Communication, 15,* 207–218.

Markus, H., & Kitayama, S. (1991). Culture and the self: Implications for cognition, emotion, and motivation. *Psychological Review, 98,* 224–253.

Martin, L. & Tesser, A. (1996). Some ruminative thoughts. In R. S. Wyer (Eds.), *Advances in social cognition.* (vol. 9, pp 1–48). Hillsdale, NJ: Erlbaum.

Martin, L. L., & Tesser, A. (1989). Toward a motivational and structural theory of ruminative thought. In J. S. Uleman & J. A. Bargh (Eds.), *Unintended thought* (pp. 306–326). New York: Guilford Press.

Masling, J. M., & Bornstein, R. F. (Eds.). (1994). *Empirical perspectives on object relations theory.* Washington, DC: American Psychological Association.

Mathews, A., & MacLeod, C. (1994). Cognitive approaches to emotion and emotion disorders. *Annual Review of Psychology, 45,* 25–50.

Mauss, I. B., Cook, C. L., Cheng, J. Y. J., & Gross, J. J. (2007). Individual differences in cognitive reappraisal: Experiential and physiological responses to an anger provocation. *International Journal of Psychophysiology, 66,* 116–124.

Mauss, I. B., Levenson, R. W., McCarter, L., Wilhelm, F. H., & Gross, J. J. (2005). The tie that binds? Coherence among emotional experience, behavior, and autonomic physiology. *Emotion, 5,* 175–190.

Mayer, J. D. (2003). Structural divisions of personality and the classification of traits. *Review of General Psychology, 7,* 381–401.

Mayman, M. (1967). Object-representations and object-relationships in Rorschach responses. *Journal of Projective Techniques and Personality Assessment, 31,* 17–24.

McAdams, D. P. (1985). *Power, intimacy, and the life story: Personological inquiries into identity.* New York: Guilford Press.

McAdams, D. P. (1993). *The stories we live by: Personal myths and the making of the self.* New York: Morrow.

McAdams, D. P., Diamond, A., de St. Aubin, E., & Mansfield, E. (1997). Stories of commitment: The psychosocial construction of generative lives. *Journal of Personality and Social Psychology, 72,* 678–694.

McAdams, D. P., Hoffman, B. J., Mansfield, E. D., & Day, R. (1996). Themes of agency and communion in significant autobiographical scenes. *Journal of Personality, 64,* 339–378.

McAdams, D. P., & Pals, J. L. (2006). A new Big Five: Fundamental principles for an integrative science of personality. *American Psychologist, 61,* 204–217.

McArthur, D. S., & Roberts, G. E. (1982). *Roberts Apperception Test for Children Manual.* Los Angeles: Western Psychological Services.

McArthur, L. Z., & Baron, R. M. (1983). Toward an ecological theory of social perception. *Psychological Review, 90,* 215–238.

McBride, C., Farvolden, P., & Swallow, S. R. (2007). Major Depressive Disorder and cognitive schema. In L. P. Riso, P. L. Du Toit, D. J. Stein, & J. E. Young (Eds.), *Cognitive schemas and core beliefs in psychological problems: A scientist-practitioner guide* (pp. 11–39). Washington, DC: American Psychological Association.

McClelland, D. C. (1987). *Human motivation.* New York: Cambridge University Press.

McClelland, D. C., Koestner, R., & Weinberger, J. (1989). How do self-attributed and implicit motives differ? *Psychological Review, 96,* 690–702.

McGrew, M. W., & Teglasi, H. (1990). Formal characteristics of Thematic Apperception Test stories as indices of emotional disturbance in children. *Journal of Personality Assessment, 54,* 639–655.

Meece, J., Anderman E. M., & Anderman, L. H. (2006). Classroom goal structure, student motivation, and academic achievement. *Annual Review of Psychology, Vol. 57* (pp. 505–528). Stanford, CA: Annual Reviews.

Meissner, W. W. (1971). Notes on identification. II. Clarification of related concepts. *Psychoanalytic Quarterly, 40,* 277–302.

Meissner, W. W. (1972). Notes on identification. III. The concept of identification. *Psychoanalytic Quarterly, 41,* 224–260.

Meissner, W. W. (1974). Differentiation and integration of learning and identification in the developmental process. *Annual of Psychoanalysis, 2,* 181–196.

Meissner, W. W. (1981). Internalization and psychoanalysis. *Psychological Issues Monograph, 50.* New York: International Universities Press.

Meltzoff, A. (1995). Understanding the intentions of others: Re-enactment of intended acts by 18-month-old children. *Developmental Psychology, 31,* 838–850.

Mendoza-Denton, R., Ayduk, O., Mischel, W., Shoda, Y., & Testa, A. (2001). Person X Situation interactionism in self-encoding (I am…when…): Implications for affect regulation and social information processing. *Journal of Personality and Social Psychology, 80,* 533–544.

Mesquita, B. (2001a). Culture and emotions: Different approaches to the question. In T. Mayne and G. Bonanno (Eds.), *Emotion: Current issues and future directions* (pp. 214–250). New York: Guilford Press.

Mesquita, B. (2001b). Emotions in collectivist and individualist contexts. *Journal of Personality and Social Psychology, 80*(1), 68–74.

Mesquita, B., & Ellsworth, P. (2001). The role of culture in appraisal. In K. R. Scherer & A. Schorr (Eds.), *Appraisal processes in emotion: Theory, methods, research* (pp. 233–248). New York: Oxford University Press.

Messick, S. (1983). Assessment of children. In P. H. Mussen (Ed.), *Handbook of child psychology, Fourth Edition,* W. Kessen (Volume Ed.), *Volume I: History, Theory, and Methods* (pp. 477–526). New York: Wiley.

Messick, S. (1989). Validity. In R. L. Linn (Ed.), *Educational measurement* (3rd ed., pp. 13–103). New York: MacMillan.

Meyer, G. J., & Kurtz, J. E. (2006). Advancing personality assessment terminology: Time to retire "objective" and "projective" as personality test descriptors. *Journal of Personality Assessment, 87,* 223–225.

Midgley, C., Kaplan, A., & Middleton, M. (2001). Performance-approach goals: Good for what, for whom, under what circumstances, and at what cost? *Journal of Educational Psychology, 93*(1), 77–86.

Miranda, J., Gross, J. J., Persons, J. B., & Hahn, J. (1998). Mood matters: Negative mood induction activates dysfunctional attitudes in women vulnerable to depression. *Cognitive Therapy and Research, 22,* 363–376.

Mischel, W. (1968). *Personality and assessment.* New York: Wiley.

Mischel, W., & Ayduk, O. (2004). Willpower in a cognitive-affective processing system: The dynamics of delay of gratification. In R. F. Baumeister & K. D. Vohs (Eds.), *Handbook of self-regulation: Research, theory, and applications* (pp. 99–129). New York: Guilford Press.

Moller, A. C., & Elliot, A. J. (2006). The 2 × 2 achievement goal framework: An overview of empirical research. In A. V. Mitel (Ed.), *Focus on educational psychology research* (pp. 307–326). New York: Nova Science Publishers, Inc.

More, S., & Gullone, E. (1996). Predicting adolescent risk behavior using a personalized cost-benefit analysis. *Journal of Youth and Adolescence, 25,* 343–359.

Morgan, C. D., & Murray, H. H. (1935). A method for investigating fantasies: The thematic apperception test. *Archives of Neurology and Psychiatry, 34,* 289–306.

Morgan, W. G. (1995). Origin and history of the Thematic Apperception Test images. *Journal of Personality Assessment, 65,* 237–252.

Moses, E. B., & Barlow, D. H. (2006). A new unified treatment approach for emotional disorders based on emotion science. *Current Directions in Psychological Science, 15,* 146–150.

Muraven, M., Shmueli, D., & Burkley, E. (2006). Conserving self-control. strength. *Journal of Personality and Social Psychology, 91,* 524–537.

Murray, H. A. (1938). *Explorations in personality.* New York: Oxford University Press.

Murray, H. A. (1943). *Thematic Apperception Test manual.* Cambridge, MA: Harvard University Press.

Murstein, B. I. (1963). *Theories and research in projective techniques: Emphasizing the TAT.* New York: Wiley.

Murstein, B. I. (1965). The stimulus. In B. Murstein (Ed.), *Handbook of projective techniques.* New York: Basic Books.

Murstein, B. I. (1968). The effect of stimulus, background, personality, and scoring system on the manifestation of hostility on the TAT. *Journal of Consulting and Clinical Psychology, 32,* 355–365.

Myler, B., Rosenkrantz, A., & Holmes, G. (1972). A comparison of the TAT, CAT, and CAT-H among second grade girls. *Journal of Personality Assessment, 36,* 440–444.

Nannis, E. D. (1988). Cognitive-developmental differences in emotional understanding. *New Directions for Child Development, 39,* 31–49.

Nelson, K., & Fivush, R. (2004). The emergence of autobiographical memory: A social cultural developmental theory. *Psychological Review, 111,* 486–511.

Neuringer, C., & Livesay, R. C. (1970). Projective fantasy on the CAT and CAT-H. *Journal of Projective Techniques and Personality Assessment, 34,* 487–491.

Newmark, C. S., & Flouranzano, R. (1973). Replication of an empirically derived TAT set with hospitalized psychiatric patients. *Journal of Personality Assessment, 37,* 340–341.

Newmark, C. S., Hetzel, W., & Freking, R. A. (1974). The effects of personality tests on state and trait anxiety. *Journal of Personality Assessment, 38,* 17–20.

Newmark, C. S., Wheeler, D., Newmark, L., & Stabler, B. (1975). Test induced anxiety with children. *Journal of Personality Assessment, 39,* 409–413.

Nezlek, J., Vansteelandt, K., Van Mechelen, I., & Kuppens, P. (2008). Appraisal-emotion relationships in daily life. *Emotion, 8*(1), 145–150.

Nigg, J. T., & Casey, B. J. (2005). An integrative theory of Attention-Deficit/Hyperactivity Disorder based on the cognitive and affective neurosciences. *Development & Psychopathology, 17,* 785–806.

Nolen-Hoeksema, S. (1999). Ruminative coping with depression. In J. Heckhausern & C. S. Dweck (Eds.), *Motivation and self-regulation across the life span* (pp. 237–256). New York: Cambridge University Press.

Nugier, A., Niedenthal, P. M., Brauer, M., & Chekroun, P. (2007). Moral and angry emotions provoked by informal social control. *Cognition and Emotion, 21,* 1699–1720.

Oatley, K. (1992). Integrative action of narrative. In D. J. Stein & J. E. Young (Eds.), *Cognitive science and clinical disorders* (pp. 151–172). San Diego, CA: Academic Press.

Oppenheim, D., Emde, R. N., & Warren, S. (1997). Children's narrative representations of mothers: Their development and associations with child and mother adaptation. *Child Development, 68,* 127–138.

Pang, J. S., & Schultheiss, O. C. (2005). Assessing implicit motives of US college students: Effects of picture type and position, gender and ethnicity, and cross cultural comparisons. *Journal of Personality Assessment, 85,* 280–294.

Parkinson, B. (1999). Relations and dissociations between appraisal and emotion ratings of reasonable and unreasonable anger and guilt. *Cognition and Emotion, 13,* 347–385.

Parry, A., & Doan, R. E. (1994). *Story re-visions: Narrative therapy in the post-modern world.* New York: Guilford Press.

Pasewark, R. A., Fitzgerald, B. J., Dexter, V., & Cangemi, A. (1976). Responses of adolescents, middle-aged, and aged females on the Gerontological and Thematic Apperception Tests. *Journal of Personality Assessment, 40,* 588–591.

Payne, B. K., Burkley, M., & Stokes, M. B. (2008). Why do implicit and explicit attitude tests diverge? The role of structural fit. *Journal of Personality and Social Psychology, 94,* 16–31.

Payne, S. C., Youngcourt, S. S., & Beaubien, J. M. (2007). A meta-analytic examination of the goal orientation nomological net. *Journal of Applied Psychology, 92,* 128–150.

Pekrun, R., Elliot, A. J., & Maier, M. A. (2006). Achievement goals and discrete achievement emotions: A theoretical model and prospective test. *Journal of Educational Psychology, 98,* 583–597.

Pennebaker, J. W. (1990). Stream of consciousness and stress: Levels of thinking. In J. S. Uleman & J. A. Bargh (Eds.), *Unintended thought* (pp. 327–350). New York: Guilford Press.

Pennebaker, J. W. (1997). Writing about emotional experiences as a therapeutic process. *Psychological Science, 8,* 162–166.

Pennebaker, J. W., Mehl, M. R., & Niederhoffer, K. (2003). Psychological aspects of natural language use: Our words, our selves. *Annual Review of Psychology, 54,* 547–577.

Pennebaker, J. W., & Seagal, J. D. (1999). Forming a story: The health benefits of narrative. *Journal of Clinical Psychology, 55,* 1243–1254.

Perkins, D. N., & Ritchhart, R. (2004). When is good thinking? In D. Y. Dai & R. J. Sternberg (Eds.), *Motivation, emotion, and cognition: Integrative perspectives on intellectual functioning and development* (pp. 351–384). Mahwah, NJ: Erlbaum.

Peterson, C. A. (1990). Administration of the Thematic Apperception Test: Contributions of psychoanalytic psychotherapy. *Journal of Contemporary Psychotherapy, 20,* 191–200.

Peterson, C. A, & McCabe, A. (1983). *Developmental psycholinguistics: Three ways of looking at a child's narrative.* New York: Plenum.

Peterson, C. A., & Schilling, K. M. (1983). Card pull in projective testing. *Journal of Personality Assessment, 47,* 265–275.

Piaget, J. (1954). *The construction of reality in the child.* New York: Basic Books.

Piaget, J. (1965). *The moral judgment of the child.* New York: Free Press.

Pinsker-Aspen, J. H., Stein, M. B., & Hilsenroth, M. J. (2007). Clinical utility of early memories as a predictor of early therapeutic alliance. *Psychotherapy, 44,* 96–109.

Pintrich, P. R., & Schunk, D. H. (2002). *Motivation in education: Theory, research, and applications* (2nd ed.). Columbus, OH: Merrill-Prentice Hall.

Posner, M. I., & Rothbart, M. K. (2007). Research on attention networks as a model for the integration of psychological sciences. *Annual Review of Psychology, 58,* 1–23.

Premack, D. (1992). On the origins of domain-specific primitives. In H. L. Pick & P. W. van den Broek (Eds.), *Cognition: Conceptual and methodological issues* (pp. 189–212). Washington, DC: American Psychological Association.

Premack, D., & Woodruff, G. (1978). Does the chimpanzee have a theory of mind? *The Behavioral and Brain Sciences, 1,* 515–526.

Pretz, J. E., Naples, A. J., & Sternberg, R. J. (2003). Recognizing, defining, and representing problems. In J. E. Davidson & R. J. Sternberg (Eds.), *The psychology of problem solving* (pp. 3–30). New York: Cambridge University Press.

Procidano, M. E., & Guinta, D. M. (1989). Object representations and symptomatology: Preliminary findings in young adult psychiatric inpatients. *Journal of Clinical Psychology, 45,* 309–316.

Rabin, A. I., & Haworth, M. R. (1960). *Projective techniques with children*. New York: Grune & Stratton.

Rappaport, D. (1947). The scoring and analysis of the Thematic Apperception Test. *Journal of Psychology, 24*, 319–330.

Rappaport, D., Gill, M., & Schafer, R. (1975). *Diagnostic psychological testing* (Rev. ed.). New York: International Universities Press.

Ray, R. D., Wilhelm, F. H., & Gross, J. J. (2008). All in the mind's eye? Anger rumination and reappraisal. *Journal of Personality and Social Psychology, 94*, 133–145.

Raynor, J. O., & McFarlin, D. B. (1986). Motivation and the self-system. In R. M. Sorrentino & E. T. Higgins (Eds.), *Handbook of motivation and cognition: Foundations of social behavior* (pp. 315–349). New York: Guilford Press.

Reese, E. (2002). A model of the origins of autobiographical memory. In J. W. Fagen & H. Hayne (Eds.), *Progress in infancy research* (Vol. 2, pp. 215–260). Mahwah, NJ: Erlbaum.

Reeve, J., Deci, E. L., & Ryan, R. M. (2004). Self-determination theory: A dialectical framework for understanding sociocultural influences on student motivation. In D. M. McInerney & S. Van Etten (Eds.), *Big theories revisited* (pp. 31–60). Greenwich, CT: Information Age Publishing.

Regner, I., Escribe, C., & Dupeyrat, C. (2007). Evidence of social comparison in mastery goals in natural academic settings. *Journal of Educational Psychology, 99*, 575–583.

Rehm, L.P. & Plakosh, P. (1975). Preference for immediate reinforcement in depression. *Journal of Behavior Therapy and Experimental Psychiatry, 6,* 101–103.

Richeson, J. A., and J. N. Shelton. 2003. When prejudice does not pay: Effects of interracial contact on executive function. *Psychological Science, 14,* 287–90.

Reisenzein, R. (2001). Appraisal processes conceptualized from a schematheoretic perspective: Contributions to a process analysis of emotions. In K. R. Scherer, A. Schorr, & T. Johnstone (Eds.), *Appraisal processes in emotion: Theory, methods, research. Series in affective science* (pp. 187–201). New York: Oxford University Press.

Riso, L. P., du Toit, P. L., Stein, D. J., & Young, J. E. (2007). *Cognitive schemas and core beliefs in psychological problems: A scientist-practitioner guide*. Washington, DC: American Psychological Association.

Riso, L. P., Maddux, R. E., & Turini-Santorelli, N. (2007). Early maladaptive schemas in chronic depression. In L. P. Riso, P. L. du Toit, D. J. Stein, & J. E. Young (Eds.), *Cognitive schemas and core beliefs in psychiatric disorders: A scientist-practitioner guide* (pp. 41–58). Washington, DC: APA Books.

Riso, L. P., McCullough, Jr. J. P., & Blandino, J. (2003). The cognitive behavioral analysis system of psychotherapy: A promising treatment for chronic depression. *The Scientific Review of Mental Health Practice, 2*, 61–68.

Ritchhart, R. (2002). *Intellectual character: What it is, why it matters, and how to get it*. San Francisco: Jossey-Bass.

Ritzler, B. A., Sharkey, K. J., & Chudy, J. F. (1980). A comprehensive projective alternative to the TAT. *Journal of Personality Assessment, 44,* 358–362.

Roberts, G. E. (2007). *Roberts-2 Casebook*. Los Angeles: Western Psychological Services.

Roberts, G. E., & Gruber, C. (2005). *Roberts-2*. Los Angeles: Western Psychological Services.

Ronan, G. F., Colavito, V. A., & Hammontree, S. R. (1993). Personal problem-solving system for scoring TAT responses: Preliminary validity and reliability data. *Journal of Personality Assessment, 61,* 28–40.

Ronan, G. F., Date, A. L., & Weisbrod, M. (1995). Personal problem-solving scoring of the TAT: Sensitivity to training. *Journal of Personality Assessment, 64,* 119–131.

Rothbart, M. K., Ahadi, S. A., & Evans, D. E. (2000). Temperament and personality: Origins and outcomes. *Journal of Personality and Social Psychology, 78*, 122–135.

Rothbart, M. K., & Bates, J. E. (2006). Temperament. In N. Eisenberg & W. Damon (Eds.), *Handbook of child psychology: Social, emotional, and personality development* (vol. 3, 6th ed., pp. 99–166). New York: Wiley.

Rothbart, M. K., & Bates, J. E. (2006). Temperament in children's development. In W. Damon, R. Lerner, & N. Eisenberg (Eds.), *Handbook of child psychology volume 3, Social, emotional, and personality development* (6th ed., pp. 99–106). New York: Wiley. Rothbart, M. K., Derryberry, D., & Posner, M. (1994). A psychobiological approach to the development of temperament. In J. E. Bates & T. D. Wachs (Eds.), *Temperament: Individual differences at the interface of biology and behavior* (pp. 83–116). Washington, DC: American Psychological Association.

Rothbart, M. K., & Jones, L. B. (1998). Temperament, self regulation, and education. *School Psychology Review, 27,* 479–491.

Rubin, K. H., Coplan, R. J., Fox, N. A., & Calkins, S. D. (1995). Emotionality, emotion regulation, and pre-schoolers' social adaptation. *Development and Psychopathology, 7,* 49–62.

Rudman, L. A. (2004). Sources of implicit attitudes. *Current Directions in Psychological Science, 13*(2), 80–83.

Rund, B. R. (1986). Communication deviance in parents of schizophrenics. *Family Process, 25,* 133–147.

Russ, S. W. (1998). Teaching child assessment from a developmental-psycho dynamic framework. In L. Handler & M. J. Hilsenroth (Eds.), *Teaching and learning personality assessment* (pp. 453–468). Mahwah, NJ: Erlbaum.

Ryan, R. M., & Connell, J. P. (1989). Perceived locus of causality and internalization: Examining reasons for acting in two domains. *Journal of Personality and Social Psychology, 57,* 749–761.

Sackett, P. R., Borneman, M., and Connelly, B. S (2008). High stakes testing in education and employment: Evaluating common criticisms regarding validity and fairness. *American Psychologist, 63,* 215–227.

Sackett, P. R., Zedeck, S., & Fogli, L. (1988). Relations between measures of typical and maximum job performance. *Journal of Applied Psychology, 73,* 482–486.

Safran, J. D., & Greenberg, L. S. (1988). Feeling, thinking, and acting: A cognitive framework for psychotherapy integration. *Journal of Cognitive Psychotherapy, 2,* 109–131.

Salz, G., & Epstein, S. (1963). Thematic hostility and guilt responses as related to self-reported hostility, guilt, and conflict. *Journal of Abnormal and Social Psychology, 67,* 469–479.

Sandler, J. (1992). Reflections on developments in the theory of psychoanalytic technique. *International Journal of Psycho-Analysis, 73,* 189–198.

Sandler, J., & Rosenblatt, B. (1962). The concept of the representational world. *The Psychoanalytic Study of the Child, 17,* 128–145.

Santostefano, S. (1991). Coordinating outer space with inner self: Reflections on developmental psychopathology. In D. P. Keating & H. Rosen (Eds.), *Constructivist perspectives on developmental psychopathology and atypical development* (pp. 11–40). Hillsdale, NJ: Erlbaum.

Schafer, R. (1992). *Retelling a life: Narration and dialogue in psychoanalysis.* New York: Basic Books.

Schank, R. C. (1990). *Tell me a story: A new look at real and artificial memory.* New York: Charles Scribner's Sons.

Schank, R. C. & Abelson, R. P. (1995). Knowledge and memory: The real story. In Wyer, R. S. (Ed.), Knowledge and memory: The real story. *Advances in Social Cognition, 8,* 1–85.

Schank, R. C., & Abelson, R. P. (1977). *Scripts, plans, goals and understanding: An inquiry into human knowledge structures.* Hillsdale, NJ: Erlbaum.

Schartau, P., Dalgleish, T., & Dunn, B. (2009). Seeing the bigger picture: Training in perspective broadening reduces self-reported affect and psychophysiological response to distressing films and autobiographical memories. *Journal of Abnormal Psychology, 118,* 15–27.

Scherer, K. R. (1992). On social representations of emotional experience: Stereotypes, proto-types, or archetypes? In M. von Cranach, W. Doise, & G. Mugny (Eds.), *Social representations and the social bases of knowledge* (pp. 30–36). Bern, Switzerland: Huber.

Scherer, K. R. (2001). Appraisal considered as a process of multi-level sequential checking. In K. R. Scherer, A. Schorr, & T. Johnstone (Eds.), *Appraisal processes in emotion: Theory, methods, research* (pp. 92–120). New York and Oxford: Oxford University Press.

Scherer, K. R., Schorr, A., & Johnstone, T. (2001). *Appraisal processes in emotion: Theory, methods, research*. New York: Oxford University Press.

Schmeichel, B. J., Vohs, K. D., & Baumeister, R. F. (2003). Intellectual performance and ego depletion: Role of the self in logical reasoning and other information processing. *Journal of Personality and Social Psychology, 85*, 33–46.

Schneider, M. F. (1989). *Children's Apperceptive Storytelling Test*. Austin, TX: Pro-Ed.

Schnell, K., Dietrich, T., Schnitker, R., Daumann, J., & Herpertz, S. C. (2007). Processing of autobiographical memory retrieval cues in Borderline Personality Disorder. *Journal of Effective Disorders, 97*, 253–259.

Schore, A. N. (2003). *Affect regulation and the repair of the self*. New York: W.W. Norton & Company.

Schroder, H. M., Driver, M. J., & Streufert, S. (1967). *Human information processing*. New York: Holt, Rinehart and Winston.

Schroth, M. L. (1977). The use of the Associative Elaboration and Integration Scales for evaluating CAT protocols. *Journal of Psychology, 97*, 29–35.

Schult, C. A. (2002). Children's understanding of the distinction between intentions and desires. *Child Development, 73*, 1727–1747.

Schultheiss, O. C., & Brunstein, J. C. (2001). Assessment of implicit motives with a research version of the TAT: Picture profiles, gender differences, and relations to other personality measures. *Journal of Personality Assessment, 77*, 71–86.

Schultheiss, O. C., Yankova, D., Dirlikov, B., & Schad, D. J. (2009). Are implicit and explicit motive measures statistically independent? A fair and balanced test using the Picture Story Exercise and a cue- and response-matched questionnaire measure. *Journal of Personality Assessment, 91*, 72–81.

Schwartz, J. C., & Shaver, P. (1987). Emotions and emotion knowledge in interpersonal relations. In W. Jones & D. Perlman (Eds.), *Advances in personal relationships* (pp. 197–241). Greenwich, CT: JAI Press.

Schwartz, L., & Eagle, C. J. (1986). *Psychological portraits of children*. Lexington, MA: Lexington Books.

Shapiro, T., & Huebner, H. F. (1976). Speech patterns of five psychotic children now in adolescence. *Journal of the American Academy of Child Psychiatry, 15*, 278–293.

Sheldon, K. M., Ryan, R., Deci, E., & Kasser, T. (2004). The independent effects of goal contents and motives on well-being: It's both what you pursue and why you pursue it. *Personality and Social Psychology Bulletin, 30*, 475–486.

Sherman, J. W., Gawronski, B., Gonsalkorale, K., Hugenberg, K., Allen, T. J., & Groom, C. J. (2008). The self-regulation of automatic associations and behavioral impulses. *Psychological Review, 115*, 314–335.

Shirk, S. R. (1998). Interpersonal schemata in child psychotherapy. *Journal of Clinical Child Psychology, 27*, 4–16.

Shirk, S. R., Boergers, J., Eason, A., & Van Horn, M. (1998). Dysphoric interpersonal schemata and preadolescents' sensitization to negative events. *Journal of Clinical Child Psychology, 27*, 54–68.

Shirk, S. R., & Russell, R. L. (1996). *Change processes in child psychotherapy: Revitalizing treatment and research*. New York: Guilford Press.

Shneidman, E. S. (1951). *Thematic test analysis*. New York: Grune & Stratton.

Shweder, R. A. (1994). "You're not sick, you're just in love": Emotion as an interpretive system. In P. Ekman and R. J. Davidson (Eds.), *The nature of emotion* (pp. 32–44). New York: Oxford University Press.

Singer, J. A., & Salovey, P. (1991). Organized knowledge structures and personality. In M. J. Horowitz (Ed.), *Personal schemas and maladaptive interpersonal patterns* (pp. 33–80). Chicago: University of Chicago Press.

Singer, J. A., & Salovey, P. (1993). *The remembered self: Emotion and memory in personality*. New York: The Free Press.

Singer, J. L. (1981). Research applications of projective methods. In A. I. Rabin (Ed.), *Assessment with projective techniques* (pp. 297–331). New York: Springer.

Singer, M. T., & Wynne, L. C. (1966). Principles for scoring communication defects and deviances in parents of schizophrenics: Rorschach and TAT scoring manuals. *Psychiatry: Journal for the Study of Interpersonal Processes, 29,* 260–288.

Skinner, E. A. (1999). Action regulation, coping, and development. In J. B. Brandtstädter & R. M. Lerner (Eds.), *Action and self-development* (pp. 465–503). Thousand Oaks, CA: Sage.

Skinner, E. A., & Zimmer-Gembeck, M. J. (2007). The development of coping. *Annual Review of Psychology, 58,* 119–144.

Slemon, A. G., Holzwarth, E. J., Lewis, J., & Sitko, M. (1976). Associative elaboration and integration scales for evaluating TAT protocols. *Journal of Personality Assessment, 40,* 365–369.

Sloman, S. (1994). When explanations compete: The role of explanatory coherence on judgments of likelihood. *Cognition, 52,* 1–21.

Sloman, S. (1996). The empirical case for two systems of reasoning. *Psychological Review, 119,* 3–22.

Smith, C. A., & Kirby, L. D. (2001a). Affect and cognitive appraisal: From content to process models. In J. Forgas (Ed.), *Handbook of affect and social cognition* (pp. 75–92). Hillsdale, NJ: Lawrence Erlbaum.

Smith, C. A., & Kirby, L. D. (2001b). Breaking the tautology: Toward delivering on the promise of appraisal theory. In K. Scherer, A. Schorr, & T. Johnstone (Eds.), *Appraisal theories of emotion* (pp. 121–138). Oxford: Oxford University Press.

Smith, C. A., & Scott, H. S. (1997). A componential approach to the meaning of facial expressions. In J. A. Russell & J. M. Fernández-Dols (Eds.), *The psychology of facial expression* (pp. 229–254). New York: Cambridge University Press.

Smith, C. P. (1992). Reliability issues. In J. W. Atkinson, D. C. McClelland, & J. Veroff (Eds.), *Motivation and personality: Handbook of thematic content analysis* (pp. 126–142). New York: Cambridge University Press.

Smith, E. R., & Neumann, R. (2005). Emotion processes considered from the perspective of dual-process models. In L. F. Barrett, P. M. Niedenthal, & P. Winkielman (Eds.), *Emotion and consciousness* (pp. 287–311). New York: Guilford Press.

Smolensky, P. (1988). On the proper treatment of connectionism. *Behavioral and Brain Sciences, 11,* 1–74.

Soenens, B., & Vansteenkiste, M. (2005). Antecedents and outcomes of self-determination in three life domains: The role of parents' and teachers' autonomy support. *Journal of Youth and Adolescence, 34,* 589–604.

Solomon, I. L., & Starr, B. (1968). *School Apperception Method (SAM)*. New York: Springer.

Spalding, L. R., & Hardin, C. D. (1999). Unconscious unease and self-handicapping: Behavioral consequences of individual differences in implicit and explicit self-esteem. *Psychological Science, 10,* 535–539.

Spangler, W. D. (1992). Validity of questionnaire and TAT measures of need for achievement. *Psychological Bulletin, 112,* 140–154.

Spear, W. E., & Lapidus, L. B. (1981). Qualitative differences in manifest object representations: Implications for a multi-dimensional model of psychological functioning. *Journal of Abnormal Psychology, 90,* 157–187.

Spinrad, T. L., Eisenberg, N., Cumberland, A., Fabes, R. A., Valiente, C., Shepard, S. A., Reiser M., Losoya, S. H., & Guthrie, I. K. (2006). Relation of emotion-related regulation to children's social competence: A longitudinal study. *Emotion, 6*(3), 498–510.

Spitz, H. H. (1988). Mental retardation as a thinking disorder: The rationalist alternative to empiricism. In N. Bray (Ed.), *International review of research in mental retardation* (Vol. 15, pp. 1–32). New York: Academic Press.

Srivastava, S., Tamir, M., McGonigal, K. M., John, O. P., & Gross, J. J. (2009). The social costs of emotional suppression: A prospective study of the transition to college. *Journal of Personality and Social Psychology, 96,* 883–897.

Stark, K. D., Rouse, L., & Livingston, R. (1991). Treatment of depression during childhood and adolescence: Cognitive-behavioral procedures for the individual and family. In P. C. Kendall (Ed.), *Child and adolescent therapy: Cognitive and behavioral procedures* (pp. 165–208). New York: Guilford Press.

Stein, M. J. (1955). *The Thematic Apperception Test* (Rev. ed.). Cambridge, MA: Addison Wesley.

Strelau, J. (1983). A regulative theory of temperament. *Australian Journal of Psychology, 35,* 305–317.

Strelau, J. (1994). The concepts of arousal and arousability as used in temperament studies. In J. E. Bates & T. D. Wachs (Eds.), *Temperament: Individual differences at the interface of biology and behavior* (pp. 117–141). Washington, DC: American Psychological Association.

Streufert, S., & Nogami, G. Y. (1989). Cognitive style and complexity: Implications for I/O psychology. In C. L. Cooper, I. T. Robertson et al. (Eds.), *International review of industrial and organizational psychology* (pp. 93–143). Chichester, England: Wiley.

Stricker, G., & Healy, B. J. (1990). Projective assessment of object relations: A review of the empirical literature. *Psychological Assessment: A Journal of Consulting and Clinical Psychology, 2,* 219–230.

Stuart, J., Westen, D., Lohr, N. E., & Benjamin, J. (1990). Object relations in borderlines, depressives, and normals: An examination of human responses on the Rorschach. *Journal of Personality Assessment, 55,* 296–318.

Suarez-Orozco, M. M. (1989). *Central American refugees and U.S. high schools: A psychosocial study of motivation and achievement.* Stanford, CA: Stanford University Press.

Suedfeld, P., Tetlock, P. E., & Streufert, S. (1992). Conceptual/integrative complexity. In C. P. Smith (Ed.), *Motivation and personality: Handbook of thematic content analysis* (pp. 393–400). New York: Cambridge University Press.

Sullivan, H. S. (1953). *The interpersonal theory of psychiatry.* New York: Norton.

Swallow S. R. (2000). A cognitive-behavioral perspective on the involuntary defeat strategy. In L. Sloman and P. Gilbert (Eds.), *Subordination and defeat: An evolutionary approach to mood disorders and their therapy* (pp 181-198). Mahwah, NJ: Erlbaum.

Symonds, P. M. (1939). Criteria for the selection of pictures for the investigation of adolescent phantasies. *Journal of Abnormal and Social Psychology, 34,* 271–274.

Symonds, P. M. (1949). *Adolescent fantasy.* New York: Columbia University Press.

Tangney, J., Stuewig, J., & Mashek, D. (2007). Moral emotions, moral cognitions, and moral behavior. *Annual Review, 58,* 345–372.

Tannock, R., Purvis, K. L., & Schachar, R. J. (1993). Narrative abilities in children with Attention Deficit Hyperactivity Disorder and normal peers. *Journal of Abnormal Child Psychology, 21,* 103–117.

Teglasi, H. (1993). *Clinical use of story telling: Emphasizing the TAT with children and adolescents.* Boston: Allyn & Bacon.

Teglasi, H. (1998). Assessment of schema and problem-solving strategies with projective techniques. In M. Hersen & A. Bellack (Series Eds.) & C. Reynolds (Vol. Ed.), *Comprehensive clinical psychology: Vol. 4. Assessment* (pp. 459–499). London, England: Elsevier Science Press.

Teglasi, H. (2006). Temperament. In G. Bear & K. Minke (Eds), *Children's needs* (327–336). Washington, DC: National Association of School Psychologists

Teglasi, H., & Epstein, S. (1998). Temperament and personality theory: The perspective of cognitive-experiential self-theory. *School Psychology Review, 27,* 534–550.

Teglasi, H., & Fagin, S. (1984). Social anxiety and self-other biases in causal attribution. *Journal of Research in Personality, 18,* 64–80.

Teglasi, H., & Hoffman, M. A. (1982). Causal attributions of shy subjects. *Journal of Research in Personality, 16,* 376–385.

Teglasi, H., Locraft, C., & Felgenhauer, K. (2008a). Empathy. In S. R. Jenkins (Ed.), *Empathy, A handbook of clinical scoring systems for thematic apperceptive techniques* (pp. 573–606). New York: Erlbaum (Taylor and Francis Group).

Teglasi, H., Locraft, C., & Felgenhauer, K. (2008b). Empathy. In S. R. Jenkins (Ed.), *Scoring manual for empathy: A handbook of clinical scoring systems for thematic apperceptive techniques* (pp. 607–632). New York: Erlbaum (Taylor and Francis Group).

Teglasi, H., Rahill, S., & Rothman, L. (2007). A story-guided peer group intervention for reducing bullying and victimization in schools. In J. E. Zins, M. J. Elias, and C. A. Maher (Eds.). *Bullying, victimization, and peer harassment: A handbook of prevention and intervention* (pp. 219–237). New York: Haworth Press.

Teglasi, H., & Rothman, L. (2001). STORIES: A classroom-based program to reduce aggressive behavior. *Journal of School Psychology, 39,* 71–94.

Thompson, A. E. (1986). An object relational theory of affect maturity: Applications to the Thematic Apperception Test. In M. Kissen (Ed.), *Assessing object relations phenomena* (pp. 207–224). Madison, WI: International Universities Press.

Thompson, C. E. (1949). The Thompson modification of the Thematic Apperception Test. *Rorschach Research Exchange and Journal of Projective Techniques, 13,* 469–478.

Thompson, J. M., & Sones, R. A. (1973). *Education Apperception Test.* Los Angeles: Western Psychological Services.

Tomkins, S. S. (1947). *Thematic Apperception Test.* New York: Grune & Stratton.

Tomkins, S. S. (1987). Script theory. In J. Aronoff, A. J. Rabin, & R. A. Zucker (Eds.), *The emergence of personality* (pp. 147–216). New York: Springer.

Trentacosta, C. J., Izard, C. E., Mostow, A., & Fine, S. E. (2006). Children's emotional competence and attentional competence in early elementary school. *School Psychology Quarterly, 21*(2), 148–170.

Uleman, J. S. (2005). On the inherent ambiguity of traits and other mental concepts. In B. F. Malle & S. D. Hodges (Eds.), *Other minds: How humans bridge the divide between self and others* (pp. 253–267). New York: Guilford Publications.

Urist, J. (1977). The Rorschach test and the assessment of object relations. *Journal of Personality Assessment, 41,* 3–9.

Urist, J. (1980). Object relations. In R. H. Woody (Ed.), *Encyclopedia of clinical assessment* (Vol. 2, pp. 821–833). San Francisco: Jossey Bass.

Urist, J., & Shill, M. (1982). Validity of the Rorschach Mutuality of Autonomy Scale: A replication using excerpted responses. *Journal of Personality Assessment, 46,* 450–454.

Vaillant, G. E. (1977). *Adaptation and life.* Boston: Little, Brown.

Vaillant, G. E. (1992). *Ego mechanisms of defense: A guide for clinicians and researchers.* Washington, DC: American Psychiatric Press.

Vansteenkiste, M., Lens, W., & Deci, E. I. (2006). To plan or not to plan? Goal achievementor interrupting the performance of mundane behaviors. *Educational Psychologist, 41*(1), 19–31.

Vansteenkiste, M., Simons, J., Lens, W., Sheldon, K. M., & Deci, E. L. (2004). Motivating learning, performance, and persistence: The synergistic role of intrinsic goals and autonomy-support. *Journal of Personality and Social Psychology, 87*, 246–260.

Vansteenkiste, M., Zhou, M., Lens, W., & Soenens, B. (2005). Experiences of autonomy and control among Chinese learners: Vitalizing or immobilizing? *Journal of Educational Psychology, 97*, 468–483.

Veroff, J. (1992). Thematic apperceptive methods in survey research. In J. W. Atkinson, D. C. McClelland, & J. Veroff (Eds.), *Motivation and personality: Handbook of thematic content analysis* (pp. 100–109). New York: Cambridge University Press.

Veroff, J., Atkinson, J. W., Feld, S. C., & Gurin, G. (1960). The use of thematic apperception to assess motivation in a nationwide interview study. *Psychological Monographs, 74*, 32.

Vitz, P. C. (1990). The use of stories in moral development: New psychological reasons for an old education method. *American Psychologist, 45*, 709–720.

Watkins, C. E., Campbell, V. L., & McGregor, P. (1988). Counseling psychologists' uses of and opinions about psychological tests: A contemporary perspective. *Counseling Psychologist, 16*, 476–486.

Watkins, C. E., Campbell, V. L., Nieberding, R., & Hallmark, R. (1995). Contemporary practice of psychological assessment by clinical psychologists. *Professional Psychology: Research and Practice, 26*, 54–60.

Watson, D., & Clark, L. A. (1992). Affects separable and inseparable: On the hierarchical arrangement of the negative affects. *Journal of Personality and Social Psychology, 62*, 489–505.

Weiner, I. B. (1966). *Psychodiagnosis in Schizophrenia*. New York: Wiley.

Weisskopf, E. A. (1950). A transcendence index as a proposed measure in the TAT. *Journal of Psychology, 29*, 379–390.

Weisskopf-Joelson, E. A., & Foster, H. C. (1962). An experimental study of the effect of stimulus variation upon projection. *Journal of Projective Techniques, 26*, 366–370.

Weisskopf-Joelson, E. A., & Lyn, D. B. (1953). The effect of variations in ambiguity on projection in the Children's Apperception Test. *Journal of Consulting Psychology, 17*, 67–70.

Weisskopf-Joelson, E. A., Zimmerman, J., & McDaniel, M. (1970). Similarity between subject and stimulus as an influence on projection. *Journal of Projective Techniques and Personality Assessment, 34*, 328–331.

Wellman, H. M. (1990). *The child's theory of mind*. Cambridge: MIT Press.

Wellman, H. M. (2002). Understanding the psychological world: Developing a theory of mind. In U. Goswami (Ed.), *Handbook of childhood cognitive development* (pp. 167–187). Oxford: Blackwell.

Wellman, H. M., & Gelman, S. A. (1998). Knowledge acquisition in foundational domains. In W. Damon (Series Ed.), & D. Kuhn & R. Siegler (Vol. Eds.), *Handbook of child psychology: Cognition, perception, and language* (vol. 2, 5th ed., pp. 523–573). New York: Wiley.

Wellman, H. M., Lopez-Duran, S., LaBounty, J. & Hamilton, B. (2008). Infant attention to intentional action predicts preschool theory of mind. *Developmental Psychology, 44*, 618–623.

Wellman, H. M., & Phillips, A. T. (2001). Developing intentional understanding. In B. F. Malle, L. J. Moses, & D. A. Baldwin (Eds.), *Intentions and intentionality: Foundations of social cognition* (pp. 125–148). Cambridge, MA: MIT Press.

Wellman, H. M., & Woolley, J. D. (1990). From simple desires to ordinary beliefs: The early development of everyday psychology. *Cognition, 35*, 245–275.

Westen, D. (1985). *Self and society: Narcissism, collectivism, and the development of morals*. New York: Cambridge University Press.

Westen, D. (1990). Towards a revised theory of borderline object relations: Contributions of empirical research. *International Journal of Psychoanalysis, 71*, 661–693.

Westen, D. (1991). Clinical assessment of object relations using the TAT. *Journal of Personality Assessment, 56,* 56–74.

Westen, D. (1993). Social cognition and social affect in psychoanalysis and cognitive psychology: From regression analysis to analysis of regression. In J. W. Barron, M. N. Eagle, & D. L. Wolitzky (Eds.), *Interface of psychoanalysis and psychology* (pp. 375–388). Washington, DC: American Psychological Association.

Westen, D. (1995). A clinical-empirical model of personality: Life after the Mischelian ice age and the NEO-lithic era. *Journal of Personality, 63,* 495–524.

Westen, D., Klepser, J., Ruffins, S. A., Silverman, M., Lifton, N., & Boekamp, J. (1991). Object relations in childhood and adolescence: The development of working representations. *Journal of Consulting and Clinical Psychology, 9,* 400–409.

Williams J. M. G., Watts, F. N., MacLeod, C., & Mathews A. (1997). *Cognitive psychology and emotional disorders* (2nd ed.). Chichester, UK: Wiley.

Williams, L. M., Hermens, D. F., Palmer, D., Kohn, M., Clarke, S., Keage, H., Clark, C. R., & Gordon, E. (2008). Misinterpreting emotional expressions in Attention-Deficit/Hyperactivity Disorder: Evidence for a neural marker and stimulant effects. *Biological Psychiatry, 63*(10), 917–926.

Wilson, A. (1988). Levels of depression and clinical assessment. In H. D. Lerner & P. M. Lerner (Eds.), *Primitive mental states and the Rorschach* (pp. 441–462). Madison, CT: International Universities Press.

Wilson, E. J., MacLeod, C., Mathews, A., & Rutherford, E. M. (2006). The causal role of interpretive bias in anxiety reactivity. *Journal of Abnormal Psychology, 115,* 103–111.

Winnicott, D. W. (1965). *Maturational processes and the facilitating environment.* London: Hogarth Press and the Inst. of Psa; Madison, CT: International Universities Press.

Winnicott, D. W. (1971). *Transitional objects and transitional phenomena.* New York: Basic Books.

Winter, D. A. (1982). Construct relationships, psychological disorder and therapeutic change. *British Journal of Medical Psychology, 55,* 257–270.

Winter, D. G., John, O. P., Stewart, A. J., Klohnen, E. C., & Duncan, L. E. (1998). Traits and motives: Toward an integration of two traditions in personality research. *Psychological Review, 105*(2), 230–250.

Woike, B. A., & Aronoff, J. (1992). Antecedents of complex social cognitions. *Journal of Personality and Social Psychology, 63,* 97–104.

Woike, B. A., Gershkovich, I., Piorkowski, R., & Polo, M. (1999). The role of motives in the content and structure of autobiographical memory. *Journal of Personality and Social Psychology, 76,* 600–612.

Woike, B. A., Lavezzary, E., & Barsky, J. (2001). The influence of implicit motives on memory. *Journal of Personality and Social Psychology, 81,* 935–945.

Woike, B. A., Mcleod, S., & Goggin, M. (2003). Implicit and explicit motives influence accessibility to different autobiographical memories. *Personality and Social Psychology Bulletin, 29,* 1046–1055.

Woike, B. A., & Polo, M. (2001). Motive-related memories: Content, structure and affect. *Journal of Personality, 69,* 391–415.

Wolk, R. L., & Wolk, R. B. (1971). *The Gerontological Apperception Test.* New York: Behavioral Publications.

Wolters, C. (2004). Advancing goal theory: Using goal structures and goal orientations to predict students' motivation, cognition, and achievement. *Journal of Educational Psychology, 96,* 236–250.

Woolfolk, R. L., Gara, M. A., Allen, L. A., & Beaver, J. D. (2004). Self-complexity: An assessment of construct validity. *Journal of Social and Clinical Psychology, 23,* 463–474.

Worchel, F. T., Aaron, L. L., & Yates, D. F. (1990). Gender bias on the Thematic Appercep-tion Test. *Journal of Personality Assessment, 55,* 593–602.

Wozniak, R. H. (1985). Notes toward a co-constructive theory of the emotion/cognition relationship. In D. Bearison & H. Zimiles (Eds.), *Thought and emotion: Developmental issues* (pp. 39–64). Hillsdale, NJ: Erlbaum.

Wyer, R. S., Jr., & Srull, T. K. (Eds.). (1994). *Handbook of social cognition* (2nd ed., Vols. 1–2). Hillsdale, NJ: Erlbaum.

Wynne, L. C., Singer, M. T., & Toohey, M. (1976). Communication of the adoptive parents of schizophrenics. In J. Jorstad & E. Ugelstad (Eds.), *Schizophrenia 75: Psychotherapy, family stud-ies, research* (pp. 413–451). Oslo: University of Oslo Press.

Young, J. E., Klosko, J. S., & Weishaar, M. (2003). *Schema therapy: A practitioner's guide.* New York: Guilford Publications.

Zelazo, P. D., & Cunningham, W. A. (2007). Executive function: Mechanisms underlying emotion regulation. In J. J. Gross (Ed.), *Handbook of emotion regulation* (pp. 135–158). New York: Guilford Press.

Zaleski, Z. (1994). *Psychology of future orientation.* Lublin, Poland: Wydawnictwo Towarzystwa Naukowego Katolickiego Uniwersyteta Lubelskiego.

Zimbardo, P. G., & Boyd, J. N. (2008). *The time paradox.* New York: Free Press, Simon & Schuster.

Zimbardo, P. G., Keough, K. A., & Boyd, J. N. (1997). Present time perspective as a predictor of risky driving. *Personality and Individual Difference, 23,* 1007–1023.

Zubin, J., Eron, L. D., & Schumer, F. (1965). *An experimental approach to projective techniques.* New York: Wiley.

Annotated Bibliography

Bellak, L., & Abrams, D. M. (1997). *The Thematic Apperception Test, The Children's Apperception Test, and The Senior Apperception Technique in clinical use.* Boston: Allyn & Bacon.
This book presents Bellak's psychodynamic interpretive approach, including pertinent literature, relevant examples, and case illustrations.

Cramer, P. (2004). *Storytelling, narrative, and the Thematic Apperception Test.* New York: Guilford Press.
This book provides a synthesis of the literature on the TAT including clinical case examples and a scholarly review of the technique's reliability and validity.

Gieser, L., & Stein, M. I. (Eds.). (1999). *Evocative images: The Thematic Apperception Test and the art of projection.* Washington, DC: American Psychological Association.
This edited volume features chapters from pioneers in the field who give their impressions about the TAT in clinical practice and research.

Jenkins, S. R. (Ed.). (2008). *A handbook of clinical scoring systems for thematic apperceptive techniques.* New York: Lawrence Erlbaum Associates.
This edited book compiles numerous clinical coding systems, providing not only the theoretical and research bases of each but also coding procedures and practice stories. Through the contributions of the editor and various chapter authors, this book offers a general theoretical background of thematic apperceptive techniques and specific information about each coding system.

Kelly, F. D. (1996). *Object relations in younger children: Rorschach and TAT measures.* Springfield, IL: Charles C. Thomas.
Focusing on object relations assessment in younger children, this book provides numerous examples demonstrating the Mutuality of Autonomy Scale (Rorschach) and The Social Cognition Object Relations Scale (TAT).

Kelly, F. D. (1997). *The assessment of object relations phenomena in adolescents.* Mahwah, NJ: Erlbaum.
This book features clinical case examples demonstrating the process of object relations assessment with two measures, the Mutuality of Autonomy Scale (Rorschach) and The Social Cognition Object Relations Scale (TAT).

Kroon, N., Goudena, P. P., & Rispens, J. (1998). Thematic Apperception Tests for child and adolescent assessment: A practitioner's consumer guide. *Journal of Psychoeducational Assessment, 16,* 99–117.
This review article notes comparative strengths and weaknesses of the 12 (of 23) thematic apperception tests currently available for use with children and adolescents. Authors observe that the well-established methods of the TAT and CAT are supplemented by various tests designed to deal with specific assessment issues.

Peters, E. J., Hilsenroth, M. J., Eudell-Simmons, E.M., Blagys, M. D., & Handler, L. (2006). Reliability and validity of the Social Cognition and Object Relations Scale in clinical use. *Psychotherapy Research, 16,* 617–626.
The Social Cognition and Object Relations Scale (SCORS), a clinician scoring system developed by Westen, is used frequently in research to rate the quality of object relations in the TAT and other forms of narrative. The dimensions of object relations include Complexity of Representations of Others, Affect Tone of Relationships, Emotional Investment in Relations and Moral Standards, and Understanding of

Social Causality. This article examines the reliability and convergent validity of the SCORS as a measure of relational narratives expressed during clinical sessions.

Smith, C. P. (Ed.). (1992). *Motivation and personality: Handbook of thematic content analysis.* New York: Cambridge University Press.

This edited volume provides the history and coding procedures for the well-known methods for content analysis of the TAT popular in the study of personality but not in clinical use.

Teglasi, H. (1993). *Clinical use of storytelling: Emphasizing the TAT with children and adolescents.* Boston: Allyn & Bacon.

Synthesizing interpretive guidelines that combine story content, structure, and narrative process, this book organizes discrete narrative elements into more general cognitive-emotional psychological processes.

Teglasi, H. (1998). Assessment of schema and problem-solving strategies with projective techniques. In M. Hersen & A. Bellack (Series Eds.) & C. Reynolds (Vol. Ed.), *Comprehensive clinical psychology: Vol. 4. Assessment* (pp. 459–499). New York: Elsevier Science Press.

This chapter outlines the relevance of current concepts and research in various subfields of psychology for assessment of schemas and problem solving with projective techniques.

Index

About the Author

Hedwig Teglasi, PhD, ABPP, is Professor in the Department of Counseling and Personnel Services at the University of Maryland, and a Fellow of the American Psychological Association, the Society for Personality Assessment, and of the American Academy of School Psychology. She has published numerous journal articles, book chapters and books on topics relevant to personality, temperament, and social competence interventions, including the use of storytelling to assess as well as to modify schemas guiding social information processing. Dr. Teglasi has served as an Associate Editor of the *School Psychology Quarterly*, as member of several Editorial Boards and as guest editor and co-editor of special topics journal issues about temperament and personality assessment. She has recently served as President of the American Board of School Psychology.

Lightning Source UK Ltd.
Milton Keynes UK
UKOW06f0128300415

250615UK00001B/37/P